Innovation and the Futureproof Bank

Innovation and the Futureproof Bank

A practical guide to doing different business-as-usual

Dr James Gardner

A John Wiley and Sons, Ltd., Publication

Registered office

John Wiley & Sons Ltd, The Atrium, Southern Gate, Chichester, West Sussex, PO19 8SQ, United Kingdom

For details of our global editorial offices, for customer services and for information about how to apply for permission to reuse the copyright material in this book please see our website at www.wiley.com.

Library of Congress Cataloging-in-Publication Data

Gardner, James.
Innovation and the future proof bank : a practical guide to doing different business as usual / James Gardner.
        p. cm.
    ISBN 978-0-470-71419-5 (cloth)
1. Banks and banking.   2. Technological innovations.   I. Title.
    HG1601.G37 2009
    332.1–dc22   2009021629

A catalogue record for this book is available from the British Library.

ISBN 978-0-470-71419-5 (H/B)

Typeset in 10/12pt Times by Aptara Inc., New Delhi, India
Printed in Great Britain by CPI Antony Rowe, Chippenham, Wiltshire.

Contents

List of Tables

List of Figures

Preface

It never ceases to amaze me how much debate the simple word 'innovation' can cause in an institution. Utter it, and one seems to touch a nerve. It causes argument about what innovation is, what sort should be engaged in, and whether, in fact, anyone is doing any innovation at all.

So personal is the term 'innovation' that I've found myself in the same discussions – sometimes even heated debates – over and over again. And all this happens before anyone even gets to the meat of the innovation problem: how to create the set of infrastructures and processes that let an institution do innovation, and do it predictably and reliably.

Most institutions recognise the urgent need for more innovation. They know there are emergent competitors coming from all directions: competitors who are small, nimble, and above all, innovative. There seems little choice but to out-innovate the innovators if one wants to compete effectively in the long term. But most institutions, whilst wanting more innovation, don't know how to go about *getting* it. They might set up an innovation team, which is then tasked with discovering everything there is to know about the innovation problem, whilst simultaneously driving expansive new ideas out the door. It will not be any surprise to discover most innovation teams fail when they are given such an insurmountable challenge.

The problem is the misconception that innovation in banks is something that can be turned on, like a switch. The truth of the matter, though, is that innovation is a corporate capability that takes time to master like any other. It is a journey that can sometimes take years. But a new innovation team rarely has years to deliver results. Institutions typically get tired of waiting for their innovation payback long before a new team is anywhere close to building the process, systems, and cultures needed to find and exploit uniqueness.

Innovation and the Futureproof Bank is a book which aims to help innovation teams and their sponsors with this problem. It is my hope that by following the advice herein, new innovation groups can spend less time learning the basics of innovation and more time driving real outcomes for their banks.

Creating predictability in the way innovation is done inside an institution is only part of the problem facing innovation teams, however. Sooner or later, it becomes necessary to consider innovation from an external perspective as well. What steps must be taken to counter that upstart new competitor, the one with the disruptive channel strategy? What consequences are likely if *no* action is taken? If it is? These are questions which will sooner or later find their way to innovation teams for an answer. And the team had better be ready with structured processes for looking into the future, or miss their chance to be part of the strategic agenda of their institutions. Here, too, this book has advice for bank innovators.

The practices and techniques described herein have been used in many institutions success-fully across the world. My approach was to examine the best innovation processes I could find, and stitch them together into something that any bank could usefully use to create a great innovation practice. The whole I call *Futureproofing*, a set of techniques that any institution can use to ensure that it gets the best from its innovation investments, whilst simultaneously watching (and reacting) to the innovation investments made by its competitors.

Of course, not everything in this book will be appropriate for every institution. It is my suggestion that practitioners take what is provided as a base, and modify it to take account of their institution's unique set of capabilities. If I've learned one thing about innovation whilst writing this book, it is that every bank is different, and consequently, the way it does innovation must be as well.

This will become especially evident when you read the stories and case studies I've included from institutions around the world. The way Bank of America approaches innovation in its joint venture with MIT Media Labs, for example, is quite different from the disruptive system of innovations that Caja Navarra of Spain calls 'customer rights'. These, and other, examples show just how diverse the innovation process can be.

Which brings me to thanking those who have collaborated in the writing of this book. A year ago, when I first stated on my blog that I was writing this book, I was surprised – and gratified – by the number of institutions that reached out to me with their innovation stories. Many of them have made their way into these pages. To them, and their innovators who were so forthcoming with information, I offer my thanks.

I must also thank those who have read parts, or all, of this manuscript during the writing process. Craig Libby, Innovation Engineer at what was then Wachovia. Steve Wakefield, of Lloyds TSB who tirelessly read every chapter as it was written, pointing out my many errors. And, of course, all those who feature in the case studies and other stories throughout. To these, I owe a debt of gratitude.

Thanks are due, also, to the readers of my blog Bankervision, whose constant stream of comments, support, and advice kept me believing that there was a need for this book, even when the words wouldn't come.

And finally, my thanks go to my employers, both past and present, for allowing me the freedom to innovate, the liberty to push the boundaries, and the chance to explore the very frontiers of innovation science in the banking context.

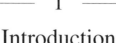

1
Introduction

What you will find in this chapter

- A useful definition of innovation that can be applied to an institution.
- Five key mistakes people make when they think about innovation in banks.
- A brief history of innovation in banks.
- An overview of the futureproofing process.
- An explanation of how it is that not all innovation is good.

There is no such thing as a bank that is innovative. At least, that is what I would believe if all I read was the popular press or the blogs of customers. Try this experiment: say the words 'bank' and 'innovation' in the same sentence to anyone in the street, and see if you get much more than a blank look in return.

Most people think of innovation in terms of breakthroughs of the sort one regularly sees coming from high technology companies. They rarely consider that, in their day, ATMs were breakthroughs. They don't think of the revolution of Internet and browser technologies combining to bring banking into the home. Nor do they realise or care that many incremental changes banks implement every day – a change to the call centre interactive voice response, or the update to queue management in the branch – are in fact innovations that other industries have, from time to time, copied.

Perhaps because their customers don't perceive the innovation all around them, bankers have started to believe they aren't very innovative as well. They accept that change will be slow. That they will react when the market demands they do so. And, in fact, that this represents the *prudent* course which will safeguard their institution and its customers.

But there is a problem with this, and that is the pace of change in financial services has accelerated markedly. When it was just regulators, competitors, and markets that were the issue, the glacial engine of *prudence* was entirely satisfactory. But the democratisation of the tools of financial services has changed that. Now *anyone* can do things banks used to think were safely behind the competitive barriers of their very special role in the economy. A savvy consumer is fully capable of using online tools to run a small loan book via emerging person-to-person lending sites. They can pick and choose from dozens of customer service experiences courtesy of the next generation of personal finance software. And they can make international or domestic payments, even to the unbanked, and do so instantly, pretty much without fees.

Many of the commercial, technical, and regulatory barriers which protected banks in the past are about to, or have already, fallen. Their fall brings a groundswell of new change which will utterly defeat *prudence* as a strategy. Prudence is simply too slow to react.

What is needed, then, is a business process which can predictably and reliably respond to all this change, and which doesn't abandon the fundamental tenet of prudence upon which banks must rely. Futureproofing, the subject of this book, is one way of doing that.

Futureproofing is the process of planning what the future might bring and doing something about it. Having read that sentence, you'd be excused for imagining these pages – as so many others at present – might concern themselves with examining doomsday scenarios in which banking no longer exists as an industry. Or if you are more positive, the happy alternative where all present threats to the special economic role of institutions have been dealt with and we continue onward indefinitely. But actually, this is a book which makes only one prediction about the future, and it is one firmly based in historical fact: change is a constant, and there is nothing that can be done to stop it happening.

Once one accepts that change is inevitable, it is only a small step further to the realisation that a business process which can systematically deal with change provides assurances against many of the challenges that might arise in the future.

This book is about building such business processes. It was born from understanding that whilst innovation might be the engine that drives progress and competitive advantage, ad-hoc innovation is, well, random. That randomness, far from providing assurances for the future, is gambling without knowing the odds in advance. Since it is possible to stack the cards in one's favour, it makes excellent business sense to do so.

So, what are the characteristics of an institution that is futureproof?

Firstly, it will have systematised a focus on tomorrow. Many organisations spend the greatest part of their operational attention seeking to optimise the business of today. A futureproof institution recognises that putting structure around future consideration is the best way to avoid surprises. This book explains how such structure can be optimised into a *futurecast*, a substantive vision of alternative futures that can be used to rehearse key strategic decisions in advance.

Secondly, it will embed a business process that actively seeks out solutions for the problems of tomorrow. A futureproof institution knows that ad-hoc, random innovation is just as likely to generate bad ideas as good ones, so it puts sophisticated tools in place to eliminate the guesswork. It recognises also that this is a process that can pay its own way, and demands that each step towards tomorrow makes good business sense.

Finally, a futureproof institution explores multiple things at once. It knows that individual innovations may be successful or may not, but taken as a portfolio, the returns can be predicted with great accuracy.

But futureproofing requires a great deal of hard work. And inevitably, there are plenty of individuals in institutions who argue that the effort, capital, and organisational bandwidth involved is better spent on core businesses. They make the point that banking has been going well since its incarnation in modern form in the late 16th century, pointing to these hundreds of years of development as proof that financial services are able to respond to change without a formal process for doing so.

They would be correct in pointing this out. But now there is an emerging body of evidence suggesting that institutions which proactively and deliberately design their future are significantly superior performers in the long term. And the interesting thing is that such superior performance is almost never about the amount of money spent. Booz Allen Hamilton, who review the top 1000 corporate spenders on R&D every year [1], found there is almost no relationship at all between spending on innovation and superior financial returns. What they did discover, though, was that those companies with a deliberate innovation process – one with links to corporate strategy and customer needs – achieved up to 40% higher growth in their operating income as a result.

With arguments such as these, it is interesting that so few financial services organisations are listed as innovative. In fact, according to Boston Consulting Group and *Business Week* [2], there are only five institutions who make the top 50 innovators globally. That *any* institution is listed alongside such famous innovators as Apple, Google, and General Electric is surprising, given the widely held view that banks aren't innovative at all.

What are those institutions doing to draw the attention of *Business Week*? What they all have in common is that they've developed robust processes to help them design their own futures, and they use them to get reliable and predictable returns from their innovation investments. They are institutions whose futures are secure.

Most banks spend years building their innovation capabilities before achieving this level of mastery. Having said that, however, the basic principles that underlie success are easily understood, and the chief concern is usually operationalising them in such a way that they become a core part of doing business. It is my hope that this book will help you do that in your own institutions.

1.1   WHAT IS INNOVATION ANYWAY?

In many financial services firms, it isn't hard to find groups that are responsible for something that is, conceptually at least, innovation. It is typical that the focus of such groups be laser-sharp on the core business operations of the organisational lines that host them. In fact, in most banks, there are many innovation teams scattered across various silos, though they might not always think of themselves as being part of the innovation function.

It is hardly unusual, for example, for a group calling itself 'Business Development' to engage in new product innovation, whilst sitting across the hall a technology team looks for innovative gadgets they can shoehorn into a banking context. Meanwhile the strategy function is undoubtedly looking at new business models and new markets, and inevitably, the CEO herself is pushing along some pet projects that have an innovative aspect to them.

Unsurprisingly, such diversity of focus leads directly to organisational confusion with respect to the corporate innovation agenda, if an institution is lucky enough to have one at all. And almost certainly, getting to an adequate definition of innovation that works for everyone is pretty much a hopeless task with so many conflicting priorities.

It is useful, then, to look first at common definitions of innovation. This will give us common language we'll be able to use throughout the remainder of this book.

With that in mind, it is possible to classify innovations in two dimensions. The first is the degree of newness incarnated in whatever-it-is. The second relates to the relationship of innovation to the competitive position of the firm. The latter of these two I'll get to in a moment, but first let us look at innovations based on the amount of uniqueness inherent in them.

Breakthrough, revolutionary, and incremental innovation

Innovations which are completely unprecedented are variously called breakthrough, radical, or discontinuous innovations depending on which book you read (I'll call them breakthroughs from now on). Breakthroughs have several attributes: they have few analogues to anything that has gone before, they change the rules of the game substantially in some way, they involve high levels of risk and reward, and they are inherently unpredictable.

History gives us a rich tapestry of breakthroughs to examine: the Wright Brothers with their first aircraft, the creation of the transistor, the discovery of penicillin. What do all these have in common? They were the result of years of thankless work with no guarantee of reward. But more importantly, they all changed the world. It is hard to imagine the inventors knew, when they started their work, how very important their efforts would be to those coming later.

A very common preconception is that innovation teams spend their days doing this kind of work: creation that is so substantially different from what has gone before that the rules of the game are completely rewritten. In fact, only unsuccessful innovation organisations spend *all* their time seeking breakthroughs, as will become evident later.

Nonetheless, there is a deceptive attraction to being first with something that completely changes the nature of a market or product. The rewards may be exceptionally large, and quite often result in a long-term sustainable competitive advantage as well. The downside, though, is that breakthrough innovations, no matter how clever they are, are extremely unpredictable. One cannot easily control when, or even if, one will make a return on what is almost certainly going to be a very large investment up front.

Breakthroughs have occurred from time to time in banking. When they have, they have substantially changed the playing field for everyone. One of the most famous was the introduction of computing to financial services by Bank of America.

As accessibility to retail banking services grew in the 1950s, especially with the rise of the credit card, banks began to struggle with the volume of paper processing required. It was becoming increasingly obvious to everyone that paper was going to put an upper limit on just how large an institution could reasonably grow. Computers seemed one answer, but the application of real computing to banking was substantially delayed by the fact that, at the time, the technology was primarily a scientific and military endeavour. Electronic machines had extremely limited input and output capabilities, which seemed to mitigate against their use in volume transaction processing environments.

Nonetheless, in 1950, Bank of America approached Stanford University regarding the possibility of an electronic machine for data processing [3]. At the time, an experienced book keeper could post 245 accounts per hour, or about 2000 per 8-hour work day. But growing volume was forcing the bank to shut its doors at 2 p.m. each day to deal with the paper backlog and checking accounts were growing at a rate of 23,000 a month. There were few alternatives but automation if the business was to continue its growth trajectory.

An early feasibility study was completed by Stanford University in 1951, leading to a first practical demonstration of a machine in 1955. This machine (called ERMA for Electronic Recording Method of Accounting) introduced several new innovations specific to banking. The first of these, Magnetic Ink Character Reading (MICR), addressed the input problem for volume cheque processing. Another parallel development was the creation of machines that could move paper at speed to the MICR reader. The use of transistors instead of valves made the machine practicable from a heat and power perspective. And magnetic memories were introduced to store instructions and intermediate data.

In 1956 the machine was tested for three months in a branch environment with loads that would be required of a central accounting facility. The tests were successful, leading to the acquisition of 32 ERMA machines by 1959.

The mechanisation of business – in which Bank of America was the pioneering innovator of the day – led to the rise of central accounting as the default mode of operation for banks globally. The breakthrough was so fundamental it was replicated by practically everyone else in short order. By 1965, almost all banks in the UK and the USA were running automated machines similar to ERMA [4].

Following breakthrough innovation (classified, as before, by the amount of uniqueness involved) is revolutionary innovation. Revolutionary innovations are sufficiently superior to what they replace that they become the default choice for a significant percentage of the market. They offer substantial advantages over what has gone before, but do not, themselves, redefine existing categories or create new ones. The Apple iPhone is a revolutionary innovation. It does not create a new product category (high end mobile phones), but it enhances the concept of an integrated phone, player, and organiser device in such a way that it has become the default choice for many people. It is revolutionary because it is winning share away from incumbent products, rather than changing the way things work fundamentally.

Revolutionary innovations tend to be less risky than breakthroughs, but as might be expected, usually have less upside. The reason? Revolutionary innovations, arising from well understood areas, are far less likely to have the kinds of entry barriers that breakthroughs have. As a result, they are copied more easily. Less than a year after the first release of Apple's iPhone, companies such as HTC of Taiwan were already releasing phones that duplicated some of its best features, for example.

Revolutionary innovations in banking are not that common, but have occurred from time to time. The launch of ING Direct, a Canadian innovation that opened its doors in 1997, is one example. At the time, Canadians had little choice but to choose a low-interest, fee-charging savings account from one of the incumbent big five banks. ING Direct's flagship product, a chargeless, high-interest savings account, was something quite new: it offered bare bones service to low margin customers, but did so at volume. It was immediately a runaway success. Apparently customers were over-served by the features of accounts they could get at their traditional banks.

In 1999, ING Direct opened in Australia, disrupting the industry there as they had done in Canada. Once again, the successful formula was repeated: provide a bare bones service and pass on those savings to customers. I recall being in a meeting with a senior banker in Australia at this time, during which he expressed his irritation that ING was 'borrowing' the use of his institution's channels without paying for them. His complaint stemmed from the fact that ING Direct offered a branchless service, and therefore customers were forced to use the facilities of his bank in order to get funds in and out of their ING accounts. Bankers' complaints aside, ING Direct in Australia went from standing start to the sixth largest retail bank in a few short years.

The next year, 2000, ING Direct opened in the USA, again repeating its successful branchless model, and except for some trademark 'ING Direct' cafes in key markets, remains relatively bricks-and-mortar free. It has now grown to become the largest direct bank in that country.

ING Direct is now operating in the UK, Spain, Germany, Italy, France, and Japan. Its revolutionary model that cut service back as much as reasonably possible and returned customers the savings is one that is, apparently, easy to transplant across cultures and geographic boundaries.

Finally, we come to the least new of all types of innovation: incremental, also known as continuous innovation. Incremental innovation takes what is well known and makes a minor improvement with a positive payback. Incremental innovations may not be visible outside an organisation: they are characteristically small, probably very specific to an institution's individual way of doing things, and are relatively low risk.

In many countries, it is possible to sign up for 'pre-pay' mobile phone contracts. Telecommunications firms provide potential customers with a free or low-cost SIM card, which is then 'topped up' with credit. Customers are allowed to make phone calls up to the value of their credit before they have to 'top up' again. Initially, the process of adding credit was available only through the shop fronts of the mobile phone operators, but in some countries, banks were quick to spot an incremental opportunity: allow mobile phone top ups through their ATM networks.

The business model that supports ATMs is very specific: one wants as much cash dispensed as possible, in the shortest amount of time. Ideally, one wants the customers of other banks to use the institution's ATMs as well, since this provides a rich source of fee income. Consequently, locations for ATMs are hotly contested, and the best spots are almost always already filled with one of the ubiquitous cash dispensing machines.

Now, most opportunities to use ATMs to dispense things other than cash have a huge downside: the time taken to operate the new dispensing function is generally greater than that for cash, and consequently revenues from individual machines tend to fall. But mobile phone top ups have none of these disadvantages. Customers simply enter their mobile phone number, and the credit is deducted from their account and added to their phone automatically. It is a nice piece of new fee revenue that institutions are able to acquire from telecommunications companies.

Mobile phone top ups at the ATM are an entirely incremental innovation. They take what is already in place – the ability to dispense cash and provide minimal account information to customers – and twist it just a little to provide a new service consumers find valuable. Unsurprisingly, in most countries that do top up at the ATM, it has become a ubiquitous offering from everyone who runs ATM networks.

If you go back over these three types of innovation I've just covered, you will probably think of examples from your own organisation. That is not unusual: it is the hallmark of an appropriate innovation strategy that things are developed from each category. But what is not generally obvious is that a much broader definition of innovation is possible: *anything* that is not presently being done by an organisation is an innovation opportunity. Market-wide uniqueness doesn't come into it. Innovation is the process of introducing new things, certainly, but it only has to be *new* to your institution for it to be an opportunity worth exploring.

Disruptive and sustaining innovation

As I mentioned earlier, it is possible to classify innovations in two dimensions. We've just looked at the first dimension: how genuinely new whatever-it-is is compared to what it proceeds. The second dimension is the way institutions and markets respond to the innovation itself. Banks react to things which are new in very different ways depending on whether the new thing *sustains* or *disrupts* their current operations. This classification was first proposed by Clayton Christensen, author of the hugely influential book *The Innovator's Dilemma* [5]. His theory of disruptive innovation has a well-established track record of explaining why it is that companies in different industries ignore some innovations and support others. We'll look at the mechanics of disruptive innovation in detail in Chapter 2.

In any event, a sustaining innovation is one that creates additional value for a firm by enhancing the products or services already being offered. By increasing the functional capabilities of existing offers, new customers can be reached or existing ones better served. Sustaining innovations create new value for banks organically in the short and medium terms. They do this by delivering growth along established trajectories in a predictable manner.

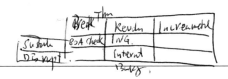

Although this may be a much disputed point, Internet banking is a sustaining innovation. It makes it possible for existing bank customers to use their products in new ways, and certainly with much greater convenience. Internet banking is also a revolutionary innovation: it applied the existing technologies of Internet networks and web-based browsers to the problem of self-service.

Internet banking, however, did not create a parallel industry of Internet-based competitors with much possibility of eroding banking business. Netbank, the most prominent online-only bank, was established in the 1990s, and roundly hailed as a disruptive innovation likely to change the face of banking forever. It was a sign, many thought, that the branch was dying, if not practically dead already.

Netbank failed in 2007. The failure, according to prominent analyst and blogger Jim Bruene, was 'primarily from poorly underwritten loans, both prime and sub-prime, and most of those originations came the old-fashioned way, through face to face broker sales' [6]. The lesson of Netbank is that whilst the reliance on Internet delivery was a novel innovation for the time, the traditional business model was still very much centre stage.

On the other hand, ING Direct, also an Internet-based bank, is extremely disruptive in any market it enters. The difference is the business model change it couples to its direct channels, represented by reducing service to the bare minimum and passing on the savings deriving from this to customers in the form of much higher interest rates.

Breakthrough and revolutionary innovations are often confused with disruptive ones. Actually, though, disruptive innovations are usually not so much about brand new capabilities, as they are about creating new value propositions. These new propositions are deceptive to an incumbent player in a particular market, who will likely ignore them as not core to their own business. They become disruptive, however, when expansion of the entrant causes the new and old value propositions to overlap.

A disruptive innovation usually starts life as a poorly performing, inferior product compared to those of incumbents. But the fact the product or service does less, means it brings with it quite a different cost and value structure than what it precedes. This is attractive to a small segment of the market, one which is probably uneconomic to a mainstream institution. The market may, in fact, be so small or so low margin that not only is it unattractive, it is actually impossible for an incumbent to enter it at all. A disruptive innovation, being less capable, and therefore less expensive, may find attractive returns in this low end space.

Over time, the disruptive innovation improves its performance, and in the end, is as capable as anything else in the market. But this time, the disruptive innovation competes against existing products from a significantly better cost base.

When UK-based Zopa became the first company in the world to launch a peer-to-peer (P2P) lending operation in March 2005, they implemented a radical concept: the 'Zone of Possible Agreement' (from which the name is derived). The term refers to that price point where both borrowers and lenders agree that a particular interest rate is fair to both sides. Zopa links both parties up at this price and facilitates the actual transaction. No bank is involved. This disruptive innovation has now been copied by companies in many countries, including the USA, Australia, Germany, and the Netherlands, and the growth of this new model seems to be gathering pace.

Initially, the facility that Zopa offered to deposit customers was significantly inferior to that of banks: depositors had a much higher risk of losing their money than they would have done using a traditional banking account. Nonetheless, a certain fringe of depositors – those early adopters who were familiar with social networking and had an appetite for risk – began to use the service.

As with all disruptive innovations, however, the capability of the product swiftly improved. Lenders were given more tools, and much more certainty about their returns, making the product a much better fit with a wider market.

In 2008, analyst firm Gartner forecasted, controversially, that peer-to-peer lending might take 10% of all retail lending volume by 2010 [7]. Initially, I was sceptical in the extreme of this, and said so on my blog [8], but when you examine the dynamics of disruption (see Chapter 2), it is possible to see a mechanism at work that might breathe truth into the prediction.

Disruptive innovations are needed to help banks deliver robust growth in the long term. As with any long-term strategy, execution is the problem. Disruptive innovations tend to have very small returns in the beginning, insignificant compared to the main business lines of any bank. But the right disruption, given time, can grow into a business with very substantial scale, as it looks that Zopa may do. An institution able to create and nurture such innovations has, indeed, futureproofed itself. Unfortunately, as we'll see later in this book, doing disruptive innovation is probably the hardest thing a bank can do.

The difference between innovation and invention

Before we leave the definitional part of this chapter, it is useful, also, to draw out the difference between *invention* and *innovation*. Joseph Schumpeter, a Harvard economist who rose to fame through his ground-breaking work in entrepreneurship, was one of the first to make a distinction between these terms. In his conceptualisation, an invention is largely a theoretical construct, an idea with, perhaps, some evidence to prove that it can be implemented in the real world. But *innovation* takes an invention and puts it into practice. It converts what was an initial theoretic construction into something that can do useful work. Another way of looking at this is that invention occurs whenever a concept is created for the first time. An innovation takes that concept and turns it into something real, something that can make real returns.

In general, institutions do not lack invention. Most people have experienced the situation where a few people in a room with a whiteboard create lots of solutions to a particular problem. Usually few, if any, of these solutions (inventions) make it from the whiteboard to practice. It is only the small number of cases that do that are innovative. Innovation is invention plus execution. And, as you'll read later in this book, the process of *killing off* inventions that aren't going to make it is a key part of ensuring a balanced return on an innovation portfolio.

1.2   WHAT HAPPENS WHEN YOU *DON'T* FUTUREPROOF

I described how futureproofing is a business process an institution can use to ensure it correctly recognises things that might affect it in the future, and then respond in an appropriate and measured way to generate a return. One question that's often asked, however, is what the consequence of *not* futureproofing might be. Have not banks been operating, with largely the same services and a fundamentally unchanged business model, for hundreds of years?

Certainly they have, but the pace of change in banking (and in most other industries as well) has increased markedly in recent times. The upshot is that the time between a trend being noticed and its implementation by a competitor is becoming increasingly short. There isn't time to dither around before making a decision: what is needed is a system that can respond routinely to change. Change is the only constant.

Recent research proves the value of having a process that looks forward. A study of North American financial services chief executives conducted in 2007 established a link between the time senior leaders in banks spent looking at the future, and the innovation success of their institutions [9].

The researchers began by examining implementations of Internet banking at 169 banks, starting from the moment it dawned on leaders that online banking on the web might be important, through to its eventual near-universal roll out. They then created a statistical analysis of public statements made by bank leaders to get an indicative measure of how much time each was spending thinking about the future.

The first thing they discovered was that as a result of focusing on potential future states, banks were not only better at making predictions about the future, they were also *much* better at responding. In the study, the average time to respond to the online banking opportunity was just over four years, but the worst performer took nearly nine and a half years before they had something customers could use.

The second, more startling thing, however, was that future-looking banks not only managed to respond more quickly, but the *breadth* of their response was superior. The first Internet banking sites in particular markets were, on average, delivering just over three new innovations each to their customers, but the best of them had up to five. Clearly, the bottom line impact of such a substantial functional difference between leaders and followers is exceptionally valuable.

Whilst evidence such as this is helpful justification of the value of futureproofing processes, one doesn't need to go much further than the rise of PayPal over the last decade to understand what can happen if an appropriate strategy for responding to change is *not* part of the way institutions do business.

In December 1998, a company called Confinity was founded on University Avenue, Palo Alto. The new company set out to explore whether the most popular digital organiser of the day – the Palm Pilot – might make a good electronic wallet that could be used to beam money between owners. Just down the road, another company, X.com, was founded to look at the opportunities surrounding online payments. When the two merged in March 2000, the combined entity, renamed PayPal, swiftly became the preferred means of payment for more than half of consumers who had begun using online auctions. Two years later, when auction giant eBay bought PayPal, its valuation was $1.5 billion. At the time of writing, it operates in 197 countries, provides payment services in 17 different currencies, and has more than 150 million accounts.

The success of PayPal was the result of the confluence of several things. Existing bank products at the time did not lend themselves to person-to-person payments. Paper cheques and direct transfers (in the countries that had them) took too long to settle in a world where auctions completed instantly, and many sellers were unable to take credit cards. Later research [10] found that payment instrument choice on eBay was influenced almost entirely by the certainty of attributes of the product being acquired (i.e., colour, size, and so forth), but in the online auction space, not only did consumers have less certainty about the product they were buying, they were dealing with uncertain individuals as well. Consumers demanded something new to go with this new shopping experience, something that enabled them to reduce all this unwanted risk when it came time to pay.

The innovation of PayPal was that it created a layer atop existing financial relationships that consumers already held. The new layer made it simple, safe, and fast to send money between people. It swiftly became ubiquitous.

As early as 2001, banking journals began to report there might be interesting things on the horizon. One went as far as to note that whilst the number of alternative payment systems was in decline, payment systems associated with inherent transaction streams (such as eBay) were thriving [11]. The publically available pre-IPO prospectus issued by PayPal around this time indicated it was processing over 165,000 transactions per day with an average value of around $50.

Competitors, not coupled with an inherent source of transaction volume (as PayPal was with eBay), swiftly found they were unable to compete. In 2003, Citibank's C2it service closed, followed closely in 2004 by the cessation of Yahoo's PayDirect offering. Then, in 2005, Western Union disposed of its person-to-person service, BidPay.

In 2006, consultancy Booz Allen Hamilton [12] made a prediction with respect to online payment providers:

'If existing providers (predominantly the card issuers and acquirers) do not find an effective counter strategy we believe they could lose 10–20% by 2008 and in the long term up to 30%.'

In my own discussions with bankers around the world on this topic, I conclude these predictions are, if not already true, very close to being so, at least in developed markets. The online payment opportunity is one that banks allowed to slip through their fingers.

Hindsight is a wonderful thing, but the attraction of a privacy and security layer above traditional payment instruments is retrospectively obvious. The problem now is that PayPal is so large (by number of accounts, the largest financial services provider in the world) that competitive responses by banks are somewhat limited.

1.3   FIVE THINGS THAT INNOVATION IS NOT

Innovation is very much on the corporate agenda of a large percentage of financial institutions. Despite that, I am surprised how often I come across misconceptions about innovation and how it is managed.

For those whose job it is to manage the innovation agenda, this can be particularly problematic. The function can often be seen in terms of way-out things new and exciting, disconnected from the core business. When that happens, innovators are liable to get labelled: geekery of any kind rarely drives business returns. Their relevance in the strategic context gets called into question.

Recently, for example, I was approached by an individual in another bank convinced an innovation programme should be all about trying to get new gadgets into the branch. His assertion was that if we weren't doing highly visible public-facing things, the whole conception of innovation in financial services was bankrupt. This individual made a mistake one often sees: he narrowed the innovation agenda to such a degree it would be hard to make a decent return no matter how good the toys were.

For institutions that are starting their innovation journey, it is critical to dispel these kinds of myths immediately. They have a negative effect that can taint efforts for ages afterwards. Such tainting is exacerbated, unfortunately, as some organisations have experienced faulty innovation attempts in the past. Getting distance from these historical issues is critical.

Here, then, are five things people believe about innovation (and about innovation teams) that should be dispelled as quickly as possible.

Innovation is only about things that are completely new

Earlier, I discussed the difference between breakthrough, revolutionary, and incremental innovations. The former two certainly get the most attention, and consequently most people believe innovators do very little incremental. Incremental is the realm of business-as-usual. In fact, people are surprised when I tell them most returns from good innovation programmes come from incremental innovation.

Perhaps the most famous incremental innovator is Toyota. The volume written about this company and its rise from relative mediocrity to global dominance on the back of small, quite basic changes is monumental. Founded in 1937, the company started commercial passenger car production in 1947, and by the 1980s was consistently ranked higher than any other manufacturer in owner satisfaction surveys. Attention to detail, and making small changes to create lasting improvements, led the company to become the largest automotive manufacturer in the world by 2007. Clearly, incremental innovation can pay, even if the individual changes aren't exciting and high profile.

Convincing people that small improvements are important is a big challenge for an innovation function. A common response to the idea that innovators should do incremental is that innovators who do so are reducing themselves to optimisers.

The emergence of instrumented methods for process improvement – Six Sigma is one – has made it easy to confuse optimisation with innovation. When product-type people create a new savings account, are they actually innovating, or are they optimising the savings category based on their expectations that making the change will result in greater market share? This thin line is the principal reason people imagine that true innovators would never concern themselves with anything which fails to change the game completely.

It's easy to understand why there is this confusion, but the difference between optimisation and innovation is really quite simple: you optimise by pulling various levers you already have to get better results. Creating a new savings product is an example: one captures a greater share by varying interest rate, fees, and terms and conditions.

True innovations, on the other hand, create *new* levers altogether, or modify the *range* of existing levers. They don't just change the position of the dials, regardless of how unique the new combination is.

ING Direct, for example, changed the range of its interest rate dial on its savings account for customers by reducing its costs and passing on the savings. This let its product managers price its savings accounts in such a way that ING was able to claim large shares of markets even when it had no traditional banking presence.

Innovation is speculative and risky

Financial institutions spend a great deal of time managing risk, and indeed, it is a core capability for any bank that wishes to lend money successfully. At the same time, banks are not known for innovation, another process which would seem to lend itself to strong risk management principles. There is a reason for this, and it is that innovation *seems* to come with risks unquantifiable in advance. Banks are good at managing predictable risk, but how is one supposed to predict the success of a radical new product? Far better to commit that capital to the lending book where, at least, the statistical return generated is well understood.

It is true that the quantitative risk associated with an individual innovation is very hard to forecast in advance. Some studies have suggested, in fact, that a new product introduction is less than 25% likely to succeed. That situation makes it *appear* as if investing in innovation is a rather poor proposition when compared to the opportunity cost of the money.

Actually, it is possible to predict – to a degree – how risky an innovation might be, and to make determinations about the likely returns. Later in this book, some of the models and other analytic tools which can be used to do that will be discussed, but the fact is, you can't always get a picture of the total risk associated with individual innovation no matter what you do.

Single innovations are risky. Which is why a portfolio of innovation investments is required.

Such a portfolio is no different from the basket of business in a loan book: some will fail, and those most likely to do so should command a higher return. Taken as a group, though, very predictable returns can be made. In fact, given a big enough portfolio, the return can be predicted pretty precisely. One invests in a range of innovations – some more, some less risky – in order to guarantee that a particular level of return is achieved.

In most cases, it is true that incremental innovations carry the least level of risk, so they are the ones that have, most of the time, small returns. By weighting your investment strategy towards incrementalism, you get lower overall returns from innovation, but much greater certainty that you will actually achieve your numbers.

On the other hand, breakthrough innovations are typically very risky. There is a lot that can go wrong: technology might need to be invented, for example, or it might not be possible to forecast the demand curve sufficiently in advance to know that the introduction will be a success. But breakthrough innovations are also the pot of gold at the end of the rainbow: they generate windfall returns when they are successful.

Let's face it, if innovation were so speculative and risky, the entire venture capital industry would be out of a job. VCs typically invest in early stage companies, most of whom will fail. Still more will persist in a kind of living/dead state – neither making nor losing money. Nonetheless, most VC firms make substantive returns for their shareholders – returns well above those available from other investment opportunities. They do it by managing a portfolio of investments.

What return is good enough? That's a difficult question, but generally, it is necessary to achieve some multiple of the institution's internal cost of capital. Obviously, if the returns of innovation efforts are less than that, questions about opportunity costs are going to rear their head. One mantra I recently heard was 'we're in the business of lending, not spending'.

However, to achieve many multiples of the internal cost of capital might involve taking an extremely high percentage of risky – disruptive, for example – innovations. A reasonable benchmark is to examine the returns of existing business-as-usual investments, and then set the bar some material way beyond. One wants to demonstrate that innovation is a preferred investment activity, whilst not accepting so much risk that it is impossible to deliver reliably.

One final point: it is absolutely key that innovation teams have a lot of activity to show for their efforts. They must have a portfolio of things going at any one time, since most will not get through the futureproofing process and generate returns. The wider the portfolio, and the better the mix of activity across breakthrough to incremental innovation, the more risk can be controlled.

One side effect of all this – which we'll discuss later – is that the innovation team will not be likely to have enough resource to do everything. It is therefore important that the innovators involved are superlative influencers: they have to be able to win support from executives to support their innovation agenda. When you go it alone, you just can't get the breadth you need to make innovation a good proposition.

Measurement is hard

Having just read the discussion of the previous section, you'd be forgiven for thinking the only innovation measure that makes any sense at all is return on investment. As I've mentioned a number of times already, unless you are creating new revenue (even if indirectly), there isn't much point in doing innovation. And the ultimate goal of the whole futureproofing process is to protect the ability to create future revenue, after all.

The reason that people think measuring innovation efforts is hard is because it *is* hard. One big problem is this: you create something new on the basis of some future return. There is inevitably a time lag between the moment of investment and the payback. The delay between investment and payback can, in real terms, be some years. This gap disconnects the innovation effort from the actual business outcome. Waiting years to know how well an innovation programme is performing is rarely acceptable to those who make the decisions about funding.

Another problem with metrics that focus only on matters financial is that they tend to make it impossible to do anything, no matter how important, that doesn't come neatly associated with a convenient cash return. Some innovations – those which drive productivity improvements, for example – are notoriously difficult to associate with hard numbers. If you have only cash-based metrics, you are likely to get only cash-based innovation. This results in leaving a great deal of opportunity on the table.

It is necessary to have measurements that touch every stage of the futureproofing process. Without defining the futureproofing process now (it is covered briefly at the end of this chapter and much more extensively elsewhere in this book), there need to be four kinds of measures. Firstly, you need to know how good you are at spotting the trends that matter to your institution. Secondly, having come to a good idea of the future, your idea-harvesting mechanism needs to be instrumented. Thirdly, you have to be able to measure how all these ideas get coupled to execution, and finally, what actual results were achieved.

Having metrics that touch every stage of the futureproofing process is important because it enables an institution to *optimise* the futureproofing process as it goes along. It is almost never the case that everything will work efficiently first try. Pulling levers to optimise is a functional necessity to ensure that an institution makes the returns it needs from its innovation efforts.

Finding the 'mega-hit' is the best way to success

I've lost count of the number of times I've had to disappoint someone when I've told them that the role of innovation programmes is *not* to do work that results in breakthroughs because they *might* be blockbusters. Innovation programmes must be about delivering predictable returns if they expect to continue in times bad as well as good.

This is an important point. In the course of research for this book, I spent a great deal of time with innovators in banks around the world, both those that were successful and those not. One key theme emerged: the average time an innovation team exists is about 18 months. Those that last longer have done so because they've managed to deliver predictably, and we'll be talking about the processes needed to get to that point later in this book. All the rest were cancelled because they failed to generate sufficient returns to justify the resources they were consuming.

With this in mind, everyone imagines that if they were to create a mega-hit, another Google, say, their careers would be made. And they'd be right. But how often does that perfect storm of technology, business model change, and consumer need happen? Answer: very, very infrequently.

Mega-hits, or the breakthrough disruptive new, is what many people imagine when they hear the word 'innovation'. The fact of the matter, however, is that real disruptions, the ones that result in long-term competitive advantage and windfall returns, don't happen all that often. Later in this chapter, I'll look at the history of disruptive and breakthrough innovations in banking. There have been some, of course, but they tend to be few and far between. Arguably, there have been only a few *really* disruptive innovations that have made a significant difference. The rest have largely been variations on a theme.

An innovation strategy that seeks returns only through disruptive breakthroughs is usually a very bad bet given how irregularly the financial services industry has actually experienced them. A far better approach is to concentrate on revolutionary and incremental opportunities.

But even revolutionary innovation has its challenges. I once had someone come up to me and explain that he'd just joined the bank and wanted to do 'revolutionary innovation'. The problem was that what he really wanted to do was *talk* about doing innovation and have someone take his ideas and implement them. Some of the things he was talking about actually *were* revolutionary. But the problem with all of them was that we'd have had to break through some pretty big barriers to execute.

Firstly, they were expensive. Revolutionary and breakthrough innovation almost always is, and money does not grow on trees. The more money you have to find to invest in a particular innovation, the less tolerant you can afford to be about risk.

But secondly, the more revolutionary something is, the more support one has to generate with stakeholders. As we'll see throughout this book, the process of doing this is a question of influence. Influence is the goodwill one has previously developed with potential sponsors. It is a scarce resource that is consumed during the process of shepherding an innovation to the point where it gets the green light. Influence and money, by the way, are often interchangeable.

So, even revolutionary innovations should be considered carefully. Does this mean that innovators should ignore them entirely? Of course not, but such investments have to be considered in the context of everything else the innovation programme is doing. A well-balanced innovation strategy will likely spend most of its money doing incremental work, certainly, but there is plenty of scope to invest in breakthrough or revolutionary innovation once the bills are paid.

Incidentally, I'm anticipating much feedback on this point. In many cases, at conferences and elsewhere, people have specifically challenged the view that banks should concentrate on incremental innovation, suggesting that incremental should be everyone's day job. Real innovation programmes, they opine, should be about changing the game. The view taken in this book isn't necessarily in disagreement with that. It doesn't matter where the innovation occurs, so long as it does. The formal innovation team might not specifically focus on it, but when you take an institution as a whole you'll likely find that most of the return on innovation investments is coming from incremental.

Ideas are the thing

Schumpeter really hit the nail on the head when he contrasted invention and innovation. It is way easier to invent than to innovate, and that's because inventing is an extremely creative, exciting exercise. Innovation, on the other hand, is mainly about hard work. It's about execution, or in other words, actually doing things.

In most companies I've worked with, there is never a shortage of ideas. In fact, every time a meeting is held in a room with a whiteboard, the probable result is a pile of invention. The thing is, few of these interesting squiggles get turned into reality.

Some years ago, I had a very personal experience with this. It was the time that people were implementing their first Internet banking solutions, and my team and I came up with something that we *thought* was a breakthrough: why not screen-scrape all these banking websites and put the results on a single web page? We sat on the idea, and were then stunned when Yodlee entered the market, simultaneously defining account aggregation as a category, a few months later. This story proves two things: firstly, that invention is pretty much valueless by itself if you don't do anything, and secondly, that invention tends to happen simultaneously in lots of different places at once.

Good ideas are prompted by market conditions that are rarely localised. That's why you often get them appearing in lots of places at once. Even if an idea is completely novel and unique, it will not generate a return if you let it sit. *Someone* has to do something with it.

In recent times, open innovation has become very fashionable. In open innovation, you collaborate with other organisations that have capabilities you do not to create the new product, process, or other change you want. But open innovation is really a shortcut from an execution perspective: you get to do the ideation (the fun part) and then buy in the stuff you need to do most of the execution. And there is nothing wrong with that, assuming the internal landscape of an institution permits it.

Perhaps the most prominent industrial example of open innovation is the latest product from Boeing: the 787 DreamLiner, an aircraft due for delivery (at the time of writing) some time in 2010. The idea was to create a faster, more fuel-efficient airliner. But execution required a host of new technologies, new supply chain techniques, manufacturing innovation, and a great deal more besides. That's a *lot* of execution for one company to come up with. So Boeing bought in a lot of what it needed from its partners. Mitsubishi Heavy Industries and other Japanese companies, for example, are responsible for the manufacture of the wing, whilst Saab makes most of the various kinds of doors on the aircraft. The end result? Boeing had a new aeroplane, but had to spend much less to realise it than otherwise.

Whilst the value of individual ideas is low, the process of capturing ideas and evaluating them is of critical importance. Without a systematic way of harvesting ideas from employees, customers, and partners, great creative wells are left untapped. An innovation programme has no connection to the business that supports it without some way of systematically harnessing all this creativity. Then, too, some of the simplest problems to solve might not be noticed at all if there is no process for stakeholders to report them.

Even solving a simple problem – like moving a check box on a form – is something that can contribute to the overall returns of an innovation programme. Unfortunately, people with innovation in their job title are unlikely to be concentrating on such things, which is a pity. You don't have to commit all that much execution to make them happen. Toyota, as mentioned earlier, rose to dominance in auto manufacturing by repeatedly making small changes.

1.4   150 YEARS OF INNOVATION IN BANKS

With all those preconceptions out of the way, we turn now to an examination of a few of the innovations that *have* been significant in our industry in the past. To this end, what follows is a potted history over the last 150 years, covering some of the most significant changes in that time. As I noted earlier, breakthrough innovations have been relatively rare in financial services, though revolutionary and incremental ones occur much more frequently. Regardless of how genuinely new these introductions were, however, there is one thing in common: some institutions led, and the rest responded. Those banks that profited were clever in spotting the emerging opportunities, and actualising them as part of their ongoing operations.

As an aside, my typification of particular innovations in what follows as incremental, revolutionary, or breakthrough is highly subjective. What is breakthrough for one organisation may, indeed, be seen as incremental for another. This, by the way, is true also for the classification of some innovations as sustaining or disruptive.

Our historical tour commences in the early part of the 19th century, with the development of the telegraph.

The late 19th century

The telegraph was first demonstrated practically on an experimental line between Washington and Baltimore. By 1846 lines were available to Philadelphia, and in 1848 to New Orleans. The effect of this innovation was electrifying (pun intended): it reduced the price associated with the information differential between New York and regional stock markets [13] hugely.

But the implications of the telegraph did not stop there. Throughout the 19th century and the early parts of the 20th century, trade between cities was governed by differing exchange rates, also the result of information differentials between cities. As a result, transactions that were geographically separated had to consider the cost of settlement. In the absence of a modern payment system, this meant physical transport of gold, the value of which could vary between geographies. The telegraph changed that, and banks were quick to recognise the potential. In fact, the *New York Herald* complained on 3 March 1846 that 'certain parties in New York and Philadelphia are employing the telegraph to speculate on stocks'.

The telegraph, then, was one of the first revolutionary innovations to be adopted by banks. No new technology was created by institutions themselves, but its application to the business of finance changed the game entirely.

The transatlantic cable (an incremental innovation on the original revolution of instantaneous messaging, from the perspective of the banks) was completed in 1866. With ten or more years' experience using the domestic telegraph in the United States, banks on both sides of the Atlantic were quick to adopt this new means of integrating their markets. They had little choice but to adopt the innovation immediately: the competitive advantage of knowing a price for a security on the same day was unimaginably significant.

The first part of the 20th century

Though these communication innovations served to unify markets, they did little to change how front- and back-office procedures were run. At the time, these operated through significant delegated authority to managers in the branch network, with a system of draconian inspections carried out by head office staff from time to time. Systems were entirely paper-based: ledgers and passbook controls being the principal means.

That worked relatively well, but communication technologies caused the volume and pace of transactions to increase. The race to process the paper was one that banks were in danger of losing. In order to address this, leading banks started to look at the possibilities of mechanisation. By the 1930s, mechanical adding machines had been introduced in a number of institutions. The technology of the time was revolutionary, but from the bank's perspective, this was an incremental innovation: making it faster to do existing work. Later, incremental innovations such as punched cards continued to enhance the speed at which paper could be processed. With eventual broad availability and declining cost of such machines, banks were poised to revolutionise their delivery of services to the public: increased worker productivity meant that more products could be offered, to more people. Both the size and number of branches expanded rapidly as a consequence.

This was the time that a new kind of financial services product started to appear (the credit card), though it wasn't, initially, noticed by banks. The rise of the automobile, and the consequent need to acquire and pay for fuel, led fuel companies to consider how they might make it easier for their customers to deal with them. In 1920, they started accepting cards, at that time little more than a place to record a reference to the customer's account, as well as cash. This innovation – perhaps the first breakthrough in recent banking history – proved popular, and by the 1930s multiple fuel companies had started to accept each other's cards.

The fifties, sixties, and seventies

The breakthrough represented by the first fuel cards went unnoticed by financial services companies for 20 years. The paper cheque was the pre-eminent non-cash payment instrument of the time, and institutions had developed mechanical means of processing them at volume. So when Diners Club invented the first modern credit card in the 1950s, banks were not expecting the effect they would have.

Diners Club was an incremental innovation on the original fuel card: rather than a card which worked for merchants of one type only (fuel stations), Diners envisaged a card which could work with any merchant at all. The Diners Club card was initially launched in New York with 14 restaurants and 200 cards in 1950. But by the end of the year, over 20,000 individuals had the card, and more than 1000 restaurants were accepting it.

Eight years later, Bank of America launched BankAmericard, which later evolved into Visa. Then Barclays, in the UK, followed some years later with a credit card of its own, largely built using systems imported from Bank of America.

Credit cards became something of a phenomenon. They were massively adopted, and suddenly, once again, banks were drowning in paper. The mechanical processing methods of that time had become the critical limiting factor that would constrain additional growth. That's when Bank of America created the first business computer, ERMA, following its initial experiments in 1950. The importance of this breakthrough innovation cannot be understated. It transformed the world of financial services completely: prior to ERMA, banks operated on the basis of paper and delegated authorities, and afterwards they didn't. It was the first time that people and manual processes were *eliminated* from the business of banking, a trend that has only recently started to reverse.

These initial steps towards electronic transaction processing didn't completely resolve the issues banks were experiencing. All credit decisions were still being delegated to skilled individuals at the branch level, a situation that put constraints on how many of the new credit cards banks could issue. There was no robust way to determine the creditworthiness of potential card applicants *at scale*.

In order to facilitate the growth of the new product, a mechanical means of determining the likelihood of default on credit needed to be found, giving rise to the breakthrough development of credit scoring. Initially pioneered by mail order and specialist finance houses in the United States during the 1950s, credit scoring was quickly picked up by a significant percentage of institutions. It was then expanded to other kinds of lending, such as mortgages, particularly in the last 20 years. The most recent innovation in this area has been the introduction of scoring for certain kinds of business lending as well [14].

But the breakthrough of credit scoring had another effect: it started the decline of branch-based decision-making, a trend that has continued till the present day, and set the scene for fully automated self-service lending.

Whilst banks were reinventing themselves in their modern image, the pace of technological development in business computing sped up. Amongst the developments of this time were high-capacity memories and magnetic disk storage, enabling the new machines to store and retrieve data at high speed. These new capabilities, in turn, led to new software techniques, primarily in the form of various database management systems.

Bankers, again drowning in paper-based systems because more customers than ever were now using cheques, immediately saw an opportunity to automate clearing operations. The first bank clearing house was established in London in 1770, but it wasn't until 1968 that institutions found a way to automate the process with their new technological capabilities. The revolutionary innovation of interbank automated clearing was first introduced in the UK in 1968. BACS (for Bankers Automated Clearing Services), as the system became known, expanded quickly, bringing with it associated advantages for member banks, and by 1976, it was handling just under 100 million items a year. At the time of writing, the network handles over 5.5 billion payments per year [15]. In the USA, meanwhile, the first Automated Clearing House (ACH) was established in California in 1972, with other regions following rapidly.

Technology quickly became the *key* enabler for the great majority of banking innovations that followed, and the pace of change began to build. 1967 saw the next breakthrough, when Barclays deployed the first ATM in London [16]. The early machine, built by De La Rue, used a mildly radioactive ink on a paper token, since the magnetic stripe would not be developed by IBM until the following year, and was capable of dispensing fixed amounts only in paper envelopes. But whilst the technology of this first ATM wasn't that advanced, it heralded momentous changes in service delivery for banks: the breakthrough was the idea that customers could *serve themselves*. The modern conceptualisation of the networked ATM was invented by Don Wetzel in 1968 in Texas [17], and included the IBM magnetic stripe innovation as well as modern cash-dispensing apparatus.

The key insight of the ATM – that customers valued convenience over relationship – led to rapid adoption of the machines globally, and forced banks to make additional investments in telecommunications. Early ATMs were entirely offline, so no balance checks were made before dispensing cash. Connecting the terminals to the centralised accounting function became essential as the customer base using the machines broadened.

Then, too, providing the capability to access the central accounting systems in an online mode required further innovations in the back office. As usual, those banks with their eyes most attuned to the new opportunity made windfall gains as they implemented – for the first time – self-service offerings. In the UK, for example, there were more ATMs than branches by 1994, and in the USA, there were 400 or more machines for every million people in the country by the same time [4].

Not all innovations of the 1970s were technological, however. In 1974, Bangladesh was struck by a famine devastating the poor of that country. Professor Muhammad Yunus, then a professor of economics at the University of Chittagong, realised that loans of very small amounts might enable the poor to bootstrap themselves out of crushing poverty. Trying an experiment, he lent less than US$1 to each of 42 impoverished bamboo stool makers in a nearby village so they could buy raw materials. He was repaid – with interest – rapidly.

Microfinance – the breakthrough discovery that lending at the bottom of the pyramid was not only practical, but could be profitable – led to the creation of the Grameen Rural Bank soon after. The founding principle of Grameen Rural Bank is that credit availability should be made on the basis of the potential of a person, rather than assets held. In order to assess such potential, a group of five potential borrowers are assembled who provide a morally binding guarantee for loans issued to two of the members. Depending on repayment performance, loans are granted to two subsequent members and, eventually, the fifth member as well.

Grameen Rural Bank presently has more than 1000 branches, and a repayment rate in excess of 98%. The economic hardship the institution has relieved, though, is incalculable. In recognition of its pioneering efforts, Professor Yunus and the bank were awarded the Nobel Peace Prize in 2006, the first and only time a financial innovation has received arguably the world's most prestigious honour.

The eighties

Although technology was the key driver for innovation in banking throughout the 1960s and 1970s, it wasn't the only thing forcing change. Distribution changes were also afoot. A breakthrough innovation in the 1980s was the entry of US retailing giant Sears Roebucks to full-service banking using its extensive stores network. This departure from traditional bank-led distribution of products was not entirely successful at the time, and led to eventual divestiture of the financial services businesses at Sears Roebucks in 1994 [18]. Nonetheless, the innovation (coupling financial services with other, only marginally related business lines) was swiftly copied by many other retailers, often with significant success. As the chairman of the American Banking Association later remarked, the evolution of non-bank players in retail financial services was leaving banks in 'the unenviable position of trying to keep up with less-regulated, non-bank competitors, while also maintaining a much more expensive infrastructure' [19]. Though Sears were unsuccessful with their play for retail financial services, the model has subsequently been proved out by major retailers such as Wal-Mart and Tesco.

Meanwhile, banks were also broadening their distribution through a range of revolutionary self-service innovations. In the late 1980s the most significant of these was the development of telephone banking. This had first been tried unsuccessfully by Banc One Corp of Ohio in 1979, and pilots continued through to 1982 [20]. The adoption of phone banking was relatively speedy after that, something that institutions could readily have expected after their previous self-service success with ATMs. Naturally, institutions such as the innovative Sanwa Bank of Japan reaped windfall rewards from being first to market: one report was that 40% of deposits and 70% of card transactions were performed through self-service channels by 1984 [4].

The rise of telephone banking next led banks to question whether they could couple telephones and televisions together to create an interactive self-service channel for customers. At the time, the technology to do this existed in the form of Videotex, an early predecessor to dial up services that used the then-developing personal computer. Introduced in 1982, Minitel, the French version of the service, actually achieved relatively high levels of adoption, but in almost all other countries, the success of Videotex was extremely limited. This did not deter banks, who could see the potential of self-service after their initial experiments with ATMs and telephone banking. By 1985, at least 37 banks in the USA offered services using the technology, but these never achieved critical mass. The vision of home-based financial self-service via personal computer had to wait more than a decade for the Internet.

The fact that Videotex was a commercial failure for most institutions does not detract from its status as a revolutionary innovation that drove banks to consider many of their operations in a fresh light. Customers with Videotex could quite reasonably demand access to their accounts in the small hours of the morning, a time when customer service centres would be closed, and even ATMs might be cycled down. Such behaviours were the result of the modal operation of the systems of the time: they could either be processing customer transactions (during the day), or carrying out various administrative tasks such as routine account maintenance and interest calculations (during the night). Most banks were simply not set up to enable both kinds of activities simultaneously. The introduction of Videotex forced institutions to think about the consequences of needing 24×7 access to systems.

Another incremental innovation of the late 1980s was the smartcard. The initial promise of the smartcard was that its embedded computer chip would be more reliable and secure than the venerable magnetic strip first pioneered by IBM more than 30 years before. The first mass use of these cards was their adoption by French authorities as a means of payment for public phones in 1983. It wasn't, however, until the early part of the millennium that the chip-based cards came into wide usage, when the chips were capable of storing not only data but applications as well.

Not all relevant innovation from this period was bank-led, however. Intuit, founded in 1983, was a small software company that sought to help households balance their chequebooks. Initially, Intuit tried to sell its new personal finance management software through banks, but quickly realised that it would have much greater success touching its customers directly. Neither was the personal finance software category unique to Intuit: a large number of competitive programs were quickly brought to market at the same time. Nonetheless, during the late 1980s and early 1990s Intuit's core product, Quicken, went from strength to strength, proving that there existed a segment of bank customers who wanted more control of their finances than that provided by paper statements.

The nineties

In 1992 Intuit added bank direct connect capabilities to Quicken, when it signed a deal with Visa to allow statement download directly into the product. Direct connect was an incremental innovation that enabled personal customers to replicate capabilities that business customers of banks had had for years. With it, they were able to reconcile their transactions electronically from home, something that wouldn't be available to the majority of customers until three years later with the rise of Internet banking.

The first precursor of modern Internet banking launched on 6 October 1995, when Presidential Savings Bank allowed customers to open new accounts over the Internet using a standard web browser. On 18 October, Security First Network Bank, launched by Kentucky-based Cardinal Bancshares organisation (backed by investments from Huntington Bancshares and Wachovia), opened its doors for business. Security First was the world's first virtual bank: it didn't have branches at all, and customers interacted with it via the Internet and call centres. During the bank's first two weeks of operation, it opened 750 accounts from customers in 32 states, more than three times the number that the founders achieved when they opened a traditional branch-based bank in Louisville a year earlier [21].

The software assets of the bank were held by a wholly owned technology development company. This was spun off as Security First Technologies, later S1 Corporation, when the banking portion of the business was acquired by the Royal Bank of Canada three years later in 1998. S1, continuing from then on as a pure technology vendor, began to deploy pioneering Internet banking solutions with other banks, operations it continues to this day.

Security First Network Bank was a traditional bank with revolutionary distribution. Although it was not especially profitable in the early years, the institution was a template subsequently copied by hugely successful direct plays such as ING Direct, launched in Canada two years later. As we've discussed elsewhere in this chapter, ING introduced its own business model innovations to enhance the direct model first pioneered by Security First.

Although it would need to wait some years for large-scale commercial success, 1998 was the year that X.com, the precursor to PayPal, was founded. PayPal was not the only alternative payment system to come into existence around this time, though it has proved to be the most successful. Other systems founded on the concept of secure digital payments, such as the much-hyped C2iT service from Citibank or BitPass from Western Union, have all subsequently closed through lack of adoption. When one examines the ostensible differences between the successful service and those that failed, the true innovation in PayPal's approach becomes clear: it coupled itself to one of the largest sources of online transactions around (online auctions), ensuring it had volume to sustain it, whilst its competitors did not. Subsequently successful online payment systems, such as Google's Checkout service, have followed the same strategy.

The closing years of the 1990s brought one final innovation based on the revolution of Internet banking: screen-scraping-based account aggregation. Technologists, recognising that if people could drive web browsers, it must be possible for machines to do so as well, quickly built automated routines that could log into Internet banking sites and extract account balances and transaction details. These were then merged together to provide a single view to customers, regardless of the number of different banking relationships they had. Yodlee Corporation, founded in 1999, was a pioneer in the industry.

Account aggregation was both an incremental innovation from a technology perspective (being based on the developing capabilities of Internet banking) and a disruptive one from the perspective of distribution. Bankers, fearful that they'd lose control of the customers they were only beginning to attract as a result of their own online efforts, spoke of 'disintermediation', whilst analysts were fulsome in their praise of the new opportunities available to those with a full picture of the 'wallet' of customers. Regulators and customers meanwhile began to worry about the legal consequences of disclosing their account information to a third party. In the end, adoption of account aggregation was slow, and had to wait for the second Internet boom surrounding the emergence of the (so-called) Web 2.0 to attract real consumer interest.

The present day

From 2000 onwards the pace of change, though not wholly driven by technological innovation, has continued. Better clearing systems have seen the emergence of decoupled debit, for example, a disruptive innovation if ever there was one. Account aggregation has led towards high-end personal finance management solutions that are entirely web-based and use the wisdom of crowds to exceed the best efforts of banks in the customer experience domain. And Internet banking has led naturally towards mobile phone banking, which will develop, inevitably, towards phone-based payments based on emerging techniques like near-field communications.

With the pace of change picking up speed, there's little hope of providing any comprehensive account of significant financial services innovations that are beginning to emerge right now. Neither would it be a sensible effort: any attempt would be completely out-of-date almost the moment the words were written.

Nonetheless, the remainder of this book will examine, from time to time, some contemporary financial services innovations, as well as those appearing just over the horizon. The reader, it is hoped, will bear in mind that their retrospective knowledge of many of these will be superior to mine at the time of writing. But that's par for the course, I suppose, when you're writing a book on innovation. No matter what you say, it is invariably out-of-date the moment the manuscript lands with the publisher.

1.5   THE INNOVATION DOWNSIDE

The historical perspective we've just explored offers an interesting insight: few single innovations described remained unique for very long. Although many were breakthrough or revolutionary, very few have generated sustainable competitive advantages. The reason is that most banking innovations are sustaining in nature. Sustaining innovations tend to be extremely replicable in financial services.

When Barclays deployed the first ATM in London, it did not retain any persistent competitive advantage, even though the breakthrough of cash self-service changed the game for the rest of the industry. And when Security First Network Bank of the United States created the first Internet banking site – a revolutionary use of web technologies – it led other major banks into the market by a few short months at the most.

Being first with an innovation does, often, mean a commercial case can be made for a limited amount of risk taking. Bank of America, for example, invested millions to build its ERMA system, and was then able to leverage year-on-year cost decreases that left its competitors scrambling to catch up. But sustaining innovations in financial services wind up being a cost of doing business eventually, since they are replicable by competitors. There is a limited period only in which the innovation will provide any differentiation.

Whatever is introduced today, especially if it is a breakthrough or revolutionary, will almost certainly be tomorrow's legacy that must be supported into the future. Over the life of an innovation (which will likely be measured in years for smaller investments, or decades for larger ones), those costs can mount up. For a sustaining innovation, financial services companies are rarely well served by going far out on a limb. This is a tricky optimisation problem that will be covered later in this book: what is the *right* time to invest in something new? The earlier one enters, the larger the windfall gains that must be available to balance the cost of supporting the innovation throughout its life.

What is the rationale for delaying the implementation of sustaining innovations (a *fast follower* strategy as some call it)? As something new becomes commoditised, its costs of implementation decline. This has the effect of reducing the barriers to entry for any particular new idea for following institutions. The later the institution comes to a particular innovation, the less its costs and risks.

This leads us to three quantitative questions which are important in the innovation selection process. Firstly, how large are the development and operating costs likely to be? Secondly, will the windfall gains for early entry plus the value of any residual advantages be enough to cover these costs? And finally, what is the risk associated with each of these two questions?

These arguments are not necessarily true, however, for disruptive innovations. A disruptive innovation becomes important, from a revenue and strategic perspective, in a much longer timeframe than a sustaining one. If the investment to deliver such an innovation can be controlled appropriately, a rational argument can often be made for early (or even first) entry with a particular innovation.

Making such arguments is one of the primary reasons that coupling a structured means of analysing the future with the innovation process is so very important. Such an analysis allows the innovator to determine whether or not a particular innovation should be framed in sustaining or disruptive modes. This, in turn, provides an important mechanism which guides the innovation selection process.

1.6   AN OVERVIEW OF THE FUTUREPROOFING PROCESS

And now, at last, we come to an overview of the business processes with which the rest of this book concerns itself. The overall process is illustrated in Figure 1.1, which shows the four main things a successful innovation function does as part of its ordinary day-to-day activity. The first, futurecasting, we'll come back to in a moment. The second, ideation, is about inventing new concepts that can reasonably be converted into new activity. Innovation is the process of converting these inventions into a funded reality, and execution, the final stage, is the set of things one does to make sure the idea finally gets into the hands of users and customers.

Figure 1.1 is quite different from the usual representation of innovation processes, which invariably uses stage gates to guide investment decisions. The fundamental concept of stage gates is that there is a 'funnel' of activity. Ideas enter the top of the funnel – often in large numbers – and proceed through various decision points. At each decision point a significant number of ideas are rejected, imposing a Darwinian 'survival of the fittest' approach to selection. At the other end of the funnel, a small number of ideas will 'graduate' to active development, with a smaller number still going on to commercial success (or, for those innovations which don't face customers, internal implementation).

Stage gates do not, by themselves, deal with some fundamental issues facing bank innovators, though. Are the ideas coming into the innovation funnel the right ones? What steps

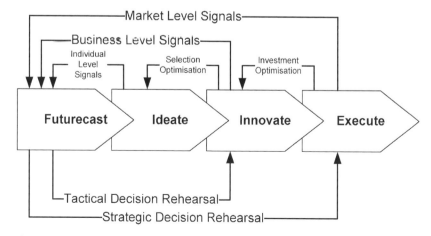

Figure 1.1   An overview of the futureproofing process

need to be taken to rehearse the decisions of senior executives before an innovation decision is made? Are the innovations that *are* being implemented the ones that the bank needs to ensure it has a future? Something beyond a robust stage-gate process is needed to answer questions such as these.

Futureproofing is probably more correctly referred to as a *phase-gate* process: it surrounds a traditional stage gate with additional mechanisms which help to ensure that what goes in (and what comes out) is connected to the strategic reality of a particular institution. And whilst stage gates send ideas through a pipeline in only one direction – towards implementation – a *phase-gate* process sends messages up and down the steps in order to optimise the predictability and returns of the whole process.

Let's now look at each of the phases shown in Figure 1.1.

The futurecasting phase

Futureproofing is a phase-gate process that adds structured mechanisms for dealing with strategic questions affecting the institution's future. This is relatively new territory for most bank innovation programmes. Many practitioners imagine that as the likely shape of the future is not amenable to accurate analysis, there is little value in devoting much attention to it at all.

But whilst one cannot predict the future with *certainty*, it is definitely possible to plan for various likely outcomes given a particular strategic scenario. For most institutions, such planning is de rigueur in any case. Economic questions, such as the likely shape of the economy in the medium term, are routinely forecast in the ordinary course of business. This is possible because the theoretical principles of economic forces are well understood.

This is increasingly the case for innovation processes as well, and the last decade has been extremely busy for innovation theorists. The consequence is that we have working models of the way that companies and their people react to innovation, and these can be used to make reasonable guesses about what is likely to happen. Such theory will be covered in the next chapter of this book. We'll also be looking at other tools – such as scenario planning – that can help guide our thinking about the likely shape of the future.

Scenario planning is a key part of the futurecast. One seeks to create several stories about possible futures. They guide decision-maker thinking, helping to inform the critical judgements that are needed to make important decisions. A scenario doesn't necessarily ascribe a particular likelihood to any particular future, but it does draw out the fundamental forces that ought to be considered before committing an organisation to a particular direction.

This mix of good theory leading to great stories about the future is the principal tool of the futurecast phase, but how does having good futurecasts help the innovation process?

Imagine that peer-to-peer lending becomes significantly successful – successful enough, in fact, that it starts to cannibalise the best customers of traditional banks. The mechanics involved in the set of circumstances which could cause that to happen are developed by the futureproofing process as part of the futurecast stage. This analysis leads the team to develop stories about likely consequences and possible responses, which are given to decision-makers to inform their thinking. They are plausible, and based on the facts that are known *now*.

Perhaps one of the stories is that P2P cracks the mortgage market and swiftly disrupts what remaining margins there are for banks in this segment of the business. A possible response is to spin off a new business to take on the entrant that utilises the superior money buying power of the institution to fend off the attack, leading to market-wide structural changes in the way that mortgages are sold and administered.

Providing such stories about the future informs the thinking of decision-makers. Then, when the innovation team presents a more realistic innovation for go/no-go approval, the issues and constraints will be well understood by those involved. The futureproofing process enables senior executives to rehearse their decision without consequences before they are actually called upon to *make* a decision.

But the benefits do not stop there. Stage-gate processes must be fed continuously with ideas, and in order to get to predictability at the other end, the gating processes need to be rigorous. The overhead in dealing with volumes of ideas is considerable.

When you use futurecasts as an input to the ideation process, the result is that you have a way to connect invention with the strategic questions facing the bank. The stories and scenarios developed by the futurecasting step deal directly with the big imperatives lying ahead. Ideas coming into the pipeline inspired by these analyses are less random, and much more likely to be helpfully applied to the big challenges.

Even during the innovation stage, when ideas are turned into reality, the futurecast is a helpful diagnostic tool. Does the implementation decision being taken now close down options that might be important in the future? Does eliminating an idea (see 'drowning the puppy' later in this book) have strategic consequences that might affect the future of the institution? Indeed, does failing to eliminate what appears to be a great idea from a stage-gate perspective lead to dead-ends later?

The ideation phase

Referring again to Figure 1.1, the second part of futureproofing is ideation. Ideation is the set of things that innovators do to marshal collective creativity around specific things that might make an institution better.

There are two main parts of the ideation phase. The first is exploratory: having a large volume of suggestions coming in from customers and staff is an excellent means of spotting opportunities for futurecasts. These individual-level signals, if they are constantly about a particular issue, are often indicative that the dynamics affecting the business are either undergoing change, or have already altered. Noticing them (and starting to write stories about consequences) results in a new wave of ideation activities that can find ways of remediating the change.

The second part of ideation, though, is collating the collective suggestions of the organisation, finding a way to prioritise and classify them, and feeding them through the futureproofing process. The great thing about ideation, as I said earlier in this chapter, is that it is a great deal of fun. Dreaming up new ways to do things is intensely creative and far less complicated than actually making things happen. Consequently, the ideation step is an excellent means of gaining broad support for the innovation agenda. Anyone can participate, and with that participation comes support, without which innovation can be like swimming uphill in treacle.

The innovation phase

Ideation naturally leads to innovation, the third part of the futureproofing process. In innovation, one seeks to create something real from the ideas that were previously prioritised during the ideation phase. Real, in this context, means everything that has to be done to get an idea from the point that it seems interesting enough to explore further to the go/no-go decision that leads to a funding decision. The set of things that must be done, practically speaking, varies from innovation to innovation. But in financial institutions, the innovation step is most likely to involve a great deal of influencing and salesmanship. Most of the time, innovation programmes themselves simply don't have control of sufficient capital to launch something in their own right. They must win the money from benefactors in the business in order to move forwards. Innovation, then, is about creating the tools necessary to convince stakeholders that whatever-it-is is a superior investment choice compared to whatever else is on the table.

The mechanism through which these tools get built necessarily involves a great deal of interaction with executives outside the innovation team. In the process of this interaction, another set of futureproofing signals surfaces: those that have to do with the responses of particular business lines to internal and external stimuli. For example, a particular innovation may be rejected on the basis that it is 'distracting' from the core business. Such rejection is informative. If the innovation has to do with an expanding business, it may be that management does not have its eye on the disruptive threats to future revenues that will inevitably emerge in the future. An appropriate futurecast would then be one which dealt with this potential for a small player to take away the future.

On the other hand, if the business line was struggling to meet its growth targets, it might indicate that management, responding rationally to a market event (such as the entry of a competitor with a cost advantage), might determine that the best strategy is focusing on protection of the existing customer base and improving margins, leaving the future hanging in the balance to ensure the present. In that case, a relevant futurecast might be one that explored the opportunities for growth inherent in a *downmarket* rather than an upmarket move.

The specific response to signals is not as important as capturing them as evidence to support the futurecasting process. The thought leadership inherent in the futurecast can then be used to improve the quality of thinking in the institution and rehearse future decisions before they must be made. In the innovation step, the future decisions of most importance are essentially tactical. Which innovations should one pursue rigorously, and which should be eliminated? Not all innovations, when subject to detailed analysis, are equally good. Selecting those most likely to be successful requires an understanding not only of the present situational state of the business, but its likely state in the future as well. The outputs of the futurecast stage enable the rehearsal of these tactical decisions as well as the ones that senior executives must make later in the process.

During the innovation phase, the quality of ideas that have arrived from the ideation step will be subject to quite deep analysis by the innovation team. The purpose of this analysis is to answer three key questions. Firstly, is the timing of the innovation right, given market and other conditions at present? Secondly, is it possible to actually make whatever-it-is work? And finally, what will it mean if the institution does? (I always paraphrase these questions as 'Can we? Should we? When?') These three questions inevitably have to be answered in the lead up to a funding decision anyway, but are also useful as a means of optimising the mix of things arriving from the ideation phase. This optimisation is a key part of balancing the innovation portfolio – a necessary step leading to predictable returns on innovation investments.

One final point on the innovation phase is that it does not often involve *actually* delivering things that can be used: prototypes and business cases may be created, certainly, but these will not be the ones that would be relied on once the actual funding has been committed to the innovation. The whole point is to create whatever needs to be done to *win funding*. It is better to do this with throwaway artefacts than fully scaled out solutions. The former are inexpensive to produce, whilst the latter aren't. Since the only way to de-risk the overall return on innovation is to have a large and diversified set of innovation investments, delaying as much of the spend as possible is a functional necessity.

The execution phase

And finally, we come to the execution phase. This commences immediately after funding is won, which is the ultimate point of the innovation stage. At this point, decision-makers have been convinced the innovation represents a superior investment choice compared with other opportunities they have had presented to them. They've had their questions satisfied about the opportunity, the technical capabilities of the team and the firm to execute, and are sure that *now* is the right time to execute.

But what happens next is determined by the kind of innovation being considered. Earlier in this chapter, I explained that innovations are either sustaining or disruptive. The former are well suited to development by core business lines using their ordinary delivery processes. But the latter are much more difficult. In most cases, existing businesses are incapable of disrupting themselves. This is because the rational choice is generally doing things in a way integrated with current business being done. But by so doing, the cost and value decisions of the main business are imposed on the disruptive one, *whether that makes sense or not*. For something truly disruptive, this usually results in failure.

Here, then, is one of the most important reasons for using futurecasts extensively: a senior manager with financial responsibilities is being asked to invest in an innovation which will – eventually – cannibalise his or her own business. Furthermore, they are asked to do so without imposing their own controls. That is a strategic decision of the first order, and most executives will simply not make such a decision without extensive preparation. Such preparation must necessarily include education about the possible consequences of *not* investing in the disruptive innovation.

The actual decision to commence investment is the first of many activities that characterise the execution phase. Along the way to launch, an innovation is subject to many compromises. Some of these are reasonable, and others not. For example, a security team well versed in the reality of large systems may impose constraints on an emerging innovation (such as special infrastructures, expensive authentication devices, or comprehensive penetration tests) which make the innovation an expensive exercise. Sometimes these compromises lead to innovation trauma, a situation where no further innovation is possible. Everyone concludes that the pain of innovation is much greater than any benefits that arise from it.

It is the role of executives (with the coaching of the innovation team inevitably) to help those assembling the parts of the innovation to understand they are doing something genuinely *new*. Old processes and procedures might work in the traditional context, but may not be appropriate now. This is especially true for disruptive innovations, but can also be the case for sustaining ones as well. Without careful nurturing during the execution phase, an innovation can simply fail under the weight of previous (even unrelated) legacy.

Why does this occur? As I will discuss later in this book, it is primarily the result of an authority asymmetry. In most institutions, there is a group of individuals who are empowered to say 'no'. The bank will be happy to let them do so, because the certain present is far less risky than the unpredictable future. Saying 'no' is the safe option.

There are far fewer people, however, who are actually authorised to say 'yes'. These individuals are the ones that give an innovation the life-support it needs during its birth. The executive who initially approved the investment in the first place is likely to be one, but he or she will not have the bandwidth to supervise every detail of implementation. Finding and engaging people on the right side of the authority asymmetry is a critical aspect of the execution phase.

Authority asymmetries are a natural consequence of all organisations, and do not reflect poorly on any particular bank. In fact, it is probably true to say that the greater the asymmetry, the more stable the bank! The natural response of any manager who has to meet a particular number in a profit and loss statement is to shoehorn anything new into a controlled, certain framework.

The strategic decision that resulted in the funding decision is not the only decision that futurecasts help rehearse. During implementation, a large number of choices must be made which have significant effects on the future success of a particular innovation, and potentially, on future ones as well. For example, a decision to implement an innovative new payments system based on the existing legacy infrastructure in place may *seem* like an architecturally sound decision. It may, even, be less expensive initially. But such a decision commits one to the legacy cost base of the entrenched infrastructure. This may be disastrous if competitors have a cost advantage resulting from, say, a brand new implementation. In this case, the futurecast enables decision-makers to see legacy cost drivers are one of the key strategic inputs they have to control in order to ensure success. IT, and other powerful interest groups, would have to be managed in a (for them) unnatural direction.

In the end, if everything has gone well, the innovation has been built into something internal users or customers can get their hands on. The response of the market (or internal user base) provides interesting signals that are input to the futurecasting process. Is the innovation interesting to the press or competitors? Do customers respond immediately, or is the take up more gradual? What is the analyst response?

These are questions which are market level in nature. They provide coarse-grained material that helps to optimise the set of questions that ought to be asked about the future. In this respect, an implemented innovation (even if it is ultimately a failure) may be seen as a probe that helps reveal interesting information about the future, and is therefore a hugely important input to determining the likely set of innovations that may be needed later.

In 2007, ING announced its Our Virtual Holland experiment – a major exploration of the use of virtual worlds. According to the company's website on the topic, 'ING is taking the virtual-world phenomenon seriously and expects that part of its future Internet activities will become three dimensional. ... ING seeks to gain a better understanding of improvements it can make to products and services by assessing valuable feedback from inhabitants who will experience ING in Second Life' [22]. By 2008, it had closed down the innovation, again remarking that it had chosen to do so because of its need to focus on merger activity it was undertaking at the time, even though 'virtual worlds continue to be an interesting and for ING a relevant development'.

That the experiment lasted only a year does not reduce its value as a lens illuminating the future, both for ING and any other institution that might be interested. Our Virtual Holland was the subject of considerable press and analyst activity, a signal of a potential market trend. Customer adoption was relatively low, but a number of substantial companies joined ING on their virtual island. These facts are indicative of an innovation released before its market was appropriately developed on the one hand, or of a technology not good enough to fulfil customer functions on the other. But regardless of the interpretation, ING has useful data that will likely make its further guesses about the future of online financial services superior to those of its competitors.

Optimisations in futureproofing

Before we leave this broad brush overview of the futureproofing process, a bit more expansion on a comment I made at the beginning of this section is in order. Whilst an ordinary stage-gate process moves ideas through to implementation in one direction only, the phase-gate process described here seeks to optimise that flow by adjusting the preceding stage using the experiences of the latter one.

The input to the execution phase is the set of things that have been funded through the activities of the innovation team. Throughout the development of the innovation, however, much will be learnt about the capabilities of the institution and its reaction to various situations, both from an internal and an external perspective. This learning provides essential *optimisations* for the innovation phase, and will almost certainly change the way the innovation team selects and pursues specific innovations.

If an innovation enters the execution phase, for example, and it is then discovered that basic technological requirements cannot be easily met within schedule and cost constraints, the effect on innovations in earlier phases of the process can be significant. Some innovations which may have been selected as incremental on the first innovation will have to be dropped. Others, which may have been unattractive given simpler opportunities available, will now become priorities. The innovation team will naturally balance its choice of what to put forward and what to ignore based on the reality of what can and cannot be done. It is usually the case that all ramifications of a particular innovation will not be understood until very late in the process. Optimising the set of investment choices presented to stakeholders with this new information is a sensible and reliable way of ensuring the overall innovation portfolio remains stable.

Similarly, input to the innovation phase is the set of ideas that have passed through whatever collective creation process has been implemented. Many of these ideas will be excellent when standing independently, but difficult or impossible to get through to funding. In order to guarantee a stable innovation portfolio, however, the innovation team will necessarily need a good flow of ideas that it can reasonably hope to develop. Over time, the team will discover additional knowledge and experiences that let it determine more accurately the chances of getting a particular concept through the process. It is therefore able to adjust selection criteria from the ideation process to ensure that this flow is adequate consistently.

1.7   WHERE TO GO NOW

Much of the rest of this book covers futureproofing processes in detail. But before we examine those, the next chapter looks at a range of innovation theories and models in the context of banking. Before you nod off to sleep at the thought of that, there is a very good reason for examining these now: theories give us a way to explain the reasons particular innovations may or may not be successful. Coupled with appropriate story telling resulting from the futurecasting tools we'll be looking at later, theory gives us a means for being robust in our expectations of the future.

Chapter 3 takes theory and examines specific innovation issues in the banking context. What sorts of innovations are available to banks? What innovation strategy is appropriate? And, in general, how do bank innovation programmes develop?

Theory aside, the main body of this book is about processes that innovation teams and their sponsors can use to get some predictability out of their innovation investments. There is a chapter on each of the phases I talked about a moment ago that provides this information in detail. You'll find this material starting at Chapter 4.

Whilst I'll mainly cover the innovation processes that lead to futureproofing, a process in isolation is just paper and abstraction. Such things have value if you are a consultant, but making things real requires people. And people, in the context of futureproofing, are just about the most critical resource there is. Time and time again, it has been shown that the difference between a successful innovation programme and the rest is the quality of the leader in charge of the programme. In Chapter 8 you'll find material that explains the roles and responsibilities of the innovation leader.

And a leader is nothing without a great team. Innovators, being creative non-conforming types (if they are any good at all, that is), are a special breed. There are many different archetypes, and it is functionally necessary to have them all in the team to ensure that the overall innovation function is a successful one. Chapter 9 has a lot to say about innovation teams.

Chapter 10 explores the systems and processes that surround an innovation team. Inevitably, the values and processes of an institution have a very big impact on the way that innovation can develop. Read this chapter if you're interested in reward systems, measurement and metrics, and the other things an innovation programme must do to fit in with the rest of the bank.

And finally, Chapter 11 presents 39 steps you can use to build an innovation team, and rounds out the rest with some final recommendations and conclusions that haven't been presented elsewhere.

I hope you enjoy this book, the result of the very hard work of many people. Many practitioners of innovation, both in financial services and from other industries, have been involved. They have been kind enough to share both their successes and failures in these pages, and I owe them a debt of gratitude. But there is another group whose work I have borrowed: the generations of scientists and academics who have been studying the problem of innovation for decades. Without their rigorous observation and theorising, the processes we'll be using in futureproofing would be more art than science. It is to their work that we will turn in the next chapter.

2

Innovation Theories and Models

What you will find in this chapter

- Models that describe how and why people choose to do new things.
- How the market reacts to innovations.
- Five key things that can describe any innovation.
- How large institutions decide what to do about innovations.
- How institutions can be overtaken by seemingly small things.

We turn now to an examination of the mechanics of innovation. Although the discipline of innovation is relatively new, the science underpinning what innovators do has been expanding for decades. There are now powerful theoretical models available which are excellent tools for driving predictability in the innovator's work.

It is interesting how often managers and practitioners discount theory as something of much value when running their day-to-day businesses. They prefer, instead, to speak of experience and intuition as the cornerstones of most of their successful decisions. Models and theories? Who needs them?

The truth is, behind the scenes, their minds have constructed their own mental models of processes they've observed and *these* are the tools they use to formulate their plans. The difference between their home-grown mental models and published theory? Practically none, excepting it most likely took years (and countless mistakes) to create those models.

What we examine in this chapter, then, is a shortcut. Why make mistakes and spend years before you are effective if you don't have to? In any case, for the purposes of futureproofing we are really interested in three kinds of models.

The first helps one understand the dynamics of an individual's choice to use an innovation or not. Designing things that are interesting and attractive to customers or end-users is often seen as a marketing exercise, especially in financial services. But as innovators, it is important to go beyond product or service attributes if one wishes to make investment decisions predictable. A model that helps us understand how an individual makes their adoption decision is, then, a useful tool when you have to decide which innovations to pursue, and which to ignore.

Another group of theories we'll examine relates to the way that end-users of something new communicate about whatever-it-is amongst themselves. It is rarely the case that an innovator is able to reach out to every single individual who might be interested. Instead, it is necessary to find ways to get particular target audiences to talk amongst themselves. Innovators need to get 'word of mouth' working for them, or risk a failure of adoption. This is innovation from the perspective of the market.

And the final set of theories we'll talk about explains how whole organisations, collectively, respond to innovations. We look at the processes that govern the internal decision-making of stakeholders in institutions, the way that institutional behaviour can select some innovations and ignore others, and how an innovation which is revolutionary or breakthrough can be mistakenly confused with one which is disruptive.

Looking at innovation from the perspective of individuals, markets, and large organisations is helpful because these are the main parties we will be dealing with from now on in our futureproofing process. At the ideation phase, we're concerned with selecting those innovations that make sense from an individual's point of view. Later on, during the innovation phase, we are about the perspectives of the market, since it will be these that determine whether or not we can create a business case that makes economic sense to fund. And in the execution phase, the perspective of the firm is essential: it is the compromises imposed by firms during development and marketing which determine how much of the original vision of the innovation actually makes it into the hands of customers or end-users. No matter how good the idea to start with, or how great the business case, a firm will tend to impose its own set of values and behaviours on something new. Unmanaged, this can happen to such a degree that the innovation fails in the market.

2.1   THE INNOVATION ADOPTION DECISION PROCESS

The failure of individual innovations is a way of life for the professional innovator. Far from being something that ought to be derided, such failures are highly informative. In fact, failure to fail quickly enough is a pretty sure way of destroying any predictability in the innovation programme at all. Early failure ensures that resources can be put elsewhere as quickly as possible.

It is therefore desirable that a large percentage of work undertaken by innovators does not make it through the early stages of the innovation process. What is highly *undesirable,* however, is that an innovation makes it to the execution phase, and *then* fails. By that stage, not only has a great deal of time and effort been wasted, the credibility of the innovation function is also in jeopardy.

What is the chief reason for a failure at the execution phase? Assuming the innovation team has been engaged throughout delivery (a functional necessity in order to manage the inevitable consequences of compromise – something that we'll talk about in Chapter 7), the most likely cause is that an innovation has failed to engage its audience appropriately in a way that supports their decision-making process prior to adoption.

Innovations, being new, demand behavioural changes from end-users or customers, and by far the greatest part of any particular market for an innovation is resistant to change. People, and by extension the organisations composed of them, are creatures of habit. Anything that changes the status quo is likely to be disagreeable, at least at first. Therefore, careful management of the decision process an individual utilises when confronted with something new is important.

An individual goes through five stages in their decision process, all occurring, more or less, in sequence. This will be news to those who hold to the commonly held belief that the innovation adoption decision is pretty much instantaneous. It is so very tempting to imagine that one can create a value proposition so compelling that it is the matter of a moment's consideration before the need to immediately adopt is obvious.

But, in fact, the adoption decision is never that fast. When one considers all aspects of each stage, considerable time can pass between the instant when an individual discovers something innovative, and the time it is actually adopted. Much of this time is spent communicating with other like-minded individuals and gathering the knowledge required to support an eventual decision and implementation process. Figure 2.1 illustrates the five stages that most people go

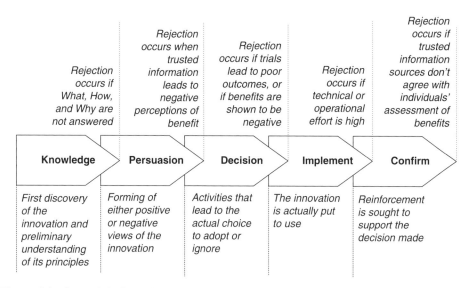

Figure 2.1   Stages in individual adoption decision process

through when trying to decide whether they should make the effort to change their behaviour by trying an innovation. Let's now look at each of these stages in a little more detail.

Knowledge

The decision process commences when an individual first becomes aware that a potentially useful innovation exists. The discovery triggers a cursory review of any information readily to hand so that a decision can be made about whether there is much point exploring the innovation further.

How this initial discovery occurs is quite dependent on the nature of the innovation. In some cases, awareness happens by accident, say, through a chance conversation with a trusted third party. This is the event that triggers the collection of additional information.

Sometimes, though, an individual might initiate activities which lead to discovery independently. People tend to expose themselves to ideas naturally similar to their present interests and belief systems, unconsciously rejecting others. During this process, they might uncover innovations which interest them.

And other times, the discovery happens because an individual realises that a need exists for which no obvious solution is available. In those cases, it might be that an active search is conducted which could lead to the discovery of an innovation that is suitable.

Regardless of the means of discovery, a potential adopter will typically seek to answer three additional questions: 'What is it?', 'How does it work?', and 'Why does it work?'

'What?' is obvious. It represents the set of assumptions and deductions an individual makes in order to create a mental model for themselves of the problem an innovation is intended to solve, and its suitability for doing so. Everyone comes to the 'What' quickly as part of the discovery process. The other questions, though, are not so easily answered in many cases.

The 'How' question is particularly important. Before a decision to adopt something can be made, it is functionally necessary that the individual understands how to operate the innovation. Acquiring that knowledge can be complicated and time-consuming, and tends to be more so if the new thing is especially different to what was familiar before. As you would expect, answering the 'How' question generally takes longer for breakthrough and revolutionary innovations than for incremental ones.

In recent years, some banks have added security tokens to online banking. These are usually devices that generate a one-time number that must be entered with a password and user id when the customer signs in. As an innovation, they are an excellent example of the 'How' question: the end-user must understand how to operate the device before they can make their adoption decision. A failure to acquire this knowledge results in loss of convenience when the online service can no longer be accessed. On the other hand, failure to adopt the device at all has the much less certain consequence that a customer *may* be exposed to additional security risks. Many customers will not adopt at all, given a choice.

The 'Why' question, though not as important to adoption in most cases as 'How', will occasionally be part of the knowledge-gathering process. 'Why does it work?' is information that isn't always required prior to adoption. But an individual who doesn't understand how something works is much more likely to discontinue use the moment something unexplained occurs. Lacking any reasonable basis to explain unexpected behaviour, the end-user concludes the innovation is unreliable (or uses any other excuse, excepting it will almost always *not* be user error!). Of course, in some situations, it is almost impossible to begin the use of an innovation without extensive 'Why' knowledge.

When Internet banking first began its widespread adoption, effort was devoted to explaining the functionality available, but most end-user attention was focused on how various security measures worked. Consumers simply wouldn't use the new service until they understood how their money was protected. It was far, far simpler for many users (in the absence of good 'Why' knowledge) to continue what they'd always done: ring their call centres and visit their branches.

The lesson for innovators at the knowledge stage: make sure an innovation is accompanied by ready information that enables potential users to easily answer their 'What', 'Why', and 'How' questions. If possible, these answers should be baked into the innovation right from the ideation phase. Frankly, if it is impossible to communicate what users might need to know succinctly, then it will certainly be much more difficult to do so once the innovation has been rolled out. And a failure to provide the right information in easily digestible form at all will cause adoption to stall at the decision stage.

Persuasion

It is tempting to imagine that with their 'What', 'How', and 'Why' questions answered, individuals would then make a decision one way or the other. Unfortunately, in most cases, this doesn't happen. People need more reason to make a behavioural change than a few well-crafted pieces of information provided by an organisation that has most to gain from their favourable decision.

At the persuasion stage, the potential adopter has become at least a little emotionally engaged with the innovation. They certainly won't be ready to make a commitment, but they might use the information they have to think about the innovation in terms of their personal circumstances. They will attempt to see it in terms of jobs they could accomplish or unmet needs they might resolve *if* they chose to adopt.

During this internal imagining process, people form positive or negative perceptions about the change they are considering. But because the innovation is something new (and will almost certainly require a behavioural change if adopted), individuals don't trust themselves to make a decision outright. Instead, they seek additional reassurances from sources they personally trust, and these either reinforce or reduce perceptions previously formed about the innovation. The reassurances come from media they believe in, from friends and colleagues, in fact, from any source *other* than the promoter of the innovation.

When a salesperson comes into an institution with a new technology, for example, it would be highly unusual if their claims are the only source of information used by a decision-maker. Instead, trusted advisors and external information sources are consulted. The salesperson starts the decision-maker down the path to adoption, but other sources of verifiable fact provide the necessary reassurance before the go-ahead is given.

The decision to do something new is fraught with uncertainties. Adopting an innovation is an exercise of taking risks with consequences that might not be predictable in advance. The persuasion process, then, is ultimately about the things people can do to eliminate, as much as possible, uncertainties about an innovation *in advance* of the decision to adopt. To see how this can work, let us return again to the example of online banking.

Firstly, let us assume a potential adopter has satisfactorily acquired the knowledge they need about the innovation to begin the persuasion process. They know, for example, that online banking will make managing their finances more convenient, that it uses their home computer and Internet connection, and that their money will be secure because of encryption.

Equipped with this knowledge, they seek the opinions of friends and family before finally signing up. One of two things can happen at this point. The first is that they encounter someone in their social network who has *bad* perceptions of Internet banking – perhaps they've been the subject of online fraud. This additional evidence *reduces* the veracity of information they've previously obtained in the context of their personal situation, and they are *less* likely to make a positive adoption decision.

On the other hand, suppose they encounter someone who used online banking and achieved significantly better personal results compared with traditional channels. In this instance, the new evidence *increases* positive perceptions, making it more likely that adoption will occur.

Depending on how innovative the person is, there can be many iterations of this process before the actual decision point arrives. Individual innovativeness is something we'll come to later in this chapter.

Decision

Finally, a conclusion is reached about whether to adopt. Until this moment, most people go through an evaluation process with a degree of see-sawing as positive and negative information arrives from sources they trust. Because of this, the point at which the actual decision must be made can be somewhat traumatic, depending on the level of riskiness inherent in the decision. This is especially so when the moment of adoption is time-bound: situations where the individual has little or no control over the timing of a decision.

Consider the case of an introductory mortgage reverting to market rates in 2008. Having enjoyed the benefit of a discounted interest rate, customers were forced to refinance in order to avoid drastic increases in their repayments. During the 2008 credit crunch, the availability of mortgages dropped to unprecedented lows as banks faced market dislocations which required them to tighten their lending criteria substantially. Faced with higher rates and unavailability of cheaper mortgages, customers were forced to examine innovative solutions, including those that involved selling partial equity in their homes at substantial discounts. The fact that these decisions were time-bound made them especially traumatic.

Because any new innovation requires effort on the part of the adopter, one way to ease the actual point of decision is providing a way to trial without consequences. Trials are known to increase the speed of adoption processes as they reduce the consequences of making a bad decision. If the innovation turns out not to be as efficacious as expected, the old solution can be returned to use without much effort.

When some banks rolled out mobile banking in the early part of the millennium they were surprised by how few consumers actually wanted the service. The problem, then, wasn't that customers weren't interested in banking on their mobile phones: it was that the inherent risks involved in trying this novel new concept without the ability to experiment first were significant.

Consider the things that could possibly go wrong. Firstly, customers were exposing their personal financial information through a new, largely unprecedented channel, with unknown consequences from a reliability and security perspective. They were not sure how mistakes would be corrected, what their liabilities might be in the event of errors, or how they could recover if they lost their phones. Then, too, there were the consequences to the phone itself: what if the software caused them to lose their ability to make calls? As a result of these and other factors, adoption of mobile banking was relatively uninspiring.

The lesson here for institutions is that a new innovation – especially one which is revolutionary or breakthrough – will most likely be successful from the perspective of the adopter if they have a way to trial the innovation first without consequences.

Implementation

With the decision made to adopt, the individual now starts those activities necessary to put the innovation to use. Remember, adopting something new typically involves a behavioural change of some sort, so the process of implementation can be likened to that of breaking a habit: it requires a great deal of personal effort and unlearning.

Innovations that require less habit breaking tend to be more successful than those that do, simply because end-users have to put in less effort to use them. This is also true at the scale of the firm: the more effort is required to instil the new thing into a culture, the slower adoption will, in general, be.

Because of the effort involved, the implementation process can easily stall if preconceptions that were formed in earlier stages of the decision process turn out to be false. Is the innovation harder to learn than expected? Does its performance match what was anticipated? Are people surrounding the adopter approving or disapproving of the change?

During the implementation process, significant mismatches of expectation can easily cause dis-adoption. When it becomes *easier* to abandon the innovation (in comparison with projected benefits that might accrue with perseverance), implementation almost always stalls.

An excellent example occurred when National Australia Bank, the largest institution in Australia (and with operations in a number of overseas markets), decided to implement its first Internet banking system in July 1998. It had lagged other major institutions in providing the facility, but this had led it to observe that the chief concern amongst potential customers was security. It determined, therefore, that it would launch with significantly better security facilities in place than those of its competitors.

It rolled out its Internet banking with a client-side digital certificate: a piece of technology that had to be downloaded from the bank and embedded into the personal computers of customers. Whilst this undoubtedly did increase the security of the initial offering, it also made it complicated and inconvenient. The installation process often failed for first-time customers, and many experienced difficulties whenever they moved computers. As the concept of a certificate was hard to explain, when things went wrong, customers weren't able to fix the issue for themselves. In the meantime, the bank's competitors were deploying online banking with simple password- and user id-based login, which led to unflattering comparisons on the usability front.

All this complexity led to a stall at the implementation point of the decision process for many customers, and the National lagged the other big banks in Australia for adoption of the Internet channel for years afterwards.

One final thing of note can occur during the implementation phase: the *reinvention* of the innovation in a way that its initial proponents never envisioned. Individuals adopting something new are often inclined to repurpose the innovation to better suit themselves and their personal situations. When Facebook, a technology for social networking, rose to prominence in late 2006, it was primarily a means for people to link up with friends and colleagues. But in 2007, Facebook added a feature it called 'Platform' – a way to enable users to add features for themselves. Savvy users of Facebook created new capabilities that made the site more relevant to themselves and their friends. They were able, in the language of innovation, to reinvent Facebook.

Reinvention, if the innovation allows it, accelerates adoption, usually because it requires less change of behaviour. In general, institutions have been slow to accept reinvention as a viable diffusion strategy for their services, mainly because they have not been able to see obvious answers to the inevitable concerns about risk and security. Nonetheless, the age of the reinventable bank is near: a savvy customer can today use a combination of non-bank products (like PayPal, pre-paid debit cards, peer-to-peer lending, and third-party product aggregation sites) to create a bank-like service out of component parts.

Assuming that inevitable misunderstandings and missteps are correctable during the implementation phase of the decision process, the change becomes institutionalised as part of the way an individual does things. It loses its distinctive newness as the idea merges with that which preceded it. This typically marks the end of the implementation part of the process, but surprisingly, is not always the end of the adoption decision.

Confirmation

When an individual starts to use something new, even if it has been well integrated with what was being done previously, he or she will continue to seek reassurance that what they've done was actually correct in the broader context of their social network. There is a feedback loop from observers that is used to *confirm* the decision was the right one. When the perceptions of others do not match those of the adopter, it sometimes leads to dis-adoption. This is the reverse of the oft-quoted word-of-mouth effect.

Later in this chapter, we'll be looking at word-of-mouth effects in detail. Suffice to say for now, however, that an individual who dis-adopts can be a very, very expensive proposition. And the earlier in the product lifecycle it occurs, the more expensive it is. Why? Because the innovation decision process requires there be other people around who can provide positive reinforcement. When someone dis-adopts at the beginning of the lifecycle, there are far fewer individuals (in comparison with the total audience) available to make up the difference with positive messages.

In recent times, financial services provided a leading example of this effect in action. In 2003, researchers began to notice that consumer adoption of Internet banking was falling short of what everyone was expecting. In an attempt to understand the phenomenon, a group of innovation scholars tried some experiments based on whole-of-market adoption data for the United States [23]. The completed analysis attempted to quantify how expensive a dis-adoption choice could be if not managed correctly. Here are the headline numbers: a customer that adopted online banking in year one and discontinued use without telling anyone about it would have cost a particular institution just over $200 in lost savings and future revenue. But assuming they reinforced their negative perceptions with five of their friends, the cost soars to more than $3000.

It is unfortunate that most customer lifetime value calculations in institutions do not account for the social effects that are core to understanding of innovation processes. The usual method, which is to compare customer spending with historical norms, fails to acknowledge that word-of-mouth effects – both positive and negative – can make a customer hugely more (or less) valuable.

This investigation of online banking provides innovators with some interesting information that is often missed by marketers engaging in lifetime value calculations. By averaging out the profitability of customers over five years, the investigators found that the first 2.5% of customers were worth 80% more than those who adopted relatively later. This additional value is derived *entirely* from their ability to influence others during and post the confirmation stage.

As you would expect, this premium declines (because the effect an individual can have in comparison with the total size of the market becomes less as more of the market has adopted) with time. By the time half the market had adopted online banking, relatively earlier individuals were worth a 30% premium. The remainder of the market has no premium at all.

Classifying individuals by the time they adopt something, it turns out, is critically important to understanding how the overall market responds to innovation. It is to this point that we turn next.

2.2   PERSONAL INNOVATIVENESS

Whilst the adoption decision process of Figure 2.2 is a good way of describing the underlying mechanics of the adoption decision, it doesn't explain why some *groups* of people adopt something and others don't. It is a model without a market context. Conveniently, though, innovation science provides us with an appropriate categorisation framework we can use to address this point.

The basic means used to do this is segmenting adopters into groups based on their responses to innovative things. From now on, I'll use the term *innovativeness* to describe these collective behaviours, which, as it turns out, are accurate for large organisations such as banks, as well as individuals.

The terms early adopter, laggard, and similar are regularly used to describe levels of innovativeness. Most people assume these are some kind of shorthand that's come into regular business use. The truth, however, is that they're part of a conceptualisation of innovation by Everett M. Rogers, famed for his theories explaining how new ideas are communicated in

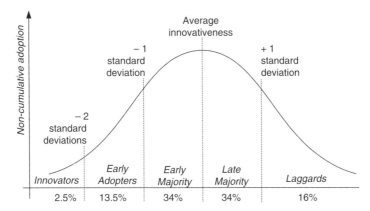

Figure 2.2 Classification of adopters of innovation

social systems. His book *Diffusion of Innovations* [24] is the pre-eminent text describing the forces governing innovation processes.

Recognising a need for an adopter classification framework, he proposed the system illustrated in Figure 2.2 whilst he was obtaining his doctorate in the early 1950s.

Rogers was amongst the first to realise that when you plot non-cumulative adoption (the number of people who take up an innovation at any point) over time, what results is a near normal distribution of adopters, with the peak rate of adoption occurring somewhere close to the middle of the graph.

With this realisation in hand, Rogers next proceeded to conceptualise the measure of innovativeness of groups based on the *time* they adopted a particular innovation. Those with average levels of innovativeness, then, would be the ones that adopted when most of their peers were also doing so – in the middle of the graph.

The conveniently normal distribution of the curve in Figure 2.2 makes it simple to divide the curve into classifications based on how much a particular group differs from those with average levels of innovativeness. Those with a background in statistics will recognise that the standard deviation – a measure of the amount of variability a particular group has – is a convenient way to do this. What Rogers did then was slice up the curve based on how many standard deviations away from the average level of innovativeness a particular individual might be.

This led to a big advantage: the normal distribution is always shaped in the same way, so the Rogers classification framework provides a good means of determining the percentage of adopters in each classification.

Proceeding from left to right in Figure 2.2, the first classification is *innovators,* representing about 2.5% of all adopters in a given market. Innovators are typified by very high tolerance of uncertainty. They are the ones who are happy to experiment with things new, and will not be dismayed if they don't work at first. They typically have significantly superior access to financial resources, are better educated, and their interest in doing things differently sets them apart from their peers. Sometimes, this means an innovator will not have the respect of these peers, and indeed, the local social network in which he or she operates. Despite this, though, individuals in this classification have a critical role in the process of innovation: they are the ones who find new ideas and impose them on a social system from the outside. Without addressing the innovators in a given population, innovation doesn't happen at all. That 2.5% is the only market that's available for things that are truly different from what has gone before.

Why is this important? For an institutional innovator, the process of rolling out something new necessarily means finding these first beachhead individuals. Because the innovation decision process *discounts* messages from the promoters of an innovation, someone has to be around to help people during their persuasion stage. Conveniently, the innovators segment likes uncertainty, so it is about the only group who will listen at first.

The next classification, comprising about 13.5% of a market, is *early adopters*. These individuals are generally more tightly integrated with a particular social system than their innovator cousins, and in fact, tend to be the opinion leaders in those systems. What is an opinion leader? In the context of innovation science, it is an individual who, when observed to adopt, is likely to influence others to do so as well. Because of this, the role of the early adopter is a critical one to address during the design of an innovation: they are the ones from whom a stamp of approval is required before the next 34% of the market is likely to follow.

How did early adopters get to be opinion leaders in the first place, though? The key attribute, it seems, is that they are judicious in their adoption patterns. They tolerate relatively high levels of uncertainty with respect to an innovation, but will be inclined to dis-adopt easily if they feel that their initial perception of an innovation was faulty. They are the denizens of the confirmation stage we spoke of earlier when examining the adoption decision process.

Opinion leaders maintain their status in the social system by being seen to be right *most of the time*. In other words, early adopters are relatively easy to *get* in the first place, but much harder to *keep*. A failure to quickly dump an innovation that doesn't seem to be working out would affect their place in the order of things.

The *early majority*, our next classification, are only slightly ahead of the average individual when deciding to adopt whatever-it-is. They are cautious in their choices, preferring to wait and see before jumping in head first. They do, however, have a certain tolerance for uncertainty, knowing that taking some risks is necessary if they wish to reap the rewards of having the innovation before the majority of their peers. In the adoption decision process, they are characterised by seeking out the experiences of opinion leaders and using them to inform their decision and persuasion stages. The early majority comprises roughly one-third of the market, and because they are so numerous, they are substantially influential on the remaining adopter categories.

An innovation is now at a substantive turning point. When you have just 16% (the innovators and early adopters) of a market using something, the effect of an individual can be very significant. That's why the online banking study we looked at previously reported such significant premiums for those customers who go online early. Their lifetime value was heavily influenced by the positive effect they had on driving demand for the innovation from later customers. Past this point, however, these individual effects become much less important, and, in fact, the innovation will be self-sustaining *regardless*. It reaches an effective critical mass point where, no matter what happens, people will continue to use the innovation. We'll talk about critical mass points and their characteristics shortly.

The late majority, on the other hand, almost never adopt anything until most of their peers have done so. They prefer to wait and see, often to the point where it becomes an economic necessity to use the innovation. The key characteristic of the late majority is that most of the uncertainty with respect to the innovation needs to have been resolved during the decision process.

The late majority comprises 34% of the market, and represents one of the biggest single segments. The fact the segment is so big is a reflection of the number of people who have already adopted that are now available to talk to. By this time, if the innovation is doing well, more than half those people who could be using an innovation *will* be using it. In other words, most personal social networks in a particular market are likely to have experience of the innovation, and will be able to contribute positive messages about it.

The final adopter classification is *laggards*, always the last to adopt any new innovation. Usually, their decisions are made on the basis of experience in the past: the traditional way of doing things. They are naturally sceptical of anything new, and delay adoption as long as possible to ensure that any remaining uncertainty about benefits is eliminated. This is entirely rational behaviour from their point of view, and the consequences of *not* adopting are generally perceived as far less than those of doing so. This segment generally accounts for about 16% of a given market.

Now, why is this theoretical framework of value to innovators in banks? In the first place, we can use it to create a map of those an innovator has to influence with positive messages to get agreement to proceed with something new. Support from many different parties has to be won before a final investment decision is made, and every one of these will likely be in a different adopter segment. For example, if the innovation is a new kind of product that will touch customers, there will inevitably be a need to involve marketing, product managers, probably IT (if they need to build new functionality), and many other groups. Not all these groups will be equally innovative, and a structured approach to dealing with this variability is required. This is something we'll examine again in Chapter 7.

The decision to support a new innovation requires funding and is, ipso facto, an adoption decision for an institution. Initially, very few people will be interested in supporting the new thing, and it is the role of the innovators to help reduce uncertainty sufficiently that early adopters (those with sufficient vision to realise the implications of whatever-it-is) can be convinced of the benefits. These, in turn, are valuable in convincing stakeholders in the early majority classification of the benefits. There is no point, conversely, in trying to target the late majority or laggards when one needs a decision with respect to an innovation *without* having first won the support of the early adopters and early majority. The late majority and laggards, with low tolerance for uncertainty, will almost always say 'no' to anything new out of hand.

The second reason the classification is useful is that it provides important guidance about what to do *after* the investment decision is made – the execution phase in the futureproofing process. With due consideration to the innovation decision process, an institution must be careful in targeting prospective end-users (for an internally facing innovation) or customers (for an externally facing one). There is, once again, little point in attempting to get the late majority or laggards to change their behaviour without first having achieved adoption in the more innovative segments. As prior segments are inevitably the gatekeepers to adoption for later ones, identifying the early adopters is a key part of the launch of anything new.

2.3   INNOVATION FROM THE PERSPECTIVE OF THE MARKET

The observation that most of the time the non-cumulative distribution of adopters of a particular innovation is close to normal (see Figure 2.2) leads to further revelations about the behaviour of markets in the presence of an innovation. When you look at the *cumulative* number of individuals who have adopted an innovation over time, the curve is always S-shaped, as shown in Figure 2.3.

The S-shaped curve is characteristic of a process in innovation science called diffusion. It explains how, from a market level, the social networks we've been talking about in decision processes and personal innovativeness work together.

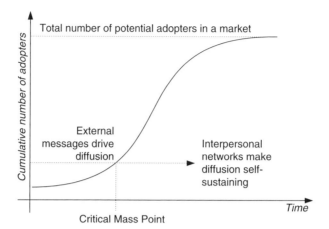

Figure 2.3 Adoption S-curve

When an innovation is first exposed, only a very small number of people change their behaviour to make use of it. These are individuals previously described as *innovators*: they are the ones who discover ideas and feed them into a particular market. Sooner or later, these innovators manage to convince a few early adopters to try out the new thing. These, in turn, convince some of the early majority to adopt.

During this process, especially during the earlier stages, the process of diffusion can stall at any time, and in order to forestall that, it's necessary to continue to push the innovation into the social system. In other words, a bank that wants to make sure its new products and services are taken up must continue to recruit from the innovators segment continuously. That way, when the innovation decision process fails to convert new individuals, others are available to make up for the loss.

Around the time significant numbers of early majority adopters gain the innovation, however, something interesting happens: the diffusion of the innovation becomes self-sustaining. This is the critical mass point shown in the figure. Adoption rapidly accelerates, and the innovation swiftly becomes ingrained across most of the market. This is the time that most of the early majority and late majority will acquire the use of the innovation.

Then, adoption begins to slow again as penetration approaches the total size of the market. That is inevitable, of course, since all that remain are laggards, who practically have to be forced into adoption in the first place.

What is the underlying mechanism that drives the kinds of curve in Figure 2.3? The answer is that individuals communicate with one another during the diffusion process: they seek opinions and form perceptions based on the feedback of those in their personal social network. This communication is the main thing that influences the innovation decision process at the persuasion and confirmation stages.

The idea of social networks has become very popular recently in the context of technology-based tools that implement ways of linking up with friends and acquaintances online. Facebook, mentioned earlier, is an example. But social networks – more traditionally called interpersonal networks – have a very long history in innovation science, and are key to understanding the diffusion process.

Around the time a new innovation is discovered by someone who might adopt, they turn to others in their network of contacts to help them evaluate the possible value of the innovation in comparison with what they presently do. Usually, such networks are formed of people who are similar in views, interests, and needs. When a likely adopter accepts new information from one of these individuals, the potential that they will accept or reject is linked to how similar the individual is perceived to be. People prefer to accept advice from those they think might have similar needs and wants to themselves.

These interpersonal networks and the communications that flow within them proceed in two stages. Firstly, new ideas are communicated to the market through one-to-many channels. These could be mass media, of course, but increasingly are direct marketing, emails, or social media such as blogs. The important point is that the party behind the innovation provides the information informing the first stage of the adoption decision process to a large number of potential adopters. Innovation scholars refer to these as external *influences* on the social network. From the perspective of the innovation decision process, this information triggers the knowledge stage. This then starts the process of gathering information from other sources considered more reliable than those coming from the promoter of the innovation.

Some of these early adopters will be *opinion leaders*, people with strong interpersonal networks, and whose opinions of whatever-it-is are unusually influential in particular interpersonal networks. These opinion leaders have the ability to cause other adopters to try out the innovation as well. Sooner or later, the process becomes self-reinforcing, leading to the critical mass point of Figure 2.3. The ability of early adopters, especially opinion leaders, to influence the social network they are part of to try out new things is known as internal *influence*.

When you plot the non-cumulative adoption curve from the perspective of internal and external influences, the way this works out becomes clear. Figure 2.4, which illustrates the process, starts at point A with almost all adoptions occurring as a result of external influence. Over time, though, this decreases as interpersonal networks start to activate. Where the critical mass point occurs, at point B, we have the first occasion at which internal influences account for more adoptions than external. There is then a sudden drop in the ratio of internal influence to external influence adoptions. At this point, the innovation would likely be impossible to contain: too many people would be using (and communicating) about it to close it down.

The work of innovation scholars had, at this point, progressed substantially from the mechanistic characterisation of adopters proposed by Rogers as part of his doctoral thesis in the 1950s. And in 1969, the next step was taken by Frank Bass, a noted American academic who is now regarded (post his death in 2006) as one of the founders of marketing science. Bass, looking at the two-step model we've been talking about, realised that expressing the process as an equation would enable an organisation to *forecast* the likely shape of innovation adoption curves. This fundamental equation has now become known simply as the Bass model [25], and has resulted in a huge number of academic studies on all manner of innovations, including the online banking study we've referred to earlier in this chapter.

In order to use the Bass model, one needs three pieces of information. The first is a parameter describing the amount of internal influence present in a particular market. This is usually represented by the letter q, and called the coefficient of imitation. The second parameter needed is one that describes how much effect external influence, like mass media, has on the diffusion process. That parameter, often called the coefficient of innovation, is represented by the letter p. And finally, the innovator needs to know the size of the market for a particular innovation, represented by the letter m.

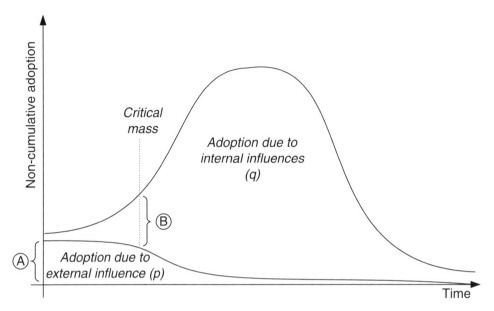

Figure 2.4   Adoptions from internal and external influences

The full specification of the Bass model is shown in Equation (2.1). y_t is the number of adopters of a particular innovation at time t, and Y_t is the cumulative number of adopters that have taken up the innovation at that time. Using this model, it is possible to predict at any time t how many people will have the innovation. This is very useful when one must know, for example, cash flows that result from a particular innovation. It is also about the only way to get to an idea of when the critical mass point will be reached. For our purposes, that is a very important thing to know: it tells an institution when it can stop pumping the potential adopter base with messages. That, in turn, provides an early indication of the amount of money that needs to be put aside for marketing of whatever-it-is.

$$y_t = \left(p + q\frac{Y_{t-1}}{m}\right)(m - Y_{t-1}) \tag{2.1}$$

But there is still a problem. How does one obtain appropriate numbers for p and q? Lots of research time has been spent on various ways to get an answer. The first thing that springs to mind is conducting some kind of survey, but because p and q represent very abstract concepts, there isn't a simple set of questions you can ask of potential adopters to get an approximation.

Another thing that doesn't work is to take the first few periods of sales (adoption) data for the innovation and use curve fitting to get the numbers needed. The problem here is that to get a stable estimate of p and q, you need to have the adoption data up to the point that critical mass is reached. But by that time, the innovation is already out in the market, and the need for a forecast is well passed.

An approach that has been used successfully, however, is to get the adoption data for an innovation as similar as possible to the one under consideration and use statistical curve fitting (such as non-linear least squares) to get the parameters from *that*. For example, if an institution has complete adoption data for their customers using Internet banking (most institutions do), and the innovation under consideration next is, say, web-based personal finance management, it is likely that the parameters will be sufficiently similar for appropriate generalisations about the likely diffusion pattern to be made.

What happens next is that definitive characteristics of the innovation are examined in comparison with the one from which the parameters were extracted. We'll be looking at these characteristics next, but the important thing is that the difference tells us whether to shift the S-curve left (faster adoption) or right (slower adoption).

Forecasting by analogy, as this is called, is a technique that should be in every innovator's toolkit, and it is a good idea to get as many complete sets of adoption data as possible. That way, innovators have a reasonable database of p's and q's to choose from.

2.4   CHARACTERISTICS OF INNOVATIONS

So far, we've looked at innovations from the perspective of the individuals adopting them, and from the more aggregate view of the whole market. But what is it about particular innovations that cause some to be widely successful and others not?

For many years, innovation researchers spent most of their efforts attempting to answer this question, looking at diffusion networks and personal behaviours of adopters. More recently, though, defining the specific attributes of the innovation itself has proved helpful. There are generally considered to be five of these attributes. Figure 2.5 shows these and their effect on the diffusion curve.

Consider, once again, the introduction of mobile phone-based banking by institutions. The idea here is that customers who have mobile phone handsets – especially those with high-end devices that also perform email, calendaring, and other office functions – would be advantaged by having access to their accounts directly from these devices. At present, the method through which this occurs is an SMS message, a cut down version of the more conventional Internet banking page, or a special program installed on the phone. But for the purposes of this discussion let us limit the means of access to a special version of the web page built especially for the mobile channel.

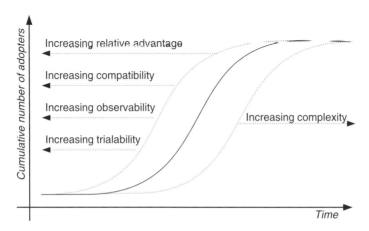

Figure 2.5   Effect of innovation attributes on speed of adoption

Continuing using the Bass-based modelling discussed earlier, we could reasonably take adoption data from Internet banking and use it to extrapolate interesting things about the likely shape of the S-curve for mobile banking.

In the context of mobile banking, then, let us examine the five key attributes of innovation.

Relative advantage

Recall from our examination of the individual adoption decision at the start of this chapter, one of the things an individual is seeking to determine is whether the new thing is *actually* better than the old one. An adopter expects, given the pain of behavioural change they must undertake in order to get the innovation to work in their personal context, that they'll achieve a substantial payoff as a result. This is the concept of relative advantage.

Although it is tempting to conceptualise relative advantage in purely economic terms, this does not always capture the total picture. Sometimes, the new thing provides superior social status. Gold, platinum, and black credit cards are considered far superior to the ordinary sort, even though their features are not that different from the standard uncoloured versions. And sometimes, the innovation provides relative advantage in terms of greater convenience, as was the case with Internet banking.

Regardless, whatever makes the new thing better than the old contributes to its overall relative advantage. If an innovation has greater relative advantage than the thing it replaces, the adoption curve should be moved to the left.

In the case of mobile banking, there are several dimensions to the relative advantage question when compared with Internet banking. The first is the added convenience of being able to bank wherever one wishes. Internet banking alone confers only *'whenever'* based access, so mobile banking has significant relative advantage on this score.

On the other hand, the small screen and poorer input capabilities of most handsets mean that customers will find it less convenient to actually *execute* the transactions they wish using the mobile channel. So for this dimension, mobile banking is actually *less* advantageous than the available alternative.

But the important question to be answered when working out the likely diffusion curve of this innovation is what *job* the customer is likely doing when he or she uses the handset to access bank services. Many studies have concluded that the most likely use is account balance enquiry and bill payment, both functions which require relatively little user input.

Overall, then, assuming most customers want mobile banking to be able to pay bills and do account balances, it is likely that the relative advantage of mobile compared with Internet banking is higher.

Compatibility

When people make their adoption decisions, they do so on the basis of existing perceptions of the problem they are trying to solve. Their sets of values, previous experience, and understanding of needs are all important inputs to the process. Therefore, an innovation which is consistent with these things is far more likely to be adopted than otherwise.

Let's consider the case of a customer whose channel choice is telephone banking. He or she is used to doing banking by telephone, so when a bank then offers mobile banking, it is a relatively small step to adopt. On the other hand, a customer who uses the branch is quite unlikely to make the leap to mobile directly. For them, the innovation is not compatible with their familiar ways of banking, which likely involve direct face-to-face contact.

How compatible is mobile banking with Internet banking? They are both self-service innovations, largely familiar in operation, and with similar outcomes. Customers who have adopted Internet banking might be expected to have addressed the uncertainties in their own mind about the security of transactions and the performance of online services in general. Furthermore, they will already have adjusted themselves to working with bank services in an interactive, though not face-to-face manner. Their perceptions of the mobile channel are likely, therefore, to be highly compatible with what they've already come to expect from their banks. In other words, mobile banking is probably about the same from a compatibility perspective as Internet banking. Following this argument, you would not expect to move the diffusion curve at all from a compatibility perspective.

An innovation with the compatibility attribute will tend to be adopted more quickly than one without it. An innovation which is compatible moves the adoption curve to the left.

Complexity

In order to realise the relative advantage of an innovation, an adopter has to be able to make whatever-it-is work. This process is either more or less difficult than the present solution. Clearly, if the new thing is harder to use, fewer consumers will choose to adopt it.

When National Australia Bank released its secure Internet banking, it was ultimately the complexity of its digital certificate solution that caused adoption to lag. Customers had simpler alternatives, and the relative advantage – better security – was insufficiently great to motivate them to put up with the additional bother.

Let us also consider our hypothetical customer with their mobile banking adoption choice. Mobile, once it is set up, is likely to have about the same complexity as Internet. But it is not usage that we are most interested in here, because adoption depends on potential customers being able to trial the innovation. Setup, then, becomes a very important question indeed. If the mobile banking application is a cut-down web page, setup should have roughly the same difficulty as Internet, though the user interface of the phone will obviously determine how true this really is. That is hardly the case for a downloaded application, however, which requires rather more user involvement, even for so-called 'over-the-air' installs.

An innovation that is more complex than what has gone before, with its associated greater understanding and learning time (the knowledge and persuasion stages of the decision process), will be adopted more slowly than what it supersedes. A complex innovation moves the adoption curve to the right.

Observability

The diffusion processes we've been examining thus far in this chapter have been driven, largely, by individuals communicating information amongst themselves about the innovation through their interpersonal networks. Another source that can inform the innovation adoption decision, however, is plain observation.

An innovation which is easily observable tends to be adopted more quickly because the evidence that it works is obvious. Such observability means the adopter is able to reduce their uncertainty much more quickly.

Banking products and experiences, in general, are not that observable. Concerned as we are with privacy and security, the idea of enabling people to 'look over the shoulder' as we conduct transactions is not that palatable. During the early days of Internet banking, institutions, perhaps instinctively, knew that this would slow down customer take up of the new channel. What did they do? Most provided a 'demo' feature on their sites, enabling their customers to have the look-over-the-shoulder experience *without* seeing real transactions. It was a positive move that sped up adoption.

How observable is mobile compared with Internet banking? Probably more so, though it is not as if one can easily look over the shoulder of a user and see what is going on. Internet banking, on the other hand, happens in the privacy of the home, and is not directly observable at all.

But the observability attribute may not be related directly to the specific experience of mobile. Mobile banking offers entirely new usage scenarios, which can be observable in their own right. An end-user with a mobile payment chip in their handset can simply tap their phone at the bar in order to pay for drinks, for example. This behaviour is itself observable, and leads to more rapid adoption as potential adopters 'discover' the innovation for the first time.

In any case, an innovation that is observable will diffuse faster than one that is not. Such an innovation moves the diffusion curve to the left.

Trialability

The final innovation attribute we'll cover here is trialability, or how easy it is to use the innovation without risk of consequences if something goes wrong. When a trial is possible, experiments are a great way for potential adopters to reduce uncertainty about the innovation before making the decision.

Trialability is especially important for earlier adopter segments than later. The earlier the adoption occurs in the product lifecycle, the fewer people in the local social network of the adopter will have knowledge of the innovation. For the innovator's segment, it is highly unlikely that *anyone* will have any knowledge of the innovation at all. To reach these segments successfully, therefore, attention to the trial scenario is essential.

In financial services, it tends to be difficult to offer trials of products, and easy for channels. After all, if a customer doesn't like a channel experience, they can always switch. But products tend to have contractual or procedural provisions that make getting out hard.

As channels, both Internet banking and mobile banking are pretty trialable, when considered in isolation. One can usually log in and play around without consequences, abandoning the exercise if the experience isn't to one's taste. Then, too, most banks provide demo versions of their Internet and mobile versions, so that customers can see what they are getting in advance.

On the other hand, getting a mobile banking application to actually work usually has a few prerequisites. You need to have a mobile handset that is capable of running the application. You need a contract with your telecommunications provider that enables the transmission of data. And, of course, you need to be registered with your bank in some way to enable access via the handset.

But once all those things are in place, trialling mobile banking is easy. In fact, as mobile banking on platforms like the iPhone has demonstrated, all you have to do is download the bank's icon from the AppStore. The experience is quite a bit easier than trying to get a browser working on a PC for the first time. In fact, if you are already an online banking user, most of the time all you have to do is put in your online banking credentials to get immediate access.

So from this perspective, mobile banking is more trialable than online.

How much should the curve move for each attribute?

Figure 2.5 shows the direction the curve should move depending on the relative attributes of an innovation, as we just discussed. But the next question is how *much* should the curve move for each of these attributes?

As we'll see later in Chapter 5, the innovation phase makes use of the adoption S-curves we're attempting to construct here because they give us a relatively robust way of guessing how many people will be using an innovation at a specific time. With that information, it is possible to construct a forecast of cash flows over time.

The first thing to know is that not all innovation attributes are equally powerful in their effect on the adoption decision. Multiple studies have shown relative advantage and compatibility are the two most important attributes from a diffusion perspective.

Since the end goal is to get to a cash flow forecast, it is best to frame the movement of the S-curve in terms of the budgetary cycles of an institution. For most banks such cycles occur annually, and one method I've used successfully is to move the curve in 6-month increments. For example, if an innovation has greater relative advantage than what it precedes, moving the curve left by about 6 months is a good way of recognising this.

The point of all this is *not* to get to a prescriptive forecast of adoption with any particular level of accuracy, by the way. These curves are all ways of classifying the likely innovation investments the team will make *in relation* to all other possible investments. As long as the same method is used to move the curves around *across the portfolio*, the results are perfectly tenable.

Let us work through an example of how this might work for our hypothetical innovation.

Firstly, we need to determine the parameters of the Bass model. Conveniently for us, the online banking phenomenon has created a fertile ground for research, so much of the statistical work has already been done for us. We'll use the parameters $p = 0.008$, $q = 0.61$ and $m = 32.4$, which are based on industry data [23].

Our analysis of mobile versus online banking leads us to believe that mobile has greater relative advantage than online. This moves the curve forward by half a year. On the other hand, we think compatibility is about the same, so that doesn't have any effect at all on curve movement.

Because of the download requirement, or maybe because the innovation requires more fiddly setup, we say that mobile is more complex than online, so this slows the diffusion curve by 6 months.

Observability, especially if there is a payment chip embedded in the mobile phone, is probably greater for mobile than for online as well, so this moves the curve forward 6 months. And trialability is also easier than for online, for another 6-month movement.

In other words, we would expect the diffusion of mobile to run approximately 1 year ahead of the analogous innovation of online banking.

Using these data, we can see how this model compares in Table 2.1.

Assuming that year 1 was 2007, it is interesting to validate these predictions against those made by experts. Online Financial Innovations, a research house that studies these trends (and on whose data the original estimates for P and Q were based, incidentally), predicts a much slower start for mobile than our estimate by analogy – some 23% less, in fact [26]. But their forecast is also for much greater adoption, more than 33% more households in year 3.

Table 2.1   Forecasts for mobile banking

Year	Known online banking penetration (millions)	Forecast mobile banking penetration (millions)
1	0.68	1.36
2	1.36	2.44
3	2.44	4.13
4	4.13	6.66
5	6.66	10.26
6	10.26	14.92
7	14.92	20.21
8	20.21	25.17
9	25.17	28.83
10	28.83	30.89
11	30.89	31.82
12	31.82	32.19
13	32.19	32.33
14	32.33	32.37
15	32.37	

2.5   INNOVATION FROM THE PERSPECTIVE OF THE FIRM

So far, this chapter has looked at innovation largely from the perspective of individuals. Larger organisational units (such as whole banks) are important for our study of innovation theories as well. Whether an innovation is aimed at individuals (such as a product or channel innovation), or is internally facing (a new communications or collaboration technology, for example), it will almost always be necessary to get organisational approval before investment in whatever-it-is can be authorised.

With this in mind, some additional principles that describe the way banks choose to accept and then implement innovation is useful. What is the primary difference between the processes described for individuals and those of firms? Chiefly, it is that the underlying dynamics are complicated by the fact firms are composed of *multiple* individuals who all influence the process collectively. There will be both champions and opponents for any particular innovation, and the way these interact determines the eventual shape of the outcome.

Though this sounds complicated, innovation science provides us with tools that can help extrapolate the behaviour of individuals to the collective outcome for an institution. The remainder of this chapter expands the models we've already looked at into the organisational situation, before closing with a look at how even the most brilliantly managed institutions can ignore things happening in their own markets to the point where their own revenues are in jeopardy.

Characteristics of organisations

An organisation, such as a bank, is an established social system that exists to serve particular goals. For most institutions, this is likely to be the financial reward of shareholders. Organisations are a way to perform the activities necessary to reach such goals in an efficient way. When broken down into its most fundamental units, an organisation is comprised of five main elements, which are shown in Figure 2.6.

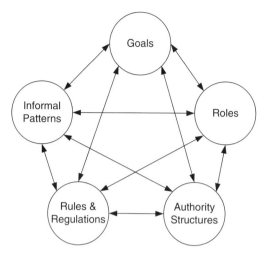

Figure 2.6   Characteristics of organisations

To the first of these, I have alluded already: the need to meet certain goals. For institutions, the goals tend to vary depending on the ownership. If the institution is publically traded, then the primary goal is usually to provide financial returns to shareholders. Credit unions, which are not-for-profit organisations, are established for the purposes of providing credit at reasonable rates. And various cooperative models, such as Grameen Rural Bank we first looked at in Chapter 1, are established to improve the welfare of participants.

The second aspect of organisations are prescribed roles; offices to which duties are assigned. These roles comprise a set of tasks which are performed by specific individuals that occupy the office. Of course, the individual office-holders may change, but the role itself does not, and neither does the set of behaviours expected by whoever holds the role.

An organisation also has an authority structure, comprised of hierarchical ordering of various roles. Usually (though not in every case) there is a chief executive of some kind, from whom all other authority devolves. Such hierarchical ordering ensures that everyone knows who is responsible for what, and dictates who can give direction to others.

But even the chief executive of an institution operates with respect to formal rules and regulations. These govern the behaviour of an organisation and are implemented in terms of policies, procedures, and other mechanisms established by the organisation. They operate as a formal memory of what is, and is not, acceptable – whether that be a quality control measure in a call centre, or a formal policy governing the behaviour of line managers when hiring and firing.

The last aspect of organisations is the set of informal patterns, the corporate culture if you like, that emerges over time. Institutions evolve ways of doing things, a set of norms and values. They are passed on through person-to-person and group-to-group interactions and can be quite malleable. A bank, whilst it might not have prescribed policy that controls absolutely how employees interact with each other in meetings, will nonetheless observe certain conventions. There might be, for example, certain norms around minute taking, addressing comments through the chair, or introducing newcomers at the start. Whilst these are not written down, they are nonetheless observed rigorously.

These five characteristics (goals, roles, authority structures, rules and regulations, and informal patterns) have been shown to affect an organisational measure of innovativeness.

Innovativeness, in this case, is defined as a measure of the likelihood an organisation might adopt something new relative to peers. Usually, this is operationalised by studying the adoption time of a basket of innovations over time.

For example, the more definite the authority structure of an institution, the less likely it is to be innovative. And if the organisation is especially command-and-control (a very typical situation for banks), with great amounts of authority held by relatively few individuals, innovation is much, much slower. This follows from common sense really. Any institution which prescribes the actions of its employees significantly is quite likely to stamp out the very behaviours that lead to innovation – creativity, experimentation, openness, and acceptance of failure.

The level of innovativeness is increased, however, in banks where individuals filling roles possess greater expertise and experience compared with their peers in similar organisations. This is so because individuals involved have greater perceptional awareness of potential opportunities that might be derived from an innovation. On the other hand, it is likely that such high-power individuals will have more difficulty than their peers in other organisations when trying to organise around a *single* innovation. Try this as an experiment: put your brightest and most creative people in a room and ask them to innovate around any particular business problem. Accustomed to standing out from the pack, it is unlikely that such a group will achieve anything very much unaided: consensus gets more difficult the cleverer the people involved.

Innovativeness in organisations is increased when employees have tightly coupled social networks. This is retrospectively obvious, given our discussion of the individual-level innovation decision. In organisations, as well, such networks enable ideas to flow more freely.

Unfortunately, social networks in banks are sometimes quite prescribed. Employees often speak of organisational silos they encounter, where individual business lines don't speak, even to units functionally aligned with their own. Luckily, recent years have seen some eroding of this traditionally difficult organisational problem, as new communications technologies (collaboration tools, instant messaging, and email, for example) have begun their diffusion in banks. These establish (and then maintain) social networks, leading (in theory) to greater innovativeness in an organisation.

And finally, researchers have found a strong correlation between organisational slack and innovativeness. Organisational slack is the degree to which resources are uncommitted to business-as-usual activities. It has been theorised that, for most industries, it is organisational slack that makes larger companies in general more innovative than smaller ones. The idea is that larger companies have more resources idle which can be usefully applied to innovative activities.

There is, in fact, substantive evidence that larger financial services companies are more innovative than their peers. In a study of 324 German banks [27], it was found that both total assets and number of employees of institutions were *highly* correlated with innovativeness. The larger these institutions were, the more likely they were to develop innovative concepts and services for customers.

This result is counterintuitive in an industry that has a mania with an accounting measure highly related to organisational slack: the cost-to-income ratio. Keenly watched by investors and analysts, institutions are considered more efficient when the number is as low as possible. In an effort to please shareholders, managers systematically optimise every resource to ensure its full utilisation. In so doing, they reduce the capacity of their bank to innovate.

The innovation decision process in firms

Earlier in this chapter (see Figure 2.1), I covered the basic process an individual goes through when making the choice-decision to use something new, given their individual circumstances. For financial services firms trying to create new products or experiences for customers, that decision process is critical when trying to design innovations that will be attractive.

Institutions as a whole also go through a decision process when evaluating whether or not to adopt, and understanding that process is similarly critical when trying to introduce innovations for internal adoption. The high-level process is shown in Figure 2.7.

Compared with the decision process for individuals, adoption decisions for firms are some-what more involved considering the additional complexity involved. Most of that complexity is the result of interplay between multiple individuals.

The innovation decision process starts when an institution develops a view of particular organisational problems it is presently facing. This is a constant process, often one which continues in a highly systematised way. Internal and external stimuli combine to establish an environment that results in various needs an institution must satisfy to ensure the future of its business. Many of these needs are satisfied during ordinary operation of the business-as-usual process, but some require innovative new methods, and these must be sought out deliberately.

A particular need often causing a search for innovative solutions is identification of a performance gap. A performance gap occurs whenever an institution decides that what it is doing *right now* is relatively worse than what *should* be occurring. Some institutions, for example, have replaced paper-based processes, many of which worked without problems for years. The performance gap was apparent when competitors began to offer automated *instantaneous* processing, particularly in core loan originations operations. The performance gap had a direct financial penalty until it was resolved.

Sometimes the agenda-setting process operates in reverse. Normally, business needs precede the identification of a solution, but on occasion, the *existence* of an innovation can trigger the creation of new business problems.

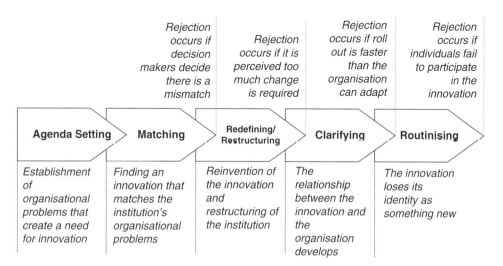

Figure 2.7   The adoption decision process for firms

When Apple released the second version of its iPhone in the latter part of 2008, many banks reacted immediately by releasing iPhone-compatible mobile banking applications. In interviews I conducted whilst preparing for this book, I often came across technology executives complaining about the sudden and 'unrealistic' priority being placed on having an iPhone capability in their online channels. The mere existence of the innovation generated a business problem – a perceived need to demonstrate innovativeness by supporting a new device – that wasn't there before.

Finally, on some occasions, an innovation is sufficiently interesting that institutions might acquire it opportunistically, *without* a particular business need identified. As part of the agenda-setting process, strategic priorities can seem to point to a need to have access to particular capabilities even though specific problems might not have emerged. It is not atypical, for example, that a bank purchases significantly more computing resource than it actually needs, knowing it may make use of those capabilities at a future time. Vendors, aware of this, make opportunistic deals bundling business-as-usual capabilities with more advanced, less adopted ones. Microsoft, for example, traditionally bundles the licences one needs for electronic mail, file & print with other licences such as collaboration and information security. The latter are optional adoption decisions for most institutions, but are acquired anyway given the likely use that will be made in the future.

Agenda setting, then, is the process banks go through to identify business issues they face, and creating the initial list of innovations that might help them resolve these issues. The actual process of selecting the innovation that fixes a particular business problem is the matching stage, and most banks go through lengthy processes to do this. As so many people are involved in selection decisions, and each has particular priorities, structured processes normally exist. Typically, there is a procurement organisation that will lead these. Their goal will be to satisfy business requirements identified whilst minimising organisational risk and cost.

Other stakeholders, such as IT, have different priorities. They are concerned with long-term maintainability, security, and consistency with enterprise architecture (if it exists). For them, matching is a process of eliminating options which do not conform to existing norms. IT people, as we will see in the next chapter, are driven by specific priorities that rarely have a great deal to do with the actual functionality the innovation is seeking to address.

As with all complicated decision processes, the matching process usually terminates with a set of compromises, diluting the innovation in various dimensions to match the priorities of powerful stakeholders. If an innovation fails to meet most of the expectations of stakeholders involved in the matching process, the usual result is the overall collapse of the innovation decision.

Over time, procurement organisations in banks have developed sophisticated methods to ensure such collapses happen infrequently. The process of scanning the market for new solutions to business problems is often facilitated through the instrument of a *Request for Information* (RFI). Universally hated by vendors, the purpose of an RFI is to motivate potential purveyors of solutions to provide sufficient information to institutions so that they are able to determine if particular business problems identified in the agenda-setting stage are actually amenable to solution.

The challenge is often (at least from the perspective of vendors) that a great deal of effort must be invested in an activity which is, regularly, simply a free fact-gathering exercise for a bank. Of course, it is necessary to respond, given that failure to be on the list of companies *capable* of providing a solution usually means any subsequent requests at acquisition time will not be forthcoming.

The *actual* matching process is often accomplished through the almost-as-hated vehicle of the *Request for Proposal* (RFP). RFPs are usually detailed, quite often to such a degree that vendors must attempt to respond without sufficient detail of any operational circumstances in which they must work. Such documents can run to hundreds of pages, and are rigorously graded using various scoring systems by stakeholders. At the end of this process, which might include high-octane presentations and competitive 'bake-offs', someone is selected to provide the solution.

Even at this point, however, things can still go wrong. Although a provider has been matched, contractual negotiations can cause the wheels to come off a deal. Achieving appropriate commercial terms is often a significant hurdle to cross as each party seeks to maximise opportunity with the least possible investment. In the end, there is no certainty about results until contracts are signed, but by this point, vendors could quite reasonably have invested significantly with no certainty of a return. A failure to win a bid generally has significant consequences for those concerned.

Assuming an innovation is selected, institutions next go through a redefining and restructuring process. When something new is introduced, firms first of all attempt to remould the innovation in ways that make it easily accessible to various stakeholders involved. For example, IT will almost certainly demand technological changes to make the innovation consistent with their architectural strategy, whilst legal and risk may have concerns of their own that need to be addressed to reduce organisational uncertainty. These changes impose the values and behaviours of the institution on the innovation, quite often diluting the original intent.

But the innovation, as it is gradually introduced, changes the firm as well. The more complicated and broad-reaching the innovation, the more likely this is to occur. It may be, for example, that new organisational units are created to manage the innovation, or particular teams have new tasks added to their portfolios of responsibilities. Perhaps new rules and regulations are required to moderate its use: most institutions have policy documents covering employee usage of Internet and email, for example.

Inevitably, these changes constitute a mutual feedback loop where both the innovation and institution are changed in unexpected ways. When the first ATMs were introduced at scale in the United States, they required entirely new processes from banks for cash provision. The notes tellers could handle could be in practically any condition at all, but this was not true of the new automated machines, which, predictably, couldn't perform reliably with worn or damaged notes. So banks had to set up specialised cash-delivery capabilities. This, in turn, motivated banks to demand better cash-handling technology from ATM manufacturers to increase reliability. The ultimate end-point in this cycle is only now being reached: cash recycling machines which are able to reuse the cash from deposits for withdrawals.

As a general rule, the more change required by both the innovation and the organisation that attempts to use it, the more likely it is that stakeholders will decide the innovation overall is too hard to adopt. At this point, the innovation decision stalls. The risk of this occurring increases with the *time* it takes to operationalise the various changes demanded for adoption.

At this point, the innovation has been matched to an overall agenda of the institution and various compromises have been made, both to the innovation itself and the structure of the organisation that will host it. It will probably be in use by a small number of people, and early gains will have been realised.

It is then that an institution enters the clarifying phase, during which the innovation enters broad and regular use by a significant percentage of the eventual audience. Depending on the level of change an organisation will need to make to accept the innovation, the duration of this phase can be highly variable. As before, the more change needed, the longer the clarifying phase.

The principal point of the clarifying phase is to convert something largely experimental into something that can be used in the day-to-day operations of an institution. This is when the time-specific operational difficulties are likely to rear their head for the first time. Prior to the clarifying phase, there are usually not enough people using the innovation day to day for every ramification to emerge. But with the entry of the innovation into this new phase, there are large numbers of people using the new thing for the first time.

Because organisations are comprised of many different people with specific agendas, the clarifying phase is usually the time an innovation runs into roadblocks from those not previously consulted during earlier phases of the decision process.

Quite often, for instance, a new way of working, particularly if it is technological in nature, will cause employees to object that their environments are being changed in some unwanted fashion. The introduction of email in banks, for example, continues to cause significant dispute: should employees manning teller counters be serving customers or dealing with messages arriving in their inboxes? Assuming email *was* allowed at the counter, it would be reasonable to imagine unions would have concerns about whether the introduction of email introduced new working conditions for employees. And even eliminating consolidated action from employee representatives, what if email *did* cause a reduction in service levels?

In the end, an employee faced with an innovation is seeking to answer significant questions about the change in the working environment from the perspective of their individual circumstances. What exactly is this change about to be implemented? Who in the institution will be affected by it? Will it affect me specifically? And if it does, how will what I do day to day be affected? There is usually significant emotion attached to the answers to such questions.

The emotional implications from the personal perspective mean that the more difficult the changes resulting from the innovation, the more time needed in the clarifying phase. Even when decisions are time-bound (such as, for example, the introduction of new regulations that must be implemented by a certain date), there is rarely any escape from a lengthy clarifying phase during which the implications of an innovation are debated in collective fashion by those involved. Ultimately, forcing speedy exit from this phase will cause adoption to falter, *regardless* of any mandate from those wielding hierarchical power over the employees.

The final phase of the innovation adoption decision for a bank is routinising. This is the process of taking an innovation and embedding it permanently in operational practices.

During the clarifying stage, most of the impacts and consequences of the new thing were examined, and resolved in some fashion acceptable to stakeholders. The period during which this occurred was likely to have been unsettled and disruptive. Routinising, however, is mainly about embedding the change in the ordinary habits of employees. The difficulty that occurs here is directly associated with how big the change is from the perspective of the individuals affected.

A good example of the difficulties inherent in routinising new things is the exceptional challenge experienced by some banks when deciding to move their teller employees from old-style green screen applications to more modern mouse- and Windows-based solutions.

Many counter employees at this time had had decades of experience using keyboard-based operating practices, and were able to navigate old systems far more quickly than the new. They objected strongly to any need to remove their hands from their keyboards to manipulate a mouse and actively sought ways to avoid doing so. And as less information could be crammed into a graphical window than a page of green-screen characters, they found themselves having to expend more effort to conduct the same amount of work. So older, more experienced employees were highly resistant to the change.

That was not true of new employees, whose operating effectiveness was vastly improved. Instead of months or years of familiarisation before full capability was reached, new employees were ready to serve customers in short order. The innovation of user-friendly interfaces was a significant improver of employee productivity for the next generation of customer-facing employees.

The most valuable, experienced employees at the counter required the greatest behavioural change before they would accept the new operating methods. Many institutions faced expensive and extensive retraining programmes to embed the innovation of graphical user interfaces in the teller environment. Routinising the innovation sometimes took years.

Routinising is by no means a certainty. It is possible that an innovation, even though all the kinks were worked out during the clarifying phase, requires too much habit changing and unlearning to ever become part of the operating routine of the firm. Some banks, for example, found that no matter what they did, they could never bring their experienced counter staff up to their former level of productivity. Dis-adoption quite often followed.

2.6   CASE STUDY: THE INTERNAL ADOPTION OF SOCIAL MEDIA

In early 2007 my own bank, based in the United Kingdom, was typical of other large banking organisations. It had, for example, an entrenched hierarchical command structure, where most significant decision-making authority was in the hands of relatively few individuals.

New employees, especially at more junior levels, took years to reach sufficiently influential positions that they could make real differences. This left many with a nascent sense of frustration. And there were few ways that employees could collaborate between themselves other than email. Paper processes were everywhere.

This was around the time that social media, social networks, and other so-called Web 2.0 technologies were reaching their peak. Other banks, such as Wachovia and Wells Fargo, for example, were quietly experimenting with blogs and other tools. The news of these innovations, when it reached the bank, encouraged it to consider whether they might be appropriate for it also.

Here is an example where knowledge of an innovation was instrumental in recognising a potential business problem not previously obvious: that command and control with rigid adherence to organisational dictates might reduce overall firm performance, at least from an innovation perspective. The bank decided it would consider whether or not it would adopt social media itself.

The basic premise was that staff would be more effective contributors to the business of the bank if they were permitted to communicate with like-minded individuals. If an employee of the bank was sufficiently motivated to create an intranet site of sufficient quality that it attracted an audience in its own right, they might be trusted to use that audience constructively to increase the rate of change in the bank as a whole.

This was a radical cultural change for the bank. The pre-eminent thought at the time was that employees, whilst they might not be deliberately malicious in their behaviour, would certainly not be sufficiently expert to determine the consequences of their actions once they were permitted to write anything they liked on internal websites. But with the launch of social media, employees would need to be delegated an unprecedented level of trust. Whilst it was not a direct challenge to the established command-and-control hierarchy, it was obvious that success in the area of social media would empower employees to an unusual degree.

The idea of a bank allowing its employees to self-publish using new communications technologies was not a universally popular one. There were a number of concerns senior managers aired immediately. How would staff have time to blog if they were doing their jobs? What if employees wrote things inappropriate? Might they write things actually damaging to the bank?

Despite these early objections, a solution was found that provisioned the new technologies in pilot form. A formal matching process was not undertaken, since an existing set of technologies being deployed for another purpose was found to have the capabilities required. Since it seemed to be a case of simply turning the new features on, the appropriate governance group in the bank gave the green light to commence a limited trial of the innovation.

With that authorisation, the bank began its redefining and restructuring phases. It turned out that the new features, as they came out of the box, didn't look anything like what would ordinarily be deployed on its intranet, so it set about a programme to rework the innovation to fix the problem. That work fell to an internal group which was already managing the existing intranet tools.

However, it was swiftly discovered that the existing group was unable to cope with the volume and complexity of changes being demanded. They were split into separate development and operations segments to better handle the new platform, and assigned to delivery units that were perceived as better able to support the new platform.

The question of how best to manage the innovation day to day then began to generate significant concern. It was realised that it would likely be inadvisable to enable such new communications tools without any controls whatsoever. Multiple committees and boards were proposed and discarded. In the end, overall ownership of the new channel was passed to existing communications functions, the custodians of most other intranet-related functionality.

But it became obvious that the workload involved in managing (potentially) thousands of sites would overwhelm any existing arrangements rather quickly. A new subordinate group was created and tasked with day-to-day management, leaving oversight in the hands of the communications team.

Eventually, the bank started its pilot, using a limited group of several thousand technology and operations professionals. Almost immediately, issues began to present themselves. Luckily, the bank was expecting things to crop up, because it had anticipated a lengthy clarifying phase whilst it worked the kinks out of its new initiative.

The first problem was what to do if staff *did* write things inappropriate. The bank issued lengthy guidelines to employees, which they needed to acknowledge electronically before using the new tools. Nonetheless, a key concern was that active technical measures were not available that would systematically examine content. If the innovation was successful, the bank might reasonably hope it would have thousands of employee-created websites – far too many to check manually.

An exhaustive search of available technologies was conducted, but did not uncover a solution. But after considerable negotiation with security and risk stakeholders, it was agreed that a solution using statistical sampling would likely be adequate. The bank would conduct a random survey of a small percentage of sites for inappropriate content, and use this information to come to an approximation of the risk it was facing through misuse.

Even then, the innovation nearly faltered when several high-profile employees began to write blogs with which certain senior managers disagreed. The result was that the bank added a 'Report this Site' link to each and every page, which staff could use to bring anything they wished to the attention of management.

This and other issues around new behaviours that employees might demonstrate when the new tools became broadly available led the bank to establish a new reporting regime in order to monitor who in the bank had actually attracted an audience of significance. It was thought these 'opinion leaders' might be a valuable new channel catalytic to employee engagement. But, during the clarifying stages, very few people showed up on this report. It would be much longer before the new internal publishers would rival the traffic generated by more traditional communications published on the intranet.

After months of trials and work-arounds, social media tools were made generally available to bank staff, excluding those in the branch network. The routinising process began relatively slowly at first, but gathered pace quickly once staff began to see their colleagues creating successful and interesting content. But the functionality used most immediately was the personal profile page every employee was assigned. This page included photographs, the opportunity to include biographical information, and was updated automatically with information from the bank's human resources systems.

Two things followed. The first was that hand-drawn organisational charts, which had previously featured everywhere on the bank's intranet, vanished immediately. The new profile pages automatically showed the organisational hierarchy of any individual, and were usually more up-to-date than anything individuals did themselves.

The second was that personal profile pages, being self-maintained, were generally more complete and timely than information in the corporate phone directory, which saw declining usage thereafter. A few months later, it was decommissioned, freeing the time of several people which had previously been devoted to the highly manual task of keeping it current.

The routinising phase of the social media innovation officially stated when the bank made its social media tools available to staff. But the new ways of communicating didn't really become routine in the organisation until they began to replace existing organisational processes, the telephone directory being the first of many examples.

2.7   THEORY OF DISRUPTION

So far, we've looked at theory which guides individual and firm decisions in respect to their choice to adopt (or not) a particular innovation. And having read this chapter so far, you might now be questioning all this rational theory, since some adoption decisions by both firms and individuals are decidedly *not* rational when viewed with the benefit of hindsight.

Why did banks ignore PayPal until it was the dominant player in the online payments market and almost immune from competitive response? How come institutions presently ignore peer-to-peer lending, even in the face of reputable analyst opinion that significant share of retail lending could be eroded in the next few years?

Believe it or not, these are rational management decisions when taken in the internal context of the dynamics of firms. The eminent thinker and Harvard professor Clayton Christensen first outlined the mechanism by which this occurs in his book *The Innovator's Dilemma* [5], a text I first referred to in Chapter 1. *The Innovator's Dilemma* illustrates how powerful, entrenched incumbents (such as banks) can fail in the presence of disruptive innovations from smaller players.

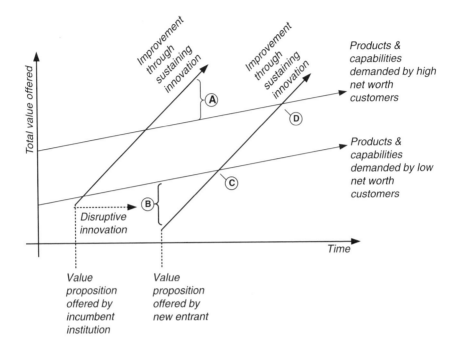

A: Overshoot of value required by high end customers of incumbent
B: Undershoot of value needed to attract low end customers of incumbent
C: Entrant is able to attract core customers of incumbent with better value proposition
D: Entrant is able to attract all customers of incumbent with better value proposition

Figure 2.8   The mechanics of disruption in financial services

Christensen's model starts with what he calls a 'failure framework', a set of observations about disruptive innovations which are characteristic of most industries that have been around long enough.

The first part of the failure framework we discussed in Chapter 1, the difference between sustaining and disruptive innovations. Recall that the former involves improving the performance of a product or service in such a way that institutions can charge more or win more customers from an established market. The latter, disruptive innovations, are about creating new value propositions, which probably only appeal to a fringe of new customers at first, but which extend to compete with mainline businesses over time.

The second part of the Christensen failure framework is concerned with the difference between what customers *actually* need, and that which is available from providers. Here is the key point: institutions expand their capabilities much faster than the pace at which customers demand improvements. This is illustrated in Figure 2.8, which is a recasting of the original diagram used by Christensen in a financial services context.

Over time, in an attempt to enhance their offerings to customers and differentiate from competitors, incumbent institutions add new capabilities, for which they attempt to charge higher prices. The process of doing this makes a product or service more appealing to ever more demanding customer segments, which are willing to pay high prices to get such capabilities.

Reaching the most demanding customers – and therefore the most attractive ones from a revenue perspective – is a key aspect of growth for financial services. It is why so many conversations are about 'share of wallet' and high net worth customers. On the other hand, the 'underbanked' are usually considered less attractive. Their needs are less demanding (that's why they may not have a bank at all), and they are therefore less likely to be profitable.

The key to expanding the capabilities of products and services to reach new customers with more demanding needs is through delivering repeated sustaining innovations. When self-service (via the ATM) was first introduced to banking in the 1960s it was disruptive. It proved that customers would not only serve themselves for some classes of transaction, but that they enjoyed doing so. It started the decline of branch- and relationship-based banking, a decline which (arguably) continues today.

On the other hand, the introduction of subsequent self-service innovations (telephone banking, early terminal-based home banking, and more recently Internet and mobile banking) has had a trajectory of capabilities that are largely sustaining. They enable banks to reach more demanding customers, but don't necessarily change the way the business of banking is done.

Over time, the requirements of customers expand. A customer who initially requires only a checking account and perhaps a student loan will eventually want mortgages and credit cards, mutual funds, and insurance products. Within each product category, consumers get more demanding as well. When credit cards became available initially, the most important thing was universal acceptance. But now customers can choose reward programmes, whether the card is charge or credit, and multiple access options in addition to plain plastic.

The rate at which customer demand for capabilities expands is much less than that provided by institutions. Low-end customers don't want new capabilities from their products as often as the institution provides them. And there are only so many higher-end customers in a particular market.

Inevitably, there is a disconnect between what the customer can use and that which they are asked to pay for. Sooner or later, around about point A in Figure 2.8, the capabilities of an institution expand beyond what even high net worth customers are able to use. Despite this, competitive pressures force the bank to continue development of its capabilities, loading more cost into the customer proposition, thereby driving increasing dissatisfaction.

Here is where the disruptive innovation comes in. A disruptive innovation, indicated by the second set of propositions towards the right of the figure, will be launched by an entrant with far less capability than even low-end customers of the main institution require. This is the gap between what is needed and what is available, shown at point B. Because of this gap, very few customers will initially be that interested in the disruptive value proposition, certainly not in sufficient numbers to cause any concern in the incumbent institution.

The disruptive innovation will have several characteristics, though, that differentiate it from other propositions in the market. It may, for example, be less expensive, or offer greater convenience. And because it is new, it will come unencumbered by the legacy of incumbent players.

Such legacies in financial services include, of course, system and procedural aspects, but might also be regulatory compliance obligations, the scrutiny of regulators, and high customer expectations. All these combine to ensure that whatever the value proposition of the entrant is, in comparison with incumbents, it will almost certainly be less expensive to run than anything a bank can do. In other words, there could be attractive margins available to the new entrant that would be *unavailable* to a traditional player. So it probably won't matter that much if there are only a few fringe customers around in the first place. They will likely be profitable anyway to the new entrant.

At this point, an ordinary bank has a couple of alternatives: it can decide fringe customers are important enough to fight for, and enter a price war with the entrant, or it can just abandon the segment altogether.

Consider it from the perspective of the traditional institution: these are customers which are very, very low end. They are probably not profitable given that a bank has built certain infrastructures which are optimised to support demanding, high-value customers. To fight for such customers will likely be costly indeed, and almost certainly the battleground will be price. Pricing battles lead to commoditisation, something that most banks are at pains to avoid.

What does a rational manager do? Exiting the segment altogether makes excellent financial sense. But the disruptive innovation swiftly expands in capability, until it reaches a point where it can serve currently profitable customers. This is point C in Figure 2.8. Suddenly, the incumbent institution has a strategic decision to make. Should it fight for these profitable customers, even though they are relatively low end, perhaps only marginally profitable? Or should it continue the development of its products and services and move further upmarket, looking for ever higher net worth customers?

Christensen characterises this as the 'fight' or 'flee' decision. It is a strategic dilemma repeated often, and in many different industries. For airlines, the emergence of budget airlines forced traditional full-service players into a 'fight' position, with disastrous consequences. For relatively undemanding customers (those who fly in coach), the battle is almost always about price. Airline seats are commodities, and margins are thin if they exist at all. Fighting a war on a price basis meant giving away seats at prices lower than cost. But what choice existed? It was unthinkable that a full-service airline would just stop flying on routes with discount competitors: their whole business model was predicated on being able to get a passenger from one point to any other. No choice existed but to fight, and profitability for most of the airline industry has plummeted.

Faced with a disruptor who achieves a capability able to satisfy profitable customers (even though they may be low end), a bank also has a fight or flee decision. Fleeing (actually, the same as ignoring the disruptor) is an easy decision, because it means that a bank can concentrate more on its high net worth customers.

It will likely even look good on the P&L: by attracting higher-end customers with fatter margins, top line numbers will probably improve. And in the meantime, fighting for low-end customers means the institution will have to compete on a price basis with the entrant. This route makes it almost certain that customers with borderline profitability will suddenly become a drain on the bottom line as the institution has to subsidise them in order to match the operational and cost advantages of the entrant. The rational decision is to flee.

The value proposition of the new entrant, however, continues to develop. Over time, it adds capabilities until, finally, the disruptor is able to reach all customers of the incumbent institution, even the most demanding (point D in Figure 2.8). If the incumbent hasn't made a fight decision at this point, it will certainly have to do so now to stay in business.

The problem, now, is that an incumbent institution is competing from a position of relative weakness, because it is *still* supporting its legacy of systems, costs, and regulations. The disruptor, on the other hand, is highly optimised and does not have many of these legacies, if at all. It is inevitable that the incumbent will be forced out of the market altogether, given sufficient time. This set of behaviours underpins the third element of Christensen's failure framework, which is that institutions will almost always find making investments in disruptive innovations themselves difficult or impossible.

Consider disruption from the perspective of an incumbent bank once again. A disruptive product will usually be simpler and cheaper to create, and enter the market at a relatively low price point. It will therefore come with lower margins, at the same time as attracting a small segment of the bank's customers. Consequently, the likely revenues will be small or insignificant compared with those resulting from the traditional businesses.

Then, too, profitable customers of the bank will be unlikely to use the disruptive innovation initially. It has too great a performance gap for them to consider switching (point B in Figure 2.8), and only those customers who are either unprofitable or marginal could possibly consider it as an alternative.

These factors combined mean that it is almost never a rational decision for an institution to invest in disruptive enterprises: existing customers can't use the innovation, and most likely will say they don't want it. The margins are low. And initial revenues will be microscopic compared with those of traditional businesses. What manager can possibly overcome such objections?

On the other hand, successful banks spend a great deal of time listening to their best customers in an attempt to find out what they *do* want. They then create products to meet those needs, systematically rooting out and eliminating any concepts which either won't be profitable, or don't appeal to the most profitable segments.

It is behaviour which ensures, in the end, they will eventually be disrupted by *someone*. When we get to the execution phase of futureproofing in Chapter 7, I will explore one avenue out of this dilemma: allowing the innovation team to pursue disruptive innovations *outside* the normal strictures of the business. But doing so requires a developed innovation function, one which has proved itself an outstanding business in its own right. We'll spend more time on the development of the capabilities of an innovation function in the next chapter.

2.8   CASE STUDY: PAYPAL'S CONTINUING DISRUPTION OF THE PAYMENTS MARKET

We've already examined the early history of PayPal in Chapter 1. Now, however, we will examine it again through the lens of Christensen's theories of disruption.

In 1998, when PayPal started its life as Confinity (prior to its later merger with X.com), the company introduced its first innovation: the ability to transfer money between Palm personal digital assistants over an infrared link. Now, clearly, only a small segment of customers actually *had* such devices at that time. Furthermore, few of those had any practical reason at all to beam money to each other. You had to be in the same room as another Palm user, and in fact, you had to be standing right next to them. Why was cash not a simpler alternative? Only a very small, technophilic segment of the market was actually interested.

If the innovation of beaming money by infrared ever showed up on the radar of any bank at that point it would have been a surprise. Why should any institution be interested? The customer segment involved was microscopic. The transactions volumes were insignificant. And with the notable (one-time) exception of a venture capital payment made to PayPal in excess of $4.5 million (and transmitted by Palm Pilot as a stunt), it seemed pretty unlikely that anyone would use the service for anything very significant.

By 1999, however, the first demonstrations of PayPal technology were being done with email addresses instead of Palm organisers. Using an email address, it became possible to move money from one individual to another easily. And the individuals involved could be at a distance from each other. The number of PayPal accounts grew, as more customers could now see a use for the service.

Getting money in and out of PayPal was also easier, but banks were either unaware or disinterested in PayPal. After all, it was hardly a reasonable substitute for an ordinary checking account, even if slightly more convenient for some fringe low-value payments. It didn't offer the real-world interfaces of a plastic card, for example, and neither did funds left in PayPal earn interest. Most customers, banks reasoned, would have no interest in PayPal.

By the end of 1999, however, PayPal had launched its Money Market Fund, an optional feature that enabled balances on PayPal accounts to earn interest. Then it started to get viral in its marketing, offering sign-up bonuses if customers referred friends. PayPal may not have been all that significant at that point, but its capability set was coming closer to what a low-end banking customer might require in an account from which payments might be made. And its viral marketing campaign was working: it soon had enough users on its books that it made sense to send money by email.

Around this time, eBay had begun its meteoric rise. Online auctions were becoming very popular indeed, and their users needed a way to pay for goods and services. Pay by email was a natural choice, and PayPal quickly made changes to its service to make it easy for eBay users to do so.

But banks were still not interested. Bankers, firmly embedded in their traditional acquiring and issuing businesses for cards, could not possibly have imagined that eBay sellers and buyers could have amounted to much. In 2000, after all, PayPal had around 100,000 accounts, and such professional sellers as were on eBay would likely have a traditional merchant account with a bank if they were of any scale whatsoever.

Two months later, though, PayPal had 1 million users, and by August 2000 that number had tripled. Banks started to wake up to the fact that PayPal might be on to something, as it rode the coat tails of the eBay wave. In the meantime, high-profile attempts to cash in on email-based payments such as those of Citibank (launched, in fact, before PayPal was even founded) were showing signs of strain or being shut down altogether.

In 2002, the service began supporting euros and pounds natively. Previously, the only currency allowed had been US dollars, but with this introduction, true international payments were possible. Foreign currency accounts, generally, were a high-end capability reserved by traditional banks for their very valuable customers. But now PayPal began to disrupt profitable remittance and other payments business as a result of operational advantages it, alone, enjoyed.

PayPal, after all, had started from a base with little or no legacy. It was initially unregulated, though later in its development it became more accountable. Even today, however, its compliance load is considerably less than that for its competitive banks. And it could settle a payment instantly, something that most banks cannot do, even today.

It still did not have, however, all the capabilities that a major bank might offer its profitable customers. Outside the online auction arena PayPal acceptance was pretty low, so most customers would have needed another form of payment in most cases. And for expensive purchases, those that would normally be made with credit, PayPal was of no help at all.

Banks, resting safely on their laurels, felt they had nothing at all to fear. PayPal was not actually touching the real-world payment market in any substantial way, where most institutions were firmly concentrated. Of course, PayPal continued to develop its product further. Credit was rectified in 2004, when PayPal launched its Buyer Credit Programme, a means to finance high-cost items even if customers didn't have funds of their own. And later, various virtual debit cards, based on the MasterCard brand, alleviated the acceptance problem as well. A customer could now buy online using PayPal whether or not a merchant chose to accept PayPal.

By the end of 2004, PayPal had global revenues of $1.4 billion dollars, making it a significant player, even in the eyes of major banks. And it had a product which had crept up the value chain to the point where it was now pretty much comparable with many of the card offerings that banks made to their less demanding customers.

PayPal was also doing quite a good business in acquiring transactions. For very small merchants dealing on the web, it had become a default, if inevitable, choice. Banks were extremely hesitant to hand out merchant accounts, given the high levels of fraud and resulting charge-backs. Small merchants, who didn't have very complicated requirements to start with, were happy to use the PayPal service.

PayPal's entry to merchant acquiring, however, took a leap forward in 2005 when it acquired VeriSign's merchant gateway. VeriSign is one of the web's biggest players in security and authentication, and with the acquisition PayPal had a product with capabilities to serve even demanding large merchants.

By the end of 2006, PayPal had more than 100 million accounts, more than all but the largest global banks. And they were taking significant share of online transaction, and not only from online auctions. Alarm bells started ringing in banks, as they projected card volume declining in previously profitable segments.

But by this time, it was too late, at least for the online payments section of banks' business. PayPal had established a disruptive layer of its own over the Internet, largely disintermediating banks altogether. If banks had any further need of evidence that PayPal was on a disruptive course, it came in 2007, when the organisation was granted a banking licence by the European Union. Now able to compete on an equal product footing with any other institution in the region, PayPal is not resting on its laurels. It has more than 150 million accounts in 190 countries and is the default means to pay for a large portion of the Internet.

Clearly, when PayPal was about transferring money from one Palm Pilot to another, it was hardly a threat to any bank. Its disruptive development from that niche capability to the mainstream happened step by step and was largely unobserved by institutions.

But the key question is whether any bank *could* actually have done anything to halt PayPal. At the beginning, before the company achieved much scale, the revenues from its payments businesses were microscopic compared with those of a traditional payments business in a bank. Then, too, the customer segment it was addressing was initially fringe in the extreme.

How on earth would it have been a rational decision for a bank profit and loss owner to commit significant funds to PayPal-compete at that point? And later, when it would have made sense from a share and revenue perspective, the operational advantages of PayPal and its ubiquitous customer base would have made any competitive response a prohibitively expensive proposition.

The game isn't over yet, however. Institutions in markets in which PayPal operate will soon face their penultimate fight or flee decision. Though nothing is certain, Christensen's theories of disruption provide us with at least some idea of a potential outcome.

2.9   THOUGHTS BEFORE GOING FURTHER

This chapter has largely concerned itself with theoretical models of innovation, which are basic tools the rest of this book will use to help build out predictable innovation processes for institutions. Using decision-making models (either at individual or firm level), for example, is helpful when selecting innovations at the ideation phase. Our diffusion model is a key part of getting to net benefit curves, which we need at the innovation stage. And our discussion of disruption helps us work out the best way to actually build an innovation, which is the focus of the execution phase of futureproofing.

But before we get to those topics, we need to answer some specific questions about banking innovation. What kinds of innovation make sense for an institution? Does the market even recognise bank innovation? How does the dominance of IT organisations influence the development process?

These and other topics are the subject of the next pages in this book, after which we will get directly to the main business at hand: the futureproofing process itself.

3

Innovating in Banks

What you will find in this chapter

- The innovation pentagram, which classifies all possible innovation in institutions.
- An explanation of the way that innovation programmes develop over time.
- How the IT organisation affects innovators.
- How large institutions decide what to do about innovations.
- Why some innovations succeed in spite of themselves in institutions.

In the previous chapter, our examination of innovation theory provided a lens into reasons why some ideas are successful and some aren't. Using those theories (and, of course, with the benefit of hindsight) it is relatively simple to explain historical innovation successes and failures. These theories would be interesting to any industry, not just financial services. But innovation in the banking context has nuances somewhat different from other industries. The products of banks, for example, are entirely digital in nature, perhaps with a bit of human personal service thrown in. The implication of this is that practically every innovation is going to involve someone from the IT organisation. Banks are also exceptionally cautious. Such innate risk aversion, whilst not endemic only to banks, is something that must be managed in a deliberate way.

And the question of what innovations to pursue is an interesting one. In a highly traditional industry such as financial services, there can sometimes be a feeling that everything worth inventing already exists. Of course, as innovators, we know that not to be true, but just *where* are all these new things supposed to come from?

So, in this chapter, I'll cover specific topics with respect to innovation in banking, things that our earlier discussion of theory didn't explore very much. Then, with that out of the way, all will be in place for us to talk about the first phase of the futureproofing process in the next chapter.

3.1 THE INNOVATION PENTAGRAM IN BANKS

Considering the breadth of historical innovations we examined in Chapter 1, it might be surprising to discover that it is possible to classify all innovations in banks using only five categories. These can be arranged in a convenient pentagram, shown in Figure 3.1.

Each slice of the pentagram represents an opportunity a bank has to be innovative: a new product, entry to a new market or expansion of an old one, an experience, something to do with the way that the bank touches its customers, or a change to a business model.

The grey shading from the centre outwards shows the probability (low, medium, or high) that new innovations (either coming from the bank itself, or from someone new) have the potential to be disruptive. And the dotted lines radiating out illustrate the likely mix of innovation types (incremental, revolutionary, or breakthrough).

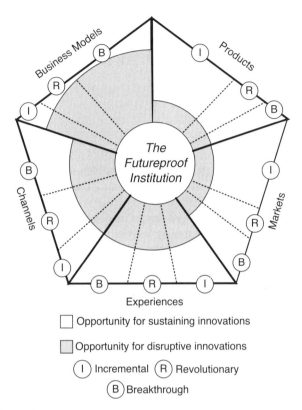

Figure 3.1   The innovation pentagram

For example, the likelihood of a serious disruption occurring to a traditional bank as a result of the arrival of a new product is low. Banks have been in the business of providing their core offers for a very long time, and it is highly unlikely that a new entrant would be able to create something presenting a serious threat to an incumbent. New products from incumbents, then, will be mostly incremental, with a smattering of revolutionary and breakthrough innovation thrown in for good measure. The mobile phone top-up innovation, where the ATM can be used to recharge a mobile phone, is an example of this.

On the other hand, the business model slice is extremely subject to disruption. The fact that banks have been providing their core services so successfully for so long means they are loath to change a winning formula. They have created highly optimised, extremely profitable processes and systems to support themselves, and are less able to change to respond to entrants competing with superior cost bases or value propositions. Naturally, that means a new entrant can serve low-margin or undesirable customers, the kind that an incumbent institution would normally abandon. These are signals that a young, disruptive competitor can enter the market and take share.

When Zopa entered the UK market, none of the major banks were concerned (and at the time of writing, probably still aren't). The Zopa business model is so different from that of entrenched banks, it just didn't seem relevant. In fact, at the time of writing, traditional lending is still vastly more profitable (from the perspective of a bank) than any P2P model yet explored. It simply doesn't make sense for a major bank to pursue peer-to-peer lending at the present time.

Another way to look at Figure 3.1 is as a threat map – a diagram that illustrates likely avenues from which real threats to banks will come in the future. Examined this way, banks would be wise to examine innovations in the business model and experience slices for breakthrough and revolutionary innovations. These are the slices in which long-term potential threats are most likely to originate.

Besides being useful as a threat map, the innovation pentagram is a helpful means of managing the overall innovation portfolio. Practitioners can use it to optimise their ideation and innovation phases to ensure a reasonable mix of activity in each sector occurs. Not only does this help by enhancing predictability (since, for example, a market downturn hitting a particular range of products can be addressed systematically through new markets or a change in a business model), it encourages broadness of thinking both from innovators and their colleagues in the wider business. We will discuss the portfolio management approach to innovation in Chapter 6.

But in the meantime, let's look more closely at each of the slices in Figure 3.1.

Products /

Product innovations are an obvious interest area for institutions. Coupled directly to revenue, they are the reason most banks have teams with titles such as 'business development' or 'propositions', teams that are innovation functions in almost all respects. Product innovations are almost always sustaining ones, and the reason is obvious given our examination of theory in the last chapter. New products are typically created by teams with strong links to groups who have major profit and loss responsibility, and two things follow from this.

The first is that large businesses demand their investments get to scale very quickly. An opportunity worth a million is rarely interesting to a group with a number measured in billions. The bandwidth of a new product team in such a group is better spent doing work on larger opportunities.

The second is that even when there is a forward-looking executive, it is a rare thing indeed that a disruptive innovation, likely to cannibalise the core profit and loss of the main business in the long term, can ever be approved.

Just as sustaining product innovation is the norm for most banks, so too are incremental, rather than revolutionary or breakthrough, developments. The fact of the matter is that whole new categories (breakthrough innovations, in our typology) are really rather rare in financial services, especially retail banking. Revolutionary innovations, the sort that immediately become the default for a majority of the market, are also infrequent.

An incremental innovation presently expanding (at the time of writing) in many countries is contactless cards. All major schemes have contactless products (proving that sustaining innovations of all sorts are readily copied): American Express has ExpressPay, Visa has payWave, and MasterCard has PayPass. Contactless cards are an incremental innovation on the magnetic stripe: they enable customers to pay for purchases by bringing their plastic close to a proximity reader attached to the ordinary point-of-sale terminals of merchants. This works even if the card is in a wallet or bag. For low-value transactions, no additional authentication is required.

Contactless cards actually provide a great deal more functionality than a simple improvement in customer convenience. But at the present time, most institutions (and their supporting schemes) are doing little with it. There are, however, some exceptions. Barclays Bank of the UK, ever the innovator, released a contactless-based product in 2007 called OnePulse. Billed as the 'one card every Londoner needs' it upped the ante on contactless by incorporating contactless travel pass functionality for the London Tube, included a Visa payWave contactless chip, and backed it all up with a supporting credit account. At the time of writing, Barclays, despite extensive selling in Tube stations around the city, had yet to achieve very substantial adoption of the product.

Contactless cards, in their various incarnations, are likely to be superseded by a revolutionary innovation with disruptive potential in the next few years. Near Field Communication (NFC) is a version of a contactless chip that can be installed in mobile phones. When handset manufacturers begin to roll these out at scale, card products will suddenly have user interfaces, communications, and processing devices attached to them. It is likely that this will result in a whole new class of payment applications as far beyond the present contactless card as contactless was beyond ordinary plastic without a magnetic stripe.

So much for the revolutionary part of NFC, but why might it be disruptive to banks? Since the invention of the credit card in the 1950s, financial institutions have controlled most non-cash forms of payment. From a credit card perspective, they've been both acquirers and issuers, a situation that has resulted in excellent profits in card operations for decades. But who will own the NFC chip – the new means of payment that replaces the card – which is embedded in the handset? Chances are, it will not be banks. Telecommunications companies, optimised to provide fashionable and current-generation handsets to their customers on contracts, have the edge here. Activation of the chip could easily result in telecommunications companies disintermediating cards as a primary means of payment.

And if it is the telecommunications company that owns the means of payment, might not the dynamics of disruption be set in train? It is not difficult to imagine that small micropayments could easily be rolled up onto phone bills, with later expansion as operators developed appropriate competencies to manage mainline credit and debit card transactions.

However, institutions are not entirely powerless in efforts to combat the innovations that NFC and network operators bring. RaboBank, of the Netherlands, commenced offering its mobile banking and airtime packages in 2006, in an arrangement that saw it step into the role of the telecommunications company itself. By buying minutes from a traditional network operator it then resold to customers, it was able to lay the groundwork for its own mobile-phone-as-wallet programme. Since many institutions have now conceded that mobile-phone-as-wallet is inevitable in the next five or so years, Rabo have shown remarkable foresight.

Markets

The second kind of innovation in which a bank can engage concerns the kinds of markets it chooses to pursue. An institution is usually not present in every market it could be, and neither will it completely serve all the customers it might do even in markets it presently concentrates on. This, then, is an opportunity to expand revenues if something innovative is done to address such untapped segments.

Perhaps one of the most interesting innovations in recent times to address new market innovation is offering services to the unbanked in Africa. Some markets in this region have mobile phone adoption significantly greater than that of bank accounts. M-Pesa, as one service is called, is offered by Vodafone affiliate SafariCom, and allows users to transfer credit from one mobile phone handset to another via SMS. Users are able to cash in and out of the system using a broad-reaching agent network, the same one they would use anyway to buy airtime. M-Pesa has been very successful – so successful, in fact, that Vodafone and Citibank announced a partnership to extend the offer worldwide [28].

The M-Pesa offer brings payment services to those who would otherwise not have them. But because this is an innovation that competes with non-consumption (customers who previously did not have any banking services at all), it has significant potential to be disruptive as well. There is nothing to stop M-Pesa expanding its services into more traditional banking products in the future using its established (and growing) base of customers. This would have the effect of eliminating banks as a factor altogether in the markets which M-Pesa serves.

Usually, though, innovations in markets tend to be skewed towards incrementalism. This is because an institution generally finds it easier to implement an existing product or process in an entirely new market than to create a new category from the start. For example, the worldwide growth in remittance businesses for institutions that are based in countries with a high percentage of migrant populations really only requires banks to repackage their existing payment relationships in an easy-to-consume way.

The predilection of banks to do more of what they are good at means that new market innovation is rarely breakthrough in nature. As usual, banks' entrenched value and cost systems enable non-bank players to take advantage of the inherent momentum of any reasonably sized institution. Microfinance is an example of a new market initiative that reflects this. At the time that Grameen Rural Bank (see Chapter 1) was founded, no one expected that poverty-stricken people in an (essentially) subsistence economy could possibly make good use of credit. But as it turned out, Grameen was able to alleviate a great deal of suffering whilst still being profitable. And of course, its founder won a Nobel Prize in the process for the astounding positive impact his invention had for disadvantaged people. Could a traditional bank have entered microfinance in this way? Probably not, since it is unlikely that its managers would have been able to adjust their cost and value structures to make borrowers at the bottom of the pyramid profitable.

Grameen showed the way for new organisations, such as Kiva.org, which takes the micro-lending model and adds a peer-to-peer aspect. We've covered peer-to-peer lending extensively in this book already, of course (refer to previous discussion on Zopa in Chapter 1), but combining the two together is an innovative way for people in First World countries to contribute to the developing world.

The story of Kiva is interesting. It was started by Matt and Jessica Flannery, two US citizens who became interested in microfinance soon after they married. Matt, an engineer in a Silicon Valley computer firm, kept in touch with his wife by mobile phone whilst she travelled in rural Africa. She had become inspired to investigate a career in microfinance after hearing Professor Yunus (the founder of Grameen and the winner of a Nobel Prize) speaking at Stanford, and was in Africa reviewing the way small loans had helped families increase their standard of living.

Both came away from this experience with a desire to make it easier to lend to budding entrepreneurs in developing countries, but found it could not easily be done at the time. There was, apparently, no way a First World lender could reach out to borrowers in the Third World. So, in 2005, they launched a website themselves. Their initiative was quickly picked up by many Internet and real-world reporters, leading to a flurry of interest globally. When they wrote their first loans, for about US$3500, it was to seven Ugandan entrepreneurs including a goat herder, a fishmonger, a cattle farmer, and a restaurateur. As Professor Yunus found when he created Grameen Rural Bank, people in the developing world are reliable repayers of debt. So it was with Kiva: all seven initial loans were repaid in six months.

Kiva is, today, the world's largest facilitator of microfinance, and channels millions of dollars worth of loans to entrepreneurs throughout the developing world. The innovation of combining microfinance and peer-to-peer lending has substantially changed the lives of thousands of people.

Experiences 体验式创新

The third kind of innovation on which a bank may concentrate is experience. Experience-based innovations are about things that make a particular interaction enjoyable (or not) for customers. For example, whilst the call centre is a channel, the way the customer is greeted by operators, whether they are culturally sensitive, accented, or know enough about the customer to ensure personalisation, are all experience issues.

A notable, and much studied, experience innovation was the work of US West Coast bank Wells Fargo, who redesigned their website home page in 2007 with a focus on customer experience and usability. Forrester, who worked with the bank afterwards to examine what they had done, found that through clever use of web page statistics, they were able to lift online applications by more than 50% [29]. The innovation in this instance was how the online channel team at Wells Fargo fed what they were seeing from their usage statistics into a user-centred development process for the website. This is quite a different approach from that normally adopted by banks. Ordinarily, a team of graphic artists creates a site design which is aesthetically pleasing, to match the brand position, or to expose the functionality that bankers *think* their customers will want. The Wells Fargo approach reversed this by *first* asking what customers wanted.

Obviously, experience-based innovations are, if anything, even easier to come up with when connected with real-world interactions with customers. In the first half of this decade, for example, banks worldwide spent a huge amount of money doing branch redesign. Innovative features such as free coffee stations, queue-busting staff complete with mobile computers, and clever use of open-plan spaces were all designed to enhance the customer experience. Deutsche Bank, in fact, went so far as to put product packages – similar to what you would find in a supermarket – on shelves in order to create an innovative experience in a store-like atmosphere [30]. Whether or not these experience-based innovations actually added to bottom-line performance, however, is still a drama being played out in many banks.

Figure 3.1 suggests a medium probability of disruption to existing bank businesses through experience-based innovation. Why is this so high? The reason is that the experience is so very core to the proposition of a banking relationship that customers are highly motivated to seek their personal optimums in this area. For example, a customer who doesn't like the Internet banking experience offered by their bank natively, is now easily able to use an online personal finance site instead. In so doing, it is unlikely the bank will have the opportunity of selling more products from its sustaining business lines. On the other hand, the disruptive personal finance website is able to use recommendations based on user-generated content to create interesting revenues for itself, without any of the costs of maintaining the account infrastructures of customers that a traditional bank faces.

Similarly, decoupled debit cards, a relatively recent phenomenon in the United States, enable customers to separate the provider of their account services from the provider of the plastic card they use to access their accounts [31]. This innovation makes it possible for the customer to choose a payment and reward experience that suits them whilst maintaining a back-end product experience with which they are familiar. From the perspective of the account-holding bank, of course, this is a terrible thing, since it disintermediates them in a very direct way from the individuals using their services. Companies providing decoupled debit, on the other hand, are free to innovate around experience so long as they manage settlement risks between the institutions.

Channels

Channels are the fourth way an institution can innovate. Reaching out and connecting with customers is one of the most important things a bank does. Innovation in the way this happens is presently a very busy area, with interest by both banks and non-bank third parties who would like to offer banking services.

Channel-based innovations are relatively simple to imagine, and are equally likely to arise through incremental, revolutionary, or breakthrough means. For example, the rise of online personal finance sites with (so-called) Web 2.0 features is a revolutionary channel innovation. Such websites allow users to manipulate their transaction information online, regardless of which bank holds their accounts. They are also quite disruptive: they take eyeballs away from the banks' own banking sites and put them firmly elsewhere.

Some personal finance sites, such as Wesabe [32], allow end-users to share useful information with one another. This sharing enables customers to create, say, a review of a restaurant, attach it to a transaction downloaded from a bank, and have this information shared with individuals in a social network. The enhancement is this user-generated content is likely to be far more targeted and relevant to the customer than anything a bank could do by itself.

Retrospectively, one of the greatest channel innovations in the last decade or so has been the combination of networks and browsers to create Internet banking. This proved that self-service in the home is something that customers desire, and will use if not too complicated. Internet banking, as it has evolved today, is one of the most important channels, both for sales and service. Many institutions go as far as making online a business unit in its own right.

Self-service at home might be desirable, but this is not necessarily true of self-service in public places. The customer, in public, has the additional complication of observability. It is usually important for individuals, when they are being watched by peers, to look like they know what they are doing – especially if there is a queue of people waiting to use whatever-it-is. When a customer makes an error in such situations, it is usually obvious to everyone. How many times have you waited in a queue for an ATM behind someone who was unfamiliar with its use? Or worse still, didn't get the result you wanted first time and had to start the transaction *again?* So irritating.

Public self-service has this kind of force field around it: one is scared to adopt a new innovation unless one can be certain of the functionality and usage. And the first few times, most people will make sure there is no one else around to ensure that if mistakes *are* made, no one will see.

Here is an example: self-service supermarket checkouts. I am yet to see queues to use these machines when a human is available. The reason? The checkout machine screams at you that you've made an error if you so much as move a product it thinks you haven't paid for. The customer is ashamed to use the machines because mistakes are so visible.

Such technologies, coupled with other more recent innovations, such as wireless access, have led some institutions down interesting roads in their quest for innovation. SNS Bank, based in the Netherlands, has a track record of novel innovation in the channel space. One experiment (conducted in 2006) was embedding a self-service kiosk into seat cushions which were then scattered across customer lounges in waiting areas of their corporate offices. This was an interesting object that customers could use without the ordinary fear of observation normally accompanying a self-service innovation. Why?

A customer sits down and places the cushion on their lap, screen side facing up. They then look downwards into the screen. They are comfortable their usage will not be observed because of social taboos involved in looking into other people's laps. Clearly, if someone is observing that particular area, it is not because they want to check the kiosk is working correctly.

So popular were the seat cushions at SNS Bank, the institution started to chain them to the seats they rested on. A fascinating message to customers, though one which illustrates just how interesting these objects were to those who used them.

Channel-based innovation can sometimes be disruptive, as in the case of the new personal finance management tools which take customers away from their home bank web pages. Or they can be sustaining, as the seat cushion at SNS.

Business models

The final area in which a bank can innovative is in business models. Business model innovation is almost always disruptive, though it is not often banks which are the cause of the disruption.

The power of business model innovation is that it enables organisations to reframe a commoditised service in light of new value propositions. These new propositions might be cost- or convenience-based, or have an inherent advantage in terms of specific niche segments they serve. And, of course, they usually start out small, but grow quickly.

Figure 3.1 indicates that the opportunity for disruption in business models is high. The problem with this is that, as we discussed in the previous chapter, the capability of organisations to disrupt themselves is quite low. In other words, looking at the figure as a threat map, this is the slice of the pentagram in which the most significant threats to the future of institutions will come.

When Zopa (see Chapter 1) launched its Zone of Possible Agreement, it was sufficiently disruptive that analysts suggested banks would sustain wholesale losses to traditional retail lending volume inside a few short years. The business model change was significant: abandon interest income and give it directly to potential depositors.

Safari Telecom's M-Pesa is similarly a business model that is disruptive. The unbanked are potentially a rich source of new revenue for banks, but by obviating the need for a bank account at all, the Telco is able to marginalise the entire banking industry for significant growth segments of whole economies.

In recent times, a business model innovation that has come particularly to the fore is the practice of securitisation. During the 1970s, banks were struggling to find sufficient funding to cope with huge demand for housing credit. At the time, institutions were forced to attract funding through deposits, and sometimes, through debt. They held all loans on their own books, throughout the entire life of the loan. Growth in lending, then, could only happen as institutions were able to borrow more money themselves or attract more depositors. It was 1970 when the US Department of Housing and Urban Development created the securitisation transaction with a mortgage-backed security. Essentially, bundles of loans of certain quality were bundled (supported by the cash flows from the underlying loans) and sold off to investors. The money from these sales could then be used to fund more loans.

Whilst the securitisation innovation initially encompassed only mortgage-backed securities, other types of credit began to be securitised as well. In 1986, in a sign of things to come, it was demonstrated (with a sale of credit card debt of about $50 million) that investors would tolerate assets sales with higher-than-expected losses if yields were high enough. This, of course, set the stage for the sub-prime boom that was to follow. Much has been written about the implosion of housing lending, but consider the result: more people than ever before were able to own their own home as lending costs fell drastically.

In the end, the frenetic competition for customers had unfortunate consequences. The lowering of costs of lending had made it economical to lend significantly more than the underlying assets were worth (based on, usually, the expectation that housing prices would continue to appreciate). And institutions found they could afford to lend to more and more risky people, and indeed, were forced to do so to continue the growth that shareholders and analysts had come to expect. But with significant drops in housing prices and a rise in interest rates, especially in the USA, individuals began to walk away from their obligations. In the end, the rate of defaults rose astronomically. As soon as it became obvious to investors that mortgage-backed securities did not have the inherent value they believed, the whole securitisation market dried up overnight.

This had a number of significant follow-on consequences, especially for those institutions that had built their businesses on the ability to fund loans *without* substantial deposit bases. Northern Rock, one such institution in the UK, would have failed in 2008 had the government not stepped in at tax-payers' expense. The bank's challenge was reacting quickly when the key assumptions of its business model – that wholesale funding of its mortgage book would be accessible and inexpensive – changed overnight. As the UK's Financial Services Authority said later, 'the failure of Northern Rock should first and foremost be attributed to the failure of its board and executive to create a durable funding model which could withstand the exceptional set of market circumstances that occurred in summer 2007' [33].

Business model innovation tends to be highly disruptive. It is the area of financial services innovation that should be of most interest to innovators, since it is here that many of the future threats to an institution will arise. Most likely, it is this slice of the pentagram that will occupy practitioners for most of their time when they begin the futurecasting phase of the futureproofing process, which is the topic of the next chapter.

3.2 THE FIVE CAPABILITY MODEL OF A SUCCESSFUL INNOVATION FUNCTION

The innovation pentagram is a useful means of classifying the kinds of innovations that practitioners might engage in, but it doesn't provide much help when one wants to understand the capabilities needed to drive particular innovations forward. This, of course, is a key theme to which much of this book is devoted. What does an innovation team need to do to drive a sustaining innovation in the business model space? A disruptive one in the experience space?

In order to answer this question, I spent a great deal of time talking with innovation leaders in banks around the world. A common theme emerging from these discussions was that innovation efforts always seemed to start small, and grew with success. It was almost never the case that programmes started big and stayed that way: in fact, big set piece innovation teams seemed to be the ones that were disbanded when they didn't deliver quickly enough. I began

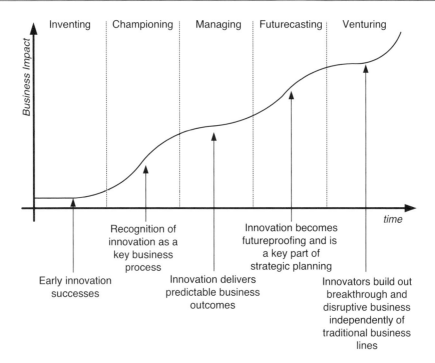

Figure 3.2   The Five Capability Model

to wonder why it was that teams with all the resources they could ever want rarely seemed to be as successful as those that had to beg for money at every opportunity.

This line of enquiry led, soon enough, to a realisation that the most successful innovation programmes developed their capabilities over time. They spent time refining and honing their skills, bootstrapping themselves into bigger, and more challenging, innovations as they were ready. They exhibited an evolution growth path to complicated, disruptive innovations, rather than attempting them at the moment of their conception. By contrast, the unsuccessful teams tried to do hard innovation immediately.

This realisation led me to what I call the Five Capability Model of innovation teams, illustrated in Figure 3.2. This model illustrates the sorts of things that innovation programmes need to do as they advance their capabilities. I've found it to be a useful way of benchmarking the capabilities of various innovation programmes I've come into contact with.

Each stage is comprised of an adoption S-curve of the kind we've already discussed in Chapter 2. S-curves, if you'll recall, describe the way an innovation's usage grows over time as people go through their adoption decision, in the meantime telling each other about what they are doing.

It was a key realisation, for me, that innovation programmes are *themselves* an innovation which follows this same kind of S-curve. Each capability in the Five Capability Model is a sustaining innovation which grows the amount of business impact of the innovation team. The amount of business impact grows slowly in each stage initially, but eventually reaches a critical mass point. This point is highly correlated with achievement of a key milestone signalling a particular capability has matured, and from then on, there is a swift rise in the business impact of the innovation team, eventually tailing off until the next milestone is reached.

Inventing

When an innovation practice is established, it will usually have sufficient influence and budget to focus on a few innovations at a time. Lacking strong relationships with other organisational units in the bank, members of the core team face the task of *personally* driving their initiatives out the door.

As an isolated team (at least initially), innovators have no choice but to invent the initial concepts on which they will focus. This is problematic, since it is difficult to determine in advance which innovations will be attractive to stakeholders and which won't when you have no means of getting feedback. A high rate of failure is usually the result of misjudging this initial selection of innovations to pursue, but unfortunately, there seems to be no way of avoiding that at the beginning.

In spite of the difficulties, the key thing at this stage is to achieve some early successes. The scale of these successes is less important than the fact they occur. Most new practitioners, however, immediately concentrate on innovations which are more significant in scope than a small programme can execute unaided. This is because the team will be seeking to create a name for itself as innovators, and incremental innovations are perceived to lack the visibility needed for that purpose.

In time, though, innovators will likely scale back their ambitions when they suffer repeated failures to actually deliver things with substantive business impact. It is critical this happens relatively quickly, because a new programme has only limited time to prove itself before sponsors worry the team is insufficiently effective to achieve the goals required.

Challenges at this stage are compounded, in many cases, by the inexperience of the new team with innovation as a discipline. Often new innovation practitioners are drawn from around the bank, perhaps with some kind of business development experience, but almost certainly little background in the processes and science that underlie what they are doing. Such recruits have a steep learning curve indeed before them.

The key inflection point for this stage is reached when innovators have achieved a body of outcomes sufficiently large that they are worthy of talking about outside the innovation team itself. One thing that often happens at this point is that the nascent innovation organisation gets very good at inventing and delivering its own concepts. There is an increasing success rate as individual team members get better at handling various stakeholders and reading the mood of potential blockers. In other words, individual innovators get very good at doing point innovations.

But this apparent success is actually a slow road to failure, because it limits teams to delivering business value in proportion to the number of people driving the innovation agenda. Because innovation will almost always be a small function at the beginning, the net impact possible is insignificant compared with other groups in a typical institution. Inevitably, this results in a waning of organisational interest. No matter how successful the innovation team is at invention, it will be irrelevant from a strategic perspective unless it finds a way to multiply the returns on its efforts.

Championing

Multiplying the efforts of the innovation team is best accomplished, in the first instance, through establishment of a proper business process to deal with the innovation challenge. Such a process eliminates the coupling between individual heroics of team members and innovation outcomes. It requires practitioners to champion innovation as a concept by building out a network of supporters.

The characteristics of an appropriate innovation process will vary from institution to institution. But such a process will almost certainly feature a means for collecting and selecting ideas, and some structured ways to put them in front of relevant business stakeholders from whom funding will need to be won.

In contrast to the inventing stage, where operations occur largely in isolation, a business process for innovation will have many touch-points. Individuals from outside the core innovation team are called on as subject matter experts, an activity which will certainly not be allowed for in the course of their ordinary goals and objectives. Stakeholders with money to invest are expected to devote their attention to things which are, in all probability, incidental to their main activities. And senior leaders are asked (sometimes begged) to look at innovation – which at this point probably hasn't delivered all that much – as a potentially strategic capability rather than a distraction.

The idea of a formal business process for innovation, consequently, can be a bit of a hard sell. This, of course, is the reason those initial wins during the invention stage are so important. They provide the principal evidence innovators use to prove a specialised business process could have significant positive consequences. Look what we did in isolation! Imagine if we could do that routinely and repeatedly!

Championing is the process that an innovation programme must go through to win support for such a business process. Innovators build networks of sponsorship in order to create the broad support they need in order to move forwards. With such broad support in place, innovators call on their sponsors to acknowledge that innovation may have a substantial role, even a strategic one, in the long-term future of an institution. Without it, of course, innovators are little more than the whizz-kids in the back room dreaming up interesting banking toys.

Here is the main problem for practitioners at this stage: whilst they are busily building their networks of sponsorship in order to get buy-in to their proposed process, they must also keep producing new innovations. Yesterday's successes lose currency very quickly, and the important thing is that stakeholders can see those initial wins weren't one-off flukes.

What signifies the critical mass point which innovators must achieve at the championing stage to get to the next? In most cases, critical mass is reached when innovators manage to get themselves assigned innovation targets. They need to get agreement from sponsors that they will be expected to achieve specific and measurable innovation outcomes, preferably ones which tie directly to the sponsoring stakeholder's agenda. Without measures and targets, an innovation function is an expensive luxury. But with them, it is a predictable business capability.

The range of possible innovation measures is very large, and much will be written about this topic later in this book. But for our purposes here, the characteristic of the target innovator's need is simple: it must be one which has direct impact on business outcomes. Usually, this means being goaled with some kind of financial objective.

Coupling innovation with the money can sometimes be problematic. It is often easier to roll out innovations which are not directly impactful on top or bottom lines. My own team did that with our implementation of social media we discussed earlier. The benefits are almost all fuzzy: increased ability to collaborate, better staff communications, and so forth. But what is the actual financial upside of social media? There probably is one, but determining it in a robust way is difficult in the extreme.

Nonetheless, innovations which are not directly coupled to the money will be less efficacious with stakeholders than otherwise. Advice to new practitioners: at this stage, select innovations where you can link whatever is delivered to the specific objectives you think you will be able to get from your sponsors. If that's going to be a financial target, make sure you have either new income or cost savings to show for your work. Various productivity or other fuzzy benefit-based innovations are best left until there is a good track record of predictability.

Managing

Until this point, the innovation programme is likely to have achieved its successes in an ad-hoc fashion. Innovations, when they've been introduced, will have been the result of heroes – people going above and beyond the call of duty – to make a difference. During the championing phase, innovators will have built a pretty good network of supporters who can see the value of a business process, so they won't have been working in the isolated splendour they did during the invention stage. They will also have achieved some robust measures that provide them with the ability to benchmark their progress.

The next key question practitioners face is how to make sure innovations are delivered predictably so that goals are met every single time. This predictability is essential if one is to establish innovation as a better investment choice than those offered by conventional business lines. Traditional business investments are generally perceived as far more certain than innovative ones, with returns that are usually large in comparison with those achievable by an early-stage innovation. Being predictable (or, in other words, less risky) is a basic competitive string to the bow when pitching for scarce funding.

There is no magic in achieving predictability in innovation. It is simply a numbers game. For every single innovation that makes it at least three others will not, on average. So if, for example, the metric is a financial one, the programme must have at least four or more times plan to ensure success.

When one is balancing a portfolio of innovation investments, it is dangerous in the extreme to have a few large projects, rather than multiple small ones. With all the eggs in one basket, so to speak, there is usually too much risk that a single failure can make the required outcomes unachievable. This is a principal reason you will find this book suggesting a focus on incremental innovation. Incremental innovations may not be visible, neither are they as sexy as the big-scope projects innovation teams might prefer to do day to day if given the choice, but the bills must be paid.

Because incremental innovations are small, and usually less risky than other sorts, the returns from each are likely to be relatively low. Many incremental innovations, delivered sausage-factory style, are needed in order to achieve a result. As I said, practitioners are primarily in a volume game: another reason the innovation network established during the championing phases is so very vital. Innovators will need help just to cope with the volume they need to run to get their numbers.

So, at this phase of development, the innovation programme is concentrating on two key activities: managing the riskiness of a portfolio of investments and putting the processes in place to enable that to happen at scale.

In Chapter 6, during our discussion of the innovation phase of futureproofing, we will talk more about the process you can use to manage the riskiness of an innovation portfolio. Suffice it to say for now, though, that many low-risk investments are used to pay for the riskiness of doing a few revolutionary or breakthrough innovations in a given period.

Linking the portfolio and the innovation process together is a well-known tool much loved by entrepreneurs and other business people: the business plan. An innovation business plan links investment to the activities that will drive returns. It is a road map for managers and stakeholders to predictability.

An innovation business plan does not have to be especially detailed, and is relatively simple to construct. One works backwards from the metrics agreed at the championing stage through each stage of the innovation process, focusing on the things that must be done to guarantee the appropriate volume. For example, it is typical that four ideas are needed as an input to the ideation phase to generate one that can be used in the innovation phase.

Getting such volume might require some kind of ideas campaign, where mass media methods are used to actualise the population inside the institution. Or you might choose to provide some kind of incentive to those who provide ideas.

A good business plan is reviewed regularly, with adjustments made to ensure that targets are met. There is a proper planning cycle during which these adjustments are made: they are never done in an ad-hoc fashion. The metrics generated by innovations flowing through the futureproofing process are examined, and these determine what tweaks must be made to ensure that returns are made.

Eventually innovation teams do achieve a stable sausage-factory of innovation. With such stability comes the ability to hit any particular return number required of the business simply by varying the volume and investment mix parameters of their innovation processes. Here is also where many innovation programmes stop their development. What more is there to achieve once you are coupled to the money and can deliver returns on demand? Let's face it, such an innovation capability is no longer something that can be considered a luxury: it has earned its stripes and is well on its way to being a significant business in its own right. But an innovation programme with a narrow focus on near-term opportunities (and therefore, on predictability) is unlikely to be part of the strategic visioning process of an institution. It is to that challenge we turn next.

Futurecasting

With stability of delivery out of the way, practitioners are free to consider themselves and their work in a strategic context. Until this point, it is likely that any attempts to do strategic, bank-changing work have failed. Innovation teams that attempt to get strategic too early tend to overreach both their influence and their budgets. Having said that, an innovation programme concentrating entirely on near-term opportunities is in danger of becoming more about 'business improvement' than innovation. Whilst there is nothing wrong with this, there are bigger fish to fry.

It is inevitable that threats to core business lines will emerge, given sufficient time. Recall our discussion of disruption theory from the last chapter: such threats might be small and seem insignificant initially. It is rational behaviour for managers in traditional business to ignore such threats and focus on sustaining innovations they can use to drive growth. Sustaining innovations tend to have short-term benefits and focus on serving existing good customers even better. This makes them very attractive.

However, someone needs to be concerning themselves with what is likely to happen in the medium and long terms. In most institutions, strategic planning cycles ordinarily contemplate such timeframes, but regularly do *not* consider the impact innovations might have given enough time. Now, although the innovation team might have a good view of likely impacts various innovations might have in the strategic context, they are unlikely to be heard until they have shown they can deliver returns predictably. Most institutions are myopic when it comes to accepting strategic advice: they prefer it to come only from those who have demonstrated capabilities at the strategic level previously.

Whilst delivering a predictable return is hardly operating at a strategic level (unless the programme is contributing revenues of a strategic magnitude in its own right), one has to start somewhere. So the futurecasting phase of development concerns itself with how innovations can impact institutions, not just at the individual business unit level, but across the board.

At this point, anticipating likely disruptions and breakthroughs becomes a key focus of the innovation team. Practitioners seek to understand the likely shape of the future, both because they need to steer the ideation process to create things that address emergent trends, and because they know that bigger plays require a lot of seed-sowing with senior leadership before decisions are made.

The principal tool innovator used to do this is story-telling. Senior leaders rarely have time to think about possible futures in any rigorous way. They are running businesses worth billions, and their attention is rightly focused on day-to-day operational issues. Consequently, they need their future thinking provided in bite-sized pieces which enable them to rehearse possible decisions and consequences without having to do all the ground work first. Stories are a great way of doing this.

Structured methods exist to create plausible stories that shape the future. A great tool is scenario planning, which we will discuss in more detail in the next chapter. When a scenario is backed up with quantitative predictions it becomes a powerful planning tool. Here is an example.

At the time of writing, green issues are a significant part of most corporate agendas. And there is an increasing focus on the cost of running data centres, especially the carbon costs of doing so. In many countries around the world, governments are considering whether to legislate to account for carbon emissions. Such legislation might impose a tax on the use of electricity in data centres, with the obvious effect of increasing the cost of running a bank's technology. Recently there have been estimates that the total cost of running a given computer system over five years in terms of power will be far, far greater than the cost of its components: the technology, the data centre, and the people. Now, given drivers such as these, what possible future scenarios can we envision for banks?

One might be rapid escalation of costs without any increase in system functionality. Depending on the legislative regime, these costs might be material to the cost-to-income ratio. This is a situation rather similar to that faced by airlines in recent decades. Historically, to start an airline, the biggest cost was getting the planes. But now it is buying the fuel needed to keep the aircraft in the air.

Bank computer systems could be facing the same inflection point, with weaker institutions finding that their IT prices them out of some low margin products. Rushing to respond to cost inflation, banks rapidly remove products and customer segments, paring themselves down to the point where the minimum IT possible is used, with a consequent contraction in the size of the institution.

An alternative scenario is one in which banks, recognising the impending cost inflection point, decide to radically adjust their IT infrastructure. With the advent of cloud computing, they move servers to geographically disperse locations, locations in which there is cheap power and where cooler climates can be used instead of air-conditioning. They share these locations with tens, perhaps hundreds, of other companies, and secure the price of their computer resource on a futures exchange. Compute cycles are traded just as carbon credits are beginning to be. Dedicated data centres become a thing of the past, as does the idea of running a process on a dedicated bit of hardware. In order to optimise their processing expenses, banks are forced to build their systems so they can run any given service anywhere, depending on which computing resources they've acquired on their futures exchange.

Clearly, the first scenario is one that could reasonably come to pass in the absence of futureproofing. Senior executives might understand the impact of carbon credits in terms of a financial services business, but will probably not have thought through the consequences of doing nothing.

The second scenario, on the other hand, couples some emerging innovations in the market with a potential positive story-line. But the point is that some very large strategic issues are illuminated by both sets of scenarios: what would an institution do if its power costs increased exponentially? And what strategic choices – some of which will most certainly be innovative – should an institution be making now to safeguard itself?

Note these issues are ones of very broad scope. Such changes to bank-wide computing practices are not something to be agreed in an eye-blink. Strategic questions such as these are subject to much analysis and deliberation. However, without the foresight of the futurecasting phase, it is rare that one starts thinking about the implications of innovations until much, much too late. By actively inserting themselves in the strategic agenda in this way, the innovation team has provided the bank with an opportunity to rehearse the decisions it must make, before things get desperate.

The critical mass point for futurecasting is that innovation inputs are part of the strategic planning process of the institution. This has significant upside for the scope of innovations the team can plan to execute as well: they have sponsors with sufficient influence to authorise practically anything, given sufficient motivation to do so.

This, then, is the time practitioners can safely begin work on their best breakthrough and revolutionary ideas, hopefully in the process resolving some of the strategic challenges of the institution identified previously as part of their thought leadership activities.

With all this achieved, however, there is one last bastion of innovation remaining: disruption. Doing disruptive innovation too early is almost always a mistake for innovators, since senior people will actively do anything they can to stop an upstart group from damaging their businesses. Combating this natural and very rational tendency is done when the innovation team reaches the venturing stage.

Venturing

The innovation team is now at an interesting point in its development. The previous four stages of development have created a capability that is predictable, linked in with the rest of the business, and demonstrated gravitas at the strategic level. It is likely the team will have grown its budgets and mandate in accordance with its success. The portfolio of innovation projects for which it is responsible will be substantial, and the overall returns from innovation might even be significant by the standards of mainline businesses. Certainly those business lines will trust the innovators to propose things which are in their best interests, even though some of them might be surprising.

The key gateway for the success of the innovation team at this final stage is that the business trusts the team to incubate disruptive innovations independently of traditional lines of management. They become sponsors of initiatives in their own right, responsible for the P&L of emerging businesses directly. Why is this independence so important?

Recall from our examination of disruption theory in Chapter 2 that incumbent businesses are usually unable to disrupt themselves. Incumbents come with a set of values and cost structures they impose on any activities under their jurisdiction, which are based on infrastructures used to serve the best, most profitable customers. But disruptive innovations usually don't address those customers, at least at first.

Disruptive innovations target, in the first instance, those customers unattractive to the incumbent business because they are low-margin, or those that are presently over-served by the current business and therefore would like a cheaper alternative. For an incumbent business line, the former situation is challenging, though not insurmountably so. These are customers that the business has already decided it is uninterested in serving. The latter, however, is much more difficult. Incumbent business lines would never allow currently over-served customers to churn downwards, since this is the slippery path to commoditisation.

The net result is that disruptive innovations will almost always be watered down by incumbent businesses until they are not disruptive any more. This means the long-term strategic advantages of whatever-it-is will likely not be realised. In the meantime, of course, the disruption will likely be introduced by a competitor. The disruption will happen regardless of any protective stance taken by incumbent business, and history has shown this to be true for *all* businesses at some time.

Programmes at the venturing stage are actually entrusted by the business to build out long-range business opportunities with material impacts to future revenues. This is one reason that large institutions have begun to create chief innovation officer roles with significant power in their own right. A chief innovation officer (or whatever the equivalent may be called) ought to be an aspirational role in every bank, considering what this level of seniority actually implies: the innovation agenda is a serious part of the ongoing business of the institution.

Unfortunately, one often sees C-level roles with innovation in their titles, whose programmes have not been through the four stages on the way to venturing I described above. It is interesting to consider the kinds of scenarios that occur when this happens, something we'll turn our attention to in a few moments.

Exceptions to the Five Capability Model

There is one set of circumstances in which the Five Capability Model does not seem to apply in the strict order I've laid it out, and that is where the CEO or board *directly* funds an innovation programme and continues to work closely with it throughout its development.

There are, apparently, a few features which make such an arrangement work. The first, obviously, is that top-level support is attached to the innovators immediately. But the real reason for success in this case is that the CEO is forced to present a strategic rationale to the rest of the institution describing *why* innovation is important and should be incorporated into the day-to-day running of the business.

As I've mentioned a few times in this book so far, it is rational behaviour for leaders in institutions to focus on the day-to-day operations of their businesses. They rarely have the time or inclination to seek innovation proactively, and must usually be laboriously won over to the idea of futureproofing. But when the CEO mandates innovation *and* presents sound strategic reasons for doing it as part of the day-to-day strategic planning of an institution, all that changes. Leaders focus their attention on thinking about the future in a structured way, and they see innovation as a key part of helping them to do this. So, the demand for the innovation practice is there right at the start, as are the resources that innovators need in order to make things happen.

That does not mean, of course, that the capabilities of an innovation team do not need to develop at all! It will still be necessary, for example, to work through getting predictable and having structured ways of thinking about the future. It is still important to be able to invent and build networks. But the advantage of a CEO-led innovation effort is that the time and resource pressures are freed up. Innovators will spend more time getting their capabilities together and less doing fire-fighting influencing to prove the group should exist. The result is that innovation happens a lot more quickly.

You may now be wondering how many examples of an innovation-led institution there are. Where a CEO decided innovation was a key strategic priority *and* then personally created and managed the team responsible for it. The answer? Very, very few. In fact, I can think of perhaps three examples where this has been the case right at the start, and none of them allowed me to mention them by name. But practically all other innovation teams have had to earn the right of existence, once they've been given their seed budgets and small head count.

Innovation strategy

This discussion of CEO-led innovation leads nicely into a topic of central importance for bank innovators – the overall innovation strategy that is to be adopted by their institution. Whether the CEO is involved directly in the day-to-day operation of innovation or not, the specific objectives of an innovation programme devolve from the overall strategic intent that an institution has when it establishes its innovation programme. There is usually a great deal of discussion about this topic, and very little agreement. Whilst everyone usually agrees that innovation is important, no one seems able to get to a consensus on what that *means,* from a strategic perspective.

Luckily, I once read a very cogent analysis of innovation strategy in a book called *Making Innovation Work* [34] that makes resolution of the question a simple one. All innovation strategies are either *Play to Win* or *Play Not to Lose.*

Play to Win (P2 W) innovation strategies occur when the answer to the question 'is the innovation investment we are making expected to be one of the key sources of long-term competitive advantage?' is an emphatic yes. It encompasses all those strategic options which move the institution towards a market-leading approach: launching new, unprecedented products and services, creating new business models, or inventing new channels. The innovation investments in this strategy will be largely revolutionary and breakthrough in nature, with the goal of always reaching beyond the grasp of competitors.

There are a number of financial services companies that have evidently adopted this innovation strategy, of which the best example, probably, is Caja Navarra of Spain. Caja Navarra was a relatively small savings bank that was in danger of being outflanked by its much larger rivals. It adopted an innovation strategy which fundamentally changed the nature of its business in a very disruptive way, resulting in spectacular growth. We'll talk about Caja Navarra again in the final chapter of this book.

P2 W strategies are usually bet-the-the-company plays for smaller organisations, but large institutions are able to balance the riskiness inherent by investing broadly in many innovations. This is the fundamental premise, of course, behind the portfolio methods we'll examine later.

If innovation is not expected to be one of the key sources of long-term competitive advantage for an institution, then all innovation strategies follow the Play Not to Lose (PN2 L) approach.

In this case, institutions take the position that being able to compete effectively *in the long term* through innovation is the best way to maximise the balance between risk and return.

Competing in the long term means doing innovation which maximises an institution's agility. It means creating new systems and processes that minimise the advantage that any competitor might obtain through releasing new breakthroughs and revolutions. And it means actively seeking out ways to improve the efficiency of current operations – finding ways to cut costs creatively, improve the speed of current business processes, or optimise the use of existing systems and technologies. As you would anticipate, PN2 L strategies tend to result in much more incrementalism in the innovation portfolio. They are also much more mechanistic, being dependent on volume to achieve sustainable rewards.

The innovation strategy decision is significant for the Five Capability Model, because it governs absolutely the way that innovation teams will structure themselves as they seek to advance through the first phases of development on the way to intrapreneuring. Then, when they have established robust and predictable returns, their futurecasting and venturing will be quite different in the P2 W scenario compared with PN2 L.

3.3   CASE STUDY: INNOVATION AT BANK OF AMERICA

Our discussion of strategy leads us now to an organisation that has a firm handle on its own innovation strategy. Bank of America, now one of the largest institutions in the world, has a long history of innovative firsts. It is illustrative to examine how these have occurred through the lens of innovators inside the bank.

Matt Calman is Head of Innovation at Bank of America, one of a triumvirate of senior innovation leaders in the bank. His perspective on the development of innovation at the bank is an interesting one, and he was good enough to share it with me for this book.

When we began our discussion, he opened with an interesting line: 'Customers don't think we are as innovative as we really are'. That is an insightful remark, and echoes my own sentiments with which I started this book. It is so often the case that innovation inside institutions goes largely unnoticed to the outside world. That can probably be said for Bank of America, whose decades of innovative achievements in banking have been covered elsewhere in this book. But though most of the innovation that goes on in this institution is probably not all that evident looking from the outside in, Bank of America has made a strategic commitment to developing its innovation capabilities. You can see this whenever you look at their annual reports, which are peppered with references to the innovative work being done across the board. But how, exactly, did innovation get so firmly on the agenda at Bank of America?

The answer is that the bank developed its innovation capabilities in line with the Five Capability Model we've been discussing in this chapter, though not necessarily in the linear order I outlined earlier. That, as it turns out, is not atypical. Some institutions start with very good innovation processes, but leave it until later to connect these with networks of innovation inside an institution. Others do a great deal of future thinking at the beginning, and only begin to concentrate on execution as the need arises. But, however it happens, practically every significantly successful innovation programme I examined has developed its five capabilities eventually.

Anyway, as we've already seen in Chapter 1 of this book, Bank of America has a significant track record of creating innovations that have changed the financial services industry. When it invested in business computing, the credit card, and had the first major deployment of ATMs, it was positioning itself as the leader which the rest of the pack must follow. But these were innovations that happened in isolation. They were innovations that were driven by the will-power of specific executives, or, as I've termed it elsewhere in this book, individual heroics.

Individual heroics are a hallmark of innovators as inventors, and as was the case at Bank of America, are signs of an innovation function that hasn't yet had the chance to develop its processes in a structured way. All innovation programmes – even if they aren't called that at the beginning – tend to start this way, even those with the highest level of executive sponsorship. It takes time for processes, systems, and influence networks to be established and operate. But Bank of America is an unusual organisation. It recognised relatively early compared with its peers that its long-term competitive advantages would be eroded without continual evolution and development. And it set about creating a capability that systematised this process.

Initially, however, these first efforts at structured innovation were led by individual business lines, which in the context of their own areas of responsibility, began creating capabilities that might result in advantages for them compared with competitors. In the pursuit of this goal, the bank created dozens of small, disconnected laboratories, all concentrated on particular business lines. Some were focused on creating new intellectual property and business concepts. Others were technology showcases for vendors to bring innovative ideas to the bank. But all were working in splendid isolation, with little, if anything, to do with each other. It is during the innovators as champions phase that institutions recognise that innovation and innovators have much more chance of success when they do not exist in a vacuum.

The initial work of Calman's innovation team, then, was to connect these creators of potentially profitable intellectual property. As he says, 'we are about creating pathways so that people can get their ideas into the mainstream execution flow. There's no point trying to do innovation separately from the business lines that have to commercialise the idea.' To this end, Calman established a 'community of innovators', an informal clustering of people involved in various labs around the bank. The idea was to cross-fertilise the best efforts across groups so that the overall pace of innovation and change would increase.

But another key aspect of the innovators as champions development stage is that key metrics for the forming innovation processes be agreed. As you will recall, this is an important step in the transition to predictability. What, after all, is the point of being able to replicate results in a consistent manner if, in the end, no one understands what the results mean?

Luckily, Bank of America has very clear goals for its innovators. 'Products and Patents', says Calman, 'are the only metrics that count for innovators. Everything else is incidental to the actual business.' Such metrics, ultimately, translate into financial benefits for an institution. Although the bank continues to pursue innovations with more fuzzy business cases, there is always a focus on making sure that the work of innovators contributes in a direct way to the bottom-line results.

In 2002, Six Sigma came to the bank in a big way, and was immediately endorsed by executives from the chairman down. The consequent focus on optimisation and process led to an interesting revelation: despite what many people had thought (or might have liked to believe, given the leadership of the bank in specific innovations such as business computing and cards), there was no real possibility that Bank of America would ever do innovation in quite the same way as, for example, Google or Apple.

Whilst these two organisations are highly optimised to produce a pipeline of breakthrough and disruptive innovations, Bank of America needed a more measured approach in its innovation-making. It wanted to ensure that its innovators were directly value-enhancing, rather than speculative. As Calman says, 'innovation is important, but it must not be too disruptive. We wanted to be a positive disruptive force, rather than a distraction.'

The clarity of focus was fortuitous for the innovators, who neatly dodged a key trap for developing innovation programmes: attempting to get big-bang innovations out the door before an institution is ready for it. Because of Six Sigma, and the consequent focus on process and optimisation, the innovators at Bank of America had another advantage: it was relatively easy to justify significant investments in innovation infrastructure. Such infrastructures included enterprise idea management systems, collaboration tools, and a raft of other things that streamline the process of taking an idea from conception to either product or patent.

In all the banks I've spoken to as part of the research for this book, I've found that the existence of innovation infrastructures – or the lack of them – is the primary predictor of whether an innovation function has reached the managing stage successfully. Those institutions that have invested in such tools tend to have much more predictable innovation efforts than those that haven't. They rely on heroics far less. And they have good visibility of the overall state of innovation in their institutions.

Another key development for Bank of America at this stage was the formation of a much more formal innovation team in 2004. In that year, a group of senior executives attended an MIT course on innovation, and came away impressed with the possibilities for Bank of America if it was truly to embrace the development of innovation as corporate competency.

The CIO of the time, one of the executives who went to MIT, decided to form an Innovation Advisory Council to support the innovation effort. Recognising a need to support the nascent new programme with seed funding, she imposed a small tax on the leaders in her organisation and amassed a kitty of 3 million dollars. And then she told her new advisory council to 'go out and do something with it'.

The Innovation Advisory Council was a successful innovation in its own right, but was populated mainly by technology leaders from Bank of America. Calman, who at this time had been working on Cheque21 and remote deposit capture, saw that the new body wasn't really as connected as it could be. 'There were a few interested individuals,' he says, 'but of 15 or so members, there were only 4 or 5 who were really engaged.' The problem was that the new organisation was relatively IT-focused, and Calman knew what was needed was to create a more direct link with the business.

His first step was to bring P&L owners onto the Innovation Advisory Council – the individuals who would, ultimately, be making go/no-go decisions on particular innovations. He then restructured his own lab to build out prototypes on its own, using concept leaders to stand between these stakeholders and technologists. Concept leaders are visionary individuals with sufficient technology training and business awareness to spot opportunities that could be reasonably implemented at Bank of America. With the concept leaders in place, Bank of America began to bridge the gap between gadgeteering and real business value. The idea was to build a small counterculture of innovation that 'added on' to the standard processes followed by business lines in any case.

Bringing the innovation function closer to the business was a key element to the success this first incarnation of the Innovation Advisory Council achieved. But Calman knew he would have to move up the value chain again if he wanted his innovation programme to truly support the strategic agenda of the bank. Consequently, he and his team started work on what he calls 'Innovation 2.0', a three-layer innovation structure that would retain the abilities previously developed, but increase the strategy and visioning piece in a significant way. Calman was seeking a way to jump to innovators as futurecasters.

His first step was to dissolve the Innovation Advisory Council, still comprised of a significant number of IT leaders, and replace it with a new body called the Innovation Community of

Practice. Instead of technologists, he invited the heads of product management and product development from every segment of the business, the individuals who actually controlled the commercial destiny of the bank. These were individuals who, in their own right, were able to give the green light to any particular innovation coming out of the programme. This was the top layer of the new innovation structure.

The bottom layer was the lab network that had previously been established at the bank. It had proven its value as a way to explore new ideas and produce outputs that could be commercialised. And the web of connections that it represented was a great way for the Community of Practice to validate its ideas and projects, no matter where they might need to be situated in the bank.

In the middle, Calman created something innovative in its own right: a new group of about 70 individuals called the 'firebrands'. The firebrands are a community of middle management associates who have proven their ability to innovate. They each have a history of creating new products and patents, and have therefore demonstrated their credentials as thought leaders able to spot interesting commercial opportunities for Bank of America.

Being a firebrand is a voluntary opportunity to contribute to the development of the bank, but they are compensated by being provided the liberty and resources to work on their own interests. Small grants are made to firebrands with interesting ideas, or they are provided with other resources they can use to explore potentially interesting ideas. In this, Bank of America has followed other leading companies such as Google, who have instituted similar programmes to ensure their most talented employees are able to make a difference on its behalf.

But the real innovation of the firebrands community was that it became part of executive decision-making. Senior leaders regularly come to the community with challenges of strategic importance. Having such a community of people they can rely on, with strong credentials for solving strategic problems in the past, is a huge advantage.

The result of a challenge is a report, essentially a catalogue of concepts for the future. Firebrands give an outside-in view of strategy, and provide that unique perspective that organisations often seek external consultants to provide. This is done in the context of the specific systems and processes of Bank of America, resulting in a very relevant output for senior leaders.

And the results have been overwhelmingly positive. When the firebrands were asked for their thoughts on the affluent customer segment and the best way to target it with new online interactions, they came back with 40 possible future states and concepts. Of these, 12 were selected by leadership for future investigation, and at the time of writing, three had been productionised, with four in implementation.

With the firebrands as the middle layer of his innovation structure, Calman has successfully grown the innovation programme through innovators as futurecasters. Where does the Bank of America innovation programme go now?

According to Calman, the need is now to reduce the time it takes to change the culture of the bank, since, according to him, everything will likely change over the next decade. 'We need to speed up the cycle time for new ideas,' he says. 'If we can reduce the year or more it takes from idea to market, and do it repeatably, we can change the culture of our organisation. What if we could double or triple the pace of change? We're trying to build the technology and people systems to make this possible now.'

Calman has a vision of moving from cloud computing to clouds of people. He realises that the investment the bank will need to make in order to achieve this will be measured in tens of millions of dollars. But the achievement of this goal will make the innovation programme at Bank of America a significant business line in its own right.

3.4   BUILDING OUT THE FUTUREPROOFING PROCESS

Bank of America may be ahead of most institutions when it comes to having developed innovation capabilities, but their development is largely typical. One starts with an innovation programme which is relatively modest, expanding into more sophisticated capabilities over time. In contrast, rushing into game-changing, high-value innovation too soon seems to be a sure-fire way to cripple the chances of success.

As you would expect, it is difficult in the extreme to get banks to talk about their failures in public (even to another banker!), so I'm unable to name the examples I am about to use. But rest assured there is a veritable graveyard of innovators and their innovation programmes in institutions. The following story of a large bank in South Africa is typical.

In an attempt to jump-start the innovation process, a large team of consultants was called in to run a day-long innovation workshop. This was attended by employees at all levels of the bank, including three members of the Executive Committee. The objective was to take five major customer issues facing the institution and come up with solutions which would then be implanted as significant innovations. The issues covered were relatively typical ones: issues with customer experience, fees and charges, some cultural aspects of human resource management. All significant, with resolution requiring a strategic level of engagement across the business.

Initially, the workshop seemed to be working well, with positive and unencumbered feedback surrounding some of the organisational issues that would be involved in making significant changes. In fact, the most radical ideas were put forward by people who would have to deal with the greatest amount of change during implementation. One extremely popular suggestion was rationalising the number of products offered to customers. At the time, more than 50 were offered, though customer research had established that even the bank's more expert customers could reasonably deal with only seven or less. In fact, the executive in charge of product went so far as to state that the bank would feel little or no pain if it sold only seven products in total, and, furthermore, there would be no revenue impact at all.

Despite all this, though, in the three years the consulting firm had done this exercise, the outcome was always the same. Some ideas were selected from workshop results by the innovation project, then presented to the Executive Committee. This body then selected the ones it could implement inexpensively and with as least disruption as possible. The remainder were abandoned.

Ultimately, whilst some innovative outcomes were the result of this process, sufficient anyway for the Executive Committee to show its employees and shareholders, our South African bank failed to deal with the key strategic issues that might be reasonably resolved by innovation. And this, despite the fact that the exercise was commenced with the *intention* of dealing with strategic issues. What was going wrong here?

Firstly, the innovation team was attempting to create strategic change in the absence of any evidence that innovation could be a significant driver of value. That is the role of innovators as managers, of course, but in advance of the workshop, there was no evidence available to the Executive Committee that innovation, some of which would likely be extremely disruptive, might actually make the bank a stronger one.

Their response was a natural one: pander to the idea of being innovative, whilst changing as little as possible. It is a typical response in the presence of uncertainty.

Then, too, the innovation team jumped straight into the strategic agenda without proving its credentials as thought leaders first. Why would the Executive Committee accept strategic advice from a team that hadn't proved itself capable of operating on their level? What was

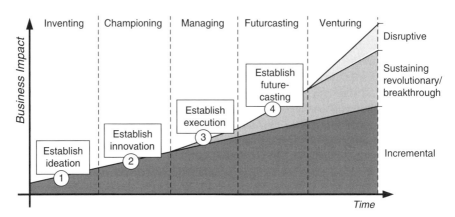

Figure 3.3   How to build out the futureproofing process

needed was that innovators extrapolated out the consequences of failing to address specific challenges through innovation. For example, with 54 products, simplification might have resulted in an opportunity to be disruptive to other competitors in the market: costs would have reduced, with the resulting possibility that the bank could target lower-margin customers, and/or steal over-served customers from its competitors. But the innovation team did none of these things.

The lesson of this story is that you have to build out an innovation programme in accordance with the Five Capability Model if you want success. That implies implementing certain parts of the futureproofing process at each stage, and varying the focus of the team depending on where you are up to. The recommended approach is shown in Figure 3.3.

During the inventing stage, innovation teams should be concentrating mainly on incremental innovations, mostly because they won't have the influence or budget to be doing much more. As I've mentioned earlier, incremental innovations are really about volume, and getting to scale means lots of ideas need to be found. This, then, is the time innovation leaders should be establishing the ideation part of their futureproofing process. Even if this entails, initially, nothing more than a simple staff suggestion scheme, it is a critical piece of infrastructure that needs to be developed sooner or later. Innovators should also start to think how their idea selection mechanisms will work, since a high-quality problem that comes with success in this area is having too many ideas to evaluate with purely manual methods.

Ordinarily, the championing stage will also be about mainly incremental innovations, since the budgetary situation won't have changed much. However, this is the time that influence networks start to get built, and it is reasonable for innovators to start thinking about some bigger innovations that might use these networks. Around now, the innovation phase of the futureproofing process would normally be established: it is functionally necessary anyway as the number of incremental innovations being managed by the innovation team grows. There is a need to have systems and processes which assist in the development of all those little projects as volume increases.

The managing stage is really the first time innovators can afford to start experimenting with larger revolutionary or breakthrough innovations. These will be done in small measure whilst they continue to build out a pipeline of incremental innovations, which are paying for the riskiness of these bigger, more visible projects. And this increased riskiness in the portfolio of projects means that innovators can no longer 'fire-and-forget' their innovative concepts, even after funding has been approved – they must take an active hand in managing the delivery process. Those activities are established as part of the execution phase, which should be implemented during the managing phase, if only to ensure all those great funded business cases actually see the light of day.

During the futurecasting stage, innovators have a chance to ramp up the innovations which make a strategic difference. As shown in Figure 3.3, this is the first time that breakthrough and revolutionary innovations will actually have much material effect on the returns the innovation team is generating. The reason such innovations can be part of the overall portfolio at this stage is that the innovators will demonstrate to senior executives the consequences of *not* considering innovation in longer-term planning as a result of the various futurecasts they will have begun to provide.

It is only with all these processes established that innovation teams can reasonably be expected to successfully take on disruptive innovations, which is a main part of the venturing stage. At this point, innovators can reasonably expect to produce disruptive ideas and be able to execute them, usually at a distance from the rest of the business.

Another interesting point coming from Figure 3.3 is the end-state mix of innovations. As I've said multiple times now in this book, doing incremental innovation pays the bills. At a minimum, it is necessary to find enough benefit from incremental innovation that you can afford the running costs of an innovation programme, plus a contribution to the overall returns the programme is expected to generate. That's why, even during the venturing stage, the majority of the business impact is shown as incremental. In most institutions, it is likely this will be true *even* if P2 W is the strategic option of choice.

Later on, as the programme builds out, more sustaining revolutionary and breakthrough innovations are introduced. The function of these is twofold. Firstly, they are what people expect innovation teams to be working on, and addressing such perceptions is something that has to happen, eventually. But more importantly, careful investment in breakthrough and revolutionary innovations is the way the team is able to generate the above-and-beyond returns it must achieve if it is to be a preferred investment choice, compared with other business-as-usual investment opportunities.

The last thing to consider is the overall business impact of disruptive innovation, started during the venturing stage. The overall contribution is quite low, because disruptive innovations always start small – perhaps microscopically so in the first instance – and grow in the medium and long terms to something substantial. A programme at the venturing level could conceivably have large returns from disruptive innovations, but not for some years. It is difficult to factor these into the year-on-year returns which most institutions demand, though such investments are often the key ones needed to avoid future competitive threats. They are the ones that make an institution futureproof.

Why big money innovation programmes usually fail

Innovation programmes are, themselves, disruptive innovations. As you will recall from our discussion of disruption theory in the last chapter, disruptions are successful when they target technologies, processes, or capabilities which are not that important to the main parts of the business.

The lack of interest from the main businesses usually results from the relatively small returns that can be made compared with business-as-usual. Senior leaders in these businesses look to spend their valuable investment budgets on very big projects that protect or enhance their existing revenues. They can do this with impunity because such investments are very predictable, being based on markets which are inherently well understood. There are often large bodies of data available that may be used to make accurate predictions, and existing processes and capabilities will already be aligned to near-term revenue production.

An innovation function cannot compete with such major investments successfully, because the returns anything truly innovative will generate in the short term will be microscopic compared with those demanded by a business leader with a significant P&L to manage.

Innovation can, on the other hand, generate value in areas not already the subject of investment by the business. It is likely that the main business will ignore such opportunities as, being mostly incremental, they won't have a material contribution to the top line it is concerned about. But with these first wins, the innovation team will grow its capabilities in line with the Five Capability Model until it becomes capable of driving business itself when it reaches the venturing stage.

The key to this process is that each previous stage is achieved before the next is attempted. This means the amount of investment required in innovation is relatively small at the beginning, and the returns, whilst large in comparison with this investment, are pretty much insignificant compared with the returns of the rest of the business.

With the achievement of each stage, however, more money is committed to the innovation programme. In order to maintain its status as the best returning business opportunity available to an institution, the actual cash returns that must be generated get larger. In other words, either volume or value must ramp up to match the investments being made. Neither of these parameters are switches that can be turned on in a binary fashion: they build over time, in a similar way to any new business experience's gradual growth.

Now consider the case of the big-investment innovation programme. Such a programme is likely to start out at the venturing stage right at the beginning, and the amount of capital under its control will be significant. The innovation team knows it must generate substantial enough returns that innovation becomes the preferred investment activity. Failing to do so will result in funding being reallocated to other opportunities where returns are more certain and profitable.

In the rush to achieve early successes, the innovators will need to invest quickly. Because the returns achieved will be compared with main-line business returns, the investment decision will almost certainly be in several very big, very risky projects. Smaller projects will not be prioritised, because they won't have big enough numbers attached to them to make the return on investment figures the team needs to stay in business.

In the meantime, these very big, risky projects will almost certainly be ones that the main-line business will take an interest in. Immediately, the leaders of those businesses will resent the innovation group stepping on their toes. Their control over major portions of revenue gives them the political clout to block projects or even shut them down altogether. The innovation team, without a track record, is unlikely to prevail in these circumstances, and their projects, if they get off the ground at all, will not have the internal support they need to achieve full commercialisation.

Whilst all this is going on, time is passing. If the innovation team is lucky, at least some of its investments will have come to fruition, and there may even have been a significant success. Regardless of that, however, the inevitable failures will be very, very obvious. The choice of prioritising a small number of very significant projects has resulted in a situation where anything other than close to 100% success is seen as a failure, and certainly the returns on capital invested will likely be less than those achievable by other investment opportunities.

Most new ideas never make it past the ideation phase, and of those, only one in four is likely to make it to commercialisation. A much smaller percentage will be successful enough that they generate windfall returns, which is what the team is counting on to support their big budgets.

Inevitably, this gamble doesn't pay off. Innovation is perceived as risky, and certainly not a preferred investment activity. Quite a lot of irritation to main-line business units will have occurred, without a lot of return. Powerful leaders elsewhere in the business will point out that the returns on investment from innovation are low. The innovation programme is cancelled after a few years at the most.

Such an innovation programme is in a lose–lose position. There is practically nothing it can do in the early stages that will provide the wins that justify the large amounts of investment poured in. On the other hand, the rest of the institution will certainly not see why, with the resources devoted to innovation, sizeable returns are not immediately forthcoming.

We've just examined two of the main traps that new innovation teams fall into: taking too much money too early, and being more ambitious in their investments than the Five Capability Model might suggest. But there is another whole area of danger which must be managed in an institutional innovation scenario: the IT organisation. As we'll see in a moment, the IT and innovation agendas are usually worlds apart. It is essential to manage and influence IT directly and immediately if one wants to be successful in the innovation game in banks.

3.5   TECHNOLOGY, BUSINESS, AND INNOVATION

Banking is an industry now so dependent on its technological underpinnings that every slice of the innovation pentagram has an IT aspect. For an innovator, this means dealing with technology professionals, and their unique outlook on the business of banking is an essential (and unavoidable) day-to-day part of the job.

Specific innovations can either be made or broken by the IT folks. If they say something is too hard or too expensive, there is often no recourse available. That is especially true for innovations which must touch primary bank infrastructures – the core banking system, channels such as the branch and Internet, or key back-office systems.

On the other hand, winning over the IT organisation can usually grease the path of an innovation. Making IT an ally is a relationship investment well worthwhile. But IT organisations are prioritised quite differently from those which are concerned directly with doing business with customers. Understanding that prioritisation is exceedingly helpful when trying to win over the IT folks.

Resource prioritisation in IT organisations

The number one priority for most IT organisations in banks is 'keeping the lights on'. This means running (the often antiquated) computer systems keeping transactions flowing is what chief information officers spend the lion's share of their resources on.

Changes to systems are hated because they are another opportunity for something to go wrong. When a system fails, there are inevitably significant consequences. Imagine the situation where a core banking system goes dark at the height of the Christmas spending period: not only are multiple business lines inside the bank screaming, retailers being served by the bank are doing so as well.

Controlling change is a mantra for IT organisations in banks. Given the opportunity to avoid a change, most IT chiefs will do so. Unfortunately, every slice of the innovation pentagram depicted in Figure 3.1 is pretty much bound up with IT change. This presents the key dilemma for an innovation professional: how to represent a change (which will likely have small short-term returns) in a way that avoids it being subordinated by changes which have significant and immediate benefits.

It has been estimated, worldwide, that up to 80% of IT budgets are spent on the task of keeping the lights on, a percentage that has been rising for some time. One of the main reasons is that yesterday's innovation, especially if it was undertaken earlier relative to peers, is likely the legacy of today, an effect we talked about in Chapter 1. Legacy systems in banks have a cost profile that increases over time, as key resources needed to maintain it become more scarce.

It is not atypical, for example, for a system that has been running an institution for decades to face a cost-inflection point during the latter part of its lifecycle. Possible reasons for this occurring are many-fold. Perhaps the hardware on which the system runs has been end-of-lifed, and the institution is reduced to scavenging parts on open markets (I know of several institutions who buy parts for old equipment on eBay because there is no other source available). Another, increasingly common reason is that individuals who have been associated with a system for decades are retiring from active service. Or perhaps the source code – the original human readable program statements forming the system – have been lost and are no longer able to be modified easily.

Whatever the reason, inevitably, computer systems become less and less transparent with age, and the risk to service levels increases. Talk to a CIO about a change to his core banking system, and there had better be a very good reason before an innovator will get much traction in the discussion.

The second priority for IT resources is almost always doing change mandated by various regulatory and compliance regimes in place. The body of regulatory pressures a typical bank must accommodate is huge and growing constantly. Regulatory changes are often expensive. For example, when Basel II compliance became an issue in the 95 countries that have indicated they will adopt it (by 2015), the IT system changes to support new capital adequacy regimes were massive.

These priorities are about sustaining existing revenues, not about creating new ones, which is the primary function of an institutional innovation function. The conflict between the goals of the two organisations can be a difficult thing to resolve at the best of times. But there are further priorities in the IT organisation which can make things even harder.

After the CIO has dealt with regulatory changes mandated to his or her systems, the next priority will be servicing specific requests of major lines of business. There is never enough resource to do everything asked for, so inevitably, the CIO will choose to do work for those business units whose revenues are most significant to the institution over all.

For the reasons we discussed in the previous chapter, large business lines will tend to make investments which are broad in scope. They will do this because the returns on those investments need to be significant in the overall scheme of the institution. Anything without material consequence will be de-prioritised in favour of such investments, even if their long-term benefit is likely to be significant. For the IT organisation, this inevitably means projects will be large, complex in scope, and affect key systems in significant ways.

The CIO, faced with such 'iconic' projects, will undoubtedly do everything possible to ensure any possible risk can be eliminated. The consequences of failing to do so are likely to be serious: future revenues are placed in jeopardy, not to mention the personal credibility issues that follow whenever something significant is delayed or fails. Steps taken at this point include cancelling anything 'distracting' to the projects delivering benefits to the core businesses.

The final thing a bank CIO usually wants to achieve is cutting costs of existing IT operations. After people, IT is generally one of the top expenses an institution incurs, so cost savings achieved here can have substantive bottom-line benefits. Chief executives, always looking for improvements in cost-to-income ratios, place constant pressure on CIOs to examine every investment carefully, cutting back to the bone as much as possible.

All this drives behaviour which is the antithesis of what innovators need in order to accomplish their jobs. Experimentation is discouraged, since investments that do not go directly to the goals of the IT organisation are a luxury that can be cost-controlled. Projects are strictly risk-managed, and laden with process to ensure they remain on track and (most importantly) run as little chance as possible of going outside their mandated budgets. Such investment monies as do exist are channelled towards rectifying critical issues that underfunding has left to ferment for years. And failure of any kind is frowned on. After all, there is no money to waste, even if such failures are instructive.

Is it any wonder, then, that innovation teams can often be seen as internally divisive, hard to control, and at the very least, best kept at arms-length for as long as possible?

Resolving the inherent conflicts between IT organisations and the critical need institutions have to do things differently is extremely challenging. There are a spectrum of solutions an innovator can employ, which range from reducing IT's need to deliver major parts of the innovation, through various models of coopertition (see page 101), to complete integration. We'll discuss these options later in this chapter. Which option is chosen for a particular innovation is, of course, innovation-specific.

A key factor is where, exactly, an innovation programme is in its development. A programme at the inventing stage, for example, is rarely, if ever, going to feature highly in the CIO agenda. Each specific invention is likely to be seen as a distraction that must be managed out of the way of iconic projects.

Innovators as venturers, however, are a completely different story. In this case, the innovation organisation is a major business line in its own right. That means it can make a call on the CIO for resources and expect to get them, once the other IT priorities are satisfied.

The IT innovation team

CIOs are not stupid. They recognise that IT's internal priorities, rational as they are, may not be consistent with the long-term strategy of their institutions. Many, however, are not in a position to change such internal behaviours, because they are driven by external forces largely beyond their control. For example, it is typical that IT organisations are given fixed budgets within which to operate, and these scarce funds are necessarily assigned in the priority order I previously described. To do anything else is irresponsible management.

In response to the discontinuity between the behaviour of IT and the desire for innovation, many CIOs have, themselves, created innovation teams. I was surprised, in fact, to discover that more often than not, IT leads its colleagues elsewhere in an institution in the creation of such teams.

The IT-based innovation team is, if anything, in a more difficult position than such teams in other areas of the business. The reason? They are not immune to the hierarchy of priorities a

CIO has, and in fact, need to demonstrate their active participation in that agenda in order to justify their budgets. The IT innovator runs the risk of being cast in the role of chief gadgeteer. The need to satisfy those who pay their salaries makes this a challenging thing to avoid. Gadgets (a prerogative term, I realise, but one that accurately describes the strategic impact IT-based innovations have in the absence of association with the business), are interesting. They are sexy. They are technological eye-candy that help the CIO address the idea that his or her organisation is little more than an expensive utility that is best left out of strategic decision-making.

Gadgets, being largely irrelevant in the overall strategic context of an institution, are a luxury easily afforded in times of plenty, and best disposed of when times get tough. Since IT organisations are so very rarely profit centres in their own right, the existence of an IT innovation team is most often a cyclical thing. Here today, and gone tomorrow, re-emerging when the CIO realises he or she is being marginalised from a strategic perspective. What, then, should an innovation team based in the IT organisation do?

As I mentioned previously, the key thing about the innovation pentagram of Figure 3.1 is that every slice is underpinned by technological imperatives. This presents the innovation team with a huge opportunity as an enabler. What other part of a bank can claim to have such a broad-reaching touch with all parts of the business? And when each and every innovation will land at the feet of IT for implementation, it may as well be the innovators who take the ball and run with it.

Functionally speaking, this means innovators in IT organisations need to move rapidly from inventing to managing (see Figure 3.2). Innovation that is as predictable as possible will please a CIO, who is dealing with uncertainty on all other fronts. So, the IT innovation team has an opportunity, but it also faces significant challenges as well. The greatest of these is tying its results to metrics which are important to the business. As I discussed previously, getting to such metrics is one of the key gateways between the championing and managing stages.

Metrics that IT cares about are somewhat incidental to the rest of a bank as long as everything is working. The business will be thinking about business outcomes represented by the innovation pentagram, not the underlying technological artefacts which make it all go. Granted, they are the ones screaming loudest when it doesn't all work, but when it does, no one worries about it all that much.

Here is one thing most IT innovation teams who have migrated through the Five Capability Model have found though: by the time they are part of the strategic agenda of an institution, their home is unlikely to be as part of the IT organisation, though the organisational chart might reflect something different. This is an almost inevitable consequence of pursing the innovation pentagram, and must be handled cautiously: one doesn't want to be accused of 'going native'.

Where does all that cost come from in IT when I want something changed?

Here's a complaint I've heard more than once in banks: 'I can buy a disk at the store and install this thing for myself for practically nothing. Why does it cost us so much to do the same thing here at the bank?'

Managers without a specific IT background don't often have visibility of the problems that come to CIOs the larger their environments get. Increasing numbers of devices, running various bits of software, all linked together, form a tangled web that gets more complex each year. In such complicated environments, it is possible to make small, seemingly inconsequential changes that have unintended consequences of very significant scale.

I once worked in a bank that made a change to the way that passwords were stored for users (for good, regulatory compliance reasons), but in the process locked out every single user in the branch environment for several days. The tellers had to revert to paper. You can imagine what pain the CIO of this institution went through during those few days, and it doesn't take much imagination to dream up what the CIO did to his people who were responsible.

IT folk spend a great deal of their time wondering what will happen to their environments every time they make a change, knowing an unexpected consequence of any kind could get them fired. The fact is, IT systems are now so complex and interrelated that it is practically impossible for any one person to understand every aspect of the technology used to run a typical bank. There are so many chances for things to go wrong.

What does a bank CIO do, when faced with such an impossible problem? The answer, of course, is that he or she seeks to reduce the level of risk by doing dry runs in advance of actual changes. This testing can, itself, be very expensive. For starters, the exact operating environment to be changed has to be replicated separately to provide a safe area from which to conduct tests. Constructing such environments can often be nearly as expensive as constructing the production system used to run the actual business. And what about the data in the system to be changed? It, too, must be replicated, possibly after scrubbing to remove customer details. More expense, and all before a change has gone live.

Even after all the testing for the actual change has been completed, things can still go wrong. Testing environments, no matter how good, are never exactly the same as the ones the business runs on day to day. So IT people have to dress-rehearse undoing the change (backing it out, they call it) in case they can't make it work once they start to implement. The back-out plan has to be tested as well.

And then, on the actual day of the change (usually at night, actually, when the load on systems is as light as possible), everyone is on hot standby – even people unrelated to the change – in case they need to come in and deal with something that's gone wrong. Think of the overtime CIOs have to pay on the off-chance that they might need help with a critical service.

Naturally, some IT organisations are better at making changes than others, but a good rule-of-thumb is the larger an institution becomes, the more complicated any IT change. That's also a good rule to apply in terms of how long an institution has been around as well: the longer, the harder any change, usually because there are so many old systems hanging around.

Architecture, standardisation, and other IT priorities

CIOs know all this cost is not that supportable in the long term. And they hear from their colleagues elsewhere in the bank how slow their IT people are to respond to needed business change. Smart CIOs have therefore begun to consider how they architect their systems in a top-down way to try and fix some of these issues.

It is presently very fashionable to have a big team in IT departments that do architecture, which really amounts to high-level technical designs at the bank-wide level of granularity. Architecture, it is thought, is a good thing because it promotes an institution-wide vision of the shape of technological change. Banks, as large organisations, have many IT projects on the go at once. Architecture is the set of guiding principles that make sure the result of all these projects is a coherent and smoothly operating whole, rather than hundreds of little investments all stitched together.

Architects, who are usually very experienced IT people, often become manic about compliance with architecture once they are given responsibility for it. And indeed, there is little point having architecture if it can be ignored the moment it becomes inconvenient. More mature organisations have reliable and rapid change processes that enable projects a certain level of flexibility in what they do, updating the architecture appropriately as the direction of the bank evolves. But many don't, and the architects cause everyone a lot of frustration as they pursue their holy grail of the 'aesthetic bank'.

Regardless of the level of maturity, architecture functions are getting increasing currency in most IT organisations today. That means architects can, without much difficulty at all, put roadblocks in the way of any innovation and prevent it from ever seeing the light of day.

For innovators, who should mainly be concerned with driving new things from the perspective of the innovation pentagram, architecture might seem like a distraction. But things go ever so much more smoothly for an innovation team if they guide their work around the principles that architects establish. For example, if the architectural decision of the bank is a particular database platform, then trying to deploy an innovation that uses something else will immediately get IT on the wrong side. Of course, there are times when it is impossible to avoid using something specific outside the architectural mandate of IT, but avoid it wherever you can.

Security and risk

Just as cost is a significant challenge for CIOs, so is their worry that their technology will leave the bank open to malicious parties, both inside and outside the bank. Failure to be cautious in this area has significant downside for banks: it has been estimated, for example, that every single record involved in a breach is worth in excess of $207 [35]. Considering that most banks have millions of records, those are very big numbers indeed.

The technological underpinnings of the innovation pentagram mean that innovators usually create significant concerns for those who need to manage the security of bank assets. The ostensible role of IT security people is to eliminate (or at least reduce) any risk an institution could be compromised through technological means. Practically speaking, the horrific consequences of a mistake mean most try to stop everything.

IT security has usually been one of the principle blockers to change for innovators. Their mandate – reduction of threat to bank assets – functionally requires them to limit or eliminate anything new with any significant uncertainties attached. As technology has broadened its application to financial services, in particular with the advent of self-service, the threats to these assets have consequentially increased. In many institutions, as a result, the word of IT security is law.

Though security folk generally wield considerable power in most institutions, there are many approaches evident in the way they exercise it. These result from philosophical differences in the management of uncertainty. At one extreme are institutions who choose to manage uncertainty by eliminating, as much as possible, any risk. In such organisations, the cost to deploy new innovations is typically very high, because stringent safeguards are demanded in order to reduce any uncertainties inherent in the innovation to as close to zero as possible. When National Australia Bank, for example, deployed a digital certificate solution as part of its first Internet banking offering, it was in stark contrast to its competitors who relied on simpler password and user-ids. As I said previously, National lagged its competitors for years afterwards, even when it dropped the requirement for the security certificate.

In the middle are institutions who accept that risk and uncertainty are inevitable. These are organisations which attempt to quantify the probability of loss and its consequences, and then make rational decisions about appropriate measures. Security teams with this approach style themselves as advisors and enablers. Some losses are unavoidable, and the key question is how much loss is acceptable before the economics of the innovation go out the window.

The most mature security personnel take this one step further. They provide advice and guidance on harm-minimisation, certainly, but then actively pursue means by which the innovation itself can be taken further than the inventor intended. The head of security architecture in one major UK bank characterised it in this way one day when I was complaining in general about security people: 'If you tell me you are going to drive a car at 20 mile per hour, I won't bother to check if you have brakes. But if you do have brakes, I will show you how to drive at 90.'

Clearly, it is preferable to have a security team in the latter category, but what steps can be taken if you don't? The safest bet for some in IT security is to say no. After all, if an innovation is blocked from proceeding, the level of loss from a breach is going to be zero. It is not the concern of security that the opportunity cost is likely to be way, way higher. It is preferable, then, to delay the involvement of security until such time as a project is practically through the innovation phase, that time an idea is at a stage it can be funded for development.

Of course, it is functionally necessary to know whatever-it-is *can* be secured, but this information can be gleaned from a water-cooler conversation rather than a formal engagement with the security organisation. A more detailed engagement will almost always result in the death of the innovation because security people, rationally performing their jobs, will attempt to reduce uncertainty to safeguard the institution. This means making compromises, and by the time the funding decision arrives, the watered-down innovation may not make sense any more.

Most practitioners find that loading up an innovation business case with funding to deliver whatever security provisions might later be required will be easier than trying to reassure stakeholders the innovation is safe enough to consider. And there are few, if any, security issues that enough money and time cannot correct. Stakeholders, when investing, want to know their investments are sensible and safe. They don't need or want to know all the details of the bits and pieces that make them so.

Before I go much further, let me make one final point. It is impossible to do without IT security, and the work those folks do is some of the most important there is. A positive relationship between innovation and security is what is needed to make things go smoothly. But also remember, security is not there to say whether or not an innovation should be investigated and funded. That is the role of the innovation team and the various stakeholders who will be, eventually, paying the bills. Security *is* there to provide the right guidance on how to make the innovation safe once the decision to proceed has been made.

Managing the IT/innovation divide

As I've alluded to throughout this section, the prioritisation of IT organisations is usually quite different from that of the rest of the institution, and for good and proper reasons. IT folk have to concern themselves primarily with making what they have today work properly. They have little time or inclination to change things unless they must. All this leaves innovators, whether they are part of the IT organisation or not, with a bit of a dilemma. Innovators are all about creating change, the antitheses of what an IT organisation needs to do. The result is often a great, wide divide between the two functional areas. This divide can be destructive. Innovators, on the one hand, can get various prerogative labels thrown at them ('cowboy!' is one I've actually had thrown at me, on occasion). And IT folk can be easily cast in the role of blockers, who will disrupt anything new because they can.

It is so very dangerous to allow matters to get to this point. Innovation and IT have to work hand-in-hand, because, as I've said previously, the whole innovation pentagram is underpinned by IT in banks. When the two parties mistrust each other, very little innovation gets done. And what *does* get done (because the innovation team have used their superior relationship skills to go around IT altogether) is likely to make sure that each success is more difficult than the last. There are really only three choices for managing this problem: reduction of IT so that it takes a peripheral role, adoption of a coopertition model, or integration with the existing IT agenda. The appropriate approach is very much dictated by the particular innovation at hand.

Reduction

I've called the first strategy 'reduction'. I prefer that term to others (such as elimination) because it is impossible to completely eliminate IT from anything in a bank. Even if one uses an outsourcer who provides a service for a fee, there are likely to be IT inputs you simply have to have: security, for example, will almost certainly be needed to review the solution from the perspective of preserving the interests of the bank.

A reduction strategy means removing dependencies on as many internal IT inputs as you possibly can. The less you depend on the IT organisation, of course, the less likely your innovation is to be caught up in the prioritisation of the IT organisation.

The evolution of technology has, of late, made this especially easy. It is now possible, for example, to rent financial services-specific applications, running on someone else's preconfigured servers, and delivered via the Internet to an institution. These reduce one's dependence on IT to the provision of network access and appropriate browser technologies on an end-user's machines.

A reduction strategy, managed well, can be something an IT organisation is pleased to support. Consider it from their point of view: it is one less system they have to worry about, and complaints about the innovation from the business will be directed elsewhere. Usually, if one is careful to influence both architects and security folk in IT, there will be few objections.

So, there is a positive side to the reduction, but there can also be a negative one as well. If the innovation concerns something that IT considers a core part of their turf – a mission-critical system, for example – they will likely fight tooth and nail against a reduction strategy. The reason IT has any influence at all with an institution is because it is entrusted to run systems that keep the bank going. They will not likely allow a mission-critical system to escape their control unless they are forced to do so.

In general, it is usually inappropriate to force the issue in these cases, and an alternative strategy should be employed. IT organisations in banks are actually very good at running mission-critical systems, far better, often, than any external provider will be. They have systems in place to manage service and availability that have developed over decades. Though all this process and rigour might make IT appear slow, it is also the reason that most banks enjoy such high levels of reliability in core operations.

Where is the reduction strategy appropriate then? Usually, reduction makes sense for innovations which are on the periphery of mission-critical systems that operate the bank *or* for breakthrough and revolutionary innovations which will likely be new build-outs in the first place. One would not consider reduction when one needs to make modifications to the core banking system to support a new channel experience, however. The core banking system is integral to the bank, and will be under the iron control of IT in most institutions.

On the other hand, it might be appropriate to consider reduction if one wishes to add a new kiosk experience in the branch, such as the clever seat cushions deployed by SNS Bank we discussed earlier. Depending on what such a kiosk does, it might be necessary to involve IT for the provision of network access and a security review only: the rest can be provided by an external supplier.

In short: consider a reduction strategy where there is an appropriate alternative to having IT provide the technological support to the innovation, *and* when the innovation does not touch something mission-critical to your institution.

Coopertition

Coopertition is a strategy where one couples external suppliers to the IT organisation to deliver an innovation. This can, itself, be an innovative approach for organisations used to all-or-nothing approaches to IT requirements. Coopertition allows your IT organisation to focus on what it is good at – driving big, reliable mission-critical systems – whilst leveraging the flexibility and agility of best-in-breed external parties.

Getting the parties to work together in the first place is one of the key challenges for coopertition strategies. In the first instance, IT will likely consider itself capable of providing the technology support to the entire innovation, though it may not be able to meet the cost and timeframe parameters of stakeholders. Nonetheless (and this will be more true, the closer to the centre of the core business the innovation is), they will insist on doing so if they are not carefully managed.

And from the perspective of managing external vendors, who will be delighted to usurp the role of the internal IT organisation at every opportunity to create more revenue opportunities for themselves, coopertition can be a relationship nightmare.

But what such a strategy does is enable the innovator to mix and match the set of capabilities required to deliver IT outcomes *independently* of the dictates of IT people, who, as I've said, are bound up in a set of priorities quite different from those of the innovator. Coopertition should be considered in circumstances where the innovation is central to the core proposition of the institution, and is either revolutionary or breakthrough in nature. In this case, it is impossible to reduce IT involvement below a certain level without making potentially serious compromises either to the innovation or the rest of the bank's infrastructure.

That is not to say that information technologists should be allowed to hold all the cards. The innovation may involve a core service proposition, but because it is *new*, almost certainly there will be parts that can be reasonably sought from outside with less cost or more speed. Whether or not external parties are chosen to provide these parts in the end is incidental to the main purpose: ensuring IT realises it must be a part of the innovation or have its control of core business lines eroded.

Whilst that description of the coopertition strategy draws battle lines between innovators and the technology folk, clever innovators will rarely be in a position where they have to be so obvious to move things forward. An understanding of the agendas of architects and other interested stakeholders can make coopertition as attractive to the IT organisation as it is to innovators.

As we discussed earlier, the way IT prioritises itself means most of the money goes to keeping the lights on, with much of the remainder being spent on making changes the business requires to further its revenue objectives, or that regulators require independently of such objectives. This leaves precious little for investments that the IT team needs in order to further its own goals.

Coopertition is valuable for IT people because it enables them to retain much of the control over the solution whilst *not* having to deliver or fund significant parts of it themselves. They can therefore watch and learn, with little risk to their own sets of priorities. And, of course, at some future time, there is always the option of bringing the externally sourced parts of the innovation back in-house.

Integration

The final strategy an innovator might employ to help get innovations out the door is integration. Integration involves attempting to couple an innovation with an existing IT agenda. As I've noted, it is practically impossible to get information technologists to do new things themselves, because their prioritisation is usually about keeping things the same. Now, although IT is often chronically underfunded, there are usually multiple streams of work going on into which an innovation can be slotted without much difficulty. In the last chapter, for example, we examined the specific case of my bank and its roll-out of social media, which is an example of the integration strategy at work.

At the start of that project, there was never any intent to have social media. The project was initially a piece of work sponsored by IT to create a decent search engine for the intranet, but it just so happened that the search technology being deployed *also* had the capability to do the kinds of things the innovation team wanted as well. Integration of the innovation with an existing project was a collaborative experience. The innovators at the bank used their relationship and sales skills to ensure that there was demand for the innovation, and IT was then able to take the credit for doing something it was doing *anyway,* though would not have publicised.

The problem for the integration strategy is that it requires deep and careful relationships with the IT folk. Innovators have to be across their own portfolios *and* those of the technology organisation, and be sufficiently IT literate they can see the appropriate match-up. In general, though, the integration strategy is most effective for small, incremental innovations. Quite often, these can be snuck into business-as-usual activities anyway, and do not impose much additional overhead on IT teams.

It is much rarer, however, that integration can be used when the innovation involved is large. Breakthroughs and revolutions inevitably require big investments in their own right. If one tries to integrate a very large piece of work with one that already exists, one runs the risk of totally derailing the original project, which is not likely to earn many favours.

3.6   AUTONOMIC INNOVATION

Having read this chapter so far, it would be understandable if you began to question how anything innovative ever gets done in any institution. Firstly, there is the challenge of finding something in the innovation pentagram which adds value to the institution. Then, it is necessary to make sure the innovation team is at the right stage in its development to be able to execute. And finally, getting the IT organisation to help deliver requires a great business case and deep relationship management. Is it any wonder that banks are so often perceived as lacking innovation?

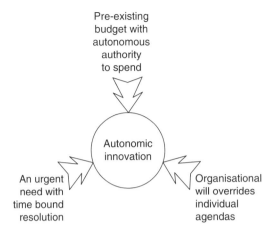

Pre-existing
budget with
autonomous
authority
to spend

Autonomic
innovation

An urgent
need with
time bound
resolution

Organisational
will overrides
individual
agendas

Figure 3.4   Autonomic innovation

Sometimes, though, innovations seem to run out the door all by themselves, and this happens *regardless* of how well the institution does innovation generally. I call such innovations *autonomic*, because they seem to happen involuntarily, almost independently of any grand design that governs their roll-out.

Now, in an ideal world, one would like all innovative activity in an institution to be auto-nomic, obviating the need for an innovation function at all. Unfortunately, however, the set of circumstances in which such innovation can occur seems relatively rare, and always involves a confluence of three factors, which are shown in Figure 3.4.

The first factor is that the institution recognises a need it must resolve with a degree of urgency. It might, for example, have to respond to a competitor's product which has begun to erode market share to an unexpected degree. After it has examined the set of capabilities it presently has and found them lacking, it determines it must look elsewhere for a solution and proceeds to do so with alacrity. This is very much in line with the firm's adoption decision process we discussed in Chapter 2 of this book.

The second factor is whether money is available in advance of a solution being defined, and if someone sufficiently senior is available with the authority to spend it. This is the reverse of what normally happens, which is that an innovation is proposed and *then* funding is sought to implement. In order for this condition to be met, either the stakeholders have ample budget not assigned elsewhere (and in a cost-to-income optimising institution, this is rarely the case), or the need is *so* pressing that a new budget is allocated a priori.

The final factor is that organisational will to respond to the urgent need is sufficiently high it overrides the agendas of those who must ordinarily be influenced to get an innovation out the door. IT, for example, might not like an autonomic innovation, but they will override most of their own controls when it makes sense to do so. Similarly, business lines who would normally not consider an innovation will do so when the will of the rest of the organisation is behind it.

Combining these three factors results in a perfect storm which practically guarantees an innovation will make it to customers or end-users. Of course, the trick is finding this confluence of factors in advance and selecting those innovations for roll-out.

For an example of how an autonomic innovation can work, we'll turn next to an examination of ChangeEverything, an online project launched in 2006 by Canadian institution Vancity.

Vancity was one of the first institutions I came across with a very public autonomic innovation, but when I wrote about this effect on my blog towards the end of 2008 [36], I was showered with stories from other financial services companies of similar experiences. This leads me to conclude that autonomic innovation isn't that rare after all, though most of the time it happens through fluke rather than any grand design.

3.7   CASE STUDY: CHANGEEVERYTHING, A PROJECT BY VANCITY IN CANADA

Vancity is Canada's largest credit union, with 400,000 members. Vancity is an institution at the heart of its community, with an objective to 'work with people and communities to help them thrive and prosper' [37]. This brand promise permeates almost everything the institution does, from its Shared Success scheme (which disburses profits to members in proportion to their business), through its participating in programmes to serve low-value and underbanked customers, to its commitment to carbon neutrality. Vancity takes its community obligations seriously, and this culture of awareness permeates it from the top down.

Although the credit union was executing well in traditional channels, it wanted to extend its social responsibility framework online. Leaders quickly recognised that extending a socially aware proposition to the online community would likely be a natural reinforcement of more traditional branding efforts. At the very least, doing so was unlikely to hinder existing initiatives underway, so it seemed like a relatively low-risk proposition.

Here, then, was the pressing need that is the first factor of an autonomic innovation. Vancity wanted to extend its proposition online, and to do so in a way quite different from that of its competitors. Then, too, social media was creating a huge buzz at the time, and institutions were already beginning to contemplate how they might harness the phenomenon towards their own ends. The opportunity was to be the *first* in its market to do something in the space.

A workshop was held, at which the idea of ChangeEverything, a social website that people might use to list the things they would like to change about themselves and their communities, emerged. The site was to be moderated, and feature the active participation of members through blogging and discussion forums. The Vancity brand would not feature prominently, though the style and colouring of the site would be highly complementary to the main Vancity online presence.

The surprising thing about this meeting, and ones that occurred subsequently, was whilst the initial objective of the programme was to build engagement with the Vancity brand, there was little direct brand relationship in the original concept, nor in the actual implementation. This happened organically. As William Azaroff, one of the principal architects of ChangeEverything at Vancity recalled later, 'The idea just built itself'.

Unusually, though ChangeEverything was the first entree of Vancity into the social media space (at least publicly), there was practically no resistance anywhere to the idea. It was so completely consistent with the brand values and overall mission of the credit union that most individual agendas were already aligned, at least with the objectives that were being resolved. By no means, however, was this novel modus operandi something that everyone immediately understood. Azaroff recalls that people either loved the idea, or they didn't 'get' it at all. Whichever camp they fell into though, objections were few and far between.

Part of the reason was that ChangeEverything wasn't going to be about products and services, which would likely have stepped on the toes of significantly powerful stakeholders. Right from the start, the value proposition was customer engagement and long-term relationships, something the community folks at Vancity were doing day-to-day anyway in support of the brand mission.

This, then, is the second factor supporting an autonomic innovation. Because ChangeEverything was an extension of the work already occurring, and this work was so central to the ethos of Vancity, there was substantive organisational will to implement. Azaroff recalls that whilst the team conducted road shows and did other things to build internal engagement, the innovation was pretty much going to walk out the door all by itself. The CEO of Vancity wasn't even shown ChangeEverything until after the launch, in fact.

Neither was there much difficulty in securing funding. The first iteration of the site was funded entirely from an existing brand marketing budget, and did not require a specific, additional authorisation. That's not to say that senior managers didn't have to display both courage and curiosity when making such an unusual investment. The idea of a financial institution doing anything in this space in 2006 was novel at the time. Some limited experiments elsewhere were showing promising, though limited results, but there was no possibility of making a business case stack up, since no one could be certain what benefits, if any, would be obtained.

Despite all this, money was allocated from an existing budget, though Azaroff admits the initial investment was not significant compared with the overall marketing budget. For an autonomic innovation, the final prerequisite is that money exists and is available for use without too much rigour in the process of spending it – something that ChangeEverything had because the initial investment required was relatively small.

Vancity agreed it would run the site as it would any other campaign: on a time-limited basis. ChangeEverything would last six months, and end towards the end of 2006. With all that in place, Azaroff and his team commenced implementation.

Two months later, they had a working site ready for launch. Azaroff's team invited selected community activists and partners, local not-for-profits, artists, politicians and bloggers, and hoped that word-of-mouth would help drive traffic. Although initial statistics were good, they were hardly earth-shattering. Vancity expected to make a reasonable return from its investment in ChangeEverything, but it seemed an experiment that would go the way of many others from financial institutions: interesting, but not significant in the overall scheme of things.

But all that changed in November that year. It was a month of particularly heavy snow-falls, and the site's full-time moderator went on a 'snow-drive', documenting the conditions for travel for that portion of Vancity's customer base who might be using ChangeEverything. They held a warm clothing and blanket drive for the homeless of downtown Vancouver, which animated great discussion and cooperation amongst the user base of ChangeEverything and attracted lots of new visitors and users to the site, as well as print, radio, and television media interest.

Even though the press fuss about snow died down quickly, many of the people who found ChangeEverything stayed around to participate in the community. It is, today, a healthy and active website on its second version, and has no chance of being cancelled.

Contrast this story with the roll-out of social media tools in other institutions. The surprising lack of these at the time of writing (end of 2008) is a testament to how difficult this kind of activity is, normally, for banks. Azaroff agrees. He suggests it would probably be impossible to do ChangeEverything again from the start, even for Vancity. The business is savvier, and wants much more rigorous business cases. ChangeEverything happened too easily, and stakeholders are wary that this success would not be replicated if innovations were just allowed to go their own way on their own.

But, actually, what happened at Vancity is collective will, money, and timely need combined. Whenever that happens, innovations will roll out the door regardless of any innovation process that might exist.

If we refer again to the innovation pentagram, it is difficult to conceive of anything new that would not be autonomic if the three prerequisites of organisation will, collective need, and money were present. Of course, the primary challenge for innovators is spotting those conditions and doing something about them. That, unfortunately, is something that happens relatively rarely.

3.8   THE BANKING INNOVATION CHALLENGE

In this chapter, we've explored a number of issues specific to banks in the innovation space. If nothing else, you would probably agree there are significant challenges for any practitioner who attempts to do new things in banks.

It is very easy to be disheartened at the beginning. Perhaps your innovation programme is trapped in the inventing stage, and no matter what you do you can't achieve the necessary recognition of metrics or business process that will enable you to move on. Maybe your IT organisation is simply unable to help you move forward at the pace you might wish. Or perhaps there are no obvious opportunities in the innovation pentagram your institution will let you work on.

Such challenges are reported by every innovation programme I spoke to whilst preparing to write this book. And my own experience bears this out. When you are starting a new programme, expect the order of the day to be frustration.

But those first successes, from which all others will eventually be derived, are very sweet indeed. They are also inevitable, given sufficient determination. Every bank says it is not innovative enough, and the fact there is an innovation programme at all is sufficient leverage to start the ball moving. Everyone *wants* to be more innovative. Sometimes, just having people around trying to show the way is enough to make surprising things happen.

4
Futurecasting

What you will find in this chapter

- What futurecasting is, and why your institution should engage in it.
- An example futurecast based on scenarios around peer-to-peer lending.
- How to construct futurecasts in a structured way.
- Methods you can use to construct predictions to support futurecasts.

Having read, thus far, about innovations in general and in institutions specifically, it is now time to start our examination of the processes a bank might use to ensure it is able to achieve a predictable level of return from its innovation investments. As I've said a few times, the ultimate goal of any innovation programme must be to create an environment in which innovation is the *preferred* investment activity compared with all other opportunities available.

In Chapter 1, I described futureproofing as a phase-gate process. Rather than a set of individual activities which comprise most innovation systems, my proposition was that a complete innovation environment is composed of phases with multiple feedback loops operating between each phase. This is in contrast to traditional stage gates, which usually feature a unitary flow of ideas from invention to innovation.

As I mentioned, though, stage gates don't really resolve all the challenges of a formal innovation system. They don't, for example, provide much guidance with respect to *which* innovations an institution ought to pursue given its present strategic imperatives. It is the purpose of futurecasting, the first material phase of futureproofing, to provide that guidance. You can see how futurecasting fits into the overall innovation system by referring again to Figure 1.1.

The futurecasting phase is all about making structured guesses about the impact that innovations and socio-economic trends will have on institutions. These guesses are the means by which the front end of the futureproofing methodology is guided towards great ideas of strategic relevance. And they are the path through which senior leaders (such as board members and their direct reports) are brought into contact with the innovation processes of their institutions.

People at the top level of banks (or, indeed, any large company) have little time to specifically consider anything even remotely speculative. They are concerned, primarily, with the day-to-day operations of what are usually substantive and expansive enterprises. Their time is taken up with the minutiae of day-to-day operations, and they have little time to worry about speculative possible futures.

The problem, of course, is that sometimes these speculative futures actually come true. And, when they do, there may have been little thought given to the best means to handle consequences. Let's face it: it was a failure to rehearse consequences that led to the financial implosion of 2007 and 2008.

Which banks weathered that storm most successfully? The ones that had considered the longer-term consequences of their actions in the light of the facts they had available at present, of course. That, actually, is the real root of the process of futurecasting.

Futurecasting, I believe, will become a key advantage for institutions. Those that are good at it will be well positioned to respond to the strategic threats which are inevitable in the medium and long terms. Those that aren't, on the other hand, will be doomed to repetitive cycles of expensive investments in order to catch up with those who have developed futurecasting capabilities.

How does futurecasting differ from forecasting, a discipline well developed in most banks, though? A forecast attempts to be a quantitative statement about the future, something that can be relied on to be at least a reasonable proxy for what might actually happen. Whole planning regimes are based on traditional forecasts. Forecasts are the outputs of an economist. Banks have lots of economists, so clearly it is redundant to add more forecasting.

A futurecast, on the other hand, is concerned with innovation-driven *trends* that might need to be addressed from a strategic perspective. Trends are broad statements about possibilities for the future that might reasonably arise given the circumstances of today. Futurecasts are important because an innovation practitioner needs to have a vision of how new things in an institutional environment might play out. They are the budgerigar in the coal-mine, an early warning signal to the rest of a bank that something important might be changing.

As a matter of fact, most innovation teams do this on a day-to-day basis anyway. Ask any innovator about the likely effect of social media on financial services, and you will be treated to a long, expansive discourse about the future. The problem is that most innovation teams don't have very much rigour in this process. They might be able to articulate a broad-brush picture of future scenarios, but when quizzed, will be unable to explain what leads them to their conclusions.

Such statements are practically useless when taken to senior people in banks. Leaders at the top of institutions are accustomed to the kind of forecasts economists do: they are based on quantitative models and hard data, and are verifiable by multiple third parties. Such forecasts are often wrong, but it is the rigour that surrounds their creation which makes them a part of the strategic planning process.

Futurecasts created by innovators need similar rigour if they are to be taken seriously. It is the purpose of this chapter to explain how that can be done.

4.1   THE PURPOSE OF FUTURECASTING

As I've mentioned, futurecasting in the innovation context has nothing to do with making definitive statements about the way things will be in the future. The fact of the matter is that there isn't any way to be certain about things that haven't happened yet, even for those highly trained economists with their expansive data-driven models to which I referred earlier. So making definitive statements means that most of the time you will be wrong, and the few times you are right will be lost in the morass of missed expectation.

Gypsy fortune tellers never make the mistake of committing to definite facts. They deal only in generalities, and most of the time, they get quite a bit right. But it doesn't take psychic power for them to do this: they ask simple questions and from the information they've been given, tell stories that could reasonably come to pass given the facts they know. Futurecasts are stories about possible futures that are easily digestible by senior management.

Of course, I'm not suggesting for a moment that innovation practitioners use crystal balls to make their futurecasts. My point is that it is possible to make generalisations about the future using facts we know now, and these can be usefully applied as a way of clarifying what is possible. How does a futurecast help the innovation process then?

As innovation groups grow through each stage of the Five Capability Model (see Figure 3.2), the innovations attempted get bigger and more complex. This process leads the innovation team, sooner or later, to a position in which they can have meaningful impact on the strategic agenda of the entire institution. Innovations with strategic connotations are rarely autonomic. Their development requires a great deal of influencing before they have much chance of successfully getting funding. And the more unprecedented or disruptive, the harder it becomes to get those who *can* authorise the innovation to actually make a decision. For truly strategic, game-changing plays, the amount of pre-work that has to be done before senior people will commit can make an innovation an impossible proposition.

Disruptive or breakthrough innovations, usually associated with very significant risks of failure or underperformance, may present an unacceptable level of uncertainty to executives, who will almost never agree to proceed if they are not carefully managed in advance of the decision. They need to understand the consequences of *not* proceeding, and what will happen to them and their businesses in the medium and long terms. Senior executives do not have the bandwidth to think about those kinds of issues, because they are running major businesses day-to-day. Innovators, on the hand, ought to be living and breathing the consequences of their innovations and those of their competitors.

The work product of innovators which informs senior executives of such consequences is the futurecast. One provides a futurecast – essentially a story recounting a *possible* future – in order to provide a framework in which critical issues can be highlighted in a concise way. Naturally, underlying the story there is a rigorous process that converts the facts of today into plausible predictions, but from the perspective of senior leaders, the story is what is important.

The story lets executives rehearse, in their own minds, the decisions they will need to take to address the future state proposed. Because they are not being asked (at least, initially) to make an actual decision, they will think through scenarios being proposed with a completely different mindset than otherwise. Then, when the innovation team brings an innovation from the story-space for an *actual* funding decision, most of the heavy lifting will have been done.

Another thing a futurecast does is guide the actual innovation process itself. As I said in Chapter 1, the traditionally implemented innovation process – stage gates – usually does not connect the strategic issues facing an institution with the actual set of things that come out the end. Stage gates take a large basket of possible ideas, and provide a methodology to whittle these down to some manageable number which can be implemented.

The problem is that stage gates are rather indiscriminate with respect to how they select things on any basis other than do-ability. What if the initial basket of ideas doesn't include any which address potential future scenarios devolving from other innovations in the market? What if the stage gate moves an idea into implementation because it is expeditious, but also locks the bank into a course which is inappropriate given what might happen in the medium or long term? For these reasons, the futurecast is an important input into each phase of the futureproofing process.

When people start thinking up ideas for future implementation, the inspiration of stories coming from a futurecast can help guide their creativity to channels which are strategically important for the institution. This is the concept of an ideation campaign, something we'll cover in more detail in the next chapter.

During the innovation phase, the process of converting an idea into something that might reasonably attract funding, the futurecast provides important guidance at an individual idea level. Whilst the fleshing out of an idea is occurring, many decisions are made which shape the eventual outcome. Some of these decisions – such as the business model supporting the idea – can have significant effects on the success of whatever-it-is in the market.

Suppose, for example, an institution wishes to create a new kind of savings product, one which appeals to an emerging demographic who are more socially responsible and wish to have a positive impact on their world. The product concept is an interesting one: the institution will declare to its customers how profitable the account is, and offer to revenue-share with the charity of the customer's choice. This, actually, is the model already offered by innovative institutions such as Caja Navarra of Spain, about whom we'll hear more in the final chapter of this book.

Here is where the futurecast can be useful. Might a story about the rise of the gift economy and how it will affect banks be important in deciding how to implement such a product? Almost certainly yes. How about the emergence of free business models – where goods and services are given away gratis, but profits made indirectly through a third party? If such models were to expand in the banking sector (given they already exist in areas such as interchange for automatic tellers), might they affect the selection of fee mechanisms supporting the innovation? Again, the answer is almost certainly yes. This leads one immediately to the question of *which* futurecasts ought to be made.

Referring again to the futureproofing process diagram in Figure 1.1, there are a number of inputs to the futurecasting phase, which I call signals. Signals can come from lots of places, but some of the best come from subsequent phases of the futureproofing process. Let us imagine your institution's innovation team has been successful in creating a decent ideation system. Ideation is the process of collecting and selecting ideas for further consideration, and as we'll see in the next chapter, the wider ranging it is, the better.

A large ideation function will routinely manage hundreds of ideas at once. When aggregated and subjected to statistical analysis, these will often reveal interesting things which can trigger a futurecast. An idea that recurs frequently over time is one that could signal the early stages of a trend.

Examine the objections coming from people during the innovation phase. During this phase, new concepts are being examined in quite a lot of detail. The idea is to get things sufficiently worked up that they can be taken to executives for funding. But during this process all manner of objections will be raised. The thematic content of objections is excellent inspiration for futurecasts. Watch for phrases such as 'cannibalistic to existing revenues', 'makes us a commodity', and 'too innovative'. The first two are key signs of a disruptive innovation, one that could reasonably be very significant in the future. And the third, of course, is indicative of something that is either breakthrough or revolutionary. All these are extremely good cases for a futurecast.

Finally, during execution, look at the way people react to the innovation as it is developed. The market reaction once whatever-it-is has been made available is also interesting. If customers and end-users don't behave as expected, there is likely some dynamic going on which merits much more exploration. For example, if the launch of a new banking channel does not result in the consumer uptake reasonably expected, there is almost certainly something *else* going on in the market which needs to be examined carefully. Perhaps a non-bank competitor already has an innovative offering in the market which performs the job the customer needs as well or better?

4.2   AN OVERVIEW OF FUTURECASTING

There is a wealth of literature that covers the business of predicting the future. All this literature attempts to define mechanisms which lead to statements about the likely shape of things to come based on what is observable today. As you would expect, in far more cases than not, people get it wrong.

Just after the Second World War, futurists began to consider the impact of the (then) leading-edge technologies such as television, telephone, and pneumatic tube on society. What effect, they wondered, might the convergence of these technologies have on society and the way we acquire and distribute goods and services [38]?

By 1935, television, telephone, and pneumatic tube were in rapid deployment. The futurists imagined a time when every home had all three. In a 1931 edition of *Forbes*, consumers were told 'Customers will tune in, watch the display of wares, and, with telephone beside them, be able to order within a few seconds of seeing the merchandise'. The goods would arrive a few moments later by air-pressure powered tube.

The futurists went so far as to predict vast central kitchens where meals would be prepared and sent by tube (after the customer had viewed a menu on TV and ordered by phone). And completing the picture, there would be central washing-up facilities to which customers would return used crockery and cutlery, also by tube. All of these, it was hypothesised, would result in massive efficiencies of scale.

Though such a vision seems fanciful today, especially given the massive investment needed in pressurised tube infrastructure, this futurecast did not seem unreasonable at the time. There had been, already, the mass roll-out of pipes for water and sewerage, and wires for electricity and telephone. Why not pressurised tubes?

The point of recounting this early attempt at futurecasting, though, is not to illustrate what was wrong about it, but what was right. Today's delivery systems *do* move product directly to the home, it's just that they are vans run by companies such as UPS, rather than air-pressured tubes. It *is* possible to order goods electronically and have them delivered, thanks to the Internet and online retailers such as Amazon. It is, in fact, easy to order meals from central kitchens (pre-prepared meals and TV dinners, for example), which are delivered in disposable packaging. The end result – electronic shopping and delivered-to-door pre-packaged meals – was correctly predicted 60 years before they would reasonably be available to a large percentage of the developed world.

When you look at this futurecast in terms of the specific technologies involved, it appears wrong. But in terms of the societal effects of communication and universal delivery systems, it was unerringly correct. The rise of Amazon and its ilk prove the value of this futurecast.

So much for historical examples. For banking innovation practitioners, though, our concern with the future is the effect innovations in any segment of the innovation pentagram might have on the strategic fortunes of our institutions (see Figure 3.1). There are really two scenarios of interest here. The first is that a particular innovation could affect the bank's strategic agenda, and the institution does something about it. The second, of course, is that the innovation is important, but nothing is done at all. These two scenarios are the focus of our futurecasting in most cases.

Of course, other scenarios can be useful too. A scenario is created by changing just one variable in a controlled way and exploring the stories that devolve from the change. Consider again, for example, our historical futurecast in the context of financial services. Cheques were rising in popularity as the economic prosperity of the post-war years began to expand. Might the combination of pneumatic delivery systems coupled with electronic communications make it simple to return to cash for many transactions? The point of cheques, after all, is to provide a token of value as a *proxy* for cash, to avoid the difficulties of providing *actual* currency. With instantaneous and private delivery by tube, why do you need cheques anymore?

So the final product of the futurecast is a set of two or more stories about possible futures. But how does one arrive at these stories in the first place in a way that has sufficient rigour they can be used as inputs to the strategic planning process? The answer to this question is that one uses one or more formal prediction methods to back up the statements one makes about the future. A prediction is a statement of a future fact that follows from the information available in the present. One combines multiple predictions together to create the various scenario stories used in the futurecasts.

In this chapter, we're going to be looking at a few methods for doing this, because a prediction has much more rigour if you can get to the same or similar results using several different means. If, for example, we are interested in making a statement about a possible future in the medium term, and we've employed both the Delphi method (a means of combining expert advice in an interactive fashion) *and* a prediction market (a wisdom of crowds approach) to come to a similar conclusion, the results have a lot more veracity than if one or the other approaches was used in isolation.

By the same token, if two methods come up with widely different results, it is often a sign that more analysis is required. It doesn't necessarily mean the prediction is *wrong*, only that the underlying assumptions and facts might need to be examined to get to the root cause of the difference.

Of course, all this leaves the practitioner with an important question. Given the possible expanse of futures, what are the best futurecasts one should be doing *right now?* It is to this question that we will turn our attention next.

4.3   WHAT FUTURECASTS SHOULD INNOVATORS BE DOING?

Futurecasting is time-consuming, and when done with rigour, quite arduous. It takes a great deal of practice both to get good stories which can be meaningful in an institution's specific context, and to educate senior executives that such stories are a useful input to their strategic planning process. Consequently, the futurecasts one attempts will usually be relatively few, and should therefore look at the key strategic issues facing an institution. Essentially, this devolves into an examination of the triggers that start a futurecasting effort. For guidance, it is useful to refer, once again, to the futureproofing process diagram in Figure 1.1. This diagram shows three inputs to the futurecasting process.

Individual-level signals are the first input. People's individual ideas can be powerful signals that the basis of competition is changing. That is especially so when multiple people separately have the *same* idea. By installing a robust ideation process, it is relatively simple to aggregate similar ideas to get a view of what is important at the front line. When reports come from multiple places simultaneously, and over a reasonable period of time, it is usually a signal that something in the business is changing.

For example, if staff in the branch environment report repeatedly that customers are asking for some new gadget they've seen at their friends' banks, it is a relatively safe bet that someone has done something interesting that might be the subject of a futurecast. You know something is going on when customers go out of their way to tell you about it.

Here's another example. What does it mean if staff in head office complain regularly they have better IT at home than work, or report that they carry their home computers to the office? These signals might be a chance to consider whether the nature of work is changing, and could trigger a useful futurecast.

The point is that when you have many individuals saying the same thing, there is invariably something to be gained from testing whether a futurecast could be a useful planning aid. At the very least, going through the process will illustrate key strategic decision points which might not have been obvious.

The second set of signals comes from the innovation phase. This is the time ideas are being developed for potential funding. Significant effort will be invested in business case development, prototypes, and other tools that support this process. Throughout, business lines have the opportunity to provide feedback to innovators, during which important insights might be revealed.

Imagine, for a moment, the team is working on a new mobile phone innovation. During the pitching process, the business reveals they are only interested in customers who have an above-average income level, and innovators are advised to reposition their mobile phone innovation to deal with that segment.

We know from disruption theory (refer again to Chapter 2) that this kind of behaviour is sometimes a sign that a fight or flee decision has been taken (perhaps unconsciously). Such decisions are signs of disruptors in the market. A futurecast based on an emergent mobile play might therefore be interesting, if a market scan reveals a dynamic innovation that serves the low end.

The final set of signals that might trigger a futurecast come from the execution phase. These are signals arriving from the market itself. During this phase, the innovation is built, and if everything goes well, released to customers or end-users. The reaction of these audiences is an important way of testing for signs that a futurecast is needed.

If, for example, the release of a new mobile phone innovation (such as mobile banking) is greeted with lacklustre uptake even though the business case for the innovation was watertight, there is a case for a futurecast. A futurecast, remember, takes what is known today and tells possible stories about the future. In this case, innovators would concern themselves with the probable reason that mobile banking was not, presently, in demand by consumers and what other innovations might be just around the corner that would address this issue. Near Field Communication chip technology, oft mentioned in this book, would be an obvious example.

In any event, market signals come when an innovation is released to the wild, but that is not the only time they are available to practitioners. Watching the Internet, for example, is a great way to know that the time for a futurecast has arrived.

One of the best resources is banking industry blogs. These are written by individuals who are often on the inside of the industry, and who will usually be very well informed about what is important, and what is not. Tracking the dialogue going on in the blogosphere is an interesting way to get a handle on what's likely to be relevant. That's especially true if more than one blogger talks about the same thing, or the discussion keeps reappearing over time. When peer-to-peer lending first came to market in 2006, for instance, it was bloggers who first started to write of its disruptive potential. You can find a list of the most important banking bloggers on my own banking blog [39].

It is not only industry-watchers who provide great input to the futurecast decision. User-generated content of any kind is an especially interesting barometer of what might make a reasonable futurecast. As a test, for example, try typing your institution's name into Google, followed by the word 'hate'. You'll be surprised at the results.

When I tried this early in my tenure at one institution, I found a long post from, purportedly, one of our own tellers. She was trying to explain to a group of angry customers what it was like working in a bank. She posted anonymously, of course, and the stories she was telling would *never* have been sanctioned through ordinary channels, even though they were overwhelmingly flattering to the bank.

The fact that such a detailed post existed at all led us to consider the effect of a trend we call 'transparency tyranny' (though we borrowed the name from the excellent *TrendWatching* publication [40]). We constructed some futurecasts based on what it would mean for the bank to participate in social media, and how we might use it internally. This led indirectly to the social media roll-out I described in Chapter 2.

It is tempting to confuse predictions about individual innovations with a futurecast. These are important, certainly, but would normally be limited to specific questions that must be answered prior to funding being agreed. Factors such as uptake, for example, are almost always required so that stakeholders can understand what the likely shape of returns might be.

An innovation futurecast, on the other hand, does not answer specific questions so much as illuminate key challenges facing an institution in the presence of emerging innovations in its markets. It may make predictions, but these are used to help quantify the message rather than lock up the future in absolutes.

4.4   AN EXAMPLE

Let us turn now to a futurecast on a topic we've been talking about throughout this book: peer-to-peer lending. At the time of writing (in late 2008) there had been a number of experiments from institutions in this space. Peer-to-peer lending organisations were reporting that due to credit crunch events starting in 2007, they were seeing increasing loan volume. None, however, were reporting profitability. In this environment, we pose the question: should banks be concerned about peer-to-peer lending? And more particularly, should they do something about it?

These two questions lead to a matrix of possible stories, which are shown in Table 4.1. Along the top, we have the possible reactions to the peer-to-peer phenomenon from the market. Customers, obviously, will either adopt such lending tools, or they won't. Both scenarios are interesting to us. Down the side, we have the key decision for banks: to do something, or not.

Examining the resulting matrix, we have three potential stories that we might like to tell, with titles selected to be explanatory of the key strategic issues they illuminate. We will get to selecting the plot and titles of the stories a little later.

All three scenarios are reasonable and devolve from data and assumptions we know to be true in the present day. They have catchy titles that communicate the essence of the strategic picture we are trying to illuminate. And they've been created using a solid process that can be backtracked with rigour. Each key statement is backed up by a reference to the underlying fact or prediction. And, later on, we will see the methodology that was used to come up with

Table 4.1   Possible scenarios for peer-to-peer lending

	P2P important	P2P not important
Banks do something	Growth gets easier	P2P experiments fail
Banks don't do something	Disconnected customers	N/A

the specific plot lines, the workings of which would normally be attached as an appendix to the document.

When confronted with this evidence of rigour, it is my experience that executives will usually find the material useful. At the very least, their reading of it will stimulate critical thinking in ways they would not have considered independently.

P2P experiments fail

It is 2012, and the year marks the twilight days for peer-to-peer lending, both for banks and the rash of start-ups that began to appear in the previous six years. Initially, the future looked exceptionally bright for peer-to-peer lending, the basic premise of which is that customers would lend money to each other via an eBay-style mechanism, taking banks out of the equation altogether. The disastrous market conditions for banks in 2008 made it seem almost certain that customers would be forced to such alternative channels, given the log-jam in wholesale money markets. Some predictions, in fact, had the new model taking up to 15% of retail lending by now.

But the problems of such individual-level participation in the lending process began to rear their head almost immediately. Consumers, having seen the failure of major banking establishments, began seeking safe havens for their capital, and became largely uninterested in participating in what was perceived to be an activity carrying even more risk than leaving deposits in competing high-interest deposit accounts. Up to 45% of all peer-to-peer loan requests remained unfunded on bank and third-party peer-to-peer sites alike. This, despite the fact that overall awareness of the peer-to-peer lending offer reached 20% by 2010, way more than the critical mass point of about 16% that it was thought would secure the future of the model.

In any event, after the initial rash of excitement generated by peer-to-peer's novel new approach, consumers found, as they had previously done with eBay, that they didn't have the inclination to spend too much of their leisure time finding depositors and validating their credentials. As consumers had previously retreated from time-intensive auction-based purchasing behaviour (exemplified, of course, by eBay), so too did they eventually retreat from peer-to-peer lending.

It had been thought that one of the principle markets for peer-to-peer lending products would be social minorities and the unbanked, who ordinarily would have faced difficulties obtaining credit. The reality, however, was that this potentially profitable segment were no more eager to use the new peer-to-peer services than their prime counterparts. Indeed, bank attempts to reach these customers via the social networks that might actualise the peer-to-peer lending offer failed miserably. Customers, it seemed, were unwilling to hand over additional details of their personal lives to banks, when viable alternatives were offered by start-ups and media companies.

In any event, normality eventually returned to the lending market, and customers needing loans were able to return to conventional channels to get them. The back-store of pent up demand for credit, initially seen as the driving force that would cause peer-to-peer to evolve to profitability, evaporated.

With all these developments, peer-to-peer lending sites, once opened in a rash of enthusiasm in a large number of developed countries, began to close. They were unable to achieve the loan volume that would have enabled them to turn a profit, and to compensate, had to raise additional revenues from fee income. These increased charges further slowed consumer adoption.

Banks, meanwhile, abandoned their peer-to-peer experiments when it became obvious that the non-bank players were no longer a significant threat. In the end, it was far more profitable to lend through conventional channels than peer-to-peer in any case.

And, in perhaps the final sign that peer-to-peer lending was increasingly irrelevant, regulators noticed the declining profile of the peer-to-peer model, and quietly dropped their efforts to supervise these start-ups directly. It was an easy decision for them to make: the political demand for increased supervision of banks was stretching their resources in the wake of the market issues of 2008.

Disconnected customers

It is 2012. Bankers are facing a nightmare scenario: their lending businesses are showing signs of decline, even though they have money to lend. It is not that there has been any contraction of the lending market (which has continued to expand rapidly after a brief hit resulting from the market dislocation of 2007 and 2008), but many borrowers have realised there are other viable alternatives.

This is a surprising discovery for many bankers, who have never had difficulties in lending before. But the numbers are unmistakeable: 15% of retail lending is going to players other than banks now, and it is possible this could rise to 20% or more by 2015. How this occurred is illustrative.

The basic premise of peer-to-peer lending was simple: let people with disposable cash lend some of it to other individuals without the intermediary of banks. Usually, a third-party website sits between the borrower and lender, grading potential applicants and handling the administrative processes supporting the process.

Peer-to-peer lending started slowly with the launch of Zopa in 2006, but the idea was copied in practically every developed market very quickly. Bankers were not concerned, however, since the loan volume involved was microscopic compared with that of their main lending operations.

What banks did not expect, however, was how the market dislocation of 2008 would affect the overall structure of the lending business. At the height of the credit crunch, the financial world was suffering from a lack of liquidity with which to fund its lending operations. The result was that institutions tightened their credit policies significantly, making it much more difficult, especially for more risky customers, to get money at all.

Coupled with this, a rising tide of anti-bank sentiment was proving difficult to manage. Consumers, not able to refinance their mortgages, were in a world of pain. Banks were perceived to have created these circumstances by chasing windfall profits, and consumers were now having to pay the bills. Consumers were eager to find an alternative.

Social networking, already booming in 2008, continued to rise in popularity during this time. Many new entrants with P2P products jumped straight into these networks as a way of reaching customers. Bankers, in the meantime, concerned themselves far more with their traditional customer service models, reasoning that their most valuable customers would hardly be looking for new credit on social networks.

This resulted in a wide gap between those who could be served by bank lenders and those who could not. The latter camp was significantly skewed towards social minorities, who began to help each other solve their credit needs via the intermediary of third-party peer-to-peer lending sites. By the end of 2011, awareness of social lending as an alternative to banks on these networks had reached 20%, well past the projected critical mass point such services required of 16%.

By the time house prices started to recover and the official lending crisis had passed, customer behaviour had changed. Social minorities, who were now used to the peer-to-peer lending model, didn't see any particular need to switch back to banks. They were well served – and increasingly able to access a full range of products – from their social networks. These customers continued to extol the virtues of the new model to others in their networks as well, resulting in continued growth of the sector.

Bankers, meanwhile, had done little, if anything, with social networks. The whole spectre of reputational injury to brand resulting from user-generated content and the uncontrollable nature of social networking had led them to conclude that this new technology was too high-risk to allow much direct participation. There were a few half-hearted attempts to enter, but realistically, it was too little too late.

In the meantime, the peer-to-peer networks were able to undercut the costs of bank operations substantially. The political fallout from events in 2007 and 2008 had led governments to rapidly increase the amount of oversight they demanded from regulators of banks. The increased load of compliance and review made providing banking services more expensive, whilst regulators struggled themselves to cope with the new demands.

In the end, regulators in many countries decided that because P2P was largely a private matter between two individuals anyway, there was little additional value to be gained from spending too much of their precious time on supervision. Even in the United States, where regulators forced the temporary closure of leading sites, they did not impose a regime that was in any way comparable with that required of banks. P2P sites were left largely unregulated, and made the most of this operational advantage over their competitors.

There are some rather obvious conclusions that follow. The lack of any substantive bank presence on social networks that offer P2P lending (and the ongoing failure of banks to develop any) has meant these are customers which are either in danger of – or have already – abandoned banking altogether. It signals the rise of a new segment – customers who have chosen to be unbanked deliberately. Any further increase in this segment will have dramatic top-line effects on bank profitability.

Growth gets easier

It is 2012. Retail banks are showing significant growth as they reach new customers with innovative models based on peer-to-peer trends in social networking. Although traditional lending is being challenged in the face of these new models, with up to 15% of volume migrating, this has resulted in net growth for banks. There are expectations that up to 20% of volume might have migrated by 2015.

Luckily, bankers were quick to note the importance of peer-to-peer models and their association with social networks, and began investing substantially in these new technologies. They were also quick to note that the then-important peer-to-peer third-party sites were suffering from chronic underfunding, with up to 70% of the loans being requested remaining unfunded. These early third-party attempts were also having a terrible time with loan quality, with one site reporting up to 20% defaults.

Proper analysis of this situation led banks to conclude that there were plenty of customers who could be well served as depositors on a peer-to-peer loan network, but they lacked time to successfully manage the overhead themselves. And there were plenty more customers with sufficient credit quality that they could be safely lent to in these new models. What banks did not expect, however, was how the market dislocation of 2008 would affect the lending business. At the height of the credit crunch, the financial world was suffering from a lack of liquidity with which to fund its lending operations, and fewer traditional loans could be written. After suffering several quarters of appalling performance, bankers began to start writing loans through this new mechanism, which meant they didn't have to fund their loan books at all.

Whilst there was a wide gap between those who could get traditional bank credit and those who could not, bankers were able to let customers help each other through their new peer-to-peer lending products. By the end of 2010, awareness of social lending as an alternative to banks on these networks had reached 20%, well past the projected critical mass point such services required of 16%.

The key factor in the success of the new peer-to-peer lending products offered by banks was that they leveraged the ability of banks to identify customers with certainty, making lending to these customers a much less risky proposition than that offered by third-party peer-to-peer lending sites. Depositors were far more comfortable with lending their own money if they knew the bank was verifying the identity of the borrowers in its peer-to-peer lending networks. Furthermore, banks, with their vast (in comparison with smaller third-party sites) customer bases, were able to collectively group baskets of customers together for depositors to invest in. This was a huge improvement over the previous arrangement, where individual depositors had to spend hours looking through loan proposals before making investment decisions. This fact alone caused many high-value customers to consider investing in banks' new P2P networks. Also, the new personal approach of customers 'helping each other' helped by the bank did much to dispel the rising tide of anti-bank sentiment devolving from the sub-prime crisis. Bankers found that launching peer-to-peer products, in fact, resulted in significant positive up-ticks to their brands, often unexpectedly so.

By the time house prices had begun their recovery and the official lending crisis had passed, banks found that customers were as happy to be offered a P2P product as a traditional one. In fact, the new P2P products were the first time a bank was able to attract a fee income stream without suffering from consumer backlash. This new source of revenue made it extremely attractive for banks to increase their focus on their new products.

In the meantime, the rise of P2P products at banks had attracted significant interest from regulators. Having been burned by the market dislocation of 2008, they were not about to stand by and allow another politically damaging financial innovation to evolve without their supervision. Many third-party sites were closed down, especially in the United States. Other countries followed suit. New compliance obligations were placed on banks, which were largely those they had been dealing with for years anyway. But this was the final straw for the independent P2P lending networks, which had no hope of building the infrastructures they needed to be compliant. Most such networks were quickly closed down.

Today, bankers are guarded about the future of their new P2P products, but are certainly happy with the growth they have created in the overall market. Furthermore, the reduction in their reliance on traditional funding models has created significant operational advantages, ultimately resulting in a situation where the only significant constraint on growth is how big they can grow their social networks.

What does this futurecast illustrate?

Although there are quantitative numbers throughout this futurecast, none of the stories included represent a complete statement about the future. Instead, they attempt to throw some light on the strategic questions we opened with at the beginning: what should banks do with respect to peer-to-peer lending?

Try this: take this futurecast (or your own one, customised to your specific institution) to any group in your bank, and ask them to discuss it. Something amazing happens: people begin to consider alternatives and options in a very open way. They challenge each other to think up ways of dealing with the issues illuminated by the futurecast. And they wonder what decisions they need to be considering right now in order to deal with the potential threat. As I said elsewhere, one of the primary roles of the futurecast is to enable leaders to rehearse their strategic decisions in their minds before they actually have to *make* their decisions.

Let us turn now to the process we used to create such futurecasts, the subject of the remainder of this chapter.

4.5 CONSTRUCTING THE FUTURECAST WITH SCENARIO PLANNING METHODS

The principal method we will be using in this book to construct the various stories that comprise a futurecast is called *scenario planning*. This is a long-range forecasting tool that has been in use for several decades, both in the military and corporate domains. The best example of the success of scenario planning is usually held to be Royal Dutch Shell, where use of the technique is advanced as the principal reason the company avoided the oil shock and other energy events of the 1970s, becoming one of the largest companies in the world in the process.

What follows here is a potted version of the scenario-planning process, suitable for use by innovators. Full-blown scenario planning is quite complicated, and requires substantive investments in both time and specialists, so it can often be overkill for the specific scenarios in which innovation practitioners are interested. Nonetheless, the full method is exceptionally interesting, and there are two key texts I would recommend you read if what follows doesn't whet your appetite enough. The first is *The Art of the Long View* by Peter Schwartz, one of the original planners at Royal Dutch Shell [41]. The second is *Scenarios: The art of the strategic conversation* by Kees Van Der Heijden, a contemporary of Schwartz [42]. The methods documented in both of these books form the recommended approach for most futurecasts, and what follows now is a summary that can be used to get started.

Step One: Determine the focal point or issue that is the subject of the futurecast

Begin by distilling down the major decision that must be made. The point of a futurecast, as I pointed out earlier, is to be able to rehearse such decisions before the time to make them arrives. It is essential, therefore, that the key decision question (though it might not be explicitly stated) is visible from the choice of scenarios that are eventually presented.

There are two clarifying questions here. Ask 'what is our worst nightmare?' Then ask 'what is our competitor's worst nightmare?' Frame these questions in terms of the innovation that is the consideration of the futurecast. The futurecast will then contemplate these nightmare questions.

Let us consider the P2P example we have been using in this chapter so far. As a banker, the worst nightmare resulting from this innovation could be that peer-to-peer lending makes traditional lending uneconomic for banks, who are forced to exit the business. And what is the worst nightmare for a competitor, including an emerging peer-to-peer lending business? One of them, surely, must be that banks enter the peer-to-peer lending game themselves, and bring their superior capital and operational resources to bear.

What follows from these two pictures then is the key decision: should we (as banks) be involved in peer-to-peer lending? And if we should, what might the shape of that involvement be?

Step Two: Examine the local environment

Having determined the key decision question in the futurecast, the next thing to do is work out what local environmental conditions would affect the success of the decision.

Firstly, define what success would look like. Let us say, in this case, it is that the threat of peer-to-peer lending is eliminated by banks, who enter the market and are successful in morphing their lending model towards the new way of doing things. In the process they find new customers and achieve good year-on-year growth.

Then, create a statement which reflects what failure might be like. In this case, it is obvious: banks begin to lose share to non-banks with peer-to-peer models, and this happens rapidly so that there is obvious decline in revenue year on year.

Step Three: Examine the driving forces

Scenario planners usually examine five 'driving forces' next. Driving forces are broad trends that affect societies, industries, and economies as a whole which will operate over the long term. For innovators, that usually means in the five- to ten-year timeframe. They are the mega-changes that are the engine of things new, such as, for example, the rise of the digital economy and the digital lifestyle. The evolution of the green agenda. Or the trend towards greater regulation of banks.

For any particular story we want to tell, there will be many driving forces, and the key here is to work out which ones are the *most* likely to be relevant for our proposed futurecast. Normally, scenario planners think in terms of five driving forces – often referred to as a STEEP analysis: Society, Technology, Economics, Ecology, and Politics. Table 4.2 lists some of the driving forces that might potentially be considered during this step.

Once again, this list is not exhaustive, but it is a good place to start. Again, using a brainstorm, one considers each of these driving forces and how they might play out in the scenario of interest. This is, perhaps, the most time-consuming step of all, since it requires substantive research and wide-ranging information-gathering.

Step Four: Ranking of forces and scenario mechanics

Once there is a list of driving forces (Table 4.2), the next thing to do is rank them in order of importance. In this example, I've suggested that the driving forces of importance are lifestyle changes and interests, culture, social exclusion, digital lifestyles, business cycles stages, and legislation and regulation. Depending on the perceptions and positioning of a particular institution, these could be quite different: it all depends on the brainstorm.

What we have at this point is a list of things that we believe will be the engines of change. Now it is time to combine these with our success and failure statements by elucidating some proposed mechanics that might result in the outcomes we're going to put in our stories. Table 4.3 is an example of doing this for peer-to-peer lending.

Table 4.2 Potential driving forces

	Driving forces	Impacts	Priority
Social	Population growth	Increase in overall demand for lending	Low
	Age distribution	Aging population, but more gen-Y borrowers who might take a P2P loan	Medium
	Education	More educated population is more likely to engage in innovative behaviour	Low
	Culture	Consumers distrust, sometimes even hate, banks. This makes non-bank alternatives attractive	High
	Lifestyle changes	Working hours increasing, less time available for time-intensive personal finance so consumers want simpler solutions	High
	Social exclusion	Unemployment rates higher for social minorities and lower education likely means that those most needing credit are least able to get it	High
	Public health	N/A	Low
	Civil safety	N/A	Low
	Attitude to foreign products and services	Increasing foreign ownership of banking causes consumers to seek local solutions	Medium
	Religious effects	Probably none, though a P2P model based on Islamic banking might be important	Medium
	Language impacts	N/A	Low
	Income levels	Economic growth slowing or recession means that income levels are static though demand for credit continues	Low
	Immigration	Increasing number of foreign workers – some who are not legal – need access to credit	Medium
	Household composition – number and type of people in households	Changes from the married couple model, and nearly a third of individuals remain single. Single parents increasing demographic. Divorces increase. Might result in greater loan demand for distress situations where normal lending can't compete	Medium
	Car ownership and public transport	More people continue to buy cars, but they are more energy-efficient models. High fuel costs cause downsizing of existing cars and switch to public transport. Cars become cheaper whilst fuel increases	Low
Technological	Internet access	Most people have Internet access, and those that don't are disadvantaged by being on the wrong side of the digital divide. Many who need loans and can't get them from traditional lenders are on the wrong side of the divide	Medium
	Mobile phone access	Practically everyone has mobile phone access and increasing numbers are using them as Internet access devices	Medium
	Business use of technology	All businesses rely on technology, but there is decreasing reliance on IT departments as more sophisticated end-users build their own systems	Low
	Personal use of technology	More and more people use technology solutions in the course of their day-to-day lives. Technology converges around the mobile phone which is a player, a file repository, a wallet, and a telecommunications device	Medium
	Digital lifestyles	Everything is done online. If you don't do everything online you miss out altogether. Decline of bank branches and traditional lending. People feel more comfortable actuating their financial needs through their social networks than traditional corporations	High

(continued)

Table 4.2   (*Continued*)

	Driving forces	Impacts	Priority
Economics	Public sector technology usage	The public sector moves to increasing self-service and begins to exceed citizen expectations. Corporations struggle to keep up and socially aware solutions are preferred over big corporate	Low
	Business cycles and stage	The economic cycle has been through a recession and is now on the upswing. But people have become accustomed to the lack of easy access to credit through traditional means, and now that they are available again, have new habits when they seek finance	High
	Economic growth rate	Trending upwards, and house prices are also recovering. People are looking for easy sources of credit again, but lending practices are still tight as a result of excessive government scrutiny resulting from the credit crunch	Medium
	Unemployment	Was climbing in previous years, but is now in decline. More people have spare capital and are looking for non-traditional, social network aware places to put it	
	Inflation rate	In decline	Low
	Interest rates	In decline, but there is still a huge difference between what people feel they should be paying and what they are	Medium
	Workforce skill levels	Have increased in the last few years. Many more people are technology literate, and the bar is being raised year on year. Systems which were far too complicated for someone without training are now the norm. The barriers to the adoption of social lending platforms decline as the technology becomes much easier to use and understand	Medium
	Labour costs	The wages paid to skilled and highly skilled workers are at their highest ever as corporations struggle to win the war for talent. But unskilled workers suffer real wage decline as increases in the cost of living make income gaps even more pronounced. This means that the well off have money to invest, and there is an ample supply of those without ready access to credit	Medium
Ecological	Environmental regulations	Possibility of carbon taxes on data centres make low-margin products even more difficult to support for banks	Medium
	Population opinion on green issues	Increasing public interest in green agendas makes products which support green policy attractive	Low
	Air pollution	N/A	
	Preservation of natural assets	N/A	
	Environmental burden of economic activities	Banks continue to create products that deal with carbon trading and carbon reduction. Consumer interest in such products continues to grow	Low
	Legislation and regulation	Increasing regulation in the wake of the credit crunch means that regulators are stretched in supervision of banks. They don't have time to manage non-bank players, and decline to do so	High
	Policy issues	Governments, burned electorally by financial instability and housing price crashes, seek to increase the availability of credit and actively support alternatives to banks. In the meantime, they direct regulators to increase scrutiny of the banking system	Medium

Table 4.2   (*Continued*)

Political	Political stability	Following the Iraq and Afghanistan campaigns, the developed world is interested in less confrontational means to resolve conflicts. The new governments of 2008/2009 actively step back aggressive policy and enjoy increasing levels of public approval and trust	Medium
	International commitments	SEPA and other international policy commitments are the sign of things to come, with increasing cooperation between governments to enhance the power of their economies	Medium
	Focus on technology	Governments are aware and nervous of increasing research and development investments, especially in Asia. They take active steps to increase innovation in their economies	Medium

Step Five: Create the stories

Finally, we come to creating the futurecast itself. Begin by examining the scenario plots already decided on and create a title for each scenario that reflects the plot. The advice of Schwartz is 'to condense a fully delineated story into a few words'. He uses the examples of 'The boy who cried wolf' and 'Johnny Appleseed': both of these titles convey a great deal of meaning and connotation. They set the stage for the scenarios that follow.

In the example futurecast, my title for the success scenario was 'Growth gets easier'. The connotations here are that bankers find a way to reverse the current-day trend of struggling against margin erosion, the lack of new customers in their particular market, and the overwhelming temptation to get growth by buying it. It is a title that suggests positive things for banks in the future.

On the other hand, I chose the title 'Disconnected customers' for the failure scenario. A present (and ongoing) strategic imperative for many institutions is to get as close to customers as they can. By so doing, strategists hope, banks will be able to build deep and profitable engagement that drives share of wallet. But what happens if all this effort is misdirected, if customers don't care about the efforts banks make to get to know them? This is the intent of my title in the failure case.

And finally, I chose the title 'P2P experiments fail' for the irrelevant attempt scenario. The use of the word *experiment* suggests that banks went into offering P2P lending with their eyes open, fully cognisant of the risks and possible rewards. Though in this instance, P2P turned out to be unimportant, at least banks were forward-thinking enough to cover their bases.

Next, we create the text of the story. Initially, write the story without being too specific about numbers. These are things we'll add later once we have plots developed. Ideally, each scenario in the futurecast should be no more than about two pages. This is about as much as you can expect a senior executive to read in a single sitting, so going on for longer means there is every chance that the messages inherent in the document will not be communicated.

Each of the dimensions identified in Table 4.3 should be explored in each futurecast. For example, the success scenario has regulators decide that peer-to-peer lending, now that banks are involved, is functionally the same as ordinary lending. The result is that many third-party sites don't have the muscle to step up to the new requirements. On the other hand, the failure scenario has little regulatory interest in peer-to-peer, with the result that third-party sites are pretty much free to do anything they like, whilst banks struggle under increased scrutiny.

Table 4.3   Scenario mechanics

	Growth gets easier	Disconnected customers	P2P experiments fail
Lifestyle changes and interests	Banks value-add the P2P process by creating an easy way for customers to lend to secure 'baskets' of customers, and P2P networks don't have the customer base to do the same thing	Whilst making deposits and writing loans using P2P networks is time-consuming and quite difficult to learn, working with these tools has the same entertainment value that stock trading and eBay have for a significant segment	As a deposit vehicle, P2P is too time-consuming for most consumers, who would rather spend their leisure time doing something else. This pattern is the same as that which emerged from eBay users in 2008
Culture	Banks leverage the new personal P2P concepts of 'helping each other' to address the inherent distrust of the experience in the market. This results in positive brand attribution and increasing participation	P2P lenders capitalise on bank-hate and make the point that their products don't support 'fat cat' bonuses when everyone else is suffering from sub-prime. Consumers readily identify and try out P2P.	Customers, having suffered the financial implosion of 2008, are wary of any kind of systematised lending and move their deposits to robust safe havens. The lack of liquidity in P2P eliminates most markets
Social exclusion	Social minorities might not be able to get loans in the traditional way, but bank P2P lending is an appropriate alternative that lets banks keep them as customers	P2P becomes firmly entrenched in niche markets for social minorities and those minorities begin to help each other through the P2P network	Social minorities change their spending patterns until increasing liquidity in the market and relaxed lending criteria return their ability to obtain credit
Digital lifestyles	Banks enable their customers to work with social networks, leveraging the identity information they already have to provide an additional level of security and trust to the process. Lenders express a preference for someone who is on a bank-backed social network over others	Banks fail to get on the social networking bandwagon at all, and find their access to customers is in decline, as those customers use their social networks rather than direct bank access	Social networking, when intermediated by a bank, turns out to be less popular than that offered by media companies and independent start-ups. Customers are simply not ready to trust banks with these additional details of their personal lives
Business cycle stages	Banks relax lending criteria significantly. But they also move customers who were unable to borrow through traditional means to their P2P sites	Banks have relaxed their lending criteria, but customers have already changed their behaviour and are now used to borrowing through social networks	The relaxation of lending criteria means that the consumers, who may previously have been forced to work with a P2P lending site, can now return to traditional ways of obtaining credit
Legislation and regulation	Regulators decide that P2P lending needs the same kind of supervision as any other financial service, and ramp up their scrutiny of third-party sites with disastrous consequences for them	Regulators don't have time to manage for anyone other than mainstream banks, leaving P2P sites with significant cost and compliance advantages	Regulators ignore P2P lending as insignificant in the overall scheme of things

In the end, there should be a great deal that is similar about each scenario, with only those differences that come from the changes in the driving forces making any substantive deviation in each case. It is essential that the audience can see the effect that different decisions can have on the eventual outcomes. One wants to avoid adding additional facts and colour so as to avoid obscuring the essential points.

Step Six: Flesh them out with predictions

Once the stories are finalised, it is then important to consider what substantive predictions might usefully be added to ground the futurecast in some reality for the reader. A story without substantive predictions is usually less impactful than one with. Of course, having numbers tends to open one to challenges of their veracity, so here is a line that must be walked carefully.

In my experience, though, a prediction can add a great deal of weight to a futurecast, so long as the prediction can be validated with appropriate rigour. On the other hand, a prediction that is weak can do a lot of damage to the overall usefulness of the futurecast. It is to the subject of getting decent predictions that we turn our attention next.

4.6   PREDICTION METHODS

The predictions made in a futurecast should be few in number. This is not a situation where more data is better! The fact of the matter is, frankly, that the more you pin down the stories about the future with numbers and other concrete facts, the less likely it is the futurecast will stand the test of time. The best thing possible is to limit oneself to that small number of predictions necessary to quantify the effect of the key decision. In our example case, the key decision is whether banks should, or should not, enter peer-to-peer lending.

There are many ways to get predictions that are helpful in a futurecast. Some, of course, take more money and effort than others. What follows is an examination of some of the more common methods that innovators might employ regularly.

Intuitive (expert) prediction

The easiest way to get statements that support a particular vision of the future is through what academics call 'intuitive' prediction, which really means asking an expert. The underlying assumption of such a prediction is that the information available to the expert, his or her academic and perceptional background, and attitudinal compatibility with the subject being considered, provides them with insights that an ordinary individual would not have.

Banks usually have batteries of individuals engaged in prediction, though they are usually called analysts. They are paid to examine publically available information both on companies and the markets they serve, and come out with statements representing likely future states. Because the intuitive prediction usually involves a single individual, it is generally easy to get. That is especially true if the appropriate expert is available in-house, though one can easily get forecasts on many subjects by subscribing to an analyst firm such as Gartner, which provides forward-looking statements for a living.

Though intuitive forecasts are easy to obtain in many cases, they are notoriously unreliable. In financial markets, for example, analysts' forecasts are wrong more than 50% of the time, and during market events (such as the credit crunch in 2008, or the dot-com bubble burst at the turn of the century), they are inevitably wrong altogether. Intuitive forecasts are usually useful for short- and medium-term predictions: the further from the present you go, the more possibilities have to be considered. Even the best expert has limited capacity to consider things, and too many variables will certainly result in a prediction that isn't useful for planning purposes.

Another key trap is to fail to consider expert bias. Inevitably, experts have formed views about their special interest areas which can be hard to shake. The problem here is that innovations often change the underlying basis of knowledge that experts rely on for their predictions. There have been some famous examples of this. In 1956, Astronomer Royal Sir Richard Woolley said that 'space travel is utter bilge', but it was only a year later than the Russian Sputnik satellite orbited the Earth.

Lord Kelvin, President of the Royal Society, also made some expert predictions which proved spectacularly wrong. In 1895 he remarked that 'heavier than air flying machines are impossible', despite the obvious evidence of birds, and was proved wrong in the following decade. Two years after that he said 'radio had no future', a prediction that was proved wrong after his death. He then wrapped up his mis-prediction trifecta with his 1900 statement that 'There is nothing new to be discovered in physics now. All that remains is more and more precise measurement.'

Both Woolley's and Kelvin's predictions were subject to significant expert bias. As an astronomer, Woolley was thinking in terms of astronomical distances and could not conceive of anything that could reasonably cross them. And Kelvin, though a noted academic and gifted theorist, was unable to stretch his thinking beyond limited applications of his own academic work. Bias and unreliability are two of the key reasons expert predictions are sometimes challenging. But because they are often quick and easy to get, they are regularly used in futurecasts.

There is one last thing to remember about expert predictions: they are included in a futurecast for the express purpose of enhancing consideration of the key decision being contemplated. It is therefore necessary to choose experts who are respected by the audience the futurecast is intended to address. There is little point selecting an expert without the appropriate reputation.

Expert consensus

The unreliability of individual expert predictions can be balanced out somewhat by asking multiple experts their opinions. Often called a 'consensus' prediction, one asks the same question of multiple experts, and averages out the answers. This is a technique often reported for predictions of company performance.

In general, it is assumed this averaging procedure results in a more reliable prediction than that of an individual forecaster. The basic rationale is that whilst some 'super star' experts get it right some of the time, they cannot be expected to do so reliably. When you put lots of experts together, however, the good predictions tend to balance out the bad.

Most of the evidence supporting the use of consensus forecasts comes from analysis of US financial markets [43]. What an examination of this evidence reveals is that predictions are most accurate when the panel of experts uses different ways to get their results, either because they have access to different information, or they use different procedures.

It is by no means clear, however, that consensus forecasts are always better than a single expert prediction in every case. One group of researchers examined the accuracy of consensus forecasts for financial performance in Japan [44]. This study found that using a panel of experts didn't actually result in better predictions compared with picking analysts at random. They did, however, verify the rather obvious conclusion that if everyone disagrees, it is likely to mean that the prediction will be rather wrong.

When confronted with the chance to use an expert prediction versus a consensus one, it is invariably better to go with the latter, assuming the budget allows it.

Delphi method

Expert consensus is all very well, but it is possible to go one step further still, using a technique known as the Delphi method. This is a more sophisticated version of the expert consensus method. The basic procedure is that an expert panel is convened, which is then asked to make a prediction multiple times, each time using the aggregated results of the previous round as an input.

There are often four phases in a Delphi method prediction. The first is an exploration of the subject under discussion by the group, during which each individual contributes any information he or she feels is pertinent to the prediction.

The second phase has the group exploring the information supporting the prediction and attempting to get to a single view of what the likely prediction is going to be. If there is significant disagreement, this is explored in the third phase to bring out the underlying reasons for the difference. And the fourth phase, which is final evaluation, occurs when all the information from the previous rounds has been analysed and individual predictions are fed back for aggregation.

The point of all this is that the prediction should reach convergence. Convergence is when the individual predictions of panel members begin to come together as a result of the cross-group feedback inherent in the Delphi method. Sometimes, it is necessary to go through the process multiple times in order to achieve this.

Whilst it is beyond the scope of this book to examine the procedural details of the Delphi method very closely, there are excellent references available online which document the procedure and its use substantively. The most referenced text is Harold Linstone and Murray Turnoff's text, available for download from the Internet [45].

There is quite a history of bankers using the Delphi method to forecast innovations in the industry. Some of these forecasts, retrospectively, were quite wrong. But others, as you will see in a moment, were surprisingly correct.

The first example we will look at was published in 1994 by two researchers [46] who were interested in the future of self-service technology in Australia and New Zealand. Recall from our examination of banking innovation historically in Chapter 1 that this was the time when banks were really beginning to understand the potential value of self-service technologies for customers. It was a year before any institution had real Internet banking, though ATMs and telephone banking were swiftly becoming the norm in the industry. In other words, banks were still tightly bound to human customer service and the branch.

Experts in the Delphi panel were given the adoption data for a range of self-service innovation at the time of study, and asked to estimate their likely penetration for 2000 and 2010. Five different panels were constructed, each of which used the Delphi technique. The panels were comprised of different kinds of experts: one, for example, had only technology vendors. Another was sourced from retail banking executives.

Here are the headline results. The Delphi study correctly predicted that self-service technologies would certainly begin to replace human intermediated transactions, with tellers becoming sellers rather quickly. It also suggested that ATM and EFTPOS would lead the way to self-service, followed up by telephone contact centres. Their estimates were conservative for these, suggesting that up to 50% of the population would use EFTPOS by 2010, for example. And their predictions for Internet banking were way short of the mark, with the most optimistic panels suggesting that only 15% of users would use the channel by 2010. Some predictions were high: one panel suggested that 23% of the population would have smartcards in the same timeframe. And predictions for some technologies (insurance, travel, loan and product profile machines) failed to account for the rise of the Internet, which made them obsolete. But considering the timeframe of the predictions – more than a decade ago – it is obvious that the Delphi study contributed in this case to an understanding of the likely shape of the future.

Another example of the Delphi method comes from a study in 2001 [47], where researchers attempted to assess the likely future of Internet banking. At the time, bankers everywhere were wondering whether the online channel was going to be 'transformational' or not, and many were attempting to determine if the rounds of branch closures they had made in expectation of customer channel migration were a strategic blunder.

The study came to the following conclusions: that 84% of banks would have an Internet channel by 2011. It also predicted that the number of transactions conducted in the channel would rise from 11% (in 2001) to 23% by 2011. These estimates are probably in line with what is currently expected from the online channel (at the time of writing, 43% of US households had online banking [48]).

But this particular Delphi study illuminated the strategic question clearly, when it said that 'While the proportion of transaction conducted on the Internet will increase... it is clear that Internet is not going to be the sole medium... the Internet is an additional channel, rather than a replacement'. This prediction, seven years ago, has proved to be resoundingly correct.

Wisdom of crowds and prediction markets

So far, we've talked of making predictions using various methods that involve experts. But there is another technique that can also be used, one that doesn't involve experts at all. You ask a large body of end-users their opinion of what will happen instead.

The easiest way of doing this is by survey. Political polls are, essentially, this kind of forecast. But there is another way of getting collective opinions about the future from people that we will look at briefly now: the prediction market.

A prediction market is a means of making guesses about the future that uses the wisdom of crowds to get to a statement about some future fact. Wisdom-of-crowd approaches have generated a great deal of interest in recent times. Amazon. com, the giant online retailer, uses the buying behaviour of crowds to make recommendations to other potential customers of products they might like to purchase. Pandora and Last.FM, two online radio stations, use the listening behaviour of crowds to make suggestions of music that new listeners might like to hear. And online resources, such as Wikipedia, use crowds of editors to build an online reference resource with much more timeliness and depth than any traditionally edited work would have.

Many of the phenomena the innovator is interested in are the result of the collective action of large groups of people. For example, the S-curve of the innovation diffusion process is driven entirely by the collective behaviour of many individuals making their adoption decisions. Consequently, the idea of harnessing this powerful tool is an attractive one for innovation practitioners.

A prediction market is a way of harnessing crowd-based opinions to get to a meaningful prediction. The basic rationale is this: end-users are provided with some proxy for money – usually a virtual currency of some kind. They use this currency to buy and sell 'stocks' in ideas. As the price rises through ordinary market forces, it tends to approximate the probability of something – the prediction – occurring. Players are rewarded for buying into ideas low and selling high – thus improving the quality of the prediction. On the other hand, players who do the reverse are punished (through a decline in the amount of currency they hold).

For an innovator, the prediction market is a very useful tool. One can pose questions (such as the likely probability that peer-to-peer lending will take 35% market share by 2012, for example) and receive a collective opinion that may be used as a prediction. Because the underlying mechanism that results in this prediction is the collective beliefs of individuals, who presumably are *also* those who would be affected by the innovation, such predictions can be surprisingly accurate.

Of course, as with all prediction methods, such markets have flaws. Firstly, a lack of liquidity in a particular prediction market can be interpreted by participants as risk aversion in the crowd: this skews the probabilities returned in a downwards direction because participants are less likely to buy into stocks with low volumes. The second major issue is countering market manipulation, where participants make trades which are counter to their best interests in order to drive the price in a particular direction. Emerging research, however, suggests that such efforts are usually short-lived, as there is significant upside to be gained for the remaining participants in betting *against* the manipulator.

Despite such flaws, however, prediction markets in various forms are beginning to become a force in many parts of the innovation process, and not just in futurecasting. Prediction markets, for example, seem to be just as good at working out which ideas to progress through an innovation system as stage gates. And crowd-based voting systems for ideas are now a de rigeur feature of practically all commercially offered ideas-management systems.

We will return to this subject in Chapter 7, where we examine the prediction market that my bank has implemented as part of its innovation process.

Statistical methods

'There are lies, damned lies and then there are statistics,' said Benjamin Disraeli in a particularly famous diatribe about the misuse of mathematical statements to bolster weak arguments. Disraeli was twice the Prime Minister of the United Kingdom, and it was his words which were then popularised by Mark Twain in his 1907 work *Chapters from my Autobiography*. This particular statement still holds true today. It is certainly appropriate to be cautious about statistical methods when looking forward: they make predictions based on historical facts, rather than human judgement about likely futures.

Historical prediction has a big history of failure. The crash of the tech-bubble in 2000 was one example. The more recent crash of the housing market was another. In both cases people looked at relatively recent history, noted continuing rises in the market, and assumed on the basis of this data that rises would continue indefinitely. They were ultimately – and very expensively – proved wrong.

Some kinds of predictions can be made with statistical methods that are intuitively obvious, however. If, for example, one notes, from previous sales history, that a particular product is adding customers, year on year, at 10%, it is reasonable to forecast in the medium term that it will continue to do so.

Historical data often illuminates patterns that can be useful for making predictions, and most people are familiar with statistical tools commonly available in spreadsheets that help make sense of them. But there is another class of statistical analysis which is of great interest to the innovator who needs to make predictions: Monte Carlo analysis.

In my experience, institutions that perform this kind of analysis always have some group which is hidden away in a back room somewhere, probably with advanced degrees in mathematics. Complicated questions are fed in, and out comes complicated, decorated with statistics, answers. The reality, however, is that Monte Carlo is a very simple technique. What you do is create some kind of model (usually in a spreadsheet) and then vary the parameters which affect the model using hundreds or thousands of iterations, substituting random numbers for each. By watching what happens to the result of the model for each random number and aggregating the results, you can draw meaningful conclusions about the likelihood of certain things. Obviously, one uses a computer programme to do all this.

Perhaps I've made that sound complicated, so let me give you an example. In one institution, my team and I were examining a new channel innovation where every transaction the customer executed caused an incremental cost to us. Clearly, then, it was important to know how many times a customer would likely execute a transaction so we would have some visibility of how the pricing would have to work so that we could make a reasonable return. The obvious statistical approach is to say something like 'on average most customers will do three transactions a week'. This gives one a point prediction, but it is completely insufficient as a model because it is reasonable to expect that many customers will do quite a few more transactions, and many less. What if some customers did ten transactions a week? How does that affect the overall profitability of the channel?

The Monte Carlo technique provides an answer to the problem. You create a model that has customer transactions per week as one of the inputs. You then tell the Monte Carlo programme to vary the input over a range of values, drawn from a range of normally distributed numbers. Those with statistical training will know that this is easily specified – you tell the programme the average value and then how much you expect it to vary around this average (the standard deviation).

The result of this exercise was that we were able to provide executives with firmly grounded predictions about the likelihood of certain events. For example, we were able to say that, given a particular price point, the probability of making a profit was about 80%, and the probability of a loss 20%. We were also able to quantify the probability of achieving particular profit levels.

None of this, by the way, need be done manually. I've had great success with Crystal Ball, a software add-in to Microsoft Excel [49]. Crystal Ball takes a spreadsheet of the kind that would ordinarily have been used for making predictions anyway, and adds the Monte Carlo technique to it. I advise this or something similar be in the kit bag of all innovators.

Adding predictions to our futurecast

As I mentioned earlier, adding specific predictions is something that adds veracity to the forecast when it can be done in a manner that doesn't bring the whole into question. Usually, therefore, one wants to limit the number used as much as possible. The main prediction in our example is that 20% of retail lending could go peer-to-peer by 2015. How is such a dire prediction supported by the data we have available right now?

Well, firstly, we know the size of the retail lending market for a given country, and it is possible to estimate the percentage of loans being written by peer-to-peer sites presently, since they conveniently publish their origination data in a way that no bank would ever do. Prosper.com, one of the largest P2P sites, for example, enables one to download their originations data in a convenient Excel form that is updated regularly. Taking this as a current point estimate, then, we know that the percentage of loans originated as a percentage of the market is a microscopic fraction of the total market.

Our next data point is based on expert opinion. Gartner forecast in 2008 that up to 10% of retail lending could go peer-to-peer by 2010 [50]. Now, Gartner as an expert is relatively credible, certainly sufficiently so that we can use it as a data point in our forecast.

With these two data points in hand, we can use our knowledge of innovation theory to construct a reasonable estimate of the adoption of the innovation. We know that innovations follow an S-shaped curve of the type shown in Figure 2.3.

It took about seven years for Internet banking to go from a standing start in 1994 to 16% penetration of all US households in 2000. 16% is a magic number – it represents (on average across many innovations) the time at which most of the innovators and early adopters have tried a particular innovation. Refer to Figure 2.2 to see why this is so. At around 16% of the market, critical mass forces take off. Let us assume for the purposes of this analysis that peer-to-peer lending would follow the same trajectory as Internet banking – a reasonable assumption given the likely similarities in the user demographic.

Using historical adoption data from Internet banking gives us a diffusion curve from which we model by analogy. Curve fitting is a statistical technique (an online search with Google can provide the details) that enables us to estimate the values of p and q for the Bass model (again, refer to Chapter 2). With these values in hand, we can use Excel's goal seek function to provide us with a curve that puts 10% of loan volume at six years after launch.

So, by 2010, six years after introduction, P2P is 10% of loan volume, and the following year, we project 16% adoption as it begins the takeoff process. Using curve fitting based on the Bass model of Chapter 2, we can come to an approximation of the takeoff curve, and by 2012 the approximate volume is 15%. Three years later, for the same curve, we're at 20%.

Does this prediction accurately reflect the most likely prospects for peer-to-peer lending? Almost certainly not. But is there science and method behind its creation? Yes. Documenting these details and adding them as a supporting appendix to the futurecast is often helpful.

And in practice, of course, one would also provide references to the additional details one has used as basic facts. For example, our futurecast suggests that up to 45% or more of loans on such sites go unfunded. This fact was initially gleaned from a paper written by Deutsche Bank analysts in 2007 [51].

4.7   CASE STUDY: AMP INNOVATION FESTIVAL

The structured approach to futurecasting presented here is, of course, only one particular approach to the problem of getting senior executives to think about the future. The challenge, as I outlined at the beginning of this chapter, is finding a way that optimises the advantage innovators can create with the limited attention span of senior leaders. In this chapter, I've advocated the construction of stories about speculative future states as one way of doing this.

Annalie Killian, the executive responsible for innovation at AMP – a leading wealth management company in Australia – has found another. The self-titled 'Catalyst for Magic' created an Innovation Festival, an opportunity for executives that concentrates all the elements of a futurecast into a corporate event. As she said when I talked about it to her, 'if Mohammad won't come to the mountain, you must take the mountain to Mohammad. I couldn't get senior leaders to come to meetings to do future thinking, so I bought the future thinking to them. The "Tyranny of the Urgent" will always defeat you otherwise.'

Innovation Festival is a smorgasbord of innovative thinking, elements of the futurecast, and cross-pollination from other industries. Typically, the institution turns the common areas and meeting rooms of its head office into a piece of innovation theatre: it is impossible for senior leaders to avoid being impacted, and it also has the added advantage of reaching the organisations they manage as well. Killian, reflecting on the economics of this, told me later 'For about the same money it costs to send 10 executives or middle managers to a Harvard executive programme, we can reach 3500 people with Innovation Festival. The result achieves a critical mass quickly in changing the thinking across the organisation.'

But the first Innovation Festival, conducted in 2005, was a much more modest affair than the immersive experiences that are now part of the programme. Killian had just visited a technology expo day and seen a technology innovation developed by the Australian Department of Fisheries. She'd been shown a raft of significant innovations in the data management space which she felt could be important in financial services.

The challenge, of course, was to get anyone else to agree that an agricultural technology had any relevance at all in an unrelated industry. Such speculative thinking, she recalls, 'was interesting, but in the end, people felt it took too much time out of their day'.

Luckily, however, the chief information officer of AMP is a visionary, and agreed to support Killian's idea to do a small-scale, one-day event that would showcase the most interesting – and outlandish – technology innovations that could be applied to financial services she could come up with. With the lobby and common spaces of AMP's prominent building on Sydney Harbour turned into an 'innovation space', executives and staff alike were exposed to a range of new concepts, innovative thought leaders, and other provocative technologies whether they were interested or not.

There was an immediate reaction from senior leadership. Killian recalls some of the key feedback from the day. 'One of our most senior leaders said that he'd realised that there were likely a whole range of significant trends and opportunities that the organisation was failing to see. It was probably eye-opening for everyone who came.'

As in the story-telling I've described throughout this chapter, the Festival has a strong focus on 'infotainment'. By making the future thinking process entertaining and easily accessible, Killian has discovered she has much better success in getting important messages across to senior leadership. 'One of our guest speakers said something very key that's stuck in the minds of several of our leaders,' she says. 'The impact of technologies is usually overestimated by organisations in the short term, but underestimated in the long.' As you would anticipate, this is a realisation that leads directly to an understanding of the importance of getting to structured considerations of the future for any financial services company.

Today, the Innovation Festival is a bi-annual event spread over a week. 'We needed the extra time because people felt they were eating a ten Christmas lunch in a day – it was too rich,' laughs Killian. 'They wanted more time to digest what they were learning.' With the extra space in the agenda, the programme was broadened to include international thought leaders, innovation from many more industries, a showcase of employee creativity, and exhibits of the most innovative employee projects of the institution's innovation programme.

And the work doesn't stop when the week is over. Killian and her team use the best concepts and ideas, as well as the feedback from participants, to construct a series of ideation campaigns to encourage creativity and innovation in the following months. It makes sure the company is a learning organisation, one that has sufficiently out-of-box thinking to deal with future change.

But the results of the Festival have not only been abstract. One of the key changes in the company has been a new focus on design thinking and an appreciation for the value of weak networks that reach outside financial services. Following from the success of products which feature design as their primary unique selling point – the Apple iPhone, Nike running shoes, or George Jensen silverware, for example – AMP has begun to think differently about its products. Rather than features and functions, it thinks in terms of experiences and customer reaction. It engages with its customers much earlier in the product development process. Even the approach to product development has changed. Faced with indisputable evidence of the new power of consumers at the Innovation Festival, executives began to think about customers as the starting point of all things new and are going outside their existing networks and industry to learn and seek innovation examples that work.

Today, AMP includes structured consideration of innovation at all levels. The Innovation Festival helped to foment a belief that innovation could be harnessed as a key engine of growth for the bank. The Festival approach might have offered more content all at once than anyone could readily digest, but it led leadership to their own realisations about the impact of change in the world.

4.8   SOME FINAL WORDS ABOUT FUTURECASTING

After reading this chapter, you may be wondering how on earth any innovation practitioner has the time to do all this work to get to a couple of speculative statements about the future. You might be thinking, in fact, that futurecasting is a waste of time.

My own experience is that futurecasting, when done right, has a powerful effect on the fortunes of an innovation team. It establishes them as thought leaders, demonstrating that they have the capability to play a role at the top table. This is especially important as the team develops through the fourth and fifth innovation capabilities (see Chapter 3). By the time stable and predictable returns from innovation have started to be routine at the managing stage, it is likely that senior executives will start to wonder where all the 'big plays' are going to come from.

An innovation team has to show up with these big plays if it ever wants to be part of the strategic agenda of an institution, of course. But, equally, the chance of getting really breakthrough or disruptive innovations approved by any executive is low when they are presented without some preparation in advance. The futurecast is a big part of getting such executives ready to make the big decisions they need to in order to get their 'big plays'.

Strategic decision rehearsal isn't the only reason to do a futurecast, of course. Another, very important, reason is that futurecasts provide an important input to more general ideation across an institution. One wants to inspire the creativity of the general population of a bank, and there are few things that do this more effectively than a set of possible stories about the future.

Ideation, which is the process used to gather the collective creativity of an institution, is where we will turn our attention next.

5

Managing Ideation

What you will find in this chapter

- An overview of the things an institution needs to do to manage ideas at scale.
- How to get the idea flow started in the campaign and create stage.
- Collecting, cataloguing, and comparing ideas.
- How to choose which ideas to work on.

The next part of the futureproofing process we will look at is ideation – the process of gathering and selecting ideas for deeper consideration in the innovation phase. Ideas are the lifeblood of an innovation team, a key building block upon which all other capability is built. Without structured ideation, innovators are left with nothing to do but dream up everything themselves.

Since no one has an unlimited fund of creativity, this approach means the innovation team runs out of things to do pretty quickly. There is another problem, however. Innovators are never likely to be expert in *every* aspect of the business of their banks. Inevitably they will miss things, which has the end result of leaving money on the table.

Luckily, the fact of the matter is that there are few organisations that lack good ideas. In multiple studies it has been repeatedly shown that most executives think they don't get the innovation results they want *not* because they don't have enough good ideas, but because they don't do enough with what they have.

Despite this, in my research for this book, I was surprised to discover how many institutions don't do structured ideas management. They are missing out on something very important by failing to master this core competency: ensuring the collective genius of their people is applied to the innovation problem.

Everyone has great ideas, but *not* everyone is in a position that will permit them to take these ideas and convert them to reality. That is why having a structured process for ideas management can help so substantially: it provides the first step in a support network that can assist those not able to push ideas forward themselves and make a significant difference to their institutions.

Why can't people push ideas forward themselves? There are many reasons, but most of the time there are two chief blockers that stand in their way.

The first is that they feel they don't have the time to drive an idea to reality given their commitments to their ordinary day jobs. Everyone is busy, and inevitably making that great idea go somewhere is going to take some personal sacrifice. Not everyone is motivated to make such personal sacrifices, and sometimes, they are unable to make them even if they wished to do so. A structured ideation system means it is possible to make sure those who come up with great ideas have the chance to realise their benefit for their bank.

The second reason people don't drive ideas forward themselves is that they don't feel they have the capability to do so. Changing something about an institution usually requires money, political savvy, and salesmanship, and all three attributes are rarely embodied in a single individual. That is especially true for more junior people who are just starting out.

The fresh perspective of the new hire, however, is often the most valuable. A failure to have a rigorous ideas management process condemns one to missing that perspective. It has another consequence too: staff who feel they can't make a difference rarely last long in a role.

But there is a third purpose to ideas management, and that is to provide signals to the other stages in the futureproofing process. Futureproofing is all about providing a systematic way to contemplate the effect that future innovations might have on a bank, and react appropriately. One of the best sources of signals is what people in the bank think is important.

What other roles does ideation have in the futureproofing process?

One is to *inspire*. As I said a moment ago, everyone has great ideas, but sometimes they need some encouragement to bring them forward. Ideas never arise in a vacuum; there is always some stimulus that causes an individual or group to say 'ah ha!' The 'ah-ha' moment is one of great emotional and intellectual joy for participants, and is the main reason why the ideation phase is a lot of fun. It is the ideation phase that establishes the conditions for such moments to occur. This is the main reason you feed futurecasts into the ideation phase, and it is also the purpose of ideas campaigns, which we will come to in a moment.

The last, and perhaps most important, part of ideation is doing preliminary screening of ideas. If an innovation function is at all successful, it will have many, many ideas to manage. Not all can be promoted to the innovation stage where they get deep consideration preparatory to implementation. There is simply insufficient bandwidth available in an innovation team to do that. So during ideation, structured processes are put in place to decide which ideas to take forward, and which not. The means of doing this is typically some kind of scoring and/or expert evaluation.

5.1 AN OVERVIEW OF THE IDEATION PHASE

It is helpful to think of the ideation phase as a system that encourages the creation of ideas at one end, classifies them in the middle, and sends out the most likely at the end. The basic premise is that a large number of ideas should be processed as quickly as possible, and ideally, for as little money per idea as possible.

The focus on cost is important: the more money a team spends on ideation, the less there is remaining for actual innovation. Keeping costs down during ideation is important, because the name of the game in the ideation phase is volume. It is a high-quality problem to struggle with the number of ideas you have to process, but only if the cost to do so leaves you some budget to progress the best of them.

An example ideation system is shown in Figure 5.1. This shows a system with four main stages, which is typical for institutions with developed ideas management processes. At one institution for which I worked, the ideation team had been running such a system for more than a decade, and were routinely processing in excess of 1600 ideas a month. And they were capable of doing it for a few pounds (less than 5 dollars) per idea. This meant the team was able to invest quite a bit more in further developing ideas before asking for funding.

Now, whilst this is one way of organising ideation, it is by no means the only option. Some institutions focus on reliable collection and scoring; Bank of America is one such, who have highly developed systems for this purpose. Others, such as business credit card firm Advanta

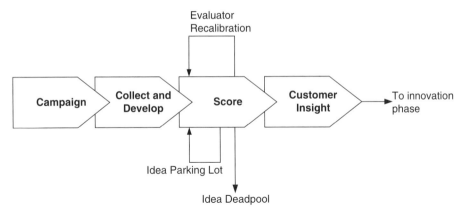

Figure 5.1   An example ideation system

(who we will meet a little later), spend a great deal of time working with customer insight. Still others, such as Royal Bank of Canada (who we'll also be looking at) do advanced work on the campaign side.

The thing to remember is that a working ideation process needs to produce only two things: insights into the current state of an institution by aggregating individual suggestions into trends (I call these individual-level signals in futureproofing) and a set of qualified ideas that merit further consideration for use later on in futureproofing.

Let us now turn to an examination of each of these four stages of the ideation phase and to the processes that surround them.

5.2   CAMPAIGN AND CREATE

The first part of the ideation phase is actually collecting ideas from customers and staff. As I intimated at the beginning of this chapter, this process is not as simple as it might appear. Some people have great ideas, but no motivation to do anything with them, perhaps not even to tell anyone they have them. You might get many ideas that suggest, for example, moving check boxes on forms (incremental improvements), but none that relate to the strategic agenda of your institution. Or you might not get enough ideas at all.

These are all factors which are managed at the campaign and create stage. The basic purpose here is to inspire people to *have* great ideas which are important for the institution, and provide them with the tools they need to *give* them to you.

Campaigns

The inspiration part of the ideation phase is the campaign. In the ordinary course of things, innovation teams will probably have a run-rate of ideas which will happen even if they do nothing to encourage them. This run-rate is valuable, but undirected. As I've said previously, a key part of the futureproofing methodology is that key strategic issues for an institution are addressed through innovation. That cannot happen unless some way is found to influence the flow of ideas, right from the start.

An ideas campaign is the way to do that. It starts with a challenge question or other stimulus. In the futureproofing methodology, such stimulus will certainly include a futurecast, but it could equally be a business problem or some local issue that needs resolution. One puts the stimulus in front of a group of people, and encourages them to contribute answers to the problem. Campaigns are usually relatively short, to the point, and high-profile.

IBM, famously, held an ideas campaign in 2006 with 150,000 people using a specially constructed online collaboration solution. During two 72-hour sessions, participants explored IBM's research lab's most advanced technologies and came up with more than 46,000 ideas. A few months later, then Chairman of IBM, Sam Palmisano, announced he would invest $100 million to create 10 new businesses resulting from the sessions [52]. Now termed *Innovation Jam*, this kind of ideas campaign is a routine business operation at IBM, and the company has started selling this service to its clients.

An ideas campaign doesn't need 150,000 people to be successful, however. The minimum requirement is that the stimulus, whatever it is, can be put in front of a reasonably targeted group, who are encouraged to give their thoughts within a certain timeframe.

Getting the ideas

Once people are inspired to give you great ideas, the next thing is having a place for them to record them. Many organisations have staff suggestion schemes. The basic idea is that people with ideas or insights are able to leave them somewhere and have them actioned on their behalf. Suggestion schemes can be as simple as a drop box into which people put their suggestions on pieces of paper. Or an online intranet page. Or anything in between. A staff suggestion scheme is usually the first iteration of the create part of ideation. I say first iteration, because most institutions quickly find a conventional suggestion scheme doesn't work very well.

The usual complaint raised by employees and customers who use suggestion schemes is 'nothing happens'. I was once talking with a front-line employee at a bank who said there was a suggestion scheme available, but there was no point putting anything in it. The reason, she said, was that the few times she'd added an idea, she heard nothing back, and furthermore, there was no way for her to check what had happened for herself. The suggestion scheme, she continued, was really there so that management could tell staff they had somewhere to put their good ideas.

The underlying problem here is that schemes which record ideas but don't have structured processes for administering them quickly get very difficult and expensive to manage. Even with the best will in the world – even, in fact, with a dedicated team – sooner or later there will be too many ideas for anyone to do more than scan and forward. Scan and forward is an onerous habit to get into: it means that stakeholders with decision-making capabilities are flick-passed new ideas as they arrive, just to get them out of the suggestion box. There is no structured way to follow up, and probably no records available that provide the idea originator with any way to check that something has happened. This is why I sometimes call such suggestion schemes 'spray and pray' – administrators spray ideas in all directions, and they pray that *something* will happen which justifies their existence.

Many institutions quickly realise they are wasting their human capital if they continue the spray and pray scheme of management and move to more collaborative approaches. More modern ideas management systems today provide, out of the box, the ability for others to search for ideas, collaborate on them with discussion forums, and track the progress at each stage. Some allow voting, which provides the innovator with early visibility of how interesting a particular concept might be.

No matter how social the ideas management system might be, there are a couple of things which have been shown to reduce the volume of ideas dramatically. The first is to require too much information up front. Some ideas management systems go into a great deal of detail before they allow you to post an idea, as much as a proper business case would do in some cases. Whilst this makes it easy for an innovator to evaluate the quality of an idea, it *also* has the effect of reducing volume considerably. The more information needed up front, the more motivated an end-user has to be to give you the idea in the first place. Experience suggests that keeping the barrier as low as possible for *submission* of the idea (and then following up with requests for more information later) is a solution which ensures you get a better contribution rate.

Having said that, however, there are some pieces of information which *should* be captured, apart from a short description of the idea itself. It is necessary, for example, to have a list of business units to which the idea might apply, some minimal classification information such as how new to bank the innovation is (i.e., whether it is incremental, revolutionary, or break-through), the organisational affiliation of the suggestor, and some keywords, or alternatively tags.

A keyword is usually system-controlled, whereas a tag is user-defined. Having one or the other is quite important, because when the idea moves to the collect, catalogue and compare stage, keyword and tag matching help determine which ideas are actually the same as others that have been submitted already. We'll come back to this subject in the next section.

Another key question important at this stage is to decide whether it should be possible to submit ideas anonymously or not. There is both an upside and a downside to whichever approach is selected. Anonymity usually results in a much higher volume of ideas. For some reason, people tend to be more forthcoming if they know their suggestions cannot be tracked back to them. However, with this increased volume comes a much higher noise-to-signal ratio: the number of ideas which are silly or sometimes even offensive, as a fraction of those which are truly useful. In one suggestions scheme I was part of, a large number of suggestions arrived one month when a senior executive had their hair redone. No one liked the new style, and they used the suggestion scheme to say so, quite scathingly, actually. Clearly, such suggestions were not helpful to the innovation programme, though the executive concerned may well have been advised to take note of the feedback. We, however, thought it best not to pass it on.

On the other hand, turning off anonymity reduces the flow of ideas, but the ideas you *do* get tend to be of higher quality, since individuals know they can be traced back. Furthermore, requiring people to take accountability for their ideas has important consequences both from a reward and recognition perspective, which we'll get to in a moment.

There is another disadvantage if an institution chooses the anonymous approach. It becomes impossible to feed back anything to the individual who proposed the idea, so immediately this anonymous individual is disconnected from the rest of the innovation process. Obviously, someone who suggests an idea was, at one stage, sufficiently motivated or inspired they went out of their way to tell the innovation programme about it. It is a great pity that innovators are then unable to keep the communication flowing in both directions.

A final question that should be included in any decisions about the campaign and create stage is how to reward participation in the idea process. This is such an important topic that we will examine it in detail in Chapter 10, where we talk about an overall process framework for innovation.

In the meantime, rewards are a useful tool for encouraging the right behaviour at the ideation phase. However, the right behaviour is *not* to reward any idea, no matter its value. Experience suggests that idea reward schemes should drive behaviours which create submissions of quality, rather than volume. That's if rewards for ideas are implemented at all, and there are several schools of thinking on that score.

Some academics argue that rewards are better delayed until later in the innovation process, so that those ideas which actually deliver benefits to the institution are the ones that attract rewards. Others counter this with the suggestion that this raises the bar so high that no one submits ideas at all. Most people agree, however, that reward and recognition is important at *some* stage in the innovation process.

5.3   COLLECT, CATALOGUE, AND COMPARE

The next part of the ideation phase is collecting and cataloguing ideas that were submitted. There are several reasons it is important to do this before any additional processing takes place. Firstly, the same idea suggested by multiple people, especially over a period of time, is an individual-level signal that ought to be considered as a candidate for a futurecast. Secondly, multiple ideas coming from the same area in the business can be a sign that there is a nascent innovation cluster developing, one which the innovation team might usefully employ in moving their agenda forwards. And finally, there is a need to ensure that an idea – which might be submitted multiple times from different sources – moves forwards in the innovation process only once.

Trends and individual-level signals

A key part of futureproofing is spotting trends which might be important subjects of futurecasts, and one of the best indicators available is the pattern of suggestions arriving from customers and end-users. These are people who, at the coal-face, deal with the reality of the competitive environment day to day. When a body of suggestions on the same topic (and at the same time) arrives, it is usually a good indicator that something interesting is happening.

More often than not, of course, such a pattern of ideas indicates an innovation opportunity, rather than being a genuine individual-level signal prompting a futurecast. What, then, are the signs that a particular group of ideas is indicative of a trend?

Most of the time, a group of similar ideas arriving all at once signals an ordinary innovation opportunity, albeit one with potentially pent up demand. One usually sees such a pattern of suggestions after a major system change as end-users react positively and negatively. A major customer experience or product change has the same effect. In any event, people motivated enough to express their opinions are usually worth listening to, if for no other reason than that the feedback can be used to create an enhanced pipeline of incremental innovation.

On the other hand, a history of similar suggestions which reoccur regularly over time should be examined carefully to determine if they are indicative of a trend. That is especially the case if there are subtle variations occurring in each suggestion, but the most important thing to look for is increasing volume over time.

If you have access to historical suggestion data at your institution, it is instructive to look at suggestion volumes with respect to Internet banking. If you plot the aggregate number of ideas against time, the likely pattern is shown in Figure 5.2. It will likely be no surprise to

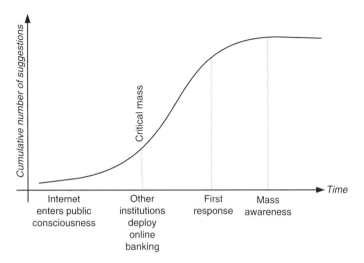

Figure 5.2   Aggregate ideas for online banking

discover that here, again, we have another S-curve. S-curves are everywhere in innovation science, actually.

Anyway, if yours is a typical institution, the first 'brainwave' from customers would have arrived in 1993 or 1994, just as the Internet began to enter the popular consciousness of many people. These well-meaning individuals would have done something that very few bankers did at the time: connect the dots between the rise of the Internet and the popularity of bank self-service. A few years later, someone local to your institution might actually have deployed a rudimentary Internet banking offering. Customers are observant, and often more aware of what is going on in the market than bankers themselves. A swiftly increasing flow of suggestions would have been the result.

Such an increase is an example of a typical innovation critical mass point. The dynamics are the same as the ones we've already covered in our examination of innovation theory: some customers adopt Internet banking, and tell others of their positive experiences. If customers cannot get online banking from their current provider, they will first ask for it. And then, if it is not forthcoming, they will leave. This is an important point. Detecting a critical mass point almost certainly means there is a trend occurring, and it would be wise to consider whether taking active steps to do something is necessary. That, of course, is the point of futurecasting.

Eventually, whatever appropriate response to the online banking idea is implemented, the flow of suggestions begins to decline. They still arrive for a while because knowledge of whatever-it-is takes time to permeate the market. And eventually they stop altogether, because customers are fully aware of the online offer and make their choice whether to adopt or not.

When you see the flow of similar ideas begin to follow an S-curve, it is an individual-level signal that should trigger futurecasting activity.

Innovation clusters and innovation antibodies

It is useful, also, to examine *where* innovative ideas are coming from. It is not atypical to find a group which submits far more suggestions than average. Such groups are a hidden treasure because they are typically composed of individuals with relatively high innovativeness compared with their peers. They will likely be innovators or early adopters, so will be highly amenable to receipt of messages concerning the innovation agenda.

In the early days of an innovation programme, at the inventing or championing stage for example, money is tight, but more importantly, so is time. One simply doesn't have the runway available to pursue innovations where there isn't at least an inherent appetite to do things differently. It is highly likely that a group with a greater than average output of ideas will also have a greater than average predilection to adopt new ideas as well. Targeting such groups is a shortcut to getting those first few wins that set an innovation programme on its path to success.

There is another reason to analyse the flow of ideas by a business group, and that is to find groups with *below* average ideas volume. What circumstances cause a group to give out fewer ideas than their colleagues elsewhere in the business?

Below average volume is often the result of a cultural imperative driven top-down. In one institution I won't name, front-line counter staff are actually discouraged from submitting their ideas. The objection of line management is that 'they are there to serve customers, not to be innovative'. Anything that takes the counter staff away from the core activity of dealing with branch queues is a negative.

But an official edict is not the only reason for reduced idea flow. Sometimes there is a senior leader who demonstrates from his or her behaviour that innovation is 'nice to have' rather than a critical determinant of forward business success. New ideas are ignored, or at best given only a cursory examination. Over time, staff learn not to bother.

Regardless of the reason, an innovation programme in the early stages should avoid groups with low idea volumes. The effort involved in fixing the problem is best delayed until the programme is secure in the managing stage, where it is properly connected to decent results.

Deduplication

Once various trends have been identified in the raw ideas data, it then becomes necessary to prepare the ideas for further evaluation. The biggest piece of work involved in doing this is working out which are similar enough to each other that they can be treated as a single idea. This is much more complicated than it seems, because one needs to compare each new idea against the *entire history* of ideas in the database.

There are several possibilities for each new idea as it arrives. The first is that it is completely original and has never been seen previously. Such ideas are assigned immediately to the scoring activity.

The second possibility is that the idea is not original and has previously been scored. What happens next depends on how well the idea was scored relative to other ideas that arrived. If the original idea achieved an approximately average score compared with all others that have arrived, the new idea should be linked to the existing one, so that they can be treated together subsequently. If, on the other hand, the original idea achieved a relatively worse score than average, what happens next depends on how often the idea has previously been raised. Clearly, an idea that scores poorly, yet is consistently put forward, can warrant further consideration if only because there is demonstrated demand. In such an instance, there is a case to be made for putting the entire group of ideas through the scoring process again. And if the idea is already being progressed through the scoring process and (subsequently) the innovation phase, joining the idea to the original one is the correct course of action so both may be progressed simultaneously.

However, none of this is simple, since ideas rarely come packaged conveniently in such a way that it is easy to identify similarities between them. And with greater ideas volume, the task becomes harder, especially as the ideas database grows.

To address this, it is necessary to have a robust keyword searching capability in the ideas management system. And when a new idea arrives, rigorous rules should be set up to ensure the correct keywords are assigned to each idea. In many organisations, there is a team that is responsible for doing this, but increasingly, end-users are able to do it themselves. In systems with such self-service capabilities, an automated search function is usually provided that makes the task easier.

In any event, once the new ideas have been sorted, analysed, and deduplicated, it is time to send them on to the next stage of the ideation process: scoring them.

5.4   SCORING

Scoring is, perhaps, the most critical part of the ideation phase after idea creation itself. It is the mechanism that determines the disposition of a particular idea, whether that be to progress it through the innovation phase, hold on to it for reconsideration later, or kill it off entirely.

Scoring is a technique that allows large volumes of ideas to be sifted quickly to find those gems which will be the main meat of the phases that follow. One is seeking, with scoring, to get an early reading on the quality and relevance of an idea *without* spending too much time (and money) in the process.

The basic procedure involved is to answer a set of questions about the idea, assigning a score to each of the questions. Then, the scores are added up and compared with those of all other innovations presently being considered. Because we know how many ideas need to go forward to the next stage (innovation) in order to fill out an innovation portfolio, the score is set at a level which enables sufficient volume of ideas to flow through to the next stage. We will come back to the question of setting this score shortly.

Now, the simple question-set methodology I've just described works at a high level, but lacks sophistication. One problem is that it doesn't recognise the fact that some business units will have different priorities from others. Often, an innovation which is exceptionally attractive to one business unit might make no sense at all to another, so it is necessary to adjust the scoring system to accommodate this. The way to do this is to add a weighting mechanism to the score. Essentially, one changes the importance of the individual components of the score with reference to the importance of each to the business unit under question.

There is another problem with this basic approach as well: the quality of the scoring is absolutely dependent on *who* is doing it. Obviously, a small team cannot be expert in everything, so it is unreasonable to expect the innovators to do all the scoring and get it right all the time. Neither can it be expected that the person who raises the idea will have perfect success either: so many of the best ideas have come from non-experts outside particular business lines. The only real answer is to refer it to an evaluator network – a group of people who are willing and able to evaluate ideas, and do so from within particular business units. I will come back to this point in a moment.

The scoring instrument

At the heart of idea scoring is a simple set of questions. Every question contributes to an overall score, which is then used to determine what will happen to the idea.

Scoring instruments can range from very simple, to very complex. However, when designing the instrument, one thing should be remembered: the people who will be using it to evaluate ideas are unlikely to be doing so full time. They are giving up their time to help the innovation agenda: too big an ask in terms of complicated scoring will cause them to avoid participation at all, or result in a massive backlog which cannot be easily cleared. In general, it is therefore sensible to ask for as little effort as possible, consistent with getting enough information to actually make a decision.

Table 5.1 is a simple scoring instrument that might be used to grade ideas. For each idea, you would answer either 'yes', 'maybe', or 'no' to each question. For each yes, assign 2 points, for each maybe, 1 point, and no points at all for no.

This scoring system results in a range of possible scores from 1 to 12 points, and can be completed very easily by evaluators. The problem, of course, is that it doesn't account very well for the range of possible innovations that might arise, and neither does it deal with the different priorities of various business groups. Let's consider a hypothetical incremental improvement now as an example.

Suppose our institution – let's call it Catch-up Bank – has a paper-based process for accepting address changes from customers. The paper-based process is quite expensive to run, but it has been working for years, and most of the bugs have been worked out of it. The problem is that customers want to be able to use online banking to notify of an address change, and practically everyone else already offers the capability. Considering this innovation in the light of our simple scoring instrument lets us find out whether it ought to be considered further.

Table 5.1   Simple scoring instrument

1	Is it aligned with our strategy?	Innovations which are unaligned with the existing strategy of an institution are much harder to execute. Usually, it makes sense to kill ideas which are at odds with strategy
2	Is it something that is consistent with what we do already?	Do we have the existing attitudes, values, and beliefs to make this idea a reality? If an idea is completely inconsistent with the values of an organisation, it will normally not be something that can be implanted
3	Is there a market or internal opportunity we can exploit?	Does the idea have a reasonable potential available that we can exploit? Will it makes sense for us to pursue this idea given what we will have to invest to make it go?
4	Is it feasible for us to implement the idea?	Technically, culturally, or environmentally, do we have, or can we get hold of, everything we need to make the idea a reality?
5	Will it give us some competitive advantage?	If we do this, will we be able to compete more effectively compared with others in our markets?
6	Can we do it with existing resources?	Is it possible to do this idea with what we have at the moment? Or will we need to acquire new capabilities and resources?

For question one, the answer is almost certainly yes, accepting online address change is aligned with strategy. Few banks are not interested in moving as much of their routine day-to-day processing to self-service as possible. So this question scores 2 points.

For question two, the answer is probably maybe. Our institution has paper-based processes in place at present, and there might be a pile of systems and people rework necessary to make an electronic process work. There might even be whole rooms of people whose jobs will now be on the line. And if this is the first time we've tried to automate a paper-based process, there will no doubt be many political and technical hurdles to get over. The thing is, we just don't know. Because the answer is a maybe, this question gets 1 point.

For question three, I'd probably say the answer is maybe. There is a cost saving to be made, of course, but we don't necessarily know how much it will cost to make all the back-office changes we would need to support the work. Without doing more numbers, it is impossible to know if this is an internal opportunity we would want to exploit. Another 1 point.

With feasibility at question four, the answer is almost certainly yes. We don't have a good handle on *what* it would take to implement the address change, but it is certain that given enough resources our institution could do it. The real question is whether the cost versus benefits case is there to justify the work. Anyway, we give this question 2 points.

Question five concerns what everyone else is doing. Everyone but Catch-up is doing online address change already. So the answer to this question is no, for 0 points.

And finally, question six has to do with the ability to do it from existing budgets. Now, this is an unknowable cost question again, but there is certainly an online banking development budget. Money is available, but we just don't know whether we have *enough*. So the answer to this question, again, is maybe for 1 point.

When you add all that up, this idea comes out with 6 points. Just about average. That's OK, but the fact of the matter is, with any large volume of ideas, the average ones will never get done.

Let's compare the same scoring for Catch-up Bank, but using a clever NFC-based mobile phone banking application. NFC lets you make contactless payments at any merchant that accepts them, so you can just wave your phone at a reader to pay for small purchases. At the time of writing, this is widely adopted in Japan, but not so much in other countries. Catch-up Bank, if it deployed NFC, would likely be doing something revolutionary. It may, even, be a disruptive innovation that affects competitors.

Question 1: It is *so* aligned with strategy. Not only has Catch-up caught up, they are outpacing the competition. The score is 2 points.

Question 2: Consistency. This is not at all consistent with what is done presently, and no doubt there will be lots of politics to get through. Many people won't 'get' mobile payments, and frankly, will be bothered by the fact that ordinary card payments will be disrupted. This is an innovation with the potential to damage existing business lines, so it gets no points at all.

Question 3: Is there a market? Most certainly there is, because studies have shown that consumers value mobile phone-based contactless payments highly. In Japan, a large number of handsets already have the feature, and it is widely used. In London, a trial found that more than 78% of people liked the service in 2008 [53]. And in France, during a similar trial, they got very high levels of acceptance as well. If Catch-up Bank did this innovation, it would certainly expand their payments business, maybe not short term, but over time. This question gets 2 points.

Question 4: Is it feasible to implement? Well, it is new technology, but there would be a lot of support from telecommunications providers who would no doubt control the handset. On the other hand, Catch-up Bank doesn't have the experience of doing anything similar, which makes this a more risky proposition. So the answer to this question is maybe, for 1 point.

Question 5: Competitive advantage. Well, no one else is doing it, so there ought to be some. 2 points.

Question 6: Can it be done with existing resources? Almost certainly not. New skills, technologies, and capabilities will have to be acquired. Or if it is going to be run externally, a vendor will have to be found that can do it. 0 points.

The total for Catch-up Bank mobile phone payments is 7 points, also just above average.

So, in other words, two innovations, one extremely incremental and the other pretty revolutionary, perhaps even disruptive, have come out almost the same. That may be OK at a high level, but what is really needed is a more advanced scoring instrument that gives us a bit more resolution in the results (Table 5.2). We need to be able to distinguish a few more factors before we can really make any statements with respect to whether this is a good idea or not.

The instrument in Table 5.3 returns a score between 0 and 12 points. Let us now look again at our two innovations and see how they fare once we start asking for all this new information. To calculate the overall score, we compute an average for each group of questions, and add up the results. Once again, a yes is worth 2 points, a maybe is worth 1 point, and a no is worth nothing. An average idea, then, will have a score of around 16 points.

With this instrument, the scores have moved much wider apart in our evaluations of each innovation. The NFC innovation is now very much below average, which would be somewhere

Table 5.2   A more sophisticated scoring instrument

Strategic fit	1	Do we have a work stream in progress already that is related to this idea?
	2	If there is a strategic work stream already, will this idea significantly enhance it?
Competitive advantage	3	Will this give us a better customer experience?
	4	Will it reduce our costs?
	5	Will it differentiate us from our competitors?
Market attractiveness	6	Will more customers join the bank if we do this?
	7	Is this a market we are already in, or would like to be in?
	8	If we do this, will it make an existing market bigger?
	9	Is it unique to us?
Core competencies	10	Can we leverage skills in things we are already good at doing to make this idea work?
Technical feasibility	11	Is this a business or technology we understand well?
	12	Do we have a similar business or technology in place already that we can use to make this idea work?
	13	Do we have an existing track record of success in this area?
Financial rewards	14	If we did this idea, would there be any noticeable effect on the annual results?
	15	Do we control all the factors that would stop us making a return on the investment?
	16	Are the returns expected to be hard numbers (as opposed to soft benefits such as productivity enhancements)?

Table 5.3 Two innovations with revised scoring instrument

		Online address change	Average score	NFC mobile payments	Average score
Strategic fit	1	2 points: online banking would be an ideal place for this to start, even if it has other implications elsewhere	Average score = 1.0	0 points: there is nothing presently in train, in fact the business is working hard just to work out what to do with contactless plastic cards	Average score = 0.0
	2	0 points: just changing an address online isn't really going to be a big strategic enabler		0 points: we don't have a programme	
Competitive advantage	3	2 points: the customer experience is improved by this innovation	Average score = 1.33	2 points: the customer experience is enhanced because customers will have a new way to pay	Average score = 1.33
	4	2 points: taking away all the paper will certainly reduce costs		0 points: it is likely, at least in the beginning, that this innovation will increase rather than reduce costs	
	5	0 points: everyone else is already doing address change – no differentiation here		2 points: first-to-market, and possibly first-mover, advantage is available	
Market attractiveness	6	1 point: it is possible that some customers will join us because they can change their address online, but this not certain	Average score = 0.75	2 points: a segment of customers is highly likely to switch banks to get this functionality	Average score = 1.75
	7	2 points: we are already doing online operations, this is an enhancement		1 point: we already do payments, but there will be reaction from the cards people about volume reduction if we do this	
	8	0 points: an address change doesn't make the number of online bankers increase across the market		2 points: there is presently not a market – Catch-up Bank will be first	
Core competence	9	0 points: we are last to market	Average score = 1.0	2 points: we are first to market	Average score = 0.0
	10	2 points: we have good experience with online banking, which should be transferable to this idea		0 points: everything will have to be designed from the ground up, and we have no people with experience in this new technology	
Technical feasibility	11	1 point: we understand the online space well, but the back-office stuff could be an issue	Average score = 1.66	0 points: we have no experience at all with this technology or business	Average score = 0.0
	12	2 points: everything should be in place already – this is an enhancement		0 points: there is nothing in place today, we would have to build everything from the ground up	
	13	2 points: we launched online banking, and customers liked it		0 points: we have no track record with mobile at this stage	

(continued)

Table 5.3   *(Continued)*

		Online address change	Average score = 1.33	NFC mobile payments	Average score = 1.33
Financial rewards	14	0 points: it's an address change, does anyone imagine it would be significant to the results?		1 point: not initially, but over time, this could be significant	
	15	2 points: everything we need to make this a success is under our direct control		1 point: there are third parties such as handset manufacturers and telecommunications providers to consider – this could be managed with contractual instruments, perhaps	
	16	2 points: the returns will be cost savings based on reduction of paper-based systems		2 points: increased card value and new customers should make this a profitable business in the next few years	
Total Score		**7.07**		**4.41**	

around 6 given the averaging system employed here. Address change, on the other hand, is around about the middle of the range. Neither idea, however, scores high enough to be considered immediately for implementation (we will see why in a little bit). NFC, on the other hand, is getting close to the level where we would throw it out altogether. Probably, though, we would keep both ideas active in case business circumstances changed.

That, of course, brings us to the next question: how do you incorporate business priorities into a scoring system so the scores reflect what the business – the ones from whom the money will have to be won eventually – actually find important?

Weightings

The answer is to weight each question group with some numerical measure that represents the importance business units place on the question. The simplest way is to ask each business unit to rate, on a scale of 1 to 10, how important they think each of the five question groups is, but this introduces problems because it then becomes impossible to compare scores across business groups: one might score tens for every characteristic, whilst the others put ones and twos.

A better method is to ask business units to distribute a number of points among each category – with more points going to the categories of most importance. Since we have six categories in each of our instruments, a good method is to distribute 12 points, with the caveat that each category must get at least one point.

Continuing with our example from Catch-up Bank, let us now imagine we have collected weightings from both online banking and cards and payments business groups. Their hypothetical answers to the weightings questions are shown in Table 5.4.

The application of weightings makes it too hard to guess what an average score is likely to be (without having a body of scores showing up from which to calculate), but it does let us see how the various innovations would be scored by each business unit. This is shown in Table 5.5.

Table 5.4 Hypothetical weightings for two business groups

	Online banking		Cards and payments	
	Points	Weight	Points	Weight
Strategic fit	2	$2 \div 12 = 0.16$	4	$4 \div 12 = 0.33$
Competitive advantage	4	$4 \div 12 = 0.33$	1	$1 \div 12 = 0.08$
Market attractiveness	2	$2 \div 12 = 0.16$	2	$2 \div 12 = 0.16$
Core competency	1	$1 \div 12 = 0.08$	1	$1 \div 12 = 0.08$
Technical feasibility	1	$1 \div 12 = 0.08$	1	$1 \div 12 = 0.08$
Financial rewards	2	$2 \div 12 = 0.16$	4	$4 \div 12 = 0.33$

Examining this table illustrates how overall business priorities can affect the scores of a particular innovation. When the NFC innovation was evaluated against the priorities of the cards and payments business, it scored the lowest. But when the same innovation was compared with the priorities of the online channel, it scored the highest.

This table is a little bit disingenuous, however, because the initial scores we created for our hypothetical innovations were the same (Table 5.3), no matter which business unit's priorities we weighted them with. In reality, the initial scores will also be different.

The obvious implication: the scoring needs to be done by the business at whom the idea is directed.

Evaluator networks

No matter how much we might wish it to be different, it is impossible for an innovator to ever be sufficiently expert that he or she can successfully score every idea that comes along. The results for scoring shown in Table 5.5 are illustrative of this. Why on earth would the payments business be less interested in NFC than the online business? The answer is that we didn't get scores from the actual business units: our hypothetical innovation team just made up their own answers. To fix this, it is necessary to rope in subject matter experts *from the businesses themselves*.

Table 5.5 Weighted scores for two innovations

	Online banking		Cards and payments	
	Address change	NFC payments	Address change	NFC payments
Strategic fit	$1.00 \times 0.16 = 0.16$	$0.00 \times 0.16 = 0.00$	$1.00 \times 0.33 = 0.33$	$0.00 \times 0.33 = 0.00$
Competitive advantage	$1.33 \times 0.33 = 0.44$	$1.33 \times 0.33 = 0.99$	$1.33 \times 0.08 = 0.11$	$1.33 \times 0.08 = 0.24$
Market attractiveness	$0.75 \times 0.16 = 0.12$	$1.75 \times 0.16 = 0.12$	$0.75 \times 0.16 = 0.12$	$1.75 \times 0.16 = 0.28$
Core competency	$1.00 \times 0.08 = 0.08$	$0.00 \times 0.08 = 0.00$	$1.00 \times 0.08 = 0.08$	$0.00 \times 0.08 = 0.00$
Technical feasibility	$1.66 \times 0.08 = 0.13$	$0.00 \times 0.08 = 0.00$	$1.66 \times 0.08 = 0.13$	$0.00 \times 0.08 = 0.00$
Financial rewards	$1.33 \times 0.16 = 0.22$	$1.33 \times 0.16 = 0.22$	$1.33 \times 0.33 = 0.44$	$1.33 \times 0.33 = 0.44$
	1.15	1.33	1.21	0.96

Building an evaluator network – a group of people that the innovation team can go to on an ad-hoc basis to get an evaluation of an idea – is critical. These should be people with enough seniority to have an idea of the strategic pictures of their business units, yet not so senior that they control the actual budgets that would implement the innovation.

You can never have too many people in this network. Individuals change jobs, or otherwise become unable to perform the evaluation function. Then, too, there is every chance there could be too many ideas to send to a single individual, no matter how simple the instrument. And sometimes, evaluators just ask to be left alone.

Evaluators, as part of the ideation process, are responsible for two things. The first is to provide timely evaluations, of course. But the second is to provide – every six months or so – their assessment of the weightings that the innovation team should use for their business unit. The reassessment of weightings ensures that ideas which didn't make it at the time of original submission are still, potentially, able to be successful down the track. Business priorities change, and by changing the weightings, automatically the scores also change.

Setting score ranges for idea destination

As with so many things in life (such as the classification of adopters by innovativeness, as we saw in Chapter 2), the distribution of scores coming from a screening instrument will approach normality over time. A normal distribution is the familiar bell-shaped curve with an average at the peak in the middle, and edges that tail off. The normality of idea scores provides us with a convenient way of deciding what to do with ideas, and is shown in Figure 5.3.

Most ideas arriving are likely to be 'average', and about 68% will be within the upper and lower boundary of one standard deviation, which is a convenient way of defining the upper and lower bounds of an average suggestion. An average idea is kept active, in case it becomes important later. In the meantime, though, ideas just sit around waiting for an evaluator to recalibrate the weightings for a particular business line. When such recalibration occurs, the idea may move from its average position and warrant further consideration.

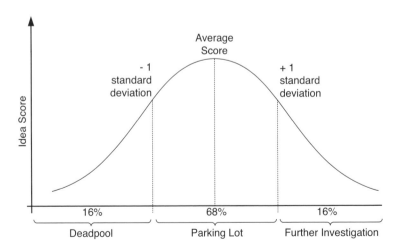

Figure 5.3 Disposition of ideas

I call the range of scores between one and minus one standard deviation the 'parking lot' in the diagram, because ideas in this range will likely be sitting around for a while.

Any idea above the average range, which will be around 16% of the total (assuming we continue with treating one standard deviation as the boundary condition), is advanced immediately to the next stage of the ideation process. These are ideas which evaluators have decided are substantially better than normal, and are ones that ought to be considered more carefully.

On the other hand, any idea which is below the average range is killed immediately, consigned to the 'deadpool'. The origins of this term are well embedded in the start-up community, who themselves borrowed it from a comic book hero. I use the term because these are ideas which are going to be dropped – they will likely never be good enough to progress.

Parking lots and deadpools

It is probably obvious that an idea which fits into the deadpool category ought to be abandoned immediately. But doesn't leaving 68% or so of ideas just floating impose a significant load on the idea management system? Well, yes it does. So it is tempting, once there is a significant idea flow, to abandon those ideas which don't lead directly to the innovation phase. But this is usually a mistake.

The strategic cycles of institutions mean that quite often great things which aren't appropriate right now become so in the future. For example, an evaluator might downgrade an idea right now because all budgets have been spent. Had they had a chance to evaluate it again in the future when money was available, it might have scored sufficiently highly to be progressed.

Of course this presents a difficulty, as with any significant ideas volume, in that it is impossible to go back and review each on a regular basis. Luckily, if you have followed the advice in the section on scoring systems, you can see the answer already: it has to do with the weightings assigned to particular business groups. When the weightings are re-evaluated for each business unit, the result is that all ideas in the parking lot will have their scores changed. An idea which was borderline before, might move into either the deadpool or further consideration segments. Or it might still be average.

Because an idea can be average enough to never move, regardless of any change to the weightings from the relevant business units, it is important that a mechanism be implemented for 'timing out' the idea. If an idea has lasted more than a few budgetary cycles without moving to the deadpool or to further consideration, it is usually time to deadpool it anyway.

It is also important to re-evaluate items in the deadpool as well. What triggers such an event? The main trigger to watch out for is that the idea continually arrives from multiple places independently. In these cases, there can be merit in sending the idea through the scoring process again.

Incremental escape hatch

Quite often, an idea will score highly, but be a very minor change. Other times, it will be a minor change, but score somewhere above average. These are changes which make sense to make, because they can be done with very little effort. But going through the rest of ideation, the whole innovation and lengthy execution phase for them would probably cost more than they are worth.

Of course, one doesn't want to just ignore these ideas altogether, because when you add them all together, they start to mount up. And, in fact, they are the lifeblood of any innovation strategy which features incremental innovations. Since incrementalism is so important for at least the first three capabilities of an innovation team (see Chapter 3), something has to be done with average, small, ideas. It is my suggestion, therefore, that an escape hatch is implemented in the scoring stage: a way that small ideas can get implemented immediately.

Escape hatch ideas are referred directly to the person who can do something about them. One continues to track the idea, but leaves it to whoever is able to make the change to do so. Sometimes they will do nothing at all. Perhaps the press of other work prohibits them devoting the time, or maybe the change, actually, is so minor it doesn't make financial sense to progress it. In these instances, the idea will time out to deadpool automatically after it has been sitting around for a few budgetary cycles. Though this sounds wasteful, it is not. Innovators *could* spend the time influencing whoever it is to make something happen, but they need to put their time where they get the most return. Forcing a small change down the throat of someone who isn't really all that interested isn't the way to do that.

However, more often than not, a good idea – coupled with a way for the originator and his or her peers to watch what happens with it – will get implemented with alacrity. It sends completely the wrong message when something simple to change isn't fixed once suggested: most managers will be very wary of sending such messages if they don't have to. This, incidentally, is another reason why the ideas management system must be able to show idea originators what the status of their idea is: it makes it impossible for those who execute the change to ignore the idea. Even better is the situation where multiple people (perhaps the peers of the originator) can see that status.

Having all ideas – and their status – available for everyone to review is very powerful. When something *does* get done, it sends a signal that individuals can make a difference. And when things *don't*, the effect is to name and shame the managers involved. An innovation team can get a lot done when external stakeholders know they will look bad if they don't participate.

Wisdom of crowds scoring

A crowd is a very, very powerful force in organisations. Groups routinely form around lots of things: gossip at the water-cooler, a project, or (not surprisingly) a great idea. These are groups that can make things happen, if the right circumstances are created to enable them to do so. For example, as I've just intimated, a group forming around a small idea can be enough to motivate a manager to make a change that otherwise might look inconsequential. Groups are a very democratic way to cause things to happen.

The power of groups, especially larger ones, has another powerful benefit: quite often, a crowd will produce a better insight than an expert evaluator. A single expert, of course, makes their evaluations based on the values and insights they personally have. And, obviously, a crowd makes the same evaluation from the perspective of multiple views at once. Crowds, then, will often approximate the true value of an idea much more accurately than an evaluator.

Because crowd-based evaluation is so valuable, many ideas management systems implement a system of 'voting' on ideas. This enables a crowd to indicate, at a very coarse level, how good it thinks an idea is. Such voting is a very interesting additional data point for an innovator. If, for example, an evaluator scores the idea as average, but 100 people vote positively for the suggestion, it is usually cause to move the idea forward no matter how it scores. It is not that the evaluator is wrong, only that their perspective on the situation could be skewed somewhere left of true value.

Of course, crowds can sometimes be wrong as well. Evaluators will typically have expert knowledge they apply to the evaluation: the strategy of their business group, for example, or deep knowledge of the systems or processes that have to change. A crowd will not often have this level of deep insight.

In order to resolve such uncertainty, one moves the idea through the next stages in the process despite its lower score from the evaluator. From a pipeline perspective, doing a little more investigation of an idea is hardly going to cost all that much more, and the idea itself may be worth a great deal, if implemented. Finding out is a worthwhile investment.

Voting isn't the only kind of wisdom of crowds scoring possible, of course. There is quite a lot of value, for instance, in enabling the crowd to use the whole scoring instrument in their own right. This gives a much finer level of detail than simple voting, which can be illustrative if only to indicate how passionate people are about the idea: it takes a bit more effort to fully score an idea than to vote on it, and if many people go ahead and do it, well, there you have an idea the crowd likes. Normally, in this circumstance, you would keep the crowd and expert evaluator's score separate. One needs both points of view before making the decision about whether to proceed.

5.5   CUSTOMER INSIGHT

Once you have an idea which gets through initial evaluation, it is time to go to end-users or customers and get a sense of whether this is something that might fly. At this point, we are interested in getting just a little bit more information that helps us make a go/no-go decision. And, to do so, we are probably going to have to spend a little bit of money and time.

Until this point, the idea has had a pretty light touch. It may have been scored by an evaluator, and perhaps a crowd has looked at it and given it thumbs up. What has *not* yet happened, however, is asking the people who will buy the innovation whether it is something they want or not. Clearly, it doesn't make sense to invest substantially in an idea in later phases of futureproofing without knowing this.

But you'd be surprised at how many innovation teams actually fail to ask their customers early enough if the idea is something they are interested in. What usually happens is that an idea gets a great score, and innovators somehow modify their thinking to imagine that if an *evaluator* likes the idea, the end customer will as well.

Then, when significant sums have been spent on the idea to get it in front of stakeholders for funding, the customer question raises its ugly head and there is no ready answer. When you are doing something truly new that needs money from a stakeholder, there is *no point* asking them to take a huge gamble that something might pay off. You need to be able to prove there is at least a reasonable chance the innovation will generate value.

Traditionally, institutions have used very expensive means to get to customer insight, such as focus groups. That is why you so rarely see innovation teams doing insight this early in the process. Far better, if you are going to invest in expensive panel research, that it be done when the number of ideas is very, very small, some time just before the money pitch to stakeholders. That way you can spend as little as possible until as late as possible. Right?

Wrong. Focus groups and panel research *are* expensive. So are complicated customer surveys and face-to-face interviews. You have to go out and find the customers, then ask them the right questions, and *then* collate the results, probably with the help of a statistician. But these are all methods designed to get deep insight into a specific concept. What we are after here is *light touch* insight into *many* ideas. There are actually several ways to do this, but all involve reaching out to customers (or end-users, if it is an internally facing innovation).

The first is a traditional research approach such as a focus group. But instead of dealing with one or two concepts in depth, you present many at once with just a few questions for each. You would then schedule multiple, recurring sessions so that a pipeline of highly scored ideas can be moved through to the innovation phase in a regular manner.

But the Internet has made doing idea screening so much easier. Today, there are companies that specialise in taking ideas and screening them for you in bulk. They use the Internet's ability to reach panels of customers in near real time, at a very, very low cost per idea. Such idea-screening organisations are immensely helpful to innovators: they remove the difficulty of finding the right consumer, presenting them with questions, and getting results. The innovation team only has to forward ideas scoring highly enough to such organisations and wait for the results to come back. My suggestion is that you find a company doing this kind of work and hire them for customer insight. Do a search in Google for Idea Screening or New Product Screening to find someone with an office locally.

There is another way to get customer insight as well: run simple experiments. Experimentation is an excellent way to find out what customers think, and can usually be done relatively inexpensively. Bank of America, famously, set up a programme that used its branches as micro-laboratories to study new customer experience innovations [54]. The idea was to take a large number of ideas for branch experience improvements, and try them quickly and often.

With this environment Bank of America experimented with queuing systems, kiosks, viewing screens to entertain customers in the queues, and a large number of other innovations. They found, not surprisingly, a lot of things that enhanced customer experiences which were later copied by other banks. For example, experiments looking at perceived customer waiting time found customers entertained with video screens thought they had been waiting in a queue a shorter time than customers without such screens.

Bank of America is not the only financial services organisation that uses experimentation as a way of getting new customer insight before taking major ideas through to funding. Advanta, the largest issuer of business credit cards in the United States, does so as well. I had the chance to meet with Dennis Alter, the CEO of Advanta, on an occasion when he was visiting London, and spent an interesting few hours with him hearing how his institution decided to be innovative and then just did it. It was an occasion that underlined for me the criticality of CEO involvement in innovation. When the CEO says innovation matters, it does. So many organisations say innovation matters, but fail to provide the strategic rationale – from the top table downwards – as to *why*.

Advanta is an organisation that has launched a number of very forward-looking innovations in recent times. In late 2007 it created IdeaBlob, a social media site rather like that launched by Vancity with ChangeEverything (see Chapter 3). But Advanta's effort specifically targets their customer demographic: small business owners. The site accepts interesting ideas, and members get to vote on the best. Every month, Advanta gives the top idea $10,000. Then they launched a Kiva.org co-branded card. We've also looked at Kiva.org in this book, and once again, Advanta touched an unserved desire in its consumer base: socially aware giving whilst driving forward a small business.

These are innovations driven out the door because the CEO decided Advanta would be innovative, created a strategic rationale for doing so, and then made innovation important by driving the behaviour downwards. That is not what happens in most organisations, of course, and most innovation programmes have to earn the right to the CEO's ear by growing through the Five Capability Model I described in Chapter 3.

When you have a CEO who wants things to be innovative, and is personally committed to make it happen, the Five Capability Model gets a shortcut. However, even a CEO can't come up with great ideas 100% of the time, and certainly not in the volume needed to make lasting changes in the business. So Advanta created a programme it calls 3D – essentially a direct mail laboratory – where it can try customer innovations quickly and easily.

Advanta acquires new customers using direct marketing methods. The problem with this says Jim Shreero, the executive leading 3D, was that it was taking months for a campaign to go from conception to the customer's letterbox. It made it impossible to do any experimentation at all. The cost and time to get any direct mail innovation out the door simply made it impossible to turn things around quickly enough.

Shreero, a long-time employee at Advanta, was moved to running 3D after some years as the institution's chief accounting officer. Though this seems a surprising job for an accounting person, it turned out to be a clever and insightful appointment. The problem before 3D was all the process and cost involved in getting a campaign from idea to customer. Who better than an accountant with deep insight into this process to unwind it for the purposes of experimentation?

Typically, the mail campaigns created by Advanta were rather conventional. But both Alter and Shreero believed that experimentation could lead them to much greater customer insight, and enable them to target their mailings to much smaller niche demographics. So, Shreero eliminated all the process surrounding new campaigns. He created light-touch systems that would enable Advanta to do small, highly targeted mail runs to small groups. And he made sure to encourage the people involved to think outside the box. All this was designed to have turnarounds of days, rather than weeks. A radical change from what existed previously.

3D let Advanta get an idea out the door in low volumes very quickly. This made it possible to try new ideas from a low cost base. What might the effect be of changing the colour on a mailing? What if black models rather than white ones were used in the creative imagery? Could there be a particular set of messages that resulted in a better return rate?

Shreero and his team started dreaming up any and every bizarre combination of attributes and features for campaigns. Many of these were tested with real customers. And the results were surprising. Says Shreero, 'we found we could gain insights into the customer that ordinary market research was never able to give us. We might discover a particular demographic responded well to a particular colour or image when conventional marketing rules told us it would never work.' By experimenting with customer insight in this way, Advanta has been able to acquire new customers that traditional mailing lists would never have allowed it to reach.

5.6   CUSTOMER CO-CREATION

Experimentation is a great way to get insight into customer needs and wants, and certainly it has worked for Advanta. But there is another way to involve customers in the ideation process, one that is getting increasing traction with many firms: customer co-creation. This is an emerging technique at the time of writing, and largely replaces the whole ideation process we've been talking about in this chapter. The idea is that you engage with customers in the development of new ideas, and have them participate through the whole process.

Customers tell you what new things they would like to see, and wisdom-of-crowds methods are often used to select the best ideas. Then, as it comes time to develop the idea for market, customers are critically involved in most of the decisions which shape the idea.

One of the posterchild organisations for customer co-creation is t-shirt company Threadless [55]. Started in 2000 by some Chicago-based designers, it is a company that releases up to four new designs per week, and it has never once had a flop. The reason? The designs are submitted by customers who work together in a community. Customers score the best designs, which then go to production. Because the scoring indicates purchase intent, Threadless never overproduces inventory. And the originator of each of the four best designs each week gets a prize of $1000. Therefore, for a cost of $1000, Threadless is able to produce a design, get customer insight, and forecast production. Obviously, the model is unparalleled from a cost basis, even if you follow all the advice in this book and take out as much cost from the ideation process as possible.

In financial services, there have been relatively few examples of customer co-creation, but things are starting to change. The best example I've found, to date, happens annually at the Royal Bank of Canada.

5.7   CASE STUDY: ROYAL BANK OF CANADA'S NEXT GREAT INNOVATOR CHALLENGE

At Royal Bank of Canada (RBC), there is decided focus on innovation as a competitive enabler. Avi Pollock, Head of Applied Innovation at the bank, is an early proponent of customer co-creation, and his team was instrumental in the creation of the 'RBC Next Great Innovator Challenge' (NGI), a competition aimed at getting college age students to help the bank create new products, processes, or concepts for its customers.

NGI was created simultaneously with the bank's Innovation Council, a group of senior leaders championing innovation across the enterprise and controlling a pot of seed money earmarked for innovation opportunities. Says Pollock, 'NGI was discussed at the first meeting of the Council. The focus was on the future of banking: what is the next generation of client going to want? And how could the bank best tap into these new needs?'

The Council chose to launch its competition to see if this new generation of customers could usefully help it create successful products and services targeting this group. An online format was decided, and the Innovator's Challenge quickly began to shape.

Surprisingly, there were few objections to this radical departure from traditional new product development processes. This is atypical in banks facing the prospect of doing something truly new, of course. But, as Pollock recalls, 'Many of the senior leaders from the IT, marketing and banking organizations are members of the Council. Anyone who could possibly object was actually part of the idea in the first place.'

In fact, the only point generating even sporadic contention was whether reaching into universities rather than high schools would provide better ideas and insights from the target demographic. Some were concerned that university students, being relatively mature, might not reflect the new Gen-Y demographic adequately. If you're trying to build the future of banking, it was thought, you really needed to touch the younger generation which would *be* that future.

In the end, though, the Council continued with its plan to target universities for the Challenge. No one knew what kinds of entries they'd get, and there were concerns about how usable the ideas would be if they came in relatively unformed. Ultimately, however, what made the decision for the bank was the difficulty in getting to large numbers of high school students. Universities were a much easier route to a significant body of educated, potential innovators. And, of course, tertiary age students have banking products whilst kids at school don't.

So, the bank reached out to campuses across Canada and asked students to participate in the development of new concepts for the next generation. Not knowing the likely response, expectations were deliberately set low, but the bank quickly got 250 teams registering for the contest and more than 100 submissions from universities and colleges across Canada.

Of course, the quality of these were variable. Many were all over the place, but others were exceptional. Regardless of the quality, though, one of the key learnings from the exercise was the value of the customer insight it generated. Says Pollock, 'the concepts themselves were interesting. But the insights each submission gave us into our target demographic was amazing. We found out lots of things we didn't expect.'

An initial win from the first year RBC ran the Challenge was its first social media site, RBC P2P [56], a social media blog for students. It turned out to be an autonomic innovation, one that just walked out the door immediately it came to light.

Pollock recalls how it happened: 'We started to show the submissions we got from the first year's competition, and the business just sat up and said "I want to do that". We provided initial seed funding from the budget of the Innovation Council, and it was out the door in less than 5 months.'

This success led the bank to repeat the competition for a second year, and this time they got more, and higher quality, submissions than previously. Now the competition is in its third year, and submissions have just closed at the time of writing. But the benefits of the programme have been far-reaching.

In the first instance, the innovation team at RBC gets a basket of fully developed ideas every year to work with. The team takes the finished ideas and distilled concepts on road-shows around the bank, and those that generate interest get developed. The process is an excellent supplement to the technical ideation systems used in the bank to capture and investigate ideas from employees but in this case customers, potential or otherwise, do most of the work.

Then, too, the earned media and other exposure generated by the competition reinforces the image of RBC as an innovative place to work. In fact, some of the first- and second-year entrants have now joined the bank full time.

The NGI Challenge is one of the best examples of customer co-creation in financial services today. And, as Pollock says, 'the competition has not only generated new ideas, it's raised the profile of the innovation team. Everyone in the bank knows it's judging day, and the best ideas get presented to a panel of senior executives for the final decision. Then we have a gala cocktail party for the winners at which the prizes get handed out by a member of the bank's Group Executive. Everyone knows the innovation team has been doing things.'

5.8   CONCLUDING REMARKS

Whether your strategy is co-creation, or the more traditional staff suggestion scheme that translates into a fully formed ideation system, getting a handle on the creative potential of your institution is the first thing an innovation team should do.

As we've seen in this chapter, capturing the thoughts of inspired and creative people in an organisation means the innovators can get onto doing what they should be: selling propositions to stakeholders in such a way that they can fill out their innovation pipelines and generate predictable returns.

No matter how creative an innovation team is, it is highly unlikely they will be able to generate sufficient numbers of ideas – with sufficient quality – to fill out any reasonable pipeline. By engaging employees and customers in the process, though, it is not difficult at all to get to volume quickly. Most people are delighted to have the opportunity to contribute to making a difference. Having a structured ideation system provides people with that opportunity.

The question then becomes, of course, what to do with all those lovely ideas. It is to this task that we turn our attention next, as we examine the innovation phase of futureproofing.

6

The Innovation Phase

What you will find in this chapter

- The three key questions an innovation must successfully answer in order to proceed.
- Managing many ideas together as a portfolio to minimise risk.
- An explanation of the benefits of failure.
- How to sell innovations and win the money.

If you've just read the previous chapter end to end, you might be wondering when it was that innovation got to be so mechanical. Scoring systems? Deadpools and parking lots, complete with bell curves to determine where ideas should go? Wasn't innovation supposed to be creative? I'm pleased to let you know that we've now come to that part of the futureproofing process where a great deal of personal judgement and creativity is required. The innovation phase, which is the subject of this chapter, requires these talents and a great deal more besides.

It is the innovation phase that is the critical determinant of the success of an innovation team (and of course, the individual members of that team). There is usually no difficulty in getting and collecting ideas, but the circumstance are few and far between where such ideas progress without any further effort. It can happen (as we saw in Chapter 3 during our examination of autonomic innovation), but such a perfect storm of factors hardly ever occurs all at once. So, it is during the innovation phase that the real mettle of an innovation team is tested. Equipped with a load of great ideas, ones that have been examined at a high level by sponsoring business lines and by end-users or customers, the problem now becomes determining which ideas to investigate more closely. This is a decision of strategic importance.

The basic premise is that the team wants to choose ideas in such a way that the expected value of returns (across a portfolio of ideas) delivers the return on investment numbers required to support the assertion that innovation should be the best investment opportunity available to stakeholders. An expected value is the return projected to result from an innovation multiplied by the probability those returns will be achieved. When you add up the expected value of every innovation in a portfolio, the sum should be close to that required to deliver the overall number for the innovation programme.

All this leaves innovators with a problem, of course. Not all innovations are easily converted to sound business cases with real numbers attached to them. It is quite often the case that the benefits of an innovation are almost all 'soft' – productivity improvements, for example. Soft benefits are challenging for stakeholders to accept in many cases, and certainly make it more difficult to justify the overall results of an innovation programme.

This leaves innovators with two alternatives: concentrate on ideas which have hard number returns only, or, in more sophisticated teams, invent a number which can reasonably be justified to stakeholders used to dealing in hard cash. But there's another issue that innovators have to face, and that is working out the best mix of innovations they should pursue across the slices of the innovation pentagram we examined in Figure 3.1. This will vary depending on the team and the institution.

The innovation pentagram, as I've said previously, provides excellent guidance to practitioners if they want to optimise their chances of futureproofing their institution. Ideally, one would have a portfolio of innovations equally balanced across all five slices, thereby maximising the potential opportunities to make a difference to the bank. Unfortunately, however, ideas rarely arrive from the ideation phase conveniently packaged in equal distribution across this pentagram. Ideas are random, and good ones even more so. Usually what happens is that ideas arrive en masse in a few slices, leaving the figurative cupboard bare elsewhere.

Though the distribution of ideas arriving might be uneven, there is another reason why innovation tends to be concentrated in some slices over others. Each institution has its own specific competences and operational capabilities, and as a result, innovations which play to these competencies are more readily accepted. Things which are truly new-to-bank, on the other hand, require a great deal more effort.

And, too, some slices of the innovation pentagram are inherently more difficult than others. Business model and market innovation, for example, require much more effort in a typical institution than, say, experience or product innovations. The reason is that the stakes tend to be much higher, and almost always the innovations involved are revolutionary or breakthrough. As we've discussed elsewhere already, the more an innovation tends away from incrementalism, the more risky and expensive it is. Such innovations are always a harder sell.

Selling, and the preparations required to do it successfully, are the point of the innovation phase. At the moment an idea arrives from ideation, it will have been validated as relatively better than most others, have been sanity-checked by a group of stakeholders, and been subject to at least some kind of customer scrutiny or insight. The task now is to flesh out the idea in sufficient detail that stakeholders have enough information to invest. Achieving such investment is the gateway milestone to execution, where the idea will actually be implemented.

There is a minimum level of detail that is needed to commence the selling process, and this can be represented by three key questions, to which we turn next.

6.1 SHOULD WE? CAN WE? WHEN?

The three questions a practitioner must answer for any idea to have a chance of getting through the innovation phase are these: 'Should we?', 'Can we?', and, finally, 'When?'

The 'Should we?' question is one, essentially, of economics. As I've mentioned, the point of an innovation function is to make money. Most innovations, therefore, will necessarily have strong positive benefits if they are to proceed. Obviously, these will not in every case be financial, but most of the time they need to be. That's because although the main part of 'Should we?' is a business case, there are often other considerations as well, especially when the idea is genuinely unprecedented.

Many new financial innovations, for example, stretch the boundaries of what is acceptable to risk and security people in institutions. The 'Should we?' question, for them, is one of prudence and operational exposure. Some ideas have fantastic business cases but come with completely unacceptable risks. These are ideas which will never make it through the innovation process intact, and it is better to know this as early as possible. Let me give you a personal example.

In the early 2000s I was involved in a project to create an account aggregation system in Australia. Account aggregation is the practice of 'screen-scraping' websites – mainly those belonging to banks – in order to get transactions and balances, which are then displayed together in a different website. To make this a reality, customers were asked to hand over their Internet banking user id and PIN numbers, which are used by automated agents to gather their data. At the time, the idea was genuinely new, and there was a great deal of speculation that the practice of account aggregation would, eventually, lead customers to abandon their banks' websites altogether.

The customer value proposition was convenience: instead of going to multiple bank websites, they could go to just one for all their details. The 'single customer view' that was talked about was to be the next killer financial services application. When we asked ourselves the 'Should we?' question, therefore, the answer was most definitely yes from a financial perspective. Although the service would, ostensibly, be free, even the most mundane projections of revenues arising from cross-selling opportunities made the new offering extremely attractive. Consider it! All that lovely customer data ready to be mined!

But, of course, a key consideration in this case was whether it was sensible to screen-scrape the websites of other banks. What if something went wrong? Nightmare scenarios including wholesale theft of PINs and user ids for other banks' customers were raised. Here, too, the answer to the 'Should we?' question was a cautious yes. It was felt that the overall benefits accruing from the service outweighed any potential risks. Especially if this was going to be the next killer financial services application.

With the 'Should we?' question out of the way, we proceeded to the second of our three questions. The determination of the 'Can we?' question is mainly technical. Often very good ideas with fantastic business cases arrive, but when the details are worked out, they prove to be impossible to implement. This is especially true when genuinely new processes or technologies are involved. Occasionally, the challenges in implementation are not even technical: they are legal or operational. That is what happened in the account aggregation project I worked on.

We determined that yes, screen-scraping was viable. We also worked out how to create a secure 'PIN vault' that would make it practically impossible for anyone to steal customer details. A myriad of other details were resolved at a high level which gave us confidence that we could, technologically, implement the service. But the real question was what the regulator would think. At the time, banking terms and conditions at most institutions specifically forbade customers from disclosing their login details to any third party, even if that was another bank. The penalty for doing so was invariably the loss of any guarantees if anything went wrong. Would the regulator countenance the situation given the potential advantages to the customer if it all worked?

This led to tense moments and some nerve-wracking meetings whilst we attempted to get a read on the likely stance the regulator would take. We knew that if we guessed wrongly we would probably invest hugely in something that would never be allowed to see the light of day. In the end, though, the answer was 'Yes', with some caveats. These were not insurmountable and we concluded that both technological and legal barriers were amenable to successful resolution with enough effort. We proceeded onward, imagining that we had, indeed, found the killer application that would change the face of online financial services.

The final question an innovator must answer before he or she can be certain of successfully getting an idea through to the execution phase is 'When?' Now, potentially, this is a question which requires the most judgement of all three, because one is seeking to understand the consequences of doing the innovation right now versus leaving it lay for a while. Not all good ideas are best executed by rushing in. Of course, the question here is whether there is significant advantage from being the first to market with something. Sometimes there is, but usually only where there is a potential network externality present.

A network externality is the situation where an innovation is worth more, when more people have the innovation. The telephone, clearly, is a great example of this. The value of the phone is that you can pick it up and talk to anyone else. But in its early days, telephonic communication was severely limited. Not everyone had the device, so it was often easier to send a letter. The value of the phone (and now, of mobiles) is directly proportional to how many people you can contact with them.

In the end, most countries experienced the same phenomenon: one large telephone operator wound up controlling practically every customer in a given market. They were the ones who moved aggressively to capture the largest possible customer base. Where a network externality is present, the organisation with the largest number of customers is most often the one that wins.

Most of the time, though, there are no network externalities present in bank innovations, so the question then becomes one of how early, relative to competitors, it is sensible to launch an innovation. In Chapter 1, we reviewed the downside of innovation: the earlier an institution is with an innovation relative to its peers, the more expensive the innovation is likely to be over its life. It is the 'When?' question that highlights this downside. Sooner or later, everyone else will have the innovation as well, but will be spending quite a bit less to make it all go. This translates into a significant competitive advantage for later entrants.

The answer to the 'When?' question, in this case, is that one must balance the long-term costs of an innovation against the likely uptake it will have, especially in the presence of a first-mover advantage. If one does something new, and many customers adopt it up front, there will almost certainly be a very good business case for an early launch.

When we finally got to the 'When?' question on our account aggregation project, we made some significant errors in judgement. Convinced of the bank-side benefits, we just assumed customers would flood into the service in order to obtain the much greater convenience of being able to access everything from one place. This was a fallacious assumption. Customers were far more concerned about their security than we had expected – the additional utility they achieved from all that convenience was more than outweighed by their fear something would go wrong. Adoption was slow, and then trailed off to nothing. We had mistaken our own excitement for the service as evidence of demand without actually checking that customers desired an aggregation service. We didn't do any detailed analysis of likely adoption behaviour of customers at all.

In hindsight, it was an obvious mistake. Customers were, after all, already getting convenience from their new Internet banking sites. Did they really need all that much more? One year after the service launched it was cancelled. None of the benefits we had promised materialised, largely because we were far too early with the innovation. We didn't understand the proposition that customers would be interested in, and completely underestimated the amount of time they would take to get on board with the idea of trusting a third party with their financial information. It was not until 2007 that account aggregation returned in force, but this time in the shape of personal finance management websites. Their unique selling proposition was not convenience (a franchise well and truly served by banks with online banking) but managing money better. They were becoming increasingly popular at the time of writing.

So, the 'When?' question is really one of timing market entry. It requires sound judgement and careful preparation to make this call well. And, of course, any error will come home to roost for the innovators in the future. An innovation that gets through the whole futureproofing process and *then* fails is a significant disaster for an innovation team: for teams that are early in their development, it is likely that no recovery is possible at all.

Before we move on to the details of how, exactly, one gets the answers to the three innovation questions, I want to make one final point. There is a very, very strong correlation between the amount of effort an innovation team puts into answering the questions and the likelihood of the idea reaching execution. Time and money invested well makes all the difference.

6.2   THE INNOVATION PORTFOLIO

Whilst the three innovation questions help us determine whether or not a specific innovation ought to be pursued, the real key to innovation success is managing the total sum of innovations under consideration as a portfolio. As I mentioned at the start of this chapter, the idea is to create a balanced mix of innovations across the innovation pentagram, where the expected value of everything in the portfolio is as close as possible to the return number one must hit in order to ensure that innovation is the preferred investment opportunity at an institution.

If you recall, expected value is the total returns achievable from an innovation multiplied by the likelihood those returns will be obtained. As you would expect, the probability of achieving a return is much greater for an incremental innovation than a breakthrough. And similarly, the probability of a sustaining innovation getting its returns is higher than a disruption. This is the reason new innovators are advised to weight their innovation portfolios strongly towards incrementalism: that certainty of return is what makes it possible to pay the bills. It is also the means by which enough certainty in the innovation function can be developed to enable one to pursue breakthroughs without a risk of the whole portfolio collapsing.

Getting to the riskiness of an innovation

From the perspective of innovators, there are two main components of innovation risk.

The first is funding risk: the situation where an idea in which the practitioner invests a lot of time and money is unsuccessful in securing investment and moving to execution. This happens rather a lot, unfortunately. It is impossible to predict, even with the best stakeholder management possible, just what the reaction of a given individual will be to a new idea.

As we saw in Chapter 2, individuals have differing appetites for new things. Those who are relatively more innovative than peers – the innovators and early adopters – will be easier to convince that the new thing will help their businesses than the rest of the organisation. But distribution of innovativeness in an institution is never even, and there will always be some people who cannot be convinced of an innovation's value, no matter how much preparation is put into it beforehand. It is possible, of course, to influence those around such individuals in such a way that even the most die-hard laggards can be convinced they should adopt something. That strategy is one we will cover a bit later in this chapter, but it is time-consuming and, therefore, expensive. It is usually appropriate only for innovations with very high expected values.

The second aspect of innovation risk is that an innovation, even if it achieves funding, does not achieve success with its target customers or end-users. Or, even worse, never makes it to customers at all because something has gone wrong during the execution phase. We'll talk about the myriad of things that can kill an innovation during implementation in the next chapter, but the key thing to know right now is that an innovation which wins funding and

Table 6.1   The likelihood an innovation will succeed

	Sustaining	Disruptive
Incremental	75%	40%
Revolutionary	60%	25%
Breakthrough	55%	5%

then fails is just about the worse thing that can happen to an innovation team. So many missed expectations and broken promises!

In order to balance the level of risk and return an innovator needs in a portfolio, then, it is essential to come to some robust way of evaluating the risk of particular innovations. Luckily, a fairly simple way to do this was created by George Day, a professor at the Wharton Business School [57]. He arranged all innovations in a particular portfolio into a grid, with the level of newness to a company on the Y axis, and the familiarity an organisation has with the target market on the X axis. Then, using a scoring system to determine the position on each axis, he provided the likelihood an innovation will fail.

For our purposes in futureproofing, I created a revised version of the Day matrix with the level of innovativeness on the Y axis (incremental, revolutionary, breakthrough) and whether the innovation is sustaining or disruptive on the X axis shown in Table 6.1. This modification provides us with an easy way of getting to an approximation of how likely a particular innovation is to succeed.

If you examine this matrix, you will see that innovations which are simultaneously disruptive and breakthrough are exceedingly risky to undertake. Does this mean an innovation team shouldn't even contemplate such ideas? By no means.

Because our portfolio works with expected values, the implication is that in order to justify the time and money to be invested in building out such an idea, the projected returns have to be significant. Very significant. Usually, it is not a problem to dream up ideas with very significant returns. The problem is working out how to sell the idea in such a way that it will get funded. The more outlandish and unusual something is, the harder this process becomes.

Calculating expected returns

Getting to an initial estimate of the returns possible from an innovation is complicated. The problem is the number of potential factors that ought to be considered before the result is anything much more than a guess. How many people will use the innovation over its lifetime? What are the likely costs of development and marketing? What price point will it need to be set at? These are questions which are fleshed out in detail during the innovation phase. But for the purposes of prioritising the portfolio, what is needed is something that can be determined much more rapidly. Something better than a guess, but less time-consuming than creating a whole business case.

A simple way of doing this is to create a proxy for returns using a score which represents the relative cost of development versus the income generated if the innovation goes to market. Table 6.2 is a matrix that lets us get to such a score.

Development costs, down the side, are classified as either low, medium, or high. This procedure is followed also for returns, which are along the top. The intersection of these two is the score that is a good enough representation of the potential of the innovation for the purposes

Table 6.2 Innovation returns matrix

Costs	Returns		
	Low	Medium	High
Low	7	8	9
Medium	4	5	6
High	1	2	3

of prioritising the innovation portfolio. As you will see, if you examine this grid, the highest scores are returned for those innovations which have a high impact but low development costs. In fact, this is a grid which prioritises ideas with low development costs. This is consistent with the advice I've given throughout this book so far: one wants a portfolio with volume, so that when an idea fails (as it inevitably will), the overall impact on the portfolio is small. Many small investments are far preferable to a few large ones.

But we still have some definitional issues. What constitutes a low development cost? A high one? How does one classify a low or high return? The development cost of an innovation is the set of things that must be done to get the innovation funded and under development. Obviously, there are other costs once the innovation is all built and ready for prime time (such as those expenses incurred in letting potential users or customers know the innovation is available), but from the perspective of practitioners, the chief output of the portfolio process is a set of projects that might reasonably make it to (and then through) the execution phase. Table 6.3 shows one way of classifying these costs.

It is reasonable to say that the development costs of a particular idea are low if the innovation team is able to fund the process entirely on its own. The development costs may also be said to be low in situations where an existing budget in a business line elsewhere is available to develop the innovation, and it can be accessed relatively easily without a lengthy approval process. Almost certainly, this means that most innovations with low development costs will be incremental in nature.

It is very typical, for example, that an institution has a process re-engineering team, or something similar. Such teams will, in the course of their ordinary business-as-usual activities, spend a great deal of time making incremental changes to business processes and other systems. When such a team exists, passing an innovation to them will likely result in its rapid implementation.

Of course, the more interesting innovations take rather more effort to sell to stakeholders than that. Usually, if there is a budget available, but there is an involved process that must be followed to gain access to the money, the innovation should be considered to have medium

Table 6.3 Innovation development costs

Development costs are...	If...
Low	The innovation team can fund the entire process end to end, or if another existing budget is available without an approval process
Medium	A budget exists somewhere, and an approval process is necessary to get access to funds
High	No budget exists and other projects have to be stopped to pay for the innovation *or* if top-table support needs to be gained to access funds

development cost. Stakeholders will naturally require a degree of reassurance they are making a sensible financial decision before they release funds. The process of producing the required artefacts to provide this reassurance is inevitably going to take some effort. And even if the required artefacts exist and are of high quality, there will be many rounds of meetings, influencing sessions, and other activities that must occur before anything will likely happen.

In one institution I worked with, for example, there was a large investment fund available to support any kind of project which had the possibility of simplifying what was then a very complex set of systems and processes. The rationale behind this investment fund was that improvements that made things simpler would have substantial payoffs in the future as the scale of operations grew. But to get the money, a very formal business case was established. Anyone seeking investment from the fund needed to demonstrate in incredible detail the returns they expected, and how it would make the ongoing operations easier to manage. Inevitably, this was a bar too high for a significant portion of ideas that might have made things better.

There was nothing wrong with this process, of course. The investment fund made sensible decisions with respect to the projects it approved. The mistake many made, however, was that they failed to factor in the effort they would need to invest to get the money in the first place. Getting through established review processes – no matter how simple – is a challenge not to be underestimated. Some innovations are so new or unusual there is no fund of money available anywhere in an institution to support their development. Such innovations will usually have very high development costs, because not only does the business justification for the innovation have to work, but senior-level stakeholders must often de-prioritise other investments to find the funds they need to pay for it. This is generally a very hard sell indeed.

An even worse situation, at least in terms of the effort an innovation practitioner must invest, is the oft-occurring case where de-prioritisation of existing investments is impossible. In these cases, the amount of effort is exceptionally great, and will sometimes involve going to the top officers in the bank. The level of preparation needed for such innovations can be titanic. One wants to be certain the returns likely to devolve from the innovation make such investments worthwhile.

So much for the effort that must be invested to develop the innovation to a point where it can be successfully pitched for funding. But is there a similarly neat classification scheme that might be used for returns? One way of classifying innovation returns that has worked in some institutions is to examine the potential scope the innovation has to change the institution. Such changes could be financial, of course, but can be efficiency- and productivity-based as well. Although the financial numbers arising from these latter cases are hard to divine in most cases, the process of categorising potential innovation returns based on their impact means that, at this early stage, we are able to avoid skewing the overall portfolio towards those ideas which are entirely revenue- or cost-based. Such a classification scheme is shown in Table 6.4.

An idea which, if developed, affects a single business process or product in some material way will probably have relatively low returns when considered in the overall context of

Table 6.4 Likely returns

Returns are...	If scope of changes will affect...
Low	A single product or business process
Medium	Multiple products or businesses process, or a whole division within an institution
High	The entire bank

an entire bank. For example, redesigning an application form for a loan product might be consequential to the product manager with responsibility for an individual product, but it is hardly likely to deliver a huge increase in revenue in the overall scheme of things. Such innovations, which are most of the time fairly incremental in nature, fit into the low-level returns category.

An innovation which affects a group of products or processes, on the other hand, is quite likely to have a material impact on an entire division or larger unit of an institution. The launch of an entirely new card product, for example, could result in a significant increase in the number of customers and their spend with the bank. Or the creation of a new channel-based application might change the dynamic of the whole sales process in branches, something that many institutions have been trying to do with various efforts to achieve a single customer view of the customer. Innovations such as these should be classified as medium return.

Finally, an innovation which is broad in scope, sufficiently large that it will impact the entire institution, may be classified as having high returns. It will usually be the case that such innovations have broad implications both financially and for the overall operating processes of a given bank. The establishment of new business lines, or the centralisation of operating functions across a bank, are examples of such innovations. They are characterised by significant changes across two or more divisions.

One final point on estimating the impact of innovations in this way: it is important to think about the effects of the innovation in terms of the total change an idea will drive over its lifetime. A disruptive new business line, for example, will start small and cause little material impact over the first few years of its life. Eventually, however, it might supersede an existing business entirely and disrupt competitors as well. The overall impact, therefore, is very high, but only if one examines the idea with a long-term outlook.

With these definitions in hand, we now have a way of estimating a proxy value for expected value. A proxy, of course, is no substitute for an actual business case, but recall that our purpose at this stage of the process is to find a reasonable way of selecting innovations for progression in a way that balances the overall portfolio and maximises our chances of getting the returns we need.

Let us examine, as we did earlier in this book, the situation with peer-to-peer lending. Assume that the idea has arrived from the innovation stage and testing with customers has determined that there is a segment that would use the new service if an institution were to make it available. Our first step, then, is to work out how risky the innovation is overall. We can do this with the matrix in Table 6.1.

As we saw in Chapter 4 in the specific futurecasts we did for peer-to-peer lending, there are several interesting scenarios here. One of them is of particular interest: the scenario in which a bank enters the peer-to-peer marketplace *and* peer-to-peer is important. Now, this is an innovation which has a great deal of potential to disrupt existing lending businesses. Clearly the model, if it takes off, is one that has at least a chance of replacing conventional lending. Using this criterion, it is obvious that peer-to-peer lending is a disruptive innovation.

The next question is whether it is revolutionary or breakthrough, since it certainly isn't an incremental innovation for a traditional institution. In my view, peer-to-peer is revolutionary for a bank, since the breakthrough was the first implementation of peer-to-peer by UK-based firm Zopa. Zopa has worked through many of the hard challenges and problems, and other P2P-based outfits have proved the model scales into other geographies.

With these two points decided, we evaluate the likelihood of successfully getting to execution in the P2P space for a bank as 25%.

The next step is to work out how much the innovation will cost to develop. Luckily there is anecdotal evidence available to support an estimate of this kind. Some peer-to-peer lending sites have started without seed capital at all, and less than six months' development. As a percentage of overall bank investments, the number involved is probably microscopic. But we are thinking here about the bank's innovation programme budget. In that context, the development probably would need some support from an external budget holder, though not to a large degree. It is probably the case that an executive with discretionary spend would be able to find the money for such an innovation. We can say, then, that there would be a medium cost to develop this innovation.

We also need to work out what the long-term returns of the innovation might be. Now, we're talking about a disruptive innovation here, one that has the potential to be a significant new income earner if it takes off. As I mentioned previously, in fact, some analysts have suggested that P2P lending could take as much as 10% of all retail lending in the next few years. And whilst peer-to-peer is useful today only for unsecured lending, there is every sign that it will expand to other credit products in the near future. In terms of returns, then, using the matrix in Table 6.2, we can say the overall returns are high.

With both these decisions in hand, we now know that the expected return for this innovation will be:

$$0.25 \times 6 = 1.5 \text{ return units}$$

We use return units at this stage, because we haven't attempted to quantify the real value of an innovation in cash. That will happen later when we attempt to answer the key questions. Right now, all we want to do is get to a standardised way of comparing innovations across the potential options available to the innovation team.

Let us examine now two other innovations we discussed in the last chapter with respect to our fictional Catch-up Bank: automated address change and NFC mobile payments. The calculations for these are shown in Table 6.5.

As we can see from this, the address change functionality scores rather higher than mobile phone payments. This is what one would expect, of course, since online address change is a relatively well-understood sustaining innovation, whilst the mobile payments play is quite likely to be complicated and expensive.

But there is one further aspect to consider in our methodology, and that is the amount of effort the innovation team would have to devote to get such innovations through the futureproofing process. In the next section, we will add innovation team effort to our portfolio approach to get a complete picture of what the team should work on.

Determining effort and prioritising innovations

The parameters of our ideation process will usually be set in such a way that far more ideas arrive from the ideation phase than can reasonably be undertaken no matter how big the innovation team is. It is therefore necessary to come to some means of determining how best to deploy the innovation team given the range of opportunities available to it. The easiest way to do this is to take the expected value of each innovation (in return units) and compare it with the amount of effort and resource that will need to be invested to drive the idea through the innovation process. There is no need to be excessively quantitative about this, and it is usually sufficient to say that the amount of effort will be low, medium, or high. Of course, there is then a definitional question as to what these terms mean for particular innovation teams. The

Table 6.5 Portfolio calculations for two innovations

	Automated address change	NFC mobile payments
Riskiness (**Table** 6.1)	The innovation is both incremental and sustaining. Therefore, the innovation is 75% likely to be successful	The innovation is sustaining to a bank, since it adds value to an existing business (payments), but is revolutionary because it changes the basis of operation from cards to mobile phones. 65% likely to be successful
Innovation development costs (**Table** 6.3)	The functionality may look easy to implement, but will require touching a large number of systems. The innovation team will need to seek budget outside its own area to proceed. Medium costs	To do mobile payments well, it may be necessary to work with both the originations and payments people to get budget, since both the in-store equipment as well as the chip in the NFC mobile phone will need to be considered. It may be there will need to be a programme to give customers handsets, as some other banks had previously done with mobile banking. The costs to do all this will likely be high
Innovation likely returns (**Table** 6.4)	The innovation will affect a number of products across a number of business groups. Medium returns	The innovation affects, primarily, the cards businesses. This could include debit and credit, so this innovation will have medium returns
Return (**Table** 6.2)	5	2
Return units	$5 \times 0.75 = 3.75$	$2 \times 0.65 = 1.3$

simplest answer to this is to return to our three innovation questions and determine how much investment it might take to answer them. Table 6.6 shows such an approach.

A low-effort innovation has obvious answers to all three questions. If the practitioner cannot see the answers for him or herself, getting them will usually be a matter of picking up the phone and asking a few questions. There will certainly be no need to invest scarce resources in any studies or other work products. Usually, a low-effort idea is so obvious that not proceeding is bad business sense. You will typically find this to be the case for ideas which are incremental and sustaining in nature. If it is necessary to go to a stakeholder at all before proceeding, convincing them to fund development is almost certainly a done deal.

A medium-effort innovation will require investment to answer one of the three innovation questions. For example, it might be necessary to retain an analyst to create a demand forecast or an adoption curve to answer the 'Should we?' question. There might be a need to acquire market research in order to answer the 'When?' question. Or, the practitioner may have to

Table 6.6 Innovation team effort

Innovation team effort is. . .	If. . .
Low	All three key questions have obvious answers that can be determined without investment
Medium	One key question needs investment to determine the answer
High	Two or more key questions need investment to determine the answer

Table 6.7 Innovation prioritisation matrix

		Return units value		
		0.0–2.4	2.5–4.8	4.9–7.0
Effort	Low	3	2	1
	Medium	6	5	4
	High	9	8	7

schedule a prototype of the innovation in order to work out whether the innovation can be implemented at all ('Can we?').

A high-effort innovation, finally, is one that requires investment to answer two or more of the innovation questions. In order to proceed with such an innovation, then, the expected returns must be pretty high. In most cases, it will make sense to select medium- and low-effort innovations in preference to high ones: an innovation portfolio with too many high-effort innovations poses significant risks to the overall number that needs to be returned by the team.

Given the typology of effort and returns outlined thus far, Table 6.7 is one way of determining the prioritisation of the innovations available to the team. It is necessary, of course, to apply judgement when using prescriptive approaches such as this one. Sometimes, for example, an innovation will be both high-effort and high-return, but have significant organisational will behind it. The innovation might event be autonomic in nature. Slavishly following the prioritisation matrix I've just presented would have resulted in such an innovation being most unlikely to move forwards.

Let us now return to our peer-to-peer lending example and work out what priority our innovation would take given this typology of effort. Firstly, we are expecting a relatively low expected return (1.5 units), but will have to spend quite a bit of time considering at least the 'Should we?' key question. As we saw back in our examination of peer-to-peer lending during futurecasting, there are several scenarios of interest. Is the innovation important in the overall scheme of things? What will happen if banks *do* enter the market? If they don't? We will need to spend money, probably, to come to reasonable statements about this.

The other key questions have relatively obvious answers. If a start-up website can build a system from scratch with practically no money, it is ridiculous to think that a bank could not do so. And the fact of the matter is, the reaction of customers and other banks to existing peer-to-peer sites tells us all we need to know about 'When?' But in the end, the innovation team will have to invest to answer two of the three key questions. That puts the amount of effort involved as high.

The other innovations we have been examining in this chapter are shown in Table 6.8. What this tells us is that the innovation team will work firstly on the address change innovation, then peer-to-peer lending, and finally mobile payments. In reality, what normally occurs is that the team works down its list of innovations until it runs out of time, money, or bandwidth, so it is highly unlikely that NFC mobile payments, with a score of 9, would be worked on at all.

It is important to review the matrices presented with a critical eye in the context of your own institution: they tend to weight the set of innovations that will be attempted towards incremental and sustaining. That is very appropriate if your innovation strategy is Play Not to Lose, of course, which is the default position of most institutions. It is a simple matter to juggle the tables to rebalance your portfolio if you are running with Play to Win. And, in any event, such modifications will be essential once the innovation programme gets beyond

Table 6.8 Priorities of three innovations

	Address change	Peer-to-peer lending	Mobile phone payments
Innovation team effort	We will probably be able to answer all three key questions without spending money. Low effort	We need to answer one key question, as discussed above. Medium effort	Both the 'When?' and 'Can we?' questions will need investment. The former because we don't know what customer and competitor response will be. The latter because we have no experience with mobile phones, or NFC. High effort.
Priority (**Table** 6.7)	2	6	9

managing to the fourth and fifth stage of the Five Capability Model (see Chapter 3). At that point, the team will be paying the bills predictably, so can afford to work on things which are much more risky, or take more effort.

6.3   WHAT HAPPENS NEXT?

At this point, the innovation team has a prioritised portfolio of ideas. This will determine where the team's effort should be concentrated in order to maximise its potential returns. The next thing to do, then, is to start the process of getting answers to the key questions I described earlier. There are a number of tools I would recommend in order to do this, and we will cover these in a moment. But first, it is necessary to talk about what to do with innovations that don't cut it, a process I call 'drowning the puppy'.

Drowning the puppy

When I present in public on the subject of innovation processes, I usually make sure to have a picture of a puppy that is so sickeningly cute that everyone immediately sighs 'ahhhh' when it comes up on screen. The thing is, ideas are quite like puppies. When you first get them, they are brand new, fresh, and just screaming out for some love. Over time, during the development process, one becomes completely attached to an idea, such that objectivity becomes very, very hard to maintain. It becomes, figuratively, impossible to drown the puppy, even when one or more of the key innovation questions have proven conclusively that proceeding is a bad idea.

I've mentioned PayPal often so far, and in one institution I worked with, some forward-thinking business leaders realised that here was a threat they needed to deal with. An innovator was tasked with coming up with a competitive response, and the one selected for investigation used a mobile phone instead of an email address as the means of specifying recipients and senders. A good idea, and one that had already proved its value in countries such as Africa, where we've already examined the success of SafariCom with its M-Pesa offering.

Unfortunately, investigation of the 'Should we?' question made it clear very early that there was never going to be a substantive business case that would stand up to scrutiny. Either the transaction cost to make the service profitable would have been prohibitive to all but a tiny segment of the market, or the bank would necessarily have needed to subsidise the offering for years, probably during a bloody battle for share, until the service built to a scale which would make it economic. Not a pretty picture.

By this time, though, the answers to the other two key questions were overwhelmingly positive. From a 'Can we?' perspective, it was possible to create a solution (and, in fact, a vendor had been located that could provide it practically out of the box). And in answer to 'When?', competitive intelligence suggested that PayPal might, itself, offer such a solution to its customers in the near term. There was a narrow window available during which a launch might be possible.

Our innovator, at this point, had committed significant resources to driving forward a mobile payments offering. The emotional and reputational investment was high. No matter what, this was going to be an innovation that proceeded. It was duly taken forward to pitch for investment funding to go live.

The result was predictable. Without a substantive business case, there was no reason to proceed. Not only was the innovation rejected outright, our innovator lost a significant amount of credibility, and had to return to the drawing board after investing significantly in something that should have been terminated much earlier.

Here is the lesson from this story: the minute there are concerns about any of the three key questions, drown the puppy immediately. Failure to fail quickly enough will result in much worse failure later.

Failure

This leads me to another point: failure is an inevitable consequence of innovation. Most ideas cannot satisfy the key questions given the particular situation of an institution. The important thing is to drown the puppy as soon as possible in order to conserve resources for ideas that have a hope of going somewhere.

One problem with this approach is that other parts of most institutions are not optimised to think of failure as a positive thing. Instead, they consider failure to be the result of a lack of judgement, a broken planning process, or even worse, personal incompetence. I was once in a meeting with a senior leader who was reviewing the metrics an innovation team was producing monthly. 'These tell me that only about four of a thousand ideas make it every month,' he said. 'Why would you be so pleased that your success rate is so low? What if one of those thousand ideas was the Next Big Thing?'

The leader in question was looking at the innovation process from the perspective of someone who has previously had a good idea or two. There is this mistaken belief that every good idea should progress or an institution is missing out on some significant potential advantages. The reality, of course, is that innovation resources are finite and some prioritisation must occur. And in order to make sure of predictability, even ideas which are exceptional cannot be progressed if there isn't much hope of getting them past the key questions.

Innovators have a significant task in front of them: they need to educate their peers and leaders about the constructive value of failure. The sooner an idea can be taken off the radar, the more likely it is that the next big thing will be found and progressed.

Another reason to make sure senior people are educated about the benefit of failure is that, sooner or later, a senior leader is going to show up with a pet idea for the innovation team to progress. This is a very difficult situation to deal with. Senior leaders are no more likely to come up with game-changing innovation than their much more junior subordinates, though their superior experience may make them think their ideas have great substantive value.

Inevitably, though, these are the people who control the funding – either for this specific idea, or for others in which the innovation team has an interest.

Obviously, it is impossible to drown the puppy out of hand in such cases, even when it is plainly evident that the key questions will not be answered substantively. There is also the question of the loss of influence with the stakeholder when outright disagreement occurs. Innovators should rarely, if ever, drown the puppies of their patrons directly. For such cases, the best approach tends to be working through intermediaries, who are trusted by the leader concerned. Intermediaries, without the specific emotional investment that arises in those who have had that creative moment, are far more likely to be objective about the idea. They are also in a position to communicate doubts effectively. By so doing, they can spare the practitioner the difficulty of dealing with an innovation that won't go anywhere directly.

Later on in this chapter, we will discuss the means of selling ideas to senior leaders who are not receptive to new things. Those same processes, used in reverse, are those I'm describing here. A senior leader can be influenced to drown the puppy just as much as they can be to fund something new.

6.4   TOOLS FOR 'SHOULD WE?'

There are quite a few tools that let us determine if, in fact, an innovation is one we should pursue. There are two dimensions to this question. The first is whether the innovation makes sense from the perspective of the whole institution, which is where we will focus most of our attention. But there is a second, less obvious, dimension as well, and that is whether the innovation makes sense from the perspective of the innovation function.

These two can sometimes be at loggerheads. It frequently occurs that a particular innovation has a very significant business case. It would make a strategic difference to the bank. At the same time, however, the innovation team is simply unprepared or unable to progress it in any reasonable way. Consider, for example, the scenario of a major, disruptive innovation that would, over time, cannibalise revenues from a core business line, such as peer-to-peer lending that we've already been examining in this chapter. Clearly, an innovation team at the inventors stage (see Figure 3.2) is not going to have the capability to drive forward such a disruptive new idea, and should place it in the parking lot immediately. As we've seen, there are usually powerful forces arrayed against those who try to promote disruptive innovations too early. It is better, by far, to leave it until the programme has developed to the venturing stage of the Five Capability Model when it has the best chance of success.

We will discuss this more a bit later when we examine the 'Can we get it up test?' further on in this chapter. Before we get there, though, let us now look at the means we can use to substantively answer the 'Should we?' key question.

The cash curve

Perhaps the most important tool we can use to answer the 'Should we?' question is the cash curve, first popularised by two partners at Boston Consulting Group's Innovation practice [58]. A cash curve is a line that measures the net benefit of an innovation over time. Throughout the conversion process of an idea into something that can be put into the hands of customers and end-users, the benefits curve is almost always extremely negative. This results from the significant investments it takes to make anything real. After the innovation begins to be used, however, the cash curve begins an upward trend. Eventually, one expects that the overall

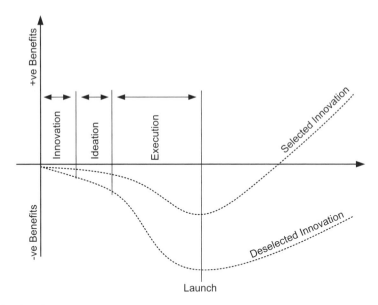

Figure 6.1   A cash curve

benefit will be positive, after the initial investments in development have been repaid. Such a cash curve is shown in Figure 6.1.

It is important, at this point, to clarify that net benefit, which is the measure on which the cash curve is based, may or may not be based wholly on actual cash. There are lots of other kinds of benefits which might usefully be incorporated here for some kinds of innovations. For example, a new collaboration tool, the result of which is productivity improvements across an organisation, might not have tangible cash benefits. The point is that measuring and quantifying the benefits of whatever-it-is against the costs of development is the essential discipline that practitioners must get to, however their numbers are derived.

Sometimes, the cash curve never ventures into the positive space of the chart, or fails to do so in a reasonable timeframe. Clearly, these are innovations which should be deselected early. They have failed the 'Should we?' question. The second trace in Figure 6.1 shows such an innovation.

There are also innovations for which the projected development costs are so substantial that there are substantive risks associated with actually achieving the magnitude of benefits required to take the cash curve into positive territory. These innovations, too, are probably ones that ought to be deselected, at least for younger innovation teams. Whenever there are substantial questions about the likelihood of achieving windfall returns or there are large up-front investments to be made, it is usually sensible to deselect. New teams cannot afford to have large blots on their copybooks, and they will most certainly get them if they don't deliver returns for a big investment in a relatively short period of time.

Of course, the cash curve leads us to an important procedural question. How does one actually get to a reasonable forecast of the net benefit of an innovation, with as little investment as possible? It is usually relatively simple to work out the costs of converting an innovation from idea to something that people can use, but what about benefits? That is where modelling the diffusion pattern of an innovation, which we covered in Chapter 2, comes in. By knowing how many people will take up an innovation at any particular point in time, one can make a guess at the cash curve of an innovation.

The business case

The cash curve is but one part of an overall document that most significant innovations will use to answer the 'Should we?' question. This document, of course, is the business case, which is usually comprised of a set of statements about the likely prospects of the innovation, its implementation cost, and a number of other sections which set out why an innovation is a good investment for an institution at a particular time.

The business case has two primary purposes. The first is obvious: it is the definitive forward-looking statement that summarises all detailed considerations taken into account before suggesting an investment is the correct one for a particular bank at a particular time. The second, though, is much less obvious: it is the document that senior leaders who make investments will use as a get-out-of-jail-free card if the investment does not perform as expected.

People, especially those with significant seniority, rarely make decisions without clarity of the consequences of failure, both to their institution and to themselves personally. Before they will commit, they need something in hand that justifies their decisions, whatever the outcome. The business case is the document that does that.

At the time of writing, many institutions are considering whether it is time to replace their aging core banking systems. Some of these systems have been around for two or more decades and are approaching an interesting inflection point: the people who built them and know how to make them run are all retired (or retiring), or even worse, dead. They face a nightmare scenario where their systems become unsupportable at worst, and hugely expensive to maintain at best. I know of a few institutions, actually, that have such old systems they've lost the source code (the original programme statements that comprise the system) and are forced to write patch after patch to the working system.

Anyway, you would think in circumstances such as these that the business case for an upgrade would be obvious. But that is rarely the case, although just looking at the raw numbers it can be hard to understand the rationale for not immediately starting replacement. The reasons for delay were neatly summarised to me by one banker thus: 'Core banking replacement is the third rail of banking projects. Touch it, and you die.'

Having a concrete analysis that summarises all the considerations that went into a decision can, indeed, save a leader when a project goes wrong. At the very least, it enables him or her to demonstrate that the failure was as a result of poor execution rather than any inherent flaw in the initial decision. No matter how Machiavellian this analysis of business cases seems, trust me when I tell you that a document targeted to work as a get-out-of-jail-free card will almost always be more successful than one that focuses only on the hard numbers.

I said at the beginning of this section that the reason for the business case was to summarise the set of forward-looking statements about what will happen as a result of introducing the innovation. But, as we've seen when we talked about futurecasting (Chapter 4), making forward-looking statements that try to predict a specific future state is a process fraught with the likelihood of error. I've yet to see a business case, actually, that was a completely correct predictor of the way things worked out in the end. Actually, as we'll see a bit later in this book, the set of things that happen during the innovation implementation process almost always changes the shape of an innovation so much that the initial business case is invalid anyway.

Given that business cases are so often inaccurate, why is so much emphasis placed on providing them at all? The answer is that once the basic numbers proving there is value in whatever-it-is have been presented, and the senior decision-maker has sufficient evidence to justify the fact that their decision was a sound one, the business case has a further role as a sales document. I'd argue, in fact, that this is the primary purpose of a business case.

For very large investment decisions, it is quite often the case that committees of senior stakeholders – the board of an institution, for example – must meet to make the decision to proceed. Now, whilst it is likely that the innovation practitioner has paved the way for a decision using the techniques I've explained thus far in this book, it is most *unlikely* that they will have relationships with everyone who is a part of making the final go/no-go decision on their nascent idea. In many circumstances, in fact, business leaders will have only the business case document to go on.

It makes sense, then, that there is a little more in this document than robust numbers. Robust numbers prove something is a good idea, but will not create the excitement that will guarantee a decision. Such excitement is the result of identifying a presently unresolved pain or need (as specific as possible to the reader, of course) and presenting a solution that is both acceptable and attractive. It helps if the decision-maker involved is personally experiencing the pain, because they will be predisposed to agree to move forwards regardless of the information in the document.

Once again, we turn to our knowledge of the innovation decision process (refer to Chapter 2) for the theoretic understanding we need to make sure decision-makers get the messages they need from the business case document.

First, decision-makers will want to know what the innovation is, how it works, and why they should care. These messages need to be communicated as if the decision-maker was personally adopting the innovation.

Second, the business case document should explain, in a personal way that relates specifically to the decision-maker, what evidence is available to *reinforce* a positive decision if they were to make one. You will recall that a key part of the adoption decision process is this kind of reinforcement: individuals like to know they are making the right decision, by seeking the assurances of those around them that they *are* making the right decision. New habits have to be formed, and old ones broken.

Then, the decision-maker will want to know how the implementation will proceed. Any change causes pain. By structuring the business case document so that specific pains are indentified and mitigated, the decision-maker will be much more likely to want to proceed.

And finally, the benefits of the change (brought on by the innovation) must be clearly communicated. These will be numbers-based, certainly, but some examination of any other benefits – especially if they relate directly and personally to the stakeholder – will always be beneficial.

Structuring the business case not as an impersonal container full of facts, but as a highly personal statement of benefits aligned to powerful individuals is highly efficacious. You will be amazed at the difference in response you get when you treat the business case document as a sales tool first.

6.5   TOOLS FOR 'CAN WE?'

Whilst the 'Should we?' question is an economic one, 'Can we?' is mainly about do-ability. Here, too, there are two dimensions to the question. The first dimension is essentially technical.

Given the current technical landscape of an institution, does the set of technological capabilities present make it possible to successfully implement the innovation? Are the right people available? Are the processes and systems that will be needed in place, or can existing ones be modified to do the job needed? The best way to answer questions such as these is to actually build something and see if it works. That's the role of the prototype, which we will cover in a minute.

The second dimension is equally important, and involves making a determination as to whether the organisational will needed to implement the innovation either exists presently or can be created. You will recall from our discussion of autonomic innovations in Chapter 3 that organisational will to do something is one of three key factors that make an innovation walk out the door by itself. But organisational will to implement is needed for all innovations, not just autonomic ones. I like to call the process of evaluating whether the necessary organisational will exists the 'Can we get it up?' test.

The 'Can we get it up?' test

There is little point pursuing an innovation without an early determination of whether or not it will be possible to handle the political context that surrounds it. And there is *always* a political context. The point of the 'Can we get it up?' test is to work out whether an innovation team is actually able to negotiate the politics surrounding a new idea or not.

When something is new, it will simultaneously assist some people, whilst threatening others. The latter group will most likely do everything in their power to ensure the innovation is impossible to move forward. Why does this happen?

Organisational units are typically built on a set of assumptions about the current state of things. Some people hate change (the late majority and laggards in particular, as we saw in Chapter 2) and they will usually be fiercely defensive of any existing assumptions upon which they rely to support their current methods of working. They will often defend these assumptions even when it is no longer reasonable to do so.

One institution I talked with had, for example, a call centre whose purpose was to accept phone calls from employees who wanted to use meeting rooms. To get a meeting room, one would ring the call centre and specify what size, location, and facilities one wanted, and a centralised booking system was used to record who was to use which. Every day, a team of people would run around the hundreds of rooms across the bank and affix small notices outside the doors to indicate the schedule for the room. When the innovation team tried to replace this labour-intensive approach with a modern electronic process attached to electronic diaries that everyone was already using, there was significant resistance. The problem was that the call centre, and indeed the entire manual booking process, were predicated on the idea that employees would not be capable of accurately self-serving room-booking, and furthermore that they wouldn't want to.

Because self-service would, in effect, end the need for a call centre at all, the underlying assumption of employee incompetence was defended vigorously. In the end, the innovation team determined they would drop the concept: they would have had to expend too much influence in order to move things forward.

What is this 'influence'?

When anyone does something that benefits someone else, the result is an increase in goodwill. Goodwill is important because it can be used as a partial offset against bad things in the future. An individual who has developed an ample store of goodwill is far more likely to have a negative message accepted than one who has not.

When one takes goodwill and applies it to the organisational unit, the result is influence. An innovation team that has previously delivered something that makes a particular organisational unit work more effectively is much more likely to be able to move something else forward which doesn't have the same benefits (to that organisational unit). There is a quid pro quo effect in operation.

When you have an innovation team at the earlier stages of development, influence is a scarce resource that must be managed as carefully as the money. Lots of effort has to be expended to make positive changes for those organisational units which have the potential to support future innovations. A new team will not have had the time or exposure to develop much influence, and must therefore be careful to pick its battles sensibly. It is far better to avoid innovations that disadvantage powerful interest groups at these early stages than to attempt them and fail. That is so even when the innovation is obviously in the best interests of the institution. With unlimited influence, it would be possible to get any innovation through the innovation stage. But even teams at the venturing capability level (see Chapter 3) are not blessed with this luxury.

Organisational will and influence are two sides of the same coin in innovation. Where one is lacking – as in the case where there are more groups that are disadvantaged by an innovation than benefit – it is possible to redress this balance by expending influence to make up the difference. The key determination of the 'Can we get it up?' test, really, is whether or not the amount of influence that must be invested in an innovation is really worth the eventual payback that is supposed to follow.

Making an accurate determination with respect to this question is simple. Examine the group that is likely to lose influence and position as a result of the innovation. Are they more powerful or more numerous than those who will gain? If so, influence will have to be expended to move the innovation forward. If the belief is that it is possible to move the situation forward without compromising the ability to innovate in any area associated with the losers, then the innovation has passed the 'Can we get it up?' test.

Prototypes and proofs of concept

Assuming an innovation has passed the previous set of tests, it then becomes important to determine if it is even possible to convert the idea into something that can used. The best way to do this, usually, is to actually try to make the idea work on a limited basis and see what happens. You will be surprised at how illuminating this process can be.

But what does 'limited basis' really mean? It is important, here, to distinguish between two kinds of limited trial: a prototype which is really an experiment to see how something works, and a pilot which is usually much more substantive and involves actual end-users, if not customers.

We will leave a discussion of pilots until the next chapter, as the level of expense and detail required to properly do a pilot makes them far too expensive to run before the key questions have been answered in a satisfactory fashion. The thing one wants to achieve with a pilot is answering very specific learning questions about how to operate an innovation once the decision to proceed has been made.

A prototype (also known as a proof of concept), on the other hand, should devote itself to resolving the technical and political ambiguity concerning the do-ability of a particular idea. Prototypes are mostly throw-away, meaning that once they have proved the single, specific point they were set up to demonstrate, they have no further value. It follows that a prototype is extremely low-cost. It doesn't make sense, after all, to spend a lot of money on something that will, in the end, be abandoned the moment funding is approved. So in what circumstances would you expect to create a prototype?

There are really three situations in which prototypes are useful. The first, of course, is the one to which I've already alluded: you need an experiment that proves the novelty in an innovation is actually something which can be implemented. Consider, for example, an innovation which includes a new algorithm to determine which customers are likely to churn. Clearly, one wants to test the algorithm against live customer data in some way to ensure its predictions are right sufficiently often that the end product, were it to be approved, would have some value.

A prototype in this circumstance would implement the algorithm in isolation, away from any real customer-facing systems. It would likely need to be hand-fed data, carefully selected from the operational data stores. And it would deliver its results in a form that proved it worked, but which would be hard or impossible to feed back to the live systems. With these compromises, the prototype can be built without much expense, but it is not really useful for anything beyond proving the algorithm works.

The second situation in which a prototype is useful is that regularly occurring circumstance where a visual demonstration of whatever-it-is is needed as an explanatory aid to executives with investment budgets or any other stakeholder who might have input into the eventual investment decision. Recall that innovations often demand a change in the way that people think about the processes and systems under their control. Sometimes, new ways of doing things cannot be explained clearly without showing the way that things will work after the innovation is implemented. A prototype that does this can be as simple as a few images of screen shots for some system. Or it can be 'fake-ware' – a working interface with pretend data that works in a very limited subset of circumstances. Once again, there will be a set of compromises that are accepted during the course of building out the prototype which will make it unsuitable for any real-world use. Fake-ware, for example, is often built with tools that are more suitable for graphic artists than high-volume transaction workloads.

The third, and final, situation in which a prototype is useful is getting a substantive reading on customer (or end-user) reaction to whatever-it-is. Because an innovation, by definition, constitutes something very new, the immediate question is whether it serves a need that customers have and will pay for.

It is quite likely that customers will already have been asked some questions about the innovation during the ideation phase. During ideation, the point of getting customer insight was to develop an early read on whether the innovation made sense at a high level. It is quite likely that any particular customer or end-user would have been presented with a large number of possible innovations all at once. A few questions – perhaps less than three – would have been asked about each idea, and the result used to gate the innovations through to the next phase.

But once an idea has arrived at the innovation stage, we need much more information, and the prototype is a useful tool to get it. Actually, the use of a prototype in the context of market research – such as focus groups or detailed interviews – really goes to answering the 'Should we?' question more than anything else. Clearly, determining if potential end-users of an innovation have an interest in changing their behaviour long term to adopt the new thing is the key question to be answered.

There are, however, other reasons to ask end-users about the idea. One of these is to see if all the right signposts are present to guide the end-user through the steps of the innovation decision process we looked at in Chapter 2. They will usually need to know what the innovation is about and how and why it works, questions for which they must easily find an answer. Then there is the persuasion stage, during which we would use a prototype to explore how readily the customer is able to form that necessary emotional engagement with the idea, and how easily they can share their thoughts about it with others. And finally, in the latter parts of the decision process, we need to see the efficacy of any trial strategy, and the ease with which the customer perceives they can actually incorporate the idea into their present way of working.

But the important thing to remember is that – even if there are detailed prototypes being presented to customers – everything done now will be thrown away. And, if it cannot be thrown away, you've built too much. Prototypes should never have so much money invested in them that they become, ipso facto, the innovation themselves. You will never get a high-quality end result if you build it out of thrown-together bits of prototypes.

High-level designs

The principal of throw-away does not extend, however, to high-level designs, which we examine next.

A high-level design is the first work product created which explains, with any level of technical veracity, how the innovation will be made to work in its entirety. It is a document that will live with the innovation for the rest of its life, though it will likely evolve as the idea progresses. High-level designs address the significant technological and strategic questions which would be involved in converting the idea into something that can actually be used. For an experience innovation, for example, the high-level design would describe the actual innovation that will result, the customer and people processes that would surround it and, of course, the technologies that will be created or installed to implement it. It is, essentially, the top-level blueprint of what will actually get built in the later phases of the futureproofing process.

The reason for creating a high-level design at this early stage of the innovation process – before funding has even been agreed, in fact – is that it is a deliverable which forces one to think in concrete terms about how a particular innovation will be implemented. Knowing how the new thing will be built is the precursor to answering the 'Can we?' question.

Now, this is not the way projects are normally initiated, I realise. So often, one gets funding and then works out how to build whatever-it-is. The problem with this, obviously, is that without knowing what is going to be built up front, one rarely has very much idea of how much money to ask for.

There is another reason to create high-level designs early, and that is to validate that the overall system is something that makes sense. Whilst the various prototypes that might have been constructed validate the uniqueness of the innovation is possible, there is still the outstanding question of having at least a high-level view of how to integrate the component parts to get a working whole.

There is one final reason that a high-level design is a very useful exercise this early, and it is mainly technological. Very few banks have the luxury of operating in a 'greenfields' environment, or, in other words, in situations where new things can be introduced without consideration of what is already in place. This consideration is exceptionally important. One cannot, for example, propose an innovation which would double or triple the transaction volume without considering whether there is enough mainframe capacity to handle the load.

Creating a high-level design forces the kind of thinking that illuminates the technological challenges the innovation will face as it goes through its development. It is also, of course, the

tool that lets us answer the 'Can we?' question in a manner so concre'
be convinced that their investment has the greatest chance of success

Open innovation

Whilst it is tempting to think that all innovation problems can be solved in-house, ι.
case that one institution has all the capabilities it needs to do something truly ground-breaκ.
at its command. When Bank of America invented the business computer (see Chapter 1), it
did not have hoards of computer scientists and electronic engineers sitting on the bench to call
upon. Instead, it had to find an innovation partner that could combine its own competencies
with those it needed to create something that was then unique. Stanford University was the
design partner, and eventually, it chose General Electric to actually manufacture the machines.

The point is that the more novel (and therefore, the larger the potential upside available)
an innovation might be, the less likely it is that all the capabilities needed will be available
in-house. The high-level design document, created as part of this phase of the futureproofing
process, is a good way of identifying such gaps. When such a document illuminates an area
where an internal capability does not exist, a workable solution is often to find someone else
with that capability who can build out what is needed.

When one UK bank decided to launch mobile banking, for example, it determined that it
would add a new feature then unprecedented in its market: the ability to transfer funds from
one account to another from the mobile application. Mobile application development was not,
however, a core capability of the bank. So, it decided to acquire the services of Monilink, a
company that specialised in that kind of development to build its application. By doing so,
the bank not only saved time, it was able to implement the solution in short order, neatly
leapfrogging its competitors in capability.

Whilst going outside an organisation for innovation expertise is not a new phenomenon,
it has recently been popularised under the sobriquet 'open innovation', a term coined by
Henry Chesbrough, the Executive Director of the Centre for Open Innovation at Berkley. The
basic premise he advanced is that companies will rarely be in a position to be competitive
from an innovation perspective when they rely on their own research entirely, and should
therefore buy in expertise, patents, and processes whenever possible. Similarly, if companies
have developed uniqueness they are not presently using themselves, this should be licensed to
other organisations who might make use of it.

Open innovation, as a paradigm, is quite different from what most institutions today do in
their innovation programmes. Most institutions take the view that all uniqueness is a trade
secret, and the way to competitive advantage is to ensure that the best brains are those working
inside your organisation creating more of it. There has been a vast amount written on open
innovation as a paradigm, and, in fact, it is presently the 'in-fashion' thing to be doing in
business. So I won't spend much more time describing it here, other than to say this: when
one has determined, through the artefact of high level designs or other means, that the answer
to 'Can we?' is no, it is useful to determine if working with competitors or other organisations
might change the answer to yes.

I realise, for banks, this is a rather titanic step. It seems inevitable, however, as more
institutions globalise, that collaboration will be an important part of the work of innovators. In
any case, the rise of powerful new tools for collaboration – the Internet is one – makes it likely
that collaboration will happen regardless of whether an institution has formally embraced
open innovation or not. Since organisations are unable to stop leakage of uniqueness through

perimeters in this connected age, there is little choice but to embrace openness to some
gree.

6.6 TOOLS FOR 'WHEN?'

The final of the key questions is 'When?', and involves making an assessment of two things:
whether, firstly, the time is right for an institution to launch an innovation and secondly, if the
market is ready for the innovation should the institution go ahead with it.

We've already discussed the 'Can we get it up?' test, which is an assessment of whether
the organisational will to implement an innovation exists. This test reflects the likelihood
that a particular innovation has a chance of getting through the innovation process from the
perspective of innovators. This is quite a different question from the ones that must be answered
now: is the timing right in the context of the strategy of this particular institution to proceed?
And if the innovation is released, what will the reaction of competitors be?

As I noted earlier, the 'When?' question also has another important point: if this is an
innovation that is relatively newer than anything introduced by competitors, the costs of
maintaining the innovation over time will also be relatively higher. Eventually, maintaining
these early-to-market innovations becomes costly enough that they constitute a competitive
disadvantage. Why is this?

It is self-evident that the more newness there is in something, the more custom development
of technologies and processes an institution must do during implementation. Developing
anything new is relatively more expensive, obviously, than buying a pre-packaged solution
off-the-shelf. Such solutions have their development costs shared across many customers, the
reason their prices tend to decline over time.

But something that has to be built from the ground up does not have this advantage. The
institution – or its partners – are forced to create everything, and then maintain it indefinitely.
In the meantime, if the innovation is one that is successful, other institutions will copy. They
will have the advantage of learning from their competitors' mistakes, certainly. But they might
also be able to take advantage of any solutions that have been developed in the meantime by
vendors, thereby sharing their development costs.

As I've mentioned elsewhere, I once worked for a consulting firm that implemented Internet
banking solutions in Australia. It was the late 1990s, and Internet banking was the brave
new frontier. The most innovative institutions had already been running their first-generation
solutions, and the remainder of the market, some years later, were readying their own for
customers. The thing was, these later institutions had quite a few vendor choices by this stage,
and out-of-the-box Internet banking was becoming something of a commodity.

When my firm was called in to one of the banks that had built their own Internet banking,
what we found did not surprise us. They had created something from the ground up, and
entered the market relatively early. What they had built served them very well, but the fact
of the matter was that it wasn't – by any stretch of the imagination – at the forefront of the
current state-of-the-art. All its competitors had, in fact, learnt lessons by watching the leader
launch its own offering, and built much more reliable and scalable platforms. They then went
to vendors who were able to leverage shared development costs and international experience
to create something with considerably more capability at a very competitive price.

What was our customer supposed to do? Though their platform had served them well, it
was swiftly becoming expensive to maintain. And yes, replacing it was a monumental cost,
considering they had something already working. They knew that to keep feature parity with

Table 6.9 Results of market entry timing

	Early launch	Fast-follower	Catch-up
Initial costs	High	Medium	Parity
Overall market position	Unique	Developing	Commodity
Recurring costs	High and increasing with time	Parity	Parity or lower
Potential for windfall gains	High	Low	None
Potential for windfall losses	Low	None	High

the other major banks in the market, they would have to spend big anyway. So, they abandoned their early platform, replacing it with something they bought from a vendor.

For them, their strategy of early entry gave them the ability to get lots of customers, when their competitors didn't have any offering at all. And then, when they determined their costs were outweighing these advantages, they adopted the same platform as everyone else in the market. It was a sensible strategy, but not one that many institutions are willing to accept. If you have something that works presently, the costs of replacement are almost always higher than the operating costs in the short term. But over the longer term, the costs of keeping parity with competitors almost always make replacement the best option.

Entry timing

When you boil it right down, for any given innovation, there are only three entry-timing windows: early launch, fast follower, or catch-up. Each of these has its own advantages and disadvantages, of course – the determination of which makes sense is very much a matter of context. These three options are summarised in Table 6.9.

The early-launch strategy is one where an institution, regardless of the riskiness of its innovation, chooses to enter a market, and is one of the first to do so. Security First Network Bank, when it launched its first online banking solution, was in this category. It didn't have much in the way of precedent to guide it, so its executives were either very foresighted, or had a particular insensitivity to risk, something alien to most institutions.

The fast-follower strategy, on the other hand, is that which adopts a wait-and-see approach to most innovations. There is far less risk involved in doing something new when someone else has already done it first. One expects, for example, that any regulatory hurdles will have been overcome. Any questions about do-ability are, ipso facto, resolved. And, of course, it is possible to judge market reaction with certainty, since the competitor's offering proves conclusively whether, after all, the new thing is something that customers and/or end-users want.

The last-entry timing strategy is catch-up. An institution waits until practically all its competitors have the innovation, and then it races to deploy it also, perhaps with some minor changes to drive some differentiation. In so doing, it does not achieve any particular windfall gains, but does restore itself to parity with its competitors.

Now, most institutions hate the idea that they would be last to market, thinking this means they are being trumped by their competitors. They feel, with some justification, that they will likely lose customers by following such a strategy, thus incurring windfall losses, especially if the innovation concerned is revolutionary or breakthrough. There are advantages, though: they will have had the time to study the market, the technical challenges of implementation, and customer reaction to the innovation to such a degree that they will be well positioned from at least a cost basis. This is especially important if the institution considers that the innovation is (or will shortly become) a commodity capability. Where a capability is held by everyone, the only thing that distinguishes it is the price at which is can be offered.

You can see, from Table 6.9, why so many institutions are considered to be fast-followers. The fast-follower timing has the advantage of practically no chance of a windfall loss, whilst there is still a chance that some residual windfall gains can be made. Note that most, if not all, of these gains will already have been taken by those courageous institutions that have already put the innovation in the market, so fast-follower really amounts to mopping up those advantages which remain on the table.

On the other hand, though, the fast-following institution will certainly have learned lessons from watching its innovative competitors, and can use these to reduce its entry costs considerably. And when it operates its innovation, the costs to do so will most likely be no more than those of the rest of the market.

Fast-follower is a safe place to be: some potential upside is available, but there is practically none of the risk. This is the reason some people feel there is so little innovation in banking. When a comprehensive assessment is made of any particular innovation, there is almost always little incentive to do anything *but* follow quickly.

To move to early launch usually takes a great deal of political and organisational will. And, as you would expect, it is the mark of a good innovation team that is able to convince its stakeholders that the increased risk of a move early is worth the eventual payoff.

Market intelligence

So far, we've been looking at the three times an institution might choose to launch an innovation from its own perspective. That, however, is only one aspect of answering the 'When?' question. Another is the impact of launch on competitors.

Now, short of engaging some kind of illegal corporate spy, there is no way of knowing with *certainty* what a competitor might do with respect to the introduction of a particular innovation. It is, however, possible to guess what competitors might do in the face of particular launch timings. Three specific scenarios are possible.

The first scenario is that the innovation is based on some specific operational or technical capability that would be difficult for any other institution to implement. For example, the network externalities inherent in PayPal give it an advantage that poses very substantial competitive barriers to entry. In this situation, a competitor has only two choices, regardless of the market entry timing. The first is to ignore the innovation entirely, something that most institutions have done with PayPal until relatively recently. Since the competitive advantage of the innovation is probably unassailable, there is no point in trying to respond. The second option for an institution in this circumstance is to attempt to change the rules of the game sufficiently that the innovation is no longer relevant. Safari Telecom with M-Pesa in Africa is an example of this. People don't use PayPal at all, because the mobile phone account with wireless transfer is a close-to-perfect substitute.

A second scenario is that the innovation is unique to a particular institution at launch, but the entry of a few competitors is possible over time. As an example, consider the launch of financial management websites based on account aggregation technologies. Now, here is an instance where there are substantive barriers to switching once the initial adoption has occurred. Customers have to move their account credentials for *all* their financial relationships from one site to another. They are unlikely to do so often.

Then, too, there is a limited market of people who will actually *use* a financial management website in the first place. In order to get to scale, an institution needs to get as many customers as possible *before* its competitors do so. Now, an institution that does launch early will almost certainly create a material response in competitors. Competitors will certainly understand enough to realise that if they don't *also* enter quickly, there will be insufficient customers available to make it a going concern. So competitors will immediately adopt the fast-follower strategy, if they enter at all.

A final scenario, of course, is that the innovation may be unique at launch, but there is no reason why it cannot be copied universally by the market. Such an innovation is one which quickly devolves into a commodity. This is the case for most innovations that are entirely product-based. Here, competitors will likely delay implementation until they are able to obtain the best optimisation of cost and revenue. There is little to be gained from an early-entry or fast-follower launch, because there are few barriers to stop them from entering any time they please. And, in fact, if we refer again to Table 6.9, there are usually substantive advantages available to them if they *don't* enter early.

6.7   SELLING INNOVATIONS

With all three key innovation questions answered satisfactorily, there remains one final part to the innovation phase of futureproofing: winning the funding necessary to take the idea into development.

As I've said elsewhere in this book, to a large degree the success of innovators depends on their ability to sell. Getting people to accept (and commit to) new ideas is a process which requires considerable acumen in this area. Business leaders, typically, will have preconceived notions about how they would like their operations run. They will defend these notions vigorously unless given good reason to think differently about what they do. Creating the environment in which new thinking can occur is one of the key predictors of the success of an innovator in most banks.

Luckily, most of the things needed to create this way of thinking differently have already been built as part of the futureproofing process. If a futurecast was done, then business leaders will already have thought through the implications of the innovation before anyone even asks them for a decision. Then, when it comes time to ask for a commitment, the answers to the key questions will have provided most of the answers that most business leaders will need.

All this sounds so simple when you put it down on paper like that. Regretfully, though, it is never so easy to get an innovation out the door. The main problem comes from the differing appetite for new things that different individuals have. It is to managing the sales process for new things, given this differing appetite, that we turn our attention next.

Innovation influence maps

The classification of adopters we examined in Chapter 2 provides us with a key tool for understanding the process that needs to be followed in order to get a new idea funded for development. When one examines Figure 2.2, there is a striking point that comes out: there is only about a 16% chance that the person who controls the money and can make a funding decision will be sufficiently receptive to new ideas that they make a commitment on the spot. That 16% is comprised of innovators and early adopters – the only segments of any population who will go through an innovation decision process without significant reinforcement from peers and other people they trust.

If you are lucky enough that the key stakeholder who can make a decision on an innovative idea is part of that 16%, you will likely have to do little more than show him or her the work products that were developed to answer the key questions. Assuming the numbers, business case, and concept stack up to scrutiny, an innovator or early adopter is very likely to make an immediate positive decision.

But most of the time, one is much more likely to meet the far more risk-averse population of individuals who prefer to consider their innovation investments very carefully, taking advice from one or more confidantes who have their trust. For these situations, a much more sophisticated influencing process is required, and it is helpful to create an influence map as a guide to the best way forwards.

An influence map for a particular stakeholder is, essentially, a chart that shows all the people who are trusted to provide advice and guidance. A sample of such a map is shown in Figure 6.2 for a hypothetical organisation reporting to the bank's CIO. As you might imagine, such a diagram bears only a partial similarity to the official organisational chart. Key people build strong, and far-ranging, networks of trusted individuals, and these usually span far beyond any official organisational boundary.

The influence map in this figure has some additional information: for both the key stakeholder and all the individuals in a position to influence him or her, a rough guess as to their likely attitude to innovation is added. One obtains this information by looking at the history of decisions an individual has made. If they have tended to be aggressive risk-takers, willing to make the hard calls in order to get the possibility of a spectacular result, they are more likely to be early adopters. But an executive who has always steered the steady course, systematically eliminating every risk whenever possible, is much more likely to be a laggard.

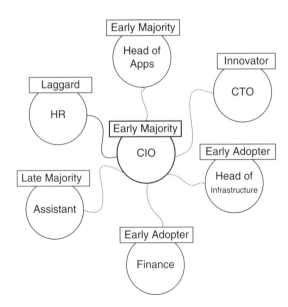

Figure 6.2   Influence map

With such an influence map constructed, it is now time to plan the campaign to convince the decision-maker they ought to consider the innovation. Eventually, this will involve direct contact, but the first step is to meet with the most likely influencers who can form an opinion early. These, obviously, are the ones you have determined are more likely to be towards the early adopter and innovator end of the curve we looked at in Chapter 2. In Figure 6.2 we would most likely approach the CTO first, followed by the head of infrastructure and finance. Such individuals will flow through the adoption process shown in Figure 2.1 much more easily than the decision-maker him or herself. They, in turn, being trusted advisors, will influence for you. With their support on board, getting agreement to pursue the innovation is likely to be much less difficult.

As a general rule, one wants two of these influencers converted to acceptance of the new idea before approaching the senior decision-maker directly, preferably with the two converts present. There is usually a declining marginal return from additional influencers, but having less than two is often insufficient evidence the idea is a good one. That is especially true if the decision-maker is a confirmed laggard.

There is still a problem, however. One often finds, when creating such an influence map, that there is a preponderance of individuals with the same proclivity for innovation as the key stakeholder one is trying to influence. This is a result of an effect that I first outlined in Chapter 2: individuals prefer to surround themselves with like-minded individuals. The people we tend to trust are often very similar to ourselves.

So what is to be done in this circumstance? The first thing is to work out whether, in fact, you have correctly answered the 'Can we get it up?' test after all. Remember, in the absence of organisational will to implement (represented, in this case, by a group of late majority or laggard individuals with pretty much no proclivity to do anything new at all), you have to spend influence to get things moving.

Assuming you are certain the innovation has decent legs, there is little choice but to extend the influence map out a level, such as shown in Figure 6.3. Once again we seek to determine, for each of the influencers of our key decision-maker, who they are influenced by.

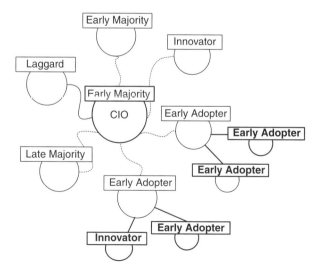

Figure 6.3   Second-level influence map

Now, because we need to convince two influencers of our decision-maker before we ask for a commitment, we must now deal with at least six new people before we can get to the point of asking for a final decision. You can see how this works out. If the key decision-maker we need is a laggard, there will be many levels of influence map that will need to be created before someone is found who will listen to new ideas with any chance of doing something about them. Frankly speaking, if it is impossible to find at least two people in the early adopter category within two levels of the stakeholder you need to convince, it is better to abandon the innovation altogether. The cost in time to convince the necessary influencers will usually be better spent doing innovations which have more immediate chance of success.

6.8   CASE STUDY: BANK OF AMERICA AND THE CENTRE FOR FUTURE BANKING

Perhaps one of the best examples of the processes we have been discussing in this chapter kicked off in 2008 at Bank of America. In early 2008, the bank announced it would create the Centre for Future Banking in conjunction with MIT's media lab. The idea of the centre is to 'serve as an idea generator, experimenting with far-reaching concepts at the cutting edge of today's technologies. Lab researchers will collaborate with the bank to determine the potential impact – and customer benefits – of implementing these ideas' [59]. Bank of America committed 25 million dollars over five years to the initiative.

Such a sizeable investment is not that unusual considering the tradition of innovation at Bank of America, some of which we looked at in Chapter 1. Innovation is a core competency and there is a central innovation function, in addition to specialised innovation centres of excellence in each line of the business.

As usual with major initiatives, however, the Centre for Future Banking started as a spark of an idea with a few people. One of these was Hans Schumacher, a graduate of MIT himself, and a relatively recent joiner of Bank of America from Ford Motor. Schumacher is an engineer, and during a routine recruiting trip on campus, managed to get a student to give him a tour of the MIT media labs at night. In Automotive, innovation is the bread and butter of success. But, as we've seen, it usually takes a great deal of effort to get much innovation done in a bank. What, thought Schumacher, might happen if Bank of America were able to get some of these students working in the lab to do internships with it? Might the innovative thinking and creativity of MIT transfer across?

Of course, there was an immediate problem. Students, used to the collegial environment and innovation-without-boundaries culture of MIT, would hardly be attracted to a bank with prescribed lines of control, significant regulation, and a 'boring' business.

Then, too, a student can't just select an internship anywhere. It is necessary that their professors also agree the experience would be valuable and that an internship might have a positive impact on their own research agendas.

Bank of America has incredible amounts of data. Universities wouldn't come close to the information stored about customers and their behaviour by any institution, and Bank of America was one of the largest. In the end, the carrot of the data was the golden nugget that convinced the first student and his professor he should come to the bank.

Initially, this caused a stir at the media labs, as students had never worked inside a bank before. It also started a process of thinking inside the bank: how might the transfer of IP between these two large institutions benefit both?

Over the course of years, Bank of America has developed elaborate pipeline processes, with sophisticated scoring systems and structured ways to transform ideas into fundable business cases. Typically for an organisation with advanced innovation methods, it noticed that whilst it was very good at delivering innovations that worked in the context of existing businesses, it had no way at all to do innovation outside them.

Jeff Carter, the executive from Bank of America who runs the relationship with the lab, was also instrumental in its creation. His interest was piqued by the embryonic student intern programme that Schumacher was attempting to get off the ground. He recalls that the bank recognised it needed to be able to come at innovation from an outside-in perspective. Innovations with long-term payoffs – breakthroughs and revolutions – often don't have good business cases at the start. They require longer-term thinking and can be speculative. There's a high chance of failure. The rigour of Bank of America's innovation processes made such innovations hard or impossible.

Disruptive innovation, Carter points out, was especially challenging. 'Imagine if the credit card business came up with something amazing, but it destroyed the deposits business,' he says. 'Disruptions have every chance of being cannibalistic to existing revenues, and banks aren't good at thinking in those terms,' he continues.

But the bank did not make the mistake of believing that, just because it found it difficult to do disruptive or breakthrough innovation, its competitors (some of whom might not yet exist) would also fail. It was for this reason that the bank began to consider its student relationship with MIT in a new way.

As we've seen in Chapter 3, it is generally complicated to get to the position where an innovation team can successfully work with disruption and get away with it. So how did Bank of America manage to counter the natural blocking behaviour of large organisations in these situations?

Carter, at the time, was working on a project to create an information architecture transformation strategy. The bank had, over many years, acquired hundreds of companies, and each of these had contributed to huge diversity in the bank's systems. Such a plethora of systems led to a confusion of data and sources, something that Carter thought the bank could solve. But there were a lot of questions. Could it be done in a short period of time, say 24 months? What would the cost be? And could the bank actually absorb so much change in a short period of time?

Along the way, Carter and Schumacher networked into the bank's community of quantitative analysts, some 3500 individuals. He found a community anticipating a tripling in size over the next three years. To help manage that, the bank built a Web 2.0 community called QuantComm.

The success of QuantComm led Carter and Schumacher from Charlotte back to MIT in Boston to see other Web 2.0 technologies and whatever else was going on at the very edge of what was possible. Here they met Frank Moss, director of the media lab at MIT. Frank was immediately invited to Charlotte, the headquarters of Bank of America, to speak on the topic of industry–academic collaborations and innovation specifically.

The discussion that followed was wide-ranging. Why were American companies – especially banks – not investing in research that would secure their futures? Might there be a perfect storm on the horizon where massive industries could be disrupted by those who were investing in research? It seemed that collaboration between Bank of America and MIT might be one way of addressing such a threat, were it to arise. An initial agreement to investigate this potential opportunity was quickly reached.

The structure of the collaboration would be a partnership. Bank employees would be embedded en masse into the lab – 10 to 20 people at a time, with hundreds rotated through over a period of years. The point was to expose as many people as possible to interesting and leading-edge concepts, and then provide the tools that would make it possible to explore them in the banking environment.

Knowing early results would have the normal business case problems of any disruptive innovation (namely, that any financial returns would be long-term, if they were available at all), the concept was framed in terms of long-term benefits, rather than short-term wins, so there would be penalties imposed for early exit. This, it was thought, would give time for the lab to breathe, to prove it was creating value for the bank.

The initial proposal took 30 days to write, but at the end, Bank of America had a robust strategy for transforming itself from outside in, with MIT as a partner. How, though, to sell such a radical idea to the senior leaders who would need to buy in to make the vision a reality?

Carter engaged with senior leaders who had access to the top table of the bank. Recalls Carter, 'They loved the plan, but didn't think it would be possible to get it up. But in the end, they were agreeable to giving it a go.' A schedule was created to socialise the strategy across the top leaders of the bank. Naturally, there were significant objections. Intellectual property protection was a key issue. Leaders wanted to know how they would protect their competitive advantage in an open academic world that encourages sharing. There was the question of patents, and what to do about people who were working outside the process. How could Bank of America possibly consider such an investment without the absolute certainty of control that its internal innovation teams gave it?

But the team countered with an argument much loved by innovators: there is no point having great ideas if you don't also have the ability to implement them at speed. The lab would provide that, in a context of working at the very edge. Bank of America, they said, needed to be faster than anyone else if it was to avoid the perfect storm that was coming.

The careful influencing paid off when several executives working for Ken Lewis, chairman of the bank, became believers. They championed the idea, authorised exploratory trips to MIT for senior people, and basically gave the project a green light.

As we've seen before in this book, the support of senior-level executives is almost always required for large, strategic innovations, and this was no exception. Once Carter had support, it was only 9 months later that the doors of the new lab opened. At the time of writing, the lab has been open for 120 days, and there is a significant portfolio of research under way. But already there are early results.

For a start, the way the bank thinks about its new ideas has changed. Says Carter, 'in research like this you are not trying to create a new product or answer a specific question... it is more about getting a complete insight into how you think about the question which might drive a breakthrough.' other words, the bank has realised it is valuable to create new questions rather than new solutions. And the ability to do innovative work outside the constraints of major business lines has also been working a subtle magic. The way the bank thinks about its business is changing, and though the changes are not pervasive in every area yet, they are being driven top-down.

Schumacher agrees. 'People were really frightened about the new world that was emerging outside the bank. You could ask people about iPhones and the threat of mobile. Or about the likely consequences if, say, Google were to buy a bank. But they wouldn't have had any answers. The lab is showing them there can be reasonable responses.'

Even the way that innovators are expected to behave is being changed. The innovator's work is traditionally kept secret. Collaborating with other organisations – especially other banks – is frowned on. But the Centre for Future Banking is an open academic environment where such secrecy isn't possible. It has demonstrated that open collaboration is a very powerful tool.

Bank of America is leading the way for innovators who are at the futurecasting stage I described in Chapter 3. It has created a way to systematically examine and react to possible futures, even if they are outside the scope of existing business lines or have disruptive potential.

6.9   WRAPPING UP THE INNOVATION PHASE

Now that we're at the end of this chapter, the innovation programme will have accomplished several things. It will, firstly, have a neatly prioritised list of innovations that it might pursue. It will have made investments in answering the key questions, and using the results of these will have approached various executives for funding. Some innovations, hopefully, will now be ready to move into the development phase. Everyone is excited to get started on whatever-it-is. And the innovators, knowing they've caused activity to occur which would not have otherwise, feel free to sit back on their laurels and recuperate before they start the next big push. They might, even, have been fooled into thinking their job is done.

The thing is, innovators can't rely on established project delivery processes – which will, in most institutions, be very mature – to support them entirely in the delivery of things which are very new. Whilst these established processes are very good at incremental improvements, particularly if they are of a sustaining nature, they tend to perform poorly the more unprecedented their deliverables might be. It is therefore necessary for innovators to act as 'gunpowder', an analogy I've often used to describe the function that innovation practitioners must perform during delivery. They aren't the gun (the foundation on which the innovation gets built), neither are they the bullet (the innovation itself). But they do need to be the gunpowder which propels it forward.

It is to the subject of being 'gunpowder' that the next chapter is devoted. We'll be talking extensively about execution, which is the last stage of the futureproofing process that is the central theme of this book.

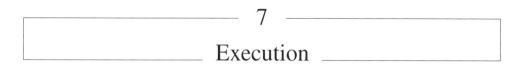

7
Execution

What you will find in this chapter

- The ways you can choose to manage the execution phase to minimise risk of failure.
- Activities for innovators whilst the new thing is being built.
- Why innovators should contribute to launch activities.
- The innovators and post-launch operations.

The execution phase commences when an idea has, finally, been given funding to build it for real. It is the time that the real work starts to convert the idea into something new that people can really use. It is also the time most innovators think their work is done, and where most books on innovation finish.

Here's the thing though: whilst puppy drowning and early failure are options *before* senior leadership has agreed to fund a project and work has started, they are certainly not afterwards. At this point, not only has the innovation team invested to answer the three key questions, leadership has committed their investment cash and reputations as well. Unfortunately, it is inevitable that innovations will not live up to expectations in every case. Left to themselves, actually, most will *not* do so.

A lot can go wrong *after* everyone has agreed a new idea should be implemented. And because innovators are judged not on what they get approved, but on what changes actually make it out the door into the hands of customers or end-users, they cannot afford, really, to step away and take a back seat whilst someone else moves things forward.

How can an idea with plenty of money behind it, the pre-work of the innovation and ideation phases done, and broad agreement go wrong? The answer is threefold.

Firstly, the process of converting an idea into reality is inherently one of compromise. The security folk, for example, will almost always want changes to minimise the risks they see to the institution. The operations people might determine they, too, need to make changes in order to ensure their costs are flat. And the technologists will have opinions which affect the idea as it goes through the development process.

All these compromises change the way the end product is delivered. Quite often, it is changed so completely there is little resemblance at all to what was initially funded. This is not a good thing, because it means the pre-work done by innovators – answering the key questions – might no longer reflect the situation faced by the innovation once it gets real use.

If one is lucky, the innovation might still be adopted sufficiently to be successful. But the purpose of the whole futureproofing process is to avoid, as much as possible, any reliance on luck: when you have to deliver hard returns dependably, eliminating luck as a factor is essential. Ensuring the innovation is true to its initial conception is the way to do that.

Another reason for innovation failure is institutional politics. In every large organisation, there are competing factions, who attempt to gain control of scarce resources to further their own agendas. Whilst this is usually done in a spirit of coopertition, it can be deadly to innovation. Failure to manage stakeholders correctly will often result in an innovation being cancelled for seemingly silly reasons.

The final reason an innovation can fail after broad support is achieved is that it fails to meet expectations after launch. Now, of all the possible failure situations that might occur this is by far the worst. Why? Because, when all is said and done, this is the time the most effort and money has been spent. If nothing comes of all that investment, it won't be the team that built the innovation, nor the ones running it post-launch that will be to blame: it is, of course, the innovators, the ones who forced the change down the throats of stakeholders against better advice.

I write that last sentence somewhat ironically, of course. It isn't always the case that the blame for a failed innovation is laid at the feet of the innovation practitioners who supported it, regardless of the reasons that the failure occurred in the first place. But one thing I can tell you with certainty: having a series of very visible flops is just as damaging to the careers of innovators as it would be to a movie star with a history of big-budget box office failures.

All three reasons we've just looked at mean innovation practitioners must be centrally involved in the implementation of their innovations. It is possible, though not always true, that innovators must also be involved in the launch and operation of their innovation as well. The execution phase of futureproofing, then, is about the set of things innovators must do during the build, launch, and operate phases of the innovation's life.

7.1   WAYS TO MANAGE EXECUTION

At the end of the day, there's no point doing innovation unless one delivers results at the end of the process. It is very tempting to imagine that by the time funding is agreed, the role of an innovator is over. This, however, does not make sure actual returns are delivered, and we've just looked at three of the most common ways an innovation can fail before it starts to deliver anything at all.

To combat this, the innovation practitioner must select a level of involvement which makes sense for the particular innovation they are pursuing. Really, when it comes right down to it, there are four levels of involvement to consider.

The first, obviously, is no involvement at all. Though I've spent the better part of this chapter thus far talking about the need for innovators to guide their innovations way past the funding decision, there are occasions when a great deal of involvement is unnecessary.

When one considers, for example, modifying a form with new imagery so it is more usable by customers (an incremental innovation, by any stretch of the imagination), there is very little for the innovators to do other than make sure the modification does, in fact, get done. I call this approach 'hands off'. One progresses the innovation to the point where everyone agrees it ought to be done, and then leaves it to others to execute. Hands off, of course, is only appropriate for some innovations, usually those that are largely incremental.

Incremental innovations, being related to existing processes, technologies, or business lines, are well understood by an institution. There will usually be well-developed processes available that have the capability to make change. And on top of all this, there will likely be people whose job is to work out how to improve things. The role of the innovator, in such environments, is to make sure the idea and its justification find their way into the hands of those who will execute.

It is usually not possible, however, to adopt such an approach for any innovation which is revolutionary or breakthrough in nature. Innovations in the former category, of course, are all about taking the existing way of doing things and remoulding them in such a way that they become the default option for a large segment of new customers or end-users. In Chapter 1, where I first characterised the difference between the kinds of innovations, I used the example of ING Direct of Canada as an example of a revolutionary innovation.

As the founder of direct banking, ING Direct offered consumers a superior financial deal on a range of products in exchange for reducing its costs of distribution. This model, unheard of at the time, was sufficiently revolutionary that ING captured sizeable deposit share in many countries and spawned a flurry of other direct banking offers from its competitors.

Revolutionary and breakthrough innovations may be difficult to get off the ground in the first place, and much investment will have to be ploughed in to answering the three key questions before anyone will agree to provide funding. For the innovator, however, the work on a revolutionary innovation has just started with such agreement.

Here is where the second way to manage execution comes in: gunpowdered implementation. The basics of this metaphor were explained earlier, so suffice it to say that innovators adopting this level of involvement are centrally involved in oversight of the process that leads from funding to launch. Why is this important at all, given that any successful institution will have mature processes for managing change? Why, actually, is a revolutionary change any different from an incremental one?

The answer to these questions may be found in the scope of the change being attempted. Whilst an incremental change (such as changing the design of a form) fits well within the existing structures and frameworks of existing processes, doing something revolutionary will almost certainly not. The innovation, therefore, not only seeks to change the way something is done, it changes the shape of the *organisation* in which it is done.

Take, for example, the historical example of Internet banking. The first banks to launch this service had little conception of the sets of things they would need to deliver to make the experience a successful one for customers. What should they do when a customer lost their password? Should they give out passwords in the first place? Who would customers turn to when their computers didn't work? And who would be responsible if the passwords got hacked and customers' accounts were emptied?

All these considerations were brand new for the institutions that launched online first. Specialised processes and teams had to be developed to address these considerations, and it wasn't long before many banks founded specialised business units to deal only with the online channel.

The innovation of Internet banking introduced a range of organisational changes. In some banks, it was the formation of entire business lines – direct banks – around the new channel. In others, the change was the centralisation of new processes and systems that overtook the old. There are few institutions today that haven't experienced substantial change as a result of this one, important innovation.

Whenever you have an organisational change of any scale, there are both winners and losers. The latter group of people, naturally, are highly motivated to ensure the innovation does not progress if at all possible. They take active steps to water down whatever-it-is, and failing to do that, will often actively work behind the scenes to discredit any potential advantages that may, eventually, emerge.

This behaviour is rarely actively planned in advance. People don't like change, especially when it impacts them negatively. For those who especially dislike change (the late majority and laggards in the innovation model we examined in Figure 2.2), they are no more able to prevent themselves from negativity during the implementation than they would be able to stop eating and drinking. Practically speaking, though, what does this mean for innovation teams?

The result of any funding decision is usually that a project team is assembled to manage the translation of an innovation into something usable by customers or end-users. There will almost always be some form of governance put in place: most often a steering committee of some kind. It is essential that innovators have a place on this committee, or at a minimum be privy to the decisions it takes and have a way to influence them.

Whilst the most visible way to 'gunpowder' an implementation is to participate in the governance of the implementation project, quite often the level of involvement needs to be even more substantial. During the day-to-day business of the implementation project, there are inevitably multiple decisions made, some of which are more significant than others. Sometimes, decisions are taken which seem minor at the time, but have substantive implications for the eventual shape of the innovation.

Consider the following scenario: your institution has chosen to add new functionality to its Internet banking channel – the ability for customers to classify their transaction into groups so they can create spending reports. Although the development costs are high, these are to be offset by a new revenue stream resulting from the data – merchants are to be able to log in and get aggregated data about the kinds of things their customers spend their money on. This is valuable new intelligence, and a number of significant corporate customers of your institution's acquiring services have already signed up. In the meantime, retail customers are expected to defect from competitors in droves. Optimism runs high.

Then, during project implementation, a seemingly inconsequential implementation decision is made. The security folk, in an effort to reduce the riskiness of the new functionality, impose a technology design that puts barriers between each customer's newly classified transaction data. Aggregation of that data into useful reports becomes impossible. Both customer and financial expectations of the innovation are missed.

From the perspective of the data involved, such a decision makes complete sense, and a security specialist was perfectly justified in making it. Recall from our discussion of this kind of thing in Chapter 3, the mandate of security people is to reduce risk. They will do so in silo fashion unless they are presented with very good arguments to do otherwise. It is the role of the innovator, acting as gunpowder, to present such reasons.

Gunpowdering, ultimately, means that innovators must provide the bigger picture view into almost *every* key decision made by the implementation team. By doing so, they are able to preserve the original intent and optimise the chances that the innovation has at least the potential to be successful after launch.

The next level of involvement an innovation team might have is the actual launch of the innovation. Launch, of course, is normally the preserve of marketing people and product managers, so why would an innovator be interested in participating in such activities? Surely such individuals will be more expert than any innovator, with their comprehensive background in developing new proposition messages for the market?

For breakthrough and revolutionary innovations, the expertise of traditional marketers and product managers in financial services is incomplete. These are professionals with very strong backgrounds in managing the launch processes of incremental innovations: a new rate savings account, superior convenience in channels, or a cheaper mortgage. When confronted with something that potentially changes the game, they do not have the complete information the innovation professional will likely be able to contribute to the process.

Innovation theory provides us with the tools we need to assist marketing and product professionals with their launch activities. Referring again to the innovation adoption model we first examined in Figure 2.1, we know there are several phases that potential adopters of any innovation go through before they make the decision to actually *use* an innovation. They need to understand the how, why, and what of the new thing. Then there's a need to provide positive reinforcement through other users and trials. And, in the end, help has to be provided to assist with actual implementation of the new innovation in daily practices. These are all areas in which the innovation professional has expertise that might assist those formally in charge of the launch.

So much for launch activities, which we will discuss in much more detail in a moment. But let us now turn our attention to the last level of involvement that innovation programmes might have in an innovation, when they own and operate the innovation in their own right. Why would any innovation team do this? Surely it is the responsibility of business executives to actually make sure the day-to-day activities that underlie the operation of any given innovation are undertaken competently? Well, that is true in all but two situations: where the innovation is disruptive, or where it is breakthrough in nature.

The breakthrough innovation is one that almost certainly has to be nurtured in the initial few years of its operational life. The reason is that it will likely be so far outside the constraints of present business and operational processes that no one will know what to do with it. Whole new capabilities may need to be developed, or new cultures incubated. For the breakthrough innovation, there is rarely, if ever, a satisfactory support structure available to make sure of success at the beginning.

The innovators, therefore, are left with the task of making sure the infrastructures needed to support an innovation (processes, people, technologies, etc.) are built over time. At the beginning, the innovation team will have as little experience as the rest of the business with the newness that is incarnated in the breakthrough. But they have one significant advantage over their colleagues: they are not tied down with day jobs that necessitate a focus on significant revenue lines critical to the operation of the broader business.

For a disruptive innovation, however, the reasons for own and operate are even more compelling. Such innovations, if you recall our discussion in Chapter 2, are rarely very interesting to mainline business units in the first instance. For a start, they tend to target unprofitable customer segments in new ways, or segments that are, at least on the face of it, not particularly strategic from an institution's point of view.

Then, too, the disruptive innovation usually won't command the kind of revenues mainline businesses are used to. Those come with time, as the innovation develops. But in the first instance, the disruptive innovation may be considered a distraction. That's especially the case during troubled times, when 'refocusing on core business' is the order of the day.

But the most significant issue facing a disruptive innovation is, if it is successful, that it will eventually cannibalise core revenue streams managed by incumbent business units. Powerful executives are highly motivated to 'drown the puppy' of anything that touches their core interests. In other words, a disruptive innovation will be too small to matter at the beginning (thereby getting none of the attention it deserves) and then will become too threatening as it begins to show success. Own and operate involvement, which we will come back to later in this chapter, is the answer to these issues.

Regardless of the level of involvement the innovation team selects once funding has been achieved, execution will always involve three critical activities: the build-out of the innovation itself, its launch, and, eventually, the day-to-day operations once whatever-it-is makes it into the hands of customers or end-users. We look at the details of each of these activities next.

7.2   BUILDING THE NEW THING

Once funding of an innovation has been achieved, the next thing likely to occur is the formation of a project team. Such teams are composed, generally, of experts both inside and outside the institution, and are tasked with converting the idea into something that can be used for real. But the project team does not start with a blank slate, and many key decisions about the innovation have already been made by the innovation team and its key stakeholders from whom funding has been obtained. Such decisions were taken, perhaps unconsciously, whilst getting the answers to the three key questions which are central to the operation of the innovation phase.

In answering the 'Should we?' question, various decisions about business and revenue models will already have been taken. The 'Can we?' question has already created high-level designs and other artefacts which shape the innovation in particular ways. And the timetable for the innovation has been laid down by answering the 'When?' question.

With so much determined, what is left for a project team to decide? The answer, of course, is quite a lot, but there is a necessary inflexibility when it comes to some key areas. It is the point of the requirements document to codify the areas in which such inflexibility exists.

The requirements document

A project with any amount of uncertainty or novelty (something innovations will certainly have in abundance) must start with detailed statements about what is to be created. The requirements document is this set of statements.

Requirements documents are much loved by IT people, who will tend to use them as justifications for any and every failure or slippage during a build process. 'It wasn't in the requirements', or 'that's a new requirement', is a mantra innovators will become familiar with during this important time in which their ideas are converted into a reality.

The fact of the matter, however, is that innovation practitioners care about requirements only in so far as they are used to codify the set of things an innovation must have to preserve the integrity of the key questions. Practically everything else should be left malleable, and indeed, exerting too much control over the requirements generation process will leave innovators too little time to manage their other projects.

Having too many requirements also ensures that when big decisions are made it is much more complicated to determine if, in fact, a key questions compromise might occur. Requirements are like the puppies we drowned in Chapters 5 and 6. Once you own one it becomes difficult, even impossible, to let it go, even when it no longer makes sense. Far better, then, to have fewer requirements and an awareness of significant implications as they change over the course of the execution phase.

Project teams have three factors under their control. They have the ability to change how much money is being spent to deliver the benefits. They have some say over the set of deliverables themselves and the exact way that they will be implemented. And, of course, they can change the schedule of deliveries. Looking at those three factors, you notice that each factor relates closely to our key questions.

This sets up a natural conflict between project managers and innovators, who will both believe they must control all three factors closely for success. However, the requirements document strikes a balance for both parties: before the project really starts, innovators have the opportunity to sketch out no-go areas through requirements, and afterwards, project managers are very much aware of what it is that needs to be delivered for success. So, how does one codify the key questions in a requirements document?

As I explained in the last chapter, the 'Should we?' question is mainly about economics. The requirements document, therefore, will normally characterise details such as the set of features required and their relationship to benefits. Elucidating this coupling in a robust way is very important, since one of the first things a project team will do when (inevitably) the project overruns or gets into other sorts of difficulties is look for features that can be cut. Often, this is done without a clear understanding of the end-game impact, so being specific about benefits at the requirements stage is very helpful later. It underlines the fact that if the shape of what the innovation does is changed, there may be no point in continuing at all.

The 'Should we?' question also demands that certain cost aspects of the innovation be detailed in the requirements document. Benefits are all very well, but the economic case for any innovation is predicated on how much money must be spent to deliver benefits in the first place, and then keep them coming later.

During the innovation phase, much consideration will have been given to the overall approach taken to building out the innovation, since this was the only way to get to specific cost data that was the foundation of the business case. Much of that work now needs to be codified as a requirement in order to avoid the project team doing something that has unintended fiduciary impacts.

The 'Can we?' question is mostly technical. Here, too, there are aspects of the work previously done during the innovation phase which must be written into the requirements document. The principle here is that the main features of the high-level design be adhered to. The high-level design defines the shape the implementation of an innovation will take. Whilst it is not necessary to adhere to such a design in every detail, the fact of the matter is that project teams must be aware that significant technical decisions have already been taken. These may, in fact, be critical to the success of the innovation.

Let me give you an example, one that has come up often recently as institutions deploy mobile banking. The technical argument is whether or not the correct interface for customers is a special web page for small screens, a simple SMS service, or an application that customers must download and install on their phones. The first has the benefit of being easy to install and manage, and SMS has the advantage of working on everything. But there are advantages to the application approach as well, not the least being availability when mobile phone coverage is poor. There are significant differences in the security models available, as well as the way features would be implemented in each.

The essential question here, though, is not a technical one. It *is* a question of which method customers prefer for bank account access. If they are proud owners of an Apple iPhone or other high-end Internet phone, they will almost certainly prefer an application. More basic handsets might work only with SMS, so their owners would be locked out of mobile banking if the more complicated approach was taken. And the remainder may well prefer the web page option. My point is that no matter what the project team (and, presumably, their technical experts) think, this is a question that has nothing to do with technology, and *everything* to do with the customer demographic being targeted. Incorporating key elements of the high-level design where they mandate a particular technological approach avoids the difficulties one encounters when an innovation has its shape unintentionally changed by a major technical decision.

The final key question is 'When?', and this too has aspects which should be incorporated in the requirements document. As we saw in the last chapter, 'When?' is comprised of consideration of the market factors that would govern adoption of the innovation. There might be, for example, a competitive release planned by another institution, and if the key questions were predicated on first-mover advantage, having the project team move the dates would likely make the innovation subject to cancellation.

'When?', of course, is the one factor over which project teams feel they have absolute control subject to the dictates of the steering committee. And it is true, to a large degree, that prescribing the delivery schedule renders the project team less able to do their jobs. But the point of adding in schedule commitments to the requirements document is that it provides focus to the linkage between timing and success. And for innovations, timing can sometimes be everything.

In the end, there is a careful line that must be walked by innovation teams when assisting in the creation of requirements documents. By prescribing too much, the innovator becomes, ipso facto, the project manager him or herself. This is rarely a core competence, and increases the likelihood that the innovation will fail to get delivered. On the other hand, specifying too little means the *shape* of what is delivered will likely not meet expectations, thereby placing the predictable returns needed by the innovation team in jeopardy.

Why innovations fail late

Unfortunately, it is impossible to argue with failure statistics. Once ideas have gotten through all the processes of futureproofing, even at the late execution phase, a surprising percentage will *still* fail. One study examined 50 innovation projects at Dutch companies and found that 39% of innovative projects failed completely or partially at this late stage [47]. Other studies, particularly those of IT projects, have reported much, much higher failure rates.

Let us assume, for a moment, the classic reasons for failure have been addressed adequately to this point. Let's face it, the amount of work that ought to have gone into the process of getting an innovation to the point of execution via the key questions will have been substantial. There is definitely a market need, an ability to execute, and the timing should be right. What, then, is the reason for these appalling failure numbers?

As it happens, most innovation research has focused on practically every stage of the innovation process *except* those specific processes which relate to turning the new thing into reality. The very few studies which are available make only broad generalisations, and there are none which have much to say about financial services. When one examines what literature *is* available, however, six key themes emerge and most are present to some degree or other when an innovation goes wrong.

The first theme is that executives perceive a lack of balance between the amount of money they are spending and the benefits they will receive. Now, although the key questions have answered conclusively whether there will be a positive return (eventually, at least), we are concerned here with *perceptions*. Because an innovation is genuinely new, executives will often feel they are being taken down a path without a map. They can easily get cold feet if they are not managed carefully.

It is usually the case that lots of investment has to occur before anything is even remotely ready to show for it. No matter how good the pre-work prior to investment, this is a scenario which will always get a competent manager nervous. And the closer the new thing is to revolution or breakthrough, the more likely this nervousness will increase to the point where executives feel they have little choice but to intervene in the project directly to safeguard themselves.

Such interventions, though not always a bad thing, are usually not desirable. They send the message that an implementation is in trouble and the project team is unable to fix the problem. These are messages which come with such interventions whether they are true or not. But it is relatively easy to avoid such situations, and the strategy that should be employed is obvious: build out whatever-it-is such that significant results appear earlier in the schedule. IT programmes, which have an especially colourful past when it comes to this particular problem, have been using early-delivery techniques for years now. They go by names such as *agile development*, or *extreme coding*, but the basic premise is making early progress as transparent as possible. This is just as important for an innovation project as it would be for an IT one.

The second theme that arises in the literature regularly when innovations fail is that information asymmetries have exhibited themselves. An information asymmetry, as you would probably guess, is any situation occurring when control of information is heavily regulated. Individuals in the know start using their inside access to knowledge for personal gain or to reinforce a particular position they have decided to take with respect to the innovation. It is inevitable that the presence of an information asymmetry results in information politics.

Most institutions, having committed funding to doing something new, then rigorously control who can know they are doing so. The idea is that competitors will, as a result of this control, be less likely to steal the march on the bank. The thinking continues with a belief that there is an increase in the duration that any competitive advantage is sustained. Human behaviour, of course, always comes directly into play, and if there is advantage to be gained from an information asymmetry, the opportunity will usually be taken.

How does this increase the chances of an innovation failure? The main reason is that the commencement of information politics slows down processes of collaboration which are essential in the development of new things. Because the process of germinating an innovation is inherently risky and subject to many unknown factors, the broadest possible collaboration across an institution will usually be the best way to mitigate the possibility of failure. Collaboration, though, does not always come easily. You can imagine a frustrated business innovator, for example, delaying the involvement of IT professionals until the last possible moment, then discovering that the systems required to launch are not available or will not scale.

Why lock out the IT folk in the first place, though? Taking our example further, one can imagine many reasons. It might be that putting the development into the ordinary technology queue would result in a delivery date too far from the present. Perhaps there is a need to circumvent a governance or architectural issue. Or maybe it is nothing more complicated than an expectation – based on past experience – that dealing with IT will be painful, so it is best put off as long as possible.

For whatever reason, segregating the information from those who might have usefully helped during the development of an innovation is one of the biggest predictors of innovation failure. And the best way to counter the effects of information asymmetries is to be as open about the innovation to as wide an audience as possible.

The third theme emerging from examples of innovation failure is the scenario in which executives, project team members, and the rest of the institution fail to develop an early enough understanding of their roles and responsibilities during the development (and subsequent operation) of the innovation. As you would imagine, this has a number of significant effects. For starters, innovators and project teams often end up doing the same jobs, with conflicts of various sorts starting fairly quickly thereafter. The actual delivery teams might confuse their role as implementers with that of innovators, especially when it comes to determinations affecting the key questions in any material way. And, as I've suggested earlier, the moment the balance of investment to benefit gets out of kilter, project sponsors will immediately think they have to be managers and implementers themselves.

Another effect resulting from role confusion is a drop in the pace of delivery. When no one knows who is doing what, a project team can get into a thrashing cycle: before any action is taken, everyone checks with everyone else to make sure no one else is doing whatever-it-is. Or, worse still, everyone waits for someone else to make a decision about whether it ought to be done at all. It is one of the principal signs of role confusion when the pace of decision-making starts to slow.

But perhaps the worst effect of role confusion – at least from the perspective of innovators – is that it clouds the processes that are so critical for managing compromise. Not only does the pace of decision slow, but the attention of decision-makers is diverted to issues which are probably irrelevant in the overall scheme of things. As I've mentioned elsewhere, the only issues that really matter to innovators are those which affect the key questions. But when there is role confusion, *every* issue becomes substantial. The consequence is that decision-exhaustion sets in, and this, unchecked, can lead to failure all by itself.

The next reason for innovation failure at the execution phase is culture gaps: those dissonances that occur as a result of the clash between the way things were done before and the way they will be done after the innovation has gone live. As I've mentioned, there are almost always winners and losers whenever change is introduced. Those on the losing side will usually not be thrilled to be so, and will take active steps to counter what they perceive to be a step backward. That is one form of culture gap that can easily defeat an innovation.

But an even more serious issue is the often-occurring situation where the whole culture of an institution must adapt to the new way of doing things. Institutionalised cultures are rarely able to move quickly. An innovation that demands quick change will certainly be met with scepticism, even panic. These forces, left unmanaged, can quickly become very powerful, gaining ground as people use word-of-mouth mechanisms to reinforce the message that 'that's not the way we do things here'.

There is an interaction here with the information asymmetries that we spoke about a moment ago. The process of managing cultural changes is one of communication, but the inherent tendency of institutions to 'lock down' the new thing in the context of retaining advantage mitigates against effective cultural change. Then, too, the more change being introduced, the more potential advantage accrues to those 'in the know', who have a powerful motivation to keep the number of people so advantaged low. Is it any wonder at all that innovations which are especially transformational fail more often than they succeed?

The final two causes for innovation failure are related. Firstly, innovation teams and their projects will often over-commit themselves in what must be delivered whilst failing to realise they've done so early enough. Secondly, there is sometimes an attempt to force the set of features and functions which are presently scoped for the innovation into adjacent problem spaces without a proper consideration of whether it is appropriate to do so. Both are defensive strategies adopted by innovators and their sponsors who are concerned they may not make adequate returns after the innovation goes live. Are there *really* enough customers in our target group to make this profitable? Will they *really* find enough utility in a first-generation effort (which is what all truly new things are) to cause them to adopt?

Faced with such uncertainty, it is easy to broaden the scope of the innovation in an attempt to broaden the market. Scope creep, as this is often known, is insidious. It seems to make sense at the time, but all it really does is dilute attention and focus from the core value of the innovation.

There are some classic examples in online banking. At one stage, for example, institutions began to believe that because their transactional websites were amongst the most visited places on the web, it would be sensible to start selling other products and services through them, just like online retailer Amazon had done. Surely, they reasoned, it would be possible to monetise all that traffic, and consumers would value the additional innovation of doing retail in a banking context.

By implementing retail in the online banking context, institutions had set themselves up to compete with established and incumbent organisations that already controlled the space. They could not hope to match the distribution, supply chain, and pure savvy of specialists in the space like Amazon.com. And they forgot the primary reason they had traffic anyway was that customers *loved* visiting their money. Multiple times every day, in some cases. This broadening of the scope of online banking, of course, did nothing for those institutions that got such offerings out the door, and everyone else quietly dropped the idea. In the meantime, though, some banks had spent millions trying to be the customer's 'one portal' on the web.

Before we leave the subject of innovation failure, however, there is one more thing that innovators and their teams must understand: a failure at this late stage will result in what some academics call innovation trauma. Innovation trauma is the situation where parties associated with the failed innovation are so badly affected that they will refuse to work on, or adopt, any further innovations no matter how well suited they might be.

Innovation trauma occurred at Sun Microsystems, a computer manufacturer well loved by many financial institutions. The case of SunRay, its innovative network-centric computer, has been exceptionally well documented [60]. Here was a way that organisations could improve the way their employees accessed computing services – basically a very low-cost terminal that offered all the ease and use of a full desktop computer, but at a fraction of the total cost of ownership. As all the computing resources were centralised, management was supposed to be simplified, efficiencies of scale realised, and end-user productivity increased. SunRay, it was said, would topple Microsoft from its dominance in the personal computing space. The thing was, it didn't do any of these things, and the reason was simple: the sales force at Sun was suffering innovation trauma from a previous, related innovation that went badly wrong: JavaStation.

JavaStation was a product flawed both in conception and execution. Sales teams who had put their necks on the line to promote it to customers had been badly burned, and reputations in the field were in tatters. When SunRay came along, no one was willing to go through the pain again, even though the new product addressed most of the shortcomings of its predecessor.

Innovation trauma, especially on the scale of SunRay, is such a significant threat to the future innovation pipeline that it must be avoided at all costs. The problem, of course, is that it is rarely obvious *in advance* that innovation trauma is the likely result of a particular project. And after the fact, all that can be done is take whatever recuperative measures seem appropriate, however ineffective they may be. When you have innovation trauma, you are staring the end of the innovation programme right in the face.

Managing compromise

The process of delivering an innovation is one of managing compromise, and it is critical that the innovation team be central to any decisions that compromise the integrity of an innovation. Compromise is inevitable, of course, because as the build-out process continues, new information comes to light that was unavailable when the key questions were first investigated. The new information might be technological or procedural, or perhaps there is a refined understanding of the environment the innovation must operate in. Whatever the case, it is data that could never have been known in advance, and plans have to change to accommodate it.

Some compromises, however, are worse than others. The most significant compromise is one that impacts the answers to any of the three key questions. For example, if an innovation's 'Should we?' question was predicated on customer reaction to a specific feature or function, and it later emerges that significant compromises have to be made, the entire premise of the innovation has changed.

Too often, however, though the basic fundamentals are now different, organisations forget to go back and ask the key questions again. They are then surprised when the innovation fails to achieve the critical mass – and hence the returns – originally projected. In many organisations, there is a kind of corporate amnesia that occurs the minute the business case is approved and funding assigned.

Innovators must be involved in the compromise process, since they were likely the ones that facilitated the development of the answers to the key questions. Whenever a compromise that touches one of these answers is put on the table, they are the ones who must make a key determination: if we accept this, does it mean we have to answer the key questions again?

If the answer is 'yes', the project should be put on hold whilst that process occurs. And it should be clear to everyone that failure to answer all three key questions positively will result in cancellation. This is a particularly difficult message both for project participants and the sponsoring executives, who both have personal credibility riding on the success of whatever-it-is. They will wonder how it was that the need for compromise was not discovered in advance of the project kick-off.

With everything material committed to a requirements document, and considering all the work that went into an innovation to get it to a position where it was funded in the first place, it is interesting to consider how a key questions compromise can happen at all. Though new information is discovered on a continual basis throughout the execution process, how is it that something as material as a key questions compromise never came up earlier?

Most of the time, significant, game-changing compromises are not the result of new information. They are, though, the result of individuals or groups taking particular positions that reinforce their positions in the light of forthcoming change. This can be the result of information asymmetries, of course, but more often than not, it is simply the way that some people respond to the prospect of significant change.

As I've said multiple times throughout this book, most people – in fact the 50% of the population who are less personally innovative than the average person (see Figure 2.2) – are uncomfortable with change, and that's especially true if there is any possibility their own circumstances will be affected negatively. In such situations, an innovation is faced with a cycle of compromise, with each significantly affected stakeholder proposing changes that make their own positions more secure. Each must be evaluated in the context of the key questions.

As a general rule, if the key questions aren't affected, it is better to allow most compromises. This increases the influence of the innovator so when the time comes that something must be blocked (and trust me, it will), the process is not overly ablative of goodwill.

This brings me to another point, and that is how the innovation team makes sure to preserve its ability to block – or at least mitigate – compromise affecting the key questions. The challenge here is project teams – and the executives to whom they report – will usually be quite adamant that it is *their* project, and they will make all the decisions needed. After all, they're the ones stumping up with the money.

A commonly implemented governance approach for projects is the steering committee, usually composed of the executives funding the project and other senior leaders who have an interest in the innovation. There will often be a process through which status reports are brought to this body, detailing progress against plans and budgets. And significant deviations from what is expected are also brought to the committee for ratification.

Getting the innovation team a role in such committees is usually not difficult. As the experts on the innovation – as they most certainly will be at the start of the project at least – steering committees will usually value their advice. This provides a platform from which strategic compromises can be managed.

In my experience, however, the really significant compromises almost never get made at steering-committee level. The steering committee is a place for project managers, most often, to talk about budgets and schedules. Members will rarely spend their full time on the innovation, and will not have the bandwidth to deal with the detail of building the new thing on a day-to-day basis. But it is in such detail that key question compromises usually get made. For innovators, who will also not be working full time on the innovation (they have a portfolio of projects to progress, remember), getting visibility of such compromises is a challenge even when they are on the steering committee.

One answer that seems to work well is insisting on a rigorous change request process. A change request is a formal statement of the set of things that either executives or project team members want to do which deviate from the previously accepted requirements documents prepared earlier in the build process. The innovation team should ensure it is part of the change request process, reviewing each against key question criteria. When a key question is affected by a change, they need to take steps, either to reject it outright or get the project held in order to re-evaluate the key questions again.

Testing

Eventually, there will be something for innovators to see and touch! This is an exciting time of course, because lots of hard work without anything very real to show for it has gone into an innovation before it reaches this point. So when, finally, it is actually working, there is usually a great deal to celebrate. But let us not break out the champagne too soon, because it is *still* possible for significant things to go wrong. Now, I am not talking here of defects and other technical problems, which are par for the course in any project. The innovation's project team will, in any case, have developed practices for dealing with those, and there will be little for an innovator to do to facilitate this process.

But testing is also the first time real people – besides the innovators and those building the thing itself – will have seen a working end-product. Consequently, it is the first time anyone will be able to gauge the innovation in the context of actual usage. The most important thing for innovation teams to observe at this juncture is how the testers respond to the innovation. Most particularly, does the innovation have the right signposts to guide the testers through the five stages of the innovation decision process we examined in Figure 2.7?

Now, testers are entering a forced adoption process (i.e., they have no choice but to use the innovation, if they are to test it), so their reactions are not a complete picture of the way one would expect *real* end-users to react, but this first insight is essential in guiding development of the launch process that follows.

Because it is a forced decision process, evaluation of the knowledge stage is probably not that helpful. After all, the testers are handed everything they need to know about the innovation in advance, and will likely have a great deal of prior information about it, especially if they were participants in the creation of the test plan. But listening and watching the testers once they have the innovation and start to use it is very instructive.

The second stage of the adoption decision process, persuasion, is all about individuals seeking reinforcement from each other. They are attempting to ensure their perceptions of the innovation are correct, and seek to justify them in the context of the impression of others they trust. This happens for testers just as much as it does for real adopters in the intended audience. So watching – and listening – to testers in the initial stages of their exposure is an excellent barometer of the potential the innovation has for word-of-mouth diffusion later. If their initial impressions of the functionality are unfavourable, there is likely to be a significant issue.

Testing, in effect, is free market research just waiting to be tapped by clever innovators. But one must be clear as to the purpose of this new information. The fact of the matter is that by this stage the innovation is so late in the process that major changes cannot be made without very considerable expense. Assuming the previous steps of the futureproofing process have been followed, major changes will not likely be needed anyway.

So, the shape of the innovation will not change very much as a result of watching the reactions of testers. What *can* change, however, are minor details that will facilitate the launch process. When the testers first started using the system, did it appear that they were able to immediately see how to operate it? What sorts of questions did they ask, and how easy was it for them to get the answers? The answers to these questions can guide an innovator in tweaking launch plans. It might be, for example, that innovators need to rethink the initial promotional material to ensure potential adopters have easy access to the answers for their 'How?', 'Why?', and 'What?' questions. Or perhaps it becomes obvious that the innovation decision process will stall unless adopters can 'taste test', in which case there may need to be a trial option built in somehow.

The point, ultimately, is that this is the very last time innovation teams will be able to make changes, and the changes available will be minor. Using them to support a launch process is the best way to reduce the risk that the innovation will fail once it is in the hands of real people.

The pilot

We come now to the further discussion of pilots to which I alluded in the last chapter. You will recall we discussed the reason for prototypes – the resolution of specific point questions about the uniqueness that comprises the core value of the innovation. A prototype is useful for answering the 'Can we?' question during the innovation phase. Pilots, on the other hand, usually involve putting whatever-it-is in the hands of actual customers or end-users. They are, therefore, usually rather complete implementations of the innovation. When you examine the investment required to get something into a state where it can actually be used as a pilot, it is obvious that pilots are only appropriate in the execution phase, once all the uncertainty about whether or not an innovation will proceed has been removed.

But why run a pilot at all? A pilot provides valuable learning opportunities for those who will eventually have to operate the innovation in the live context. For incremental innovations, there is generally no problem managing the day-to-day operations of an innovation, since it will likely exist inside the context of established processes and frameworks anyway. That is not the case for breakthroughs, however, and may not be for revolutions. In both these cases, as I mentioned earlier in this chapter, not only is the innovation itself new, but the environment into which it must be integrated is new as well. No one has sufficient experience with the new thing to professionally operate it, certainly not at scale.

Since no one knows how to operate the innovation, learning how to do so becomes a critical dependency. This can be an especially painful time, by the way, as real people tend to be much harsher critics than will have been faced before the pilot starts. But this, of course, is the point. The pilot lets an institution find out what works and what doesn't, before any significant segment of its customers or end-users base find out themselves.

There are several learning dimensions to any pilot. The first is operational. The institution is able to test its processes and support systems in the context of the newness incarnated in the innovation. What happens when a customer has a problem? Who do they call? Who gets the escalation in the bank when a major problem demanding immediate resolution occurs?

Getting the answers to such questions is, in my experience, delayed until the very last moment. Everyone is so busy making sure the innovation works, they forget that the infrastructures surrounding the innovation need attention too. The pilot is a great way of forcing an institution to address this.

The second learning dimension of a pilot is technical. A theme recurring throughout this book is that technology, whilst it is not the point in itself, actually underpins every segment of the innovation pentagram we looked at first in Chapter 3. Because technology is involved, there are significant questions to be answered in advance of any real launch. Will the technology scale up to the number of users that might be expected after launch? Can it be secured to an appropriate level acceptable to the risk people? Are all the bugs out of the system?

Now, whilst most projects don't consider the surrounding infrastructures until the last minute, they *do* tend to focus minutely on technology questions such as these, and one wouldn't schedule a pilot without a satisfactory resolution to all of them. But pilots do illuminate certain operational questions: the technology must be operated competently, and if the innovation is very new, new systems will need to be put in place to make sure of this.

Let us return again to the first-generation account aggregation solution I described earlier in this book. In account aggregation, customers are handing over their PINs and passwords to their bank so the system can get their transaction details from other institutions on their behalf. Such a list of PINs and passwords is, obviously, something that must be secured robustly.

Our implementation employed multiple smartcards (chip cards) which were used together to secure the PIN list. Two cards were required to initiate the system, and the security rules we put in place meant that an operator could only have one of the two cards physically in their possession at any time. This implementation of the two-man rule, we thought, would safeguard the list from any attack

During our initial pilot, however, we discovered something significant: there was a need to restart the servers on which the system ran from time to time. Every restart required access to the smartcards. And that required two people to be on duty to handle them. Guess what? The ordinary schedule for that part of the data centre didn't have two people available.

Such issues are only discovered when you actually have to run the innovation for real, and that's why pilots are so valuable: you can address any major technical impact before the number of customers or end-users involved makes failure a news item.

The final learning dimension for pilots is experiential. And by this I mean the way the innovation is incarnated in reality for customers. When one is doing something truly new, there are any number of decisions made during implementation which are based on assumptions about what the audience *might* think or do. The pilot is about the first time that all the pieces come together sufficiently that customer reaction can be tested.

Such tests can, and often do, mean going back to the implementation and changing a few things. For example, if a pilot illuminates the fact that customers aren't adopting the innovation at all (when, in fact, the answer to the 'Should we?' question in the innovation phase was resoundingly clear that they should), there may be a need to examine the innovation adoption decision as I described earlier. Ultimately, it is generally good practice to schedule a pilot somewhat before the official launch. The pilot is a dress rehearsal for live, and the learning that one gets cannot be obtained in any other way.

One final point about pilots: it is almost never appropriate to give customers or real end-users an unfinished innovation to *test*. Testing – the removal of defects before the innovation is ready to go out the door – should always happen internally to the project team that is implementing the innovation. To see why, one returns to our theories of innovation diffusion that we first discussed in Chapter 2. Recall that individuals *talk* to one another about their experiences with whatever-it-is, and these communications are used to reinforce the decision process of others. Bad experiences at the beginning – during testing, for example – will linger around an innovation indefinitely.

The problem is much heightened when the innovation is tested with early adopters and innovators. These people – the beachhead demographic that is absolutely essential to trigger further adoption of the innovation – are highly susceptible to dis-adoption if they feel the new thing is unable to do the job for which it was intended. Having formed such an opinion, they will almost never pass on positive messages to those in their influence network.

Betas

In more recent times, many companies – especially Web 2.0-based ventures – have begun a practice of allowing customers access to their products before they are completely ready for prime time. In fact, even large organisations like Microsoft have begun to adopt this practice, which they call 'beta testing' their new offerings. And Google has its labs website, where its new innovations can be tried out by customers before they are officially ready for launch.

On the face of it, it looks as if an organisation running beta tests is attempting to get free testing from their customers. Invariably, there is at least an option to report any defects that are found. But the fact of the matter is that beta tests are actually not tests at all. The product is usually nearly feature-complete. If there are defects, they will be relatively minor, and certainly not sufficiently impactful that they will stop end-users finding value. In some cases, in fact, customers have to queue for access to the beta, especially if the innovation is an especially high-profile one.

This leads to only one conclusion. A beta test is actually a launch, rather than a pilot or test activity. One seeks to provide early access to the innovation in order to access the innovator and early adopter segment (Figure 2.2) earlier than an official launch. The hope is that one can build a body of people sufficiently enthused about the innovation that when the launch *does* occur, there is a strong base of people who can provide the positive word-of-mouth messages needed for the early majority and later adoption decision process.

7.3   THE LAUNCH

I cannot think of a time more exciting – and more scary – than the moment an innovation is placed in the wild. You wonder initially if everything will work as planned. You cross your fingers and hope your new users will be able to get through the adoption decision process. And then, you spend the rest of your time checking whatever management reports are available to see how people are using (or not) the innovation. The first users are celebrated, and their initial usage held up by everyone as the precursors of the success that will surely follow.

As we've seen, though, many innovations fail once they get to the market. There are many reasons for this. Sometimes it is because the intended audience doesn't want the innovation in the first place. Other times because the execution of the innovation is poor, or has been compromised so severely during development that it no longer resembles what was initially dreamed of back at the ideation phase.

The fact of the matter is, if you've been following the steps of the futureproofing process, all these reasons for failure are eminently controllable. A lack of interest is something that should have been caught during ideation, or at the very latest, during the innovation phase. And compromise is something that is actively managed during execution. This leaves the launch as the final hurdle for the innovation, and it is this last leap that is so often muffed by the innovation team. Their usual error, as I mentioned earlier in this chapter, is to assume that product managers and marketing people have the background necessary to launch something unique. And all innovations, by their nature, have something which is unique about them.

I do not suggest for one minute that innovation teams should be *solely* accountable for launch. In fact, the innovators will rarely have the skills needed to create interesting collateral, run launch events, or have access to the specific channels through which messages can be put in front of audiences. These are all aspects of the launch phase that are best left to professionals. But what innovators bring to the table is a deep understanding of two things: the process through which new things are diffused in markets, and an underlying understanding of the way individuals make their adoption decisions when faced with something new.

Viral marketing

Let me first turn to the somewhat distastefully named *viral marketing* approach to launch. This is the idea that whatever-it-is will be launched in such a way that word-of-mouth will cause lots of people, given enough time, to adopt the innovation. Typically, proponents of this approach suggest that little, if any, marketing must be done up front, because the innovation 'sells itself'. Special techniques are usually recommended to increase the 'viral' nature of whatever-it-is, such as trials and mechanisms to facilitate 'tell-a-friend'-type features. All these things, purportedly, replace conventional marketing approaches where mass marketing is used to put messages in the hands of potential adopters.

I have news for proponents of viral marketing: *all* innovations, whether they are named 'viral' or not, are adopted by the vast majority of people through word-of-mouth processes. The tiny percentage – it is actually the 2.5% of a given market in the innovator segment (see Figure 2.2) – who respond to mass-marketing messages without reinforcement from word-of-mouth is hardly a big enough market to justify the massive investments most organisations make in launch activities.

The basic mechanics of viral marketing are those we've already discussed earlier in this book. People tell each other their experiences of an innovation, resulting in more people who make the decision to use it. Eventually that process becomes self-sustaining. Here's the thing though, which is obvious if you think about it. Viral or not, there is *still* a time no one will know about the innovation, and you have to use other methods to get people to agree to try it. Before critical mass occurs, somewhere between 2.5% and 16% of the total market available for an innovation needs to be using the new thing. Prior to that being achieved, reaching out to the people who will initially be most interested in using the innovation is the critical aspect of launch.

Refining launch to optimise the adoption decision process

A theme throughout this book has been the application of the theory of innovation to the practice of getting something new out the door and into the hands of customers or end-users. From the perspective of launch, the key material from Chapter 2 is that which helps us understand how individuals (and organisations, for some innovations) make their decision processes. Crafting a launch strategy in terms of this understanding is one way to make sure that any residual risks remaining in the innovation are controlled tightly.

Now, from a launch perspective, there are different audiences that must be targeted depending on how many people are using it at a given time. One size most certainly does not fit all when you want customers or end-users to adopt something new.

At the earliest stage, when the innovation is unveiled for the very first time, there are likely to be few, if any, people much interested, probably somewhere short of 2.5% of the total. These are the innovators, that segment of the population with market little aversion to risk, who are adventurous enough to try out the innovation *without* the positive reinforcement of peers.

Considering the size of this initial group, mass media is the least efficient way possible to create the circumstances for a successful launch. Certainly, such a mass-media scattergun approach gets the message in front of the right sets of eyes, but at what cost? Let's face it, for every hit there will be hundreds of misses. The consequence is that each successful introduction winds up costing a great deal. Sometimes the costs are so high it precludes launching at all.

Bank marketers, especially those who have come up through the ranks on the retail side, rarely have many tools *besides* mass marketing. They will seek to structure a launch programme that uses television, print, and perhaps in-branch methods. They might hire PR firms to achieve positive press mentions. Or use any one of the hundreds of other ways to get their messages into the heads of as many people as possible. This is true even of internal innovations, where the scattergun approach is equally prevalent. Blanket emails, foyer signage, and impersonalised messages on intranets are de rigeur in most banks.

But the modern institution has a lot of ways of reaching the innovator segment, if it would only break out of its historical habits. Innovators, being adventurous, are likely to be present in lots of places, for which the data is easily available. Who were the first 2.5% of customers that signed up for Internet banking when it first launched? They are all likely to be innovators, or at least early adopters. When your institution first launched contactless cards, who were the customers that first rang in wanting them? Not those who waited for them to be sent out, but actually picked up the phone and sought them out specifically? If you have a corporate blog, who are the readers? Who are the ones who contribute and participate in the conversation?

Chances are, these are all individuals who are not only open to new things, they actively seek out innovative experiences. Our understanding of the dynamics of the adoption process makes it likely that initial messages targeted at such people will get that initial foothold of adoption we need to get across the first chasm.

At my bank, we launched an innovative new way of collecting and executing ideas towards the end of 2008. *Innovation Market*, as it is called, is a fundamental shift in the way staff approach the process of innovation, and it is radical in the extreme: we created a virtual currency, complete with a virtual stock market, and told everyone that each new idea would be treated as a nascent company, with the eventual chance of an initial public offering on the virtual exchange. For those of you who are interested in the story of Innovation Market, I'll talk more about it towards the end of this chapter, but the point is, we coordinated our launch activities around getting innovators and early adopters on board early. How did we do that?

Luckily, there was already a channel to the innovators in the bank. Every month, we published *Innovation Digest*, a newsletter sent out by email, that covered a topic close to the heart of those interested in innovation in financial services, coupled with a news round-up of things innovative from other institutions. The recipients of *Innovation Digest* all self-selected to join the mailing list. In other words, they telegraphed to the innovation team that they were likely to be innovators or early adopters.

So, prior to launch, we scheduled a beta test. Now, though this was billed as a way of getting rid of any final defects in Innovation Market before launch, it was *really* a means of getting the innovators on board before the actual launch activities took place. People on the *Innovation Digest* mailing list were invited early into Innovation Market. Many of them took the opportunity to come in and 'play', looking for defects (and they were very few, because we'd already done all the testing we needed). During their 'playing', however, they were able to form positive (and negative) perceptions about Innovation Market. Their play was really carefully camouflaged opinion-making. We hoped that we would be able to take these early opinions and use them to reinforce the perceptions of those less able to accept change – the early majority and later.

When the bank launched Innovation Market to a broad audience, there was already a nice core of users – the ones who could provide the positive reinforcement necessary during the persuasion stage – on board and ready to talk about their experiences. As a result, we did not face a long, uphill battle to get our end-users on board, even though Innovation Market was a radical concept, and had not been tried anywhere else.

Of course, awareness of an innovation is only one part of what must happen at the start of the adoption decision. Potential customers and end-users must also answer their 'How?' and 'Why?' questions, in addition to 'What?'

Although not often seen in financial services, especially in product, offering potential adopters the no-risk trial is a very important way of making it as simple as possible to progress through the five stages of the decision process. Individuals, when making their decisions to try something new, are actually most interested in risk reduction. The risk, in this case, is that the new thing fails to meet their expectations. When you create an obvious and easy-to-execute exit path, innovators are able to eliminate the consequences of a missed expectation. In so doing, the innovation is more easily able to negotiate the knowledge and persuasion stages.

The next time an innovator can make a real impact on the launch process is considering the implementation mechanics that will be required for the innovation. Because the new thing changes the way a customer or end-user does something, there is a level of pain involved in adoption. It is similar to the difficulty involved in breaking a habit. It requires, for example, constant attention to give up smoking, and may even require special medicines or therapies. Though the pain involved may not be as great as this in the case of the financial services innovation, active steps must still be taken by adopters to use the new thing. And the more difficult it is to break previous habits, the more likely it is that the innovation adoption decision process will stall.

It is therefore necessary, when formulating launch plans for innovations, to consider means by which habit-breaking can be facilitated. For many innovations, this will be as easy as providing a simple way to, essentially, 'flip the switch'. For a credit card product with balance transfer, for example, one might provide a simple form that can be used by the customer to instruct the bank to make the transfer occur. You can imagine how take-up of such a product would fall if the customer were required to move their balance from one card to another personally.

But some innovations need rather more support during the implementation process. Consider a checking (or current) account with specific rewards attractive to the young professional segment – say free airline lounge access and discount two-for-one partner seats on a range of airlines. The innovation may be extremely attractive to the target market, but there is *very* considerable pain in making the decision to adopt. The issue is the standing orders and direct debits associated with the customer's existing accounts. They may have recurring bills which automatically deduct from the balance. Their gym memberships might be paid automatically. Their salaries paid in by their employers. Or their monthly savings transfers to a high-interest-rate account might execute on a given day of every month, after all the other bills are paid.

All these automatic operations need to be updated by the customer if they are to adopt the new checking account. For most people, the bother involved in trying to unravel the wiring of their financial relationships to get a few free hours in an airline lounge or a partner seat on a discount airline will simply not be justified. The adoption decision process will likely stall.

That is why, increasingly, institutions are offering switching services for a range of products. Because the pain of moving financial products around – with all their attendant interconnections to other products and suppliers the customer values – is the primary barrier for adopters, institutions that have implemented switching services have been able to increase the rate of churn to their products substantially.

Switching services are all very well, but the principle applies to *all* innovations, whether they are product-related or not. The key questions innovators must answer when designing their launch strategies are these: what are the key habits that adopters will have to break before they will be able to use the innovation? And how can the innovation itself facilitate the breaking of these habits?

There is a final contribution to the launch process innovators can make, and that is providing some insight into the timing of the entire launch sequence. During the work that was done to answer the 'Should we?' and 'When?' key questions, a demand forecast will have been created, ideally based on the diffusion models we examined in Chapter 2. This forecast, if you recall, results in a chart that shows cumulative demand for an innovation over time. Figure 2.3 illustrates the familiar S-shaped curve that is associated with most successful innovations. Such a curve always has two inflection points: the first is the critical mass point, when the innovation takes off and becomes self-sustaining. The second happens towards the end of the process, when the explosive growth of the innovation tends to tail off, as fewer and fewer of the late majority remain, and only laggards continue to resist adoption.

Our interest, from the perspective of launch, is with the former: the timing of the critical mass point. Having an approximation of this time is important because it determines the moment at which it is possible to cease recruiting new users from the innovator and early adopter category. Prior to achieving the critical mass point, there aren't enough people using an innovation to be certain that word-of-mouth effects won't stall. But afterwards, there is nothing that will prevent diffusion from proceeding. The innovation begins to sell itself.

A key mistake many innovators and their marketing colleagues make is imagining that the launch is a single event that happens at the beginning, and the innovation will then just roll out itself. The truth is that a programme of work has to be planned that takes the innovation from its first availability to the moment it reaches critical mass.

Knowing the critical mass point has another key advantage: it enables the innovator to predict how many individuals need to have adopted the innovation for critical mass to occur. As it is generally the case that one knows how many people are using an innovation at a given time, this makes it simple to instrument the launch process in such a way that one can judge the relative success (or not) of the measures that one has implemented to facilitate the innovation adoption decision.

One final point remains to be said on this topic. You will find, when suggesting an innovation might need a launch programme that runs into months – maybe years – there will be incredulity, perhaps even the suggestion to cancel the innovation altogether. The fallacy that new things 'sell themselves' is deeply ingrained in the minds of many people who believe all that is required is the right innovation. They look at the performance of smash hit innovations such as Apple's iPhone as evidence of this.

Diffusion processes were just as active for the iPhone, though, as for any other innovation. The key difference in this case was the number of adopters required to reach critical mass was reached extremely quickly. Then, too, the consumer segment Apple addresses is typically more innovative than average, with a disproportionate number of innovators and early adopters. It was these factors – and not the phone itself – that resulted in the surge of adoption.

For most innovations, however, a much more leisurely course to critical mass must be expected. Setting this expectation appropriately will head off much frustration – even innovation trauma – when the new thing does not immediately become the 'smash hit' that everyone imagines is the future for their pet idea.

7.4   OPERATIONS POST-LAUNCH

Getting customers or end-users to adopt a new thing is only part of the battle, however. All those new users and customers won't stay around – no matter how innovative they are – if whatever-it-is doesn't work properly. It is to the task of ensuring the innovation gets through its first operational challenges that we turn our attention next.

Earlier, I suggested that own and operate is an appropriate strategy for any innovation which is either breakthrough or disruptive in nature. The underlying reasons for this differ, though, depending on which kind of innovation is being managed.

A breakthrough is usually so new that procedures, systems, and cultures have to be built around it to ensure success. Without these efforts, you have an interesting gadget, not a profitable business. Creating the set of things needed to ensure the breakthrough is fit for purpose is the primary reason for own and operate.

Disruptions are different though. Quite likely, they do not incarnate anything especially difficult technologically. They may not require brand new skills in the organisation either. But what they *do* require is protection from powerful executives and other leaders who will first of all consider the disruption too insignificant to be bothered with, and *then* too threatening to live with once success begins to be evident. Own and operate in this case is a way of protecting the innovation until the politics of the institution catch up.

Now, as a general rule, innovators *do not* want to be owning and operating innovations. Their position, usually, must be to find and nurture new things which have positive impacts for an institution rather than spending their time running yesterday's innovation. But making the decision to *never* own and operate functionally limits a team to small revolutions and increments.

This is a perfectly good strategy, by the way, until the team gets beyond the managing stage of its development (see Figure 3.2). But once futurecasting and venturing become part of the innovation team's mandate, own and operate will become very difficult to avoid.

Consider what is likely to be occurring here: at the futurecasting stage, innovators have injected themselves into the strategic planning process of an institution. They will be providing input on matters that affect the future of their institutions, and it will be practically impossible for them to avoid being part of the solution as well. And, at the venturing stage, they have created a business based mainly on incremental innovations, but achieving the growth they need to stay ahead of the game (remember, innovation must be the most attractive investment opportunity at any given time) will necessitate taking some larger risks.

The ultimate difference in approach for breakthrough versus disruptive innovations is simple. In the former case, innovators are seeking to protect their investment through the formative stages until it becomes successful and is self-sustaining. In the latter case, though, they are seeking to protect the innovation once it *starts* to be successful. For a disruptive innovation, success is usually the first nail in the coffin unless active steps are taken. Protections must usually be in place until the innovation is so successful it *cannot* be killed off.

The breakthrough innovation

Let us first consider the breakthrough innovation, a thing of such uniqueness that it is quite unlike anything that's ever gone before. Such innovations, of course, are relatively rare in financial services, but, nonetheless, occur from time to time.

Breakthroughs tend to be very expensive to implement up front, and start making returns at a relatively slow pace in the beginning. With success, of course, the breakthrough is likely to become an ipso facto standard, generating windfall returns, but there will ordinarily be a wasteland period of poor revenues before anything so serendipitous occurs. It is during this wasteland period that innovators need to involve themselves.

Perhaps the best example of a real breakthrough in financial services is one we've looked at already in Chapter 1: ERMA, that first Bank of America computer which changed the way financial services conducted its operations forever.

In 1951, when ERMA was conceived, business computing was practically non-existent. Such machines as did exist were primarily the preserve of the military and scientific establishments, but Bank of America, with a clarity of purpose that is so rarely seen in financial services, realised it needed to do something to ease the mountain of paper it was facing. A computer, fanciful though it must have seemed at the time, was a supposed answer.

The introduction of the new machines, when it occurred a few years later, radically changed the workforce of the bank. Using the machines, one worker could be as productive as 50 had been with paper. The labour force reduction was significant. But so too were the organisational changes that surrounded the innovation. Imagine the new skills the bank had to acquire, from scratch. Technicians who could operate the machines. Mechanics who knew how to repair them. Mathematicians who could write the programs. And, not least, a set of processes and cultures to support automatic operation.

These are all radical new capabilities for an organisation that was previously optimised for managing paper. The likelihood of failure was very high, and the organisational forces that permeated the roll-out at the bank must have been extraordinary. Protecting the innovation during its early years cannot have been a simple task, given the millions of dollars that were being spent.

Luckily, Seth Clark Beise, then project sponsor and later president of the bank, intuitively knew that they needed to have a handle on such things. He was active in supporting and protecting the innovation, especially during its initial years. Remarking later, he said, 'ERMA is a new concept in banking. Its effects will be far reaching, touching such things as bank architecture and new banking services undreamed of today. Because of electronics, we have an eighteen months' lead time over all other banks in this amazing era' [61]. His rapid promotion through the ranks at the bank subsequent to being proved astoundingly correct in his assessment of the potential of ERMA is the testament to his tenacity in managing the organisational change surrounding the introduction of computing to business.

There are really three areas that need focus from innovators when considering how to operate a breakthrough and they are these: technology, process, and people. Failing to manage each correctly for the breakthrough will result in significant, and probably fatal, early failure of adoption. Those early customers – the innovators and early adopters – are like gold. They have such a huge impact on subsequent success that losing even a few can significantly slow diffusion of an innovation. Imagine the consequences of losing many!

Actually, there is quite good data on the actual quantitative effect of this. Researchers, using online banking diffusion data and the theoretical principles we looked at in Chapter 2, have been able to estimate the cash value of customer losses by innovator category [23]. The results of their research are summarised in Table 7.1.

As you can see from this data, the quantitative effect of making mistakes early is very significant. Innovators, who are the principals influencing later segments, are worth almost 30% more than early adopters. And early adopters, that segment of the market which will cause almost half the rest to use the innovation, are worth nearly 50% more than those that follow. As I said, every early customer is like gold. With that in mind, then, let us turn first to a consideration of the people aspect of operations.

There will usually be few relevant skills inside an institution applicable to a breakthrough when it is first dreamed up. ERMA, for example, was conceived at SRI (Stanford Research Institute), a part of Stanford University, since Bank of America lacked its own technological research and development capability. And later, when it came time to build the actual machines, General Electric was the partner the bank selected to do the engineering. Both parties were essential to the project, since Bank of America had no capability on its own beyond those required to manage a paper-based banking operation. In other words, it hired an organisation that could provide it with scientists to design its computer, then a contractor with experience in doing one-off development to build it.

The more unique the breakthrough is, the harder it becomes to find people who know what they are doing. It is entirely possible, in fact, that the innovators – who have spent their time

Table 7.1 Approximate value of a lost customer in Internet banking

Segment	Approximate value of a lost customer
Innovators	$850
Early adopters	$675
Early majority	$290
Late majority	$220
Laggards	$210

answering the key questions – have the only expertise available, despite its limited depth. In these cases it will likely be necessary for the innovators to step into the breach themselves to operate whatever-it-is, at least until the appropriate level of understanding has been developed elsewhere in the institution.

This isn't a sustainable position to be in, even if the innovation team is providing broad management direction only. As they are accountable for a portfolio of innovations, devoting too much time to just one has the predictable consequence that potential future uniqueness is ignored and predictability goes out the window. The practitioner, therefore, needs to be clear on what steps must be taken to up-skill the institution to operate the innovation without their input.

The development of new skills in organisations is the subject of whole books, and I don't propose to cover the specific details of how that occurs here. But there are a few points of relevance to innovators which are helpful when trying to build out the people side of a breakthrough.

The first is that operating a breakthrough in a large organisation is very similar to operating a start-up company. The kind of person that suits a start-up is very, very different from the sort that prefers the comfort of a large institution. People who work well in start-ups don't expect anything to be done for them: they know there is no infrastructure available, so they actively seek solutions to problems on their own. In the case of the breakthrough innovation, there will likely be no ready source of solutions anyway.

Jack-of-all-trades people are pretty rare in most large institutions, though. For most banks, promotion systems are structured to eliminate generalists. When a new graduate enters a bank, they are put onto a path that encourages greater levels of expertise in ever-narrower specialities. This occurs for most of their formative years as individual contributors. Then, when they are promoted to management, the remainder of their career is spent becoming more generalised so they can manage greater numbers of specialists, and later, increasingly more generalised managers. Now, the kind of generalised manager this system breeds is probably not well equipped to deal with a breakthrough. Lacking specialist skills that would actually be relevant to fostering the innovation directly, they must always call in external expertise to resolve any problem, costing money.

This leads to another problem. When you begin with a breakthrough, there is an initial period during which few will have adopted the innovation. The consequence is that there won't be much revenue coming in the door, so there is little alternative but to find solutions that don't cost much. Calling in external expertise to solve problems all the time is not a cheap solution.

The upshot of all this is that the selection of people to develop a breakthrough must be careful. On the one hand, there must be sufficient experience in the people selected that *stupid* things are avoided. You cannot, for example, bring in an entrepreneurial founder from the start-up community with a few years' experience and expect good results. They won't have the political nous to successfully develop the innovation in a big company context without being squashed flat, even though they might be able to resolve any technical difficulties that might arise. On the other hand, a senior and experienced manager will likely build things that cost too much, or try to shoehorn the breakthrough into an existing institutional context because it is expeditious politically, two alternatives that will likely spell the end of the innovation anyway.

What is the answer to this dilemma, then? In my experience, you can find people very well suited to working on breakthroughs in many unexpected places. Look for the ones who don't fit in, whose careers seem to be limited because they fail to conform to the organisational norm, or who refuse to 'play the game'. Quite often, appropriate individuals will have a track history of mediocre or average performance ratings, and in fact an excellent track history of performance in a large institution is almost always a sure sign that the individual will *not* perform well in a breakthrough setting. This is because the process of getting star-performer status in most banks is one that optimises behaviour to *conform* with norms – something that is most definitely not desired when you have to incubate a breakthrough. Here is the lesson for innovators: cherish the talent that appears (on paper) to be non-performing.

The second aspect of operations that needs to be considered from a breakthrough perspective is technology. Now, more often than not, the breakthrough idea will have been incarnated in some kind of technological newness which is largely unprecedented for an institution. This makes the first few months and years of operation of whatever-it-is somewhat like driving at night down a country road in an unfamiliar car without headlights. You don't always know what is going to come at you from around the next bend. And sometimes, it is going to be a massive Mack truck going at full speed.

The figurative Mack truck is avoided readily, however. All you have to do is attend to security, reliability, and scalability.

Now, as to security, I've spent a great deal of time in this book moaning about security people, and their predilection to shut down innovations prematurely in an attempt to minimise institutional risk. However, as with all things, a balance is required. It is impossible to have an innovation which leaves wide, gaping holes in the defences of customers and institutions. So, planning a decent security strategy – and having the resources to implement it – is a key part of operating a breakthrough. The problem, of course, is that the breakthrough is so new that most security people will have as little idea of what to do about it as anyone else. Probably, this will not be that important when the innovation is launched, since relatively few people will be using it. But the attack surface of whatever-it-is is proportional to the number of people who have adopted it. The more successful, the more likely a successful attack will cause damage both to the institution and to the innovation itself.

This is what occurred, obviously, in Internet banking. Initially, when there were relatively few people who used the new channel, there was hardly any reason for thieves and scoundrels to spend all that much time trying to hack their way through bank defences. Security people, consequently, were happy to secure their websites with password and user id combinations. In the early days, indeed, that is probably as much as they knew how to do. The situation today – with practically everyone on Internet banking – is quite different. The security people at institutions have resorted to a range of techniques to control access and theft. These range from issuing specific devices (buttons that generate unique, one-time codes, for example) to multiple random questions asking for personal information, and sending of secondary pin codes to mobile phones. As the attack surface of Internet banking increased, so too did the necessary security measures taken to protect it.

Having an appropriate plan – the result of a detailed risk assessment – for a breakthrough is critical in avoiding the Mack truck which will be just around the corner, especially if an innovation involves the potential for thieves to get their hands on large amounts of money.

With security concerns out the door, the next thing to worry about is reliability. Reliability is making sure that an innovation is available to customers when they expect it to be. That it provides most of its functionality most of the time. And that the functionality provided works as customers and end-users expect.

For a breakthrough that relies on technology, these are challenging questions. If there are many moving parts incarnated in the innovation – multiple servers, databases, and communications links, for example – the engineering for reliability can be complex. Sometimes, a failure mode isn't obvious until *after* the failure occurs.

The effects of a failure in an innovative service or product are much more significant when the innovation is young than later. At the beginning, the only people who are likely to use the new thing are those with high levels of personal innovativeness. They are seeking to ascertain whether whatever-it-is is able to fulfil expectations, and are quite happy to abandon it when it does not. The problem here is that these early adopters are the ones who carry the message to later segments – the early and late majority. Losing the first few users can have a dramatic effect on the pace of take-up, as we saw in the case of Internet banking earlier (see Table 7.1).

Later on, as well, the effects of failure can be significant. A popular service, such as Internet banking, will almost certainly make the news if customers lose access often. And, especially during troubled times, service failures send messages that customers process unfavourably. ATMs down? Is the bank about to fail as well? So, reliability is something that's key to the technology part of the own and operate model. The temptation, however, given the downside when things go wrong, is to over-compensate.

If you ask for three-nines reliability (that means the service or product is available 99.9% of the time – or offline just under nine hours per year), there is a certain cost involved. Probably, you will need to duplicate every single point of failure to achieve such a number – with a massive increase in the technology cost involved. But imagine you need four nines – just under one hour of downtime a year. The implication will almost certainly be that it is necessary to duplicate *everything,* and make sure both instances are immediately available anytime there's a problem. Every scrap of data, every network wire, every server. The costs mount geometrically.

Five nines of reliability is equivalent to less than six minutes of downtime each year. Theoretically, modern transaction systems can reach this number today, but at what cost? Triple? Quadruple? The point is this. Each additional nine is exponentially more expensive than the previous one. The diminishing return on reliability investments means that it is critically important to determine the tolerance for downtime as a function of where the new thing is in terms of adoption.

Getting the balance right is tricky: the effects of downtime at the beginning – in terms of the speed of take-up – will be hugely significant, but the revenues involved are low. On the other hand, once lots of people have the innovation, an outage will most likely not materially affect growth, but will almost certainly have significant financial consequences.

Reliability and security are important things to get right up front, because they have direct consequences for the innovation in its early stages. Later on, though, scalability will likely become the key consideration for innovators doing the own and operate model.

Scalability refers to the ability of the innovation to cope with expanding workloads as the number of users grows. Technology systems tend to have choke points – system constraints that limit the growth of the system. They can occur in lots of places. It might be, for example, that a specific record is updated in a database very frequently – and since only one person can be updating at any one time, everyone else has to wait. Or maybe there is finite capacity on a network, so requests are delayed or slowed to share out the capacity. Storage and processing capability are other places that choke points can exhibit themselves.

Architecturally, there are usually specific measures needing implementation right from the start to ensure scalability. Some design decisions can have significant implications for the future of an innovation. Here is an example. One commonly implemented Internet banking system used to store secure bank emails from customers in text files on hard disks. Each email was given a filename based on a unique number. This was fine at the start, when there were few customers sending emails. But eventually, secure email became a very well-adopted feature, and the hard disks were only able to store so many emails in each directory before they ground to a halt. The result was an extensive – and expensive – redesign of that functionality. Meanwhile, customers lost access to secure email, not a situation optimised to create a good impression. So, designing for scalability right from the start is important for any innovation.

But there is another consideration even though architectural scale questions may have been resolved, and that is the ease with which new capacity can be added to a particular innovation as its usage increases. The unfortunate thing is that the more reliable and more secure a particular technology innovation is, the more expensive it becomes to add capacity. This can have consequences for the overall business case that supported the innovation in the first place. Ultimately, when answering the 'Should we?' key question, making sure that scalability and capacity questions are resolved means ensuring that costs do not outpace revenue. There's not much point building the most widely celebrated banking breakthrough of all time if it can never be profitable.

The final aspect to be considered with breakthrough innovation is the set of processes that need to surround it for success. There will certainly be processes needed to support even the most incremental of innovations. I often joke that much of the innovation programme at my bank is about moving check boxes on forms – but even such a small innovation needs its process. The form has to get out of the design shop and into the branches, for example.

The thing about breakthrough innovations and the processes that surround them is that they are often not obvious before the innovation is launched. Customer behaviour is very rarely entirely what one predicts, and this means innovators have to be ready to create new processes to deal with unexpected circumstances often.

Consider the NFC mobile phone innovation we've been discussing in this book. Introduction of mobile phone payment technology of this kind will require a whole new set of unfamiliar business processes. What will the process of associating a new mobile phone with an existing account be? And what if the customer loses their phone? What if they switch telco providers, or cancel their phone contracts altogether? Even worse, how will an institution deal with the situation when the customer hasn't paid their phone bill (so the mobile phone is taken off the network), thereby making it much harder to use the payment chip inside the handset?

For the breakthrough innovation, the fact of the matter is that surrounding processes have to evolve, rather than be designed up front. This evolution will likely happen in a piecemeal, rather than a consistent way. As a new situation presents itself, a process will usually be developed on the fly, and sometimes that will work well. Other times, naturally, it will result in a very poor customer or end-user experience.

The key thing here, however, is to make sure these 'on-the-fly' processes are replicable. Having defined how something will be done for the breakthrough *once* it should thereafter be done in the same way. The principle that needs to be followed is this: new processes are created on the spot, but subsequent changes to processes are *designed.*

Now, at the start, this means that the breakthrough can seem as if it is limping from one crisis to another. Every time a customer or end-user shows up with something new that needs attention, everyone has to scramble to work out the best way to accommodate the new request. The frequency with which this occurs, however, declines with time as the process infrastructure surrounding the innovation gets better. In the end, everything tends to self-optimise for the best results.

The disruptive innovation

If the challenge of making a breakthrough innovation successful is great, it is nothing compared with that of shepherding a disruptive one. Whereas the chief problem for the breakthrough is that it exists in an environment poorly equipped to deal with whatever uniqueness it brings, the disruptive innovation is far more threatening to incumbent players in a bank.

The threat comes from the possibility that the new thing will interfere with existing revenue streams, eventually supplanting what may have been a stable operation for years. For those associated with the incumbent business line, there is a great deal to be gained by getting rid of the disruption, and the dirty tactics that will likely follow are pretty much inevitable.

Now, this may not happen immediately with a disruptive innovation. In the first instance, the innovation will likely be something of an amusing sideline for those in incumbent businesses. After all, its initial revenues will be absolutely insignificant in comparison with those the institution is used to. And the business model involved will certainly be substantially different from that with which everyone is familiar. It is highly likely that incumbents will put up with the presence of the disruption, so long as it doesn't interfere with their operations.

But what happens when customers – who may have been paying premiums for features of the incumbent business line that they didn't really need or want – start to defect? That's inevitable in the presence of a disruption, of course, but incumbents don't see this as a new opportunity in the scheme of the overall institution. It will be represented, instead, as an attempt to move an institution *down-market*, something that practically everyone is conditioned to treat with trepidation at the very least. The fact that customers would eventually defect anyway to someone else being disruptive is irrelevant.

PayPal is such a great example of the mechanics of disruption at work. Even today, there are institutions who don't believe that alternative payment systems are that much of a threat. And, having tried and failed to build alternative payments initiatives in *two* institutions, I can say with authority that the internal resistance to such innovations is very high. For the innovation practitioner who has decided to go after a disruptive innovation (as will inevitably be the case as the programme reaches the futurecasting and venturing stage), there is a need to investigate innovative methods, both to deliver and operate the innovation.

Because of the organisational forces inherent in large institutions, such methods involve insulating the innovation from the main business for that part of its life during which it germinates. Failing to do so will result in the early demise of whatever-it-is.

Corporate venturing is one approach that has worked in some institutions as a means of dealing with these issues. As you might expect from the name, a separate business unit is established which has all the hallmarks of a venture capital firm: it evaluates innovations, funds them through the build and operate stages, and then sells them off when they are successful.

The corporate venturing operation is quite a different beast from the innovation team and its processes described in this book. Whereas an innovation team directs its attention towards winning funding for its efforts (being without large-scale funding of its own), corporate venturing organisations can fund innovations in their own right. Their attention is directed much more towards the nurture and eventual disposal (either through drowning the puppy or sale to another business unit) of new business opportunities surrounding an innovation. This makes them ideal for creating disruptive innovations, of course, because corporate venturing teams are largely independent and isolated from the political forces which will seek to eliminate a threatening innovation before it germinates into something valuable.

As you might imagine, the level of responsibility and trust placed with the corporate venturing team is significant. The reason? The team must be trusted to do the best thing for an institution in the long term, *even when* short-term goals may be compromised by whatever-it-is. Countering short-termism requires powerful relationships and a significant track record of success for the innovators. Which is why, actually, you don't normally see corporate venturing that's successful in banks until the innovation team has reached the venturing stage of the Five Capability Model.

Here is another difference between corporate venturing and the ordinary process of innovators: it is normal for a fully-funded venture to fail, and indeed, the costs of these failures are factored into the portfolio of investments that a corporate venturing team will make. The innovation process described here, on the other hand, recommends that any failures happen early, that 'drowning the puppy' be a key discipline executed as soon as possible.

The thing is, a disruptive innovation will probably be subject to puppy drowning rather earlier than it should be. When it comes to answering the key questions, almost certainly 'Should we?' and 'When?' will come out on the negative side. This is because an innovator needs to evaluate the answers in the context of the current state of an institution and the likelihood he or she will win funding. Inevitably, the disruption won't make the grade.

The corporate venturing team, on the other hand, is set up to take calculated risks with things that might fail *after* funding. This is why they have their own money, after all: they can take such risks without the political fallout or the innovation trauma that usually follows a fully-funded failure.

A well-studied case of corporate venturing is Nokia's Venture Organisation (NVO), a corporate venturing division that was established by the company as its core products – mobile phone handsets – were maturing, and senior leaders recognised they would need to disrupt their own markets to achieve future growth [62].

In the four years following 1998, Nokia's success was highly variable. Fully 70% of all investments were either discontinued or sold off altogether. But 21% were absorbed into mainline businesses, where they proceeded as part of business as usual. And senior executives evaluated 25% of the investments that NVO made as having contributed brand new capabilities or important new intellectual property. But here is the headline statistic: 16% of investments turned into – one way or another – new products that Nokia was able to sell.

The reason for this high rate of success, it turns out, is twofold. Firstly, Nokia was aware of the fact that the value proposition of the innovations it was nurturing in NVO would be very different from those that might ordinarily have come from the mainline businesses. Short-term revenue opportunities would be limited, and costs expected to be relatively high. By freeing NVO from the need to inappropriately escalate commitments resulting from its innovations, Nokia made it possible for the organisation to pursue opportunities with a long-term timeframe. This, obviously, is an ideal setting for disruptive innovations.

The second reason that Nokia was successful with NVO was that it adopted a portfolio, rather than a project, mindset. You will be familiar with this approach from the advice given throughout this book. When you put all your innovatory eggs in one basket, you are unlikely to get predictable successes. Innovation can be treated statistically when you have volume, and this is true for corporate venturing just as much as it is for the innovation processes described in this book. Nokia realised this, and made sure its distribution of investments was broad.

Corporate venturing isn't the only way to own and operate a disruptive innovation, though. Other models include incubators, where individuals are taken out of mainline businesses and allowed to work on their innovations, freed of their ordinary work pressures. Or open innovation, where core capabilities are bought into the organisation already fully formed and ready to use.

But every successful model for doing disruptive innovation has one element in common: they always involve separating out the team and funding supporting the new thing from the rest of the business. Failing to do so inevitably results in organisational politics killing the innovation off long before it has a chance to mature into something of value.

7.5 SIGNALS FOR FUTURECASTING

Before we come to the discussion of Innovation Market that I promised earlier, there is one final topic we need to cover, and that is how the execution phase contributes market-level signals to the futurecasting process I described in Chapter 4.

Market-level signals are those that innovators – both internally and externally to an institution – can see when they put their innovations in the market for the first time. They are useful to the futurecasting process because they illuminate the way that driving forces may change over time.

Let us imagine a specific scenario. An institution creates a new kind of mortgage in the wake of sub-prime: one where payments are tied to the *future* disposable income of the borrower. At the start of the mortgage, the interest rate is subsidised by payments that will occur later in the loan. The rationale behind this is that a new borrower – perhaps starting a family – is least able to afford a new home in the earliest phases of their career, but will certainly be able to do so later. This new mortgage, then, targets those who cannot afford a home *now*, and who would be considered sub-prime under traditional lending criteria. This mortgage, though, is *not* subject to traditional lending criteria, which don't work for considerations of the total lifetime value of the customer.

In compensation for this consideration of future income, the mortgage is based on a long-term contract which cannot be exited for a much greater period than normal without substantial penalties – say ten years or more. This enables the institution to recover its interest-rate subsidies in the initial years. Supporting this new mortgage product is an enhanced way to evaluate the future potential of customers to pay, based on a number of non-traditional measures: payment history on utility bills and rent, coupled with demographic data based on expected earnings for similarly educated and located individuals. These new scoring methods complement those already utilised extensively by institutions, such as the well-known FICO algorithm popularised by Fair Issac in the United States.

Let us further imagine that the innovation team gets this product launched in the market, and then watches the result. Several things can happen. Institutions who adopt the fast-follower strategy rush in with competing products, perhaps with some minor variations to drive differentiation. In this event, market-level signals drive particular kinds of futurecasts. What is the effect of new ways of evaluating the lifetime value of a customer? What does it mean if it is possible for some institutions to cherry-pick (seemingly) sub-prime customers with relative safety? And how might the demographics of the housing market change if young professionals are able to buy their own home much more quickly than would otherwise be the case?

On the other hand, perhaps no one enters with a product that can compete with this new kind of mortgage. Consideration of the underlying reasons for this is relevant. Perhaps other institutions aren't feeling any need to enter the new market, believing they have ample growth opportunities in more traditional lending. Since the set of customers in any market that can obtain a suitable credit score for lending purposes is essentially finite, this is an important signal that a futurecast may be important. What new markets might competitive institutions be considering that have escaped notice?

The response of institutions to an innovation is one aspect of market-level signals. But equally relevant is the response of consumers and end-users themselves. Usually, there will be three scenarios of relevance. Firstly, consumers adopt en-masse the new innovation, and it becomes an ipso-facto standard which everyone else seeks to emulate. The second is that consumers adopt a much more traditional S-shaped adoption pattern. And the third is that no adoption occurs at all. The first and last of these are opportunities for futurecasts.

In the first case, the innovation has successfully addressed significant pent-up demand that previously had no satisfactory outlet. This is a market-level signal that attention should be directed to adjacent market spaces to see if similar demand can be reached with incremental changes added to the initial innovation. Usually, the fit of the innovation will be less good in adjacent markets, so relatively slower adoption will occur. Nonetheless, the futurecast provides interesting opportunities to multiply revenues significantly.

In the case where no adoption at all has occurred, the role of the futurecast is diagnostically very helpful. Often, by examining the innovation in terms of driving forces, it is possible to understand *why* adoption didn't occur. For example, at the time of writing, the UK market was failing to adopt mobile phone banking, despite the fact that every single main street bank had a service offering in the market. This behaviour was distinctly at odds with that experienced overseas, where growth of the new channel was exceeding expectations, especially in Asian countries.

From a social perspective, might it be that UK consumers were more branch-bound than their overseas cousins? Technologically, perhaps the distribution of handset capability didn't match the service offerings promoted by banks? Economics, such as the marginal utility available to consumers using the mobile channel, *compared* with available substitutes might have been unfavourable. Or politically, perhaps customers felt they didn't have clarity on the bank's obligations if something went wrong.

Whenever anyone does *anything* new in a particular market, the ranges of signals generated are usually extensive. Applying the futurecasting process will usually be illuminating, even if it clarifies only that an institution *should not* be a fast follower to someone else's innovation.

7.6   CASE STUDY: INNOVATION MARKET

However ideas get generated, through futurecasting or some other ideation process, it will certainly be clear by now that being successful at innovation is never about having the best ideas. It *is* about having the best execution, though, and herein lies the core problem an innovation team faces: there is never enough execution capability to go around.

All resources are finite, and those which can be acquired for use by an innovation team even more so: the fact of the matter is that business as usual will always have more right to money, people, and technology than an innovation team, since it is concerned with doing things that make an institution money *right now*. Innovators, on the other hand, must beg for the scraps that are left over. That is the situation, certainly, when there is a central innovation team that is accountable for doing everything. But what if it were possible to find a way to motivate those with great ideas to follow up with execution as well? In theory, at least, it would mean that the amount of innovation that could reasonably be attempted by an institution would be limited only to the number of great ideas collected.

This was the thinking that led my innovation team to create Innovation Market, an internal stock exchange for ideas. Innovation Market is several things. It is an open website where anyone can contribute their ideas for improving the institution. Individuals are able to comment, vote, and review ideas, and their contributions are visible to everyone. In this respect, Innovation Market is an ideation platform with the features of a modern consumer website.

But all this activity is instrumented in the system, and those ideas which get the most attention automatically promote to a second stage. In this second stage, teams are able to form around an idea. Teaming is accomplished through the issuance of preferred shares. A preferred share entitles the holder to specific compensations should the idea ever reach the hands of end-users or customers. For example, if someone created an idea that resulted in significant cost savings for the bank, the preference share might entitle them to a cut of the savings in the first year.

With preference shares, Innovation Market encourages the person with the idea to create a team that might be able to make things move forward. Potentially, a preference share can be very, very valuable. But the real motivation for preference shares is that they encourage teaming with the intent of doing something new.

As you might have guessed, the teaming stage of Innovation Market results in most of the activities we've previously discussed in the innovation phase of futureproofing. The team doesn't, at the start, have any access to money. They have to win that competitively from stakeholders who hold budgets. In order to do so, they will prepare business cases, sales documents, and prototypes, just as a traditional innovation team would do.

Successfully getting an idea funded moves it to the final stage of Innovation Market – trading. As an idea commences its transformation into something people can use, it is listed on an internal stock market, at a price which reflects the buzz around it. Interestingly, the price of an idea is a very good predictor of how likely it is to get through all the activities involved in execution. At the start, the price of the idea is relatively low. But as status updates and progress reports come to light, the price rises. By the time the innovation is ready to roll out, this price difference can be substantial. Those who acquired shares in the idea at the start are likely to make windfall gains at the end.

Underlying all this is a virtual currency, known as Bank Beanz. Wages, in Bank Beanz, are paid to anyone who contributes. A small number are awarded for comments and votes, and there are larger awards for good ideas and reviews. None of these awards are especially substantial. In order to acquire Bank Beanz in large amounts, it is necessary to trade in ideas on the market.

Another innovation introduced with Innovation Market was making the Bank Bean worth real cash. Users are able to 'cash-out' of the market and use their Bank Beanz for real-world rewards, such as shopping vouchers. We'll be looking much more closely at reward systems later in this book, but for our purposes here it is enough to say that this mechanism encourages a particular sort of behaviour: finding great ideas and doing things which make it likely their price will rise.

Now, the introduction of real-world money to what is, essentially, a prediction market (see Chapter 4) resulted in a number of things which were unexpected at the beginning. One of these was hyper-inflation of the Bank Bean, but this was easily addressed with the same sort of controls that would normally be instituted by a central bank in a real economy. But more interestingly, insider trading in ideas became prevalent.

Now, insider trading is banned in real-world markets for very good and proper reasons, and the innovation team immediately started to consider what measures they should implement to ensure it didn't happen in their nascent virtual economy as well. But, it turns out, insider trading is a very powerful way to couple the idea to execution. Individuals who have invested their hard-earned Bank Beanz are naturally motivated to ensure the price of an idea rises. In order to do that from a position of knowledge, they have to join the team that is working on the idea, and actively do things that make it progress. In other words, anyone who has an interest in the idea is highly motivated to *work* on the idea as well. What the innovation team achieved was the ability to couple the idea to execution.

Innovation Market is an example of the way that the futureproofing process can be implemented in a way that engages a broad base of people across an institution. And since it launched, both the number of ideas arriving and the percentage that progressed were on the rise.

7.7   THE END OF FUTUREPROOFING

Now we've come to the end of the formal process descriptions that comprise this book. If you've been reading the chapters sequentially, you will have seen how to couple a structured determination of the likely shape of the future with a process that generates useful ideas. And how to turn those ideas into a reality you can put in front of customers or end-users. With any luck, the innovation that results has been a substantial success, and contributed to the overall predictability of returns.

With the process out of the way, we now turn our attention to a dimension of innovation that we have not spent much time on so far: the people who will actually make this process work. It doesn't matter how good your innovation process is, nor how accurate your futurecasting, if at the end of the day, the people in innovation roles don't have what it takes to create predictability. Then, too, there is the question of the leadership of all these highly creative, deeply passionate people. It takes a special kind of leader to make an innovation team work, and we'll be looking at some of the characteristics of such individuals in the next few chapters.

8
Leading Innovation Teams

What you will find in this chapter

- The kinds of styles an innovation leader can adopt.
- Activities an innovation leader needs to undertake.
- How you know your innovation leader is a bad one.

When you look around the world at bank innovation groups, something is immediately obvious. Some institutions seem, inherently, better at innovation than others. And, you will probably not be surprised to learn, this success has practically nothing to do with the size of the innovation budget, or the scope of the innovation programme. Apparently, some institutions have discovered a 'secret sauce' which makes them better than their peers when they are doing new things.

It is tempting to imagine this difference is the result of some cultural or environmental influence beyond the control of management. When asked why a particular bank is not innovative, for example, one often hears excuses such as 'We are fast followers', or 'Banks are risk averse'. In fact, I've actually heard professional *innovators* make remarks of this kind when attempting to explain why it is difficult to be innovative in a bank. However, if one examines the history of innovation in financial services (refer back to Chapter 1), what is clear is that there *have* been monumental innovations in the industry. Some of these were – at the time – both exceptionally risky and ground-breaking.

When Bank of America, for example, created ERMA in the 1950s, it had no reason to believe that the project would deliver anything at all. It was a risky endeavour. Yet it proceeded, and with the success of its cheque-processing machine created business computing as a category. ERMA was unprecedented not only for bankers, but in all other industries as well. By no means was Bank of America a fast follower, though it could hardly be said to have been more accepting of risk than its peers. It did, however, have Seth Clark Beise, the leader credited with mechanising the bank, and who later went on to become its president.

And when Barclays deployed the first cash-dispensing machine, based on a radioactive paper cheque, they had no evidence to expect that it would amount to anything significant. At the time – around the same time Bank of America was building ERMA, actually – self-service wasn't even a concept in financial services. Is this an example of a bank so concerned with avoiding risk that it kills innovation completely? Hardly, and it also had the benefit of John Shepherd-Barron – the man who invented the device – who was then managing director of De La Rue Instruments. Shepherd-Barron was an innovator and *also* a key supplier and confidante of the CEO of Barclays.

As you will probably guess from these examples, the secret sauce that makes some innovation programmes more successful than others is the quality of leadership brought to bear on the innovation challenge.

In 2007, McKinsey published a survey of 600 global business executives and found that practically everyone they asked cited leadership as the key predictor of innovation performance

[63]. McKinsey looked mainly at firm-level outcomes, but the innovation leader has an impact at the individual level as well.

Everyone has great ideas from time to time. Sometimes they are big, potentially game-changing and sometimes small, perhaps an incremental improvement to a local workgroup process. But most of the time, nothing happens to all these ideas. The hurdles involved in going from invention to innovation are simply too great for most people. But a good innovation leader has the knack of working out how to motivate people to jump the hurdles needed to make their ideas into something. And they also know how to make the hurdles lower in the first place, so people don't have to jump as high. By doing these two things, an innovation leader can create a culture of innovation where previously management thought there was none.

The McKinsey study obtained the feedback of hundreds of executives who all complained about the quality of their innovation leadership. There is one conclusion that follows: getting a leader who is capable of doing innovation well is a challenge. Just where, exactly, does one find such a leader? What are the qualities that such a person should have? What background and experience are required?

It is commonly assumed that innovation leaders should, themselves, be great innovators. How could anyone expect to create success in an innovation function without having spent years going through the process themselves? Surely what is needed is a firm hand with lots of experience that knows stage-gate processes back to front and the ability to move the levers on the innovation process to optimise outputs?

This is a misconception, of course, because the *process* of innovation is only one part of the job of the innovation leader. He or she must also be a great influencer. As we've seen during the innovation and execution phases of futureproofing, there will be many times when it is the leader who will have to negotiate some very tricky situations if they are to ensure that innovations reach their full potential. They need to be visionary enough to understand when and how to lead the futurecasting process. And they have to be sufficiently entrepreneurial that they can make the decisions needed to ensure innovation delivers the returns needed to make it the preferred investment choice most of the time. That's a difficult mix, and quite different from the leaders one normally hires for any other business process.

But there is yet another challenge that makes the role of the innovation leader especially difficult, and that is changing the cultural surrounding of the innovation function to one that accepts early failure as success. This is in stark contrast to other business processes, where failure is most definitely not an optimal outcome. But for innovators, 'drowning the puppy' (or, in other words, failing fast) is a key skill that must be accepted if one is to achieve predictable returns.

In risk-adverse organisations such as financial institutions, a culture of celebrating failure rarely exists. So here, too, the leader has a key role in making sure that failures are recognised as the successes they actually are.

With all of that to take care of, is it any wonder that leading an innovation team is a job that is rarely done well? And the consequences of *not* doing it well are pretty significant: at best the innovation programme won't be very predictable. At worst? It will be cancelled outright the minute such a 'luxury' investment has to be justified.

8.1 LEADERSHIP STYLES

It is firstly useful to consider the style of leadership an innovation team might respond well to if one wants to create an optimum environment for predictable and reliable futureproofing. Innovation leadership styles are somewhat a superset of the leadership styles that most people are familiar with. Everyone knows the autocratic leader, who gives orders and expects things to be done. The democratic leader, who always seeks the counsel of subordinates before making any decision. And the bureaucratic leader, who follows every process to the letter.

These styles (and the hundreds more which are documented in the leadership literature) are appropriate for ordinary processes which relate to business-as-usual activities in an institution. But innovation is something that must be encouraged to happen *outside* these ordinary frameworks. This requires new styles which are somewhat unique.

Much academic research has been completed on this topic in the past few years, in a range of industries [64, 65]. The result is that we can conveniently divide the set of behaviour styles adopted by innovation leaders into four broad archetypes, which we examine now.

Charismatic leadership

The first is the charismatic leader. Everyone knows the type: an individual who creates energy whenever he or she is in the room. In an innovation team, the charismatic leader is the fuel: he or she motivates team members towards new objectives, values or aspirations. Charismatic leaders generate commitment, and because of this, they can often ignore organisational boundaries and official roles and get away with it. Not surprisingly, studies have found the presence of a charismatic leader results in a greater perception that the innovation team is, actually, innovative.

A number of years ago, I was lucky enough to work in a start-up company with a lady named Janet Parker, founder of Australian and New Zealand Internet banking provider Parker's Edge. Janet was, and still is, the most charismatic leader I've ever worked closely with. On one occasion, during a presentation in which she was outlining her vision for the company (using all the correct aspirational, visionary, and values-based factors available), I actually had a tear in my eye.

As an innovator, the experience was an influential one. At the time, we were building Australia's first account aggregation solution, and were rushing to deliver against tight, even impossible deadlines. Despite late nights and many weeks without a single weekend off, Janet was still able to excite and motivate the team to create new things. Though Parker's Edge is no longer in business, I have sought ever since to replicate Janet's ability, though must reluctantly admit I am not as good at it as she is.

It is interesting to consider the charismatic leader in the context of the earliest stages of an innovation programme. Referring to Figure 3.2, our oft-mentioned Five Capability Model of innovation programmes, the charismatic leader has a specific role to play during the invention phase. Such individuals have the capability to create belief and vision in a *specific* innovation. So often, and especially at the start of the innovation journey, the key hurdle to overcome is inherent inertia in an institution. If you *expect* to hear 'we're a bank, you'll never get something *that* innovative to happen', then what's needed is a bit of charisma to drive things forward. Inevitably, before wins are on the board, every initiative of a new innovation programme is treated with suspicion. This is one of the main reasons many organisations find that getting started with innovation is much harder than they expect.

In any event, it is the charismatic inventor who is able to come up with something that tests previous boundaries *and* is able to generate enough support to see it through to implementation. Creating support is not the same thing as actually *delivering,* of course. For that you need the instrumental leadership style, which I'll cover in the next section.

The charismatic style is especially at the fore when the innovation programme is at the champion stage. What can a charismatic champion achieve? He or she will make those at the interface to the innovation programme, *want* an innovation programme. Creating an innovation programme is a simple act of assigning people and resources. But success demands the organisation surrounding the new team buy in to a shared set of goals. Bridging the gap between the act of creation and organisational adoption is one of the first things that a charismatic champion will be able to accomplish.

Now, let's turn to the charismatic manager. Recall that the managing stage is all about creating a plan for innovation that delivers predictably. This predictability in the innovation process is fundamental to the longevity of the innovation function. But what about the people who work for the innovation leader? As part of any move towards predictability, they are likely to be required to sign up for specific financial or other targets, and will certainly have to operate in a more accountable manner than they may have been used to. Their roles will necessarily shift towards a more procedural style of innovation: they won't be creating (inventing) so much as running portfolios and managing processes. As I will discuss in the next chapter, the mix of people in the innovation organisation will determine how palatable this kind of change actually is. Regardless of team composition, however, the charismatic style will make the move to procedural innovation way more palatable.

And during the final two stages of development, charismatic leadership is also important. One cannot expect the results of a futurecast, for example, to be well accepted by senior leaders initially. They will be wondering how these sets of stories created by the innovation team have any relevance to their operations day to day. In point of fact, they may read the outputs of futurecasting, and not recognise the positive effects they have on their consideration processes.

This is much more common that you would expect, actually. I've been in many situations where, upon accepting a futurecast, the leaders involved have duly considered the points which were brought out, and actually discussed the potential decisions they might have to make should the predicted things come to pass. But it wasn't until it was pointed out to them that their thinking about issues had changed that they realised this to be so. The futurecast is a subtle tool.

Anyway, it requires a charismatic leader to get senior executives to realise the futurecast is something they should consider as part of their strategic process. And then, of course, to take meaningful actions based on the thinking it generates.

Even at the venturing stage, there is a role for the charismatic leader. Now, although a programme at this stage is quite likely to be in a position where it can authorise major innovations in its own right, it will certainly be working on things which are controversial at best. If it has decided to progress a portfolio of disruptive innovations, for example, it will be necessary for the innovation leader to spend a great deal of time working with those these innovations will eventually affect.

That is especially so the first time an innovation programme makes the jump from sustaining to disruptive. A sustaining innovation, you might recall, will usually be one that adds value to an existing business in some way. But a disruption seeks to establish something completely new, something that will probably take business *away* from the incumbents in the institution over time. That is a complicated and difficult message for any senior executive to accept. The importance of the charismatic innovation leader in these circumstances cannot be over-stated.

Instrumental leadership

Whilst the charismatic style is about obtaining buy-in to a vision for innovation, the instrumental style is mainly about process and objectives. It is only in the earliest phases of the development of an innovation programme that one can afford to be without metrics and measures. With them, there is evidence to prove that innovation is a valuable activity, and, indeed, the preferred way to spend investment resources. But without them, stakeholders are unlikely to see progress that would justify their investments, even if there *is* such progress. Mostly, they don't have the time to be taken through the latest and greatest change in the business: they need numbers that summarise results.

Getting to such results means implementing – and then managing – a process. Let's face it, it is all very well to be able to motivate a team through the power of one's raw charisma, but what are all those excited people supposed to be doing once they've been fired up? The instrumental leader is the one who makes sure that people know what they are doing and when they have to do it. As you would expect, this is particularly to the fore when the leader is running an innovation programme that is at the managing stage.

When is instrumental leadership most important? Or perhaps a better question, when is it *not* important?! Execution is always the difference between actually achieving something and not: instrumental leadership isn't managing by numbers, but it is about a focus on outcomes. Consider the invention phase of the Five Capability Model. The leader is, at this time, communicating the technical know-how to create a specific innovation, if they are not creating the innovation themselves. That is all very well, and a charismatic leader may have an excited staff, but not provide much guidance with respect to *how* things should be delivered.

An innovation programme that is at the championing stage needs instrumental leadership too. Building out the interdepartmental connections and senior-level influence that it takes to advance an innovation programme is not a scatter-gun activity. Some relationships are more important than others. Some organisational units need more attention. The staff in the innovation group may not have visibility of the political landscape they are operating in. Adopting the instrumental style makes sure that the nascent relationships the team is building are the right ones.

And, of course, the predictability needed at the managing stage is all about instrumental leadership. At this stage, the innovation team will be running innovation by numbers. The game will be about volume, about achieving metrics reliably, and delivering predictable returns.

Once a programme has reached the futurecasting and venturing stage, the importance of instrumental leadership is somewhat reduced, however. By this time, predictable returns and process are well established, and the innovation leader has to focus on other things to drive the next stage of success. He or she will, for example, need to be creating the environment in which disruptive innovations, as opposed to the sustaining ones which will have been the bread and butter of a programme until this time, can be reliably undertaken.

Interactive leadership

Whilst the charismatic leader is about motivating innovative behaviour through inspiring vision, and the instrumental leader gets results by making sure the right processes are in place, our next leadership style is much more concerned with establishing an environment in which everyone has the skills and values which make it possible to do innovation well.

The interactive leadership style is very communicative, almost democratic. The leader attempts to empower his or her team whenever possible, and spends a great deal of time in cooperative tasks that aim to develop the innovation capability.

Interactive leadership is about involving innovators in the set of decisions that affect them and their work. That does not mean that an interactive leader is unable to make significant decisions themselves, just that their primary motivation is the achievement of a collegial working environment. Such environments tend to be important for the retention of innovative behaviour. The fact of the matter is that most innovators, creative people with their own ideas and goals, do not respond well to autocratic leadership of any kind. The idea that management would direct them in the minutiae of their daily work lives grinds on them.

This is most obvious when you deal with younger innovators, especially those recent graduates who have just joined an institution. This new talent operates in a way which is quite different from that most managers are used to. They are used to making their own decisions, even to deciding for themselves what might be interesting to work on. When they join an institutional innovation function, they are likely in for a rude shock, especially if the innovation leader is not a practitioner of the interactive leadership style.

During 2008, I had the opportunity to speak at a 'geek dinner' – a function created by young technology geeks, for other young technology geeks. The format is simple: book out a restaurant, and get some speaker in to talk on a subject of interest. Usually, the speaker is an older, more experienced professional, and the geeks get to marvel at how very disconnected the older workforce is from their reality.

Geeks, in case you are wondering, are those individuals who have a passionate interest in technology. They often work in very small, very innovative start-up companies. Many are generation-Yers (I'll have more to say about this in the next chapter), whose work practices are quite different from the traditionalist approaches normally seen in banks. And they're full of fresh ideas, and a burning ambition to make a difference. They realise that ideas without execution aren't worth much, especially since they have new ideas every few seconds. Perfect innovators, in other words.

Anyway, so I went to this geek dinner and spoke, and what I found reinforced for me the absolute importance of the interactive leadership style when dealing with very innovative people. *None* of the geeks were even remotely interested in working for a large bank. The reason? They didn't feel they would have any opportunity to work on things that were interesting to them. One attendee even went so far as to tell me 'yes, I'm working in a big company now, but won't be for long. Why would I bother with being told what to work on when I can work on anything I like if I work for myself?'

The moral of this story is that the more innovative an individual, the more likely the interactive leadership style is the sort which will get the best response.

The desire of innovators to do interesting work and be managed loosely presents some difficulties for an innovation leader, of course. When one is at the managing stage, for example, maintaining predictability of returns requires a level of discipline and coaching that can sometimes be at odds with the creative ideals of the innovation team. But once the future-casting stage is reached, interactive leadership becomes the critical determinant of success. Futurecasting, as we saw in Chapter 4, is really all about garnering the opinions of many knowledgeable people with the idea that these inputs contribute to stories which have strategic merit for an institution. In this environment, only collaborative working results in any outputs that are worthwhile.

Strategic leadership

The next leadership style an innovation leader can adopt is the strategic style, which is really about using one's hierarchical position to enhance the innovation journey. Usually, the strategic style is associated with a very senior executive. The sort that people sit up and listen to when they give directions or make comments.

As an innovation programme becomes more significant in the strategic tapestry of an institution – say at the futurecasting or venturing stages – the strategic leadership style becomes the critical determinant of how successful the innovators can be.

Some innovations are so risky and expensive, it is *only* by exercising the strategic style that you can get them approved at all. Much research has been conducted on this with a single conclusion: when you have the support and commitment of top management to innovation, the organisation itself is likely to be innovative. A leader exercising the strategic style is likely to have the authority to approve ideas in his or her own right. Their strategic imperative is innovation, and they make bold decisions despite the uncertainty of outcomes.

Now, it must be said here that strategic leadership has nothing at all to do with autocratic dictatorialism. As we just saw, innovators rarely respond well to such leadership anyway, and the point is to *encourage* innovative behaviour, not constrain it. The strategic leader, instead, knows they have official sanction to do things which would otherwise be challenging for an institution *and* uses this power to support the progress of the innovation agenda. Innovation teams, working for a leader who is able to exercise the strategic style, are in a lucky position indeed. Because of the mandate given to their leader, there is generally a great deal less influencing to be done in order to get to the execution phase for any particular innovation.

Of course, getting to the position where the leader has hierarchical authority to make things happen doesn't occur all by itself. In fact, one usually finds strategic leaders only in innovation programmes which have reached the venturing stage. At this point, not only does the innovation programme know how to deliver reliable and predictable returns, it has a seat at the strategic table as well. Innovators are consulted on significant questions that devolve from innovations and market adoption of them. And the leader is an important part of the planning process for an institution.

Recognition of the importance of strategic leadership has resulted in an emerging trend: appointing very senior individuals in banks to roles entitled chief innovation officer or similar. This is quite often accompanied by universal acknowledgement that an institution will adopt a Play to Win innovation strategy. Everyone is thrilled that *finally* innovation is getting the senior-level attention it deserves, and quite rightly assume the result will be a new revival of the fortunes of whichever institution is involved.

Unfortunately, most of the time, such initiatives are quietly terminated in 18 months or less, that magical stretch of time which most innovation programmes have to live before senior executives decide they aren't worth the resources being spent on them. How can this happen *even* when a leader capable of executing the strategic leadership style is in place?

The fact of the matter is that even when very senior-level support of an innovation programme is put in place, and even when large budgets are committed, innovation doesn't just happen. Strategic leadership is all very well once you have fundamental innovation infrastructure in place, but is practically useless before that time.

No matter how senior the individual appointed to lead innovation, or how much money is thrown at the problem, if there is no pipeline of ideas, nothing will happen. Nothing will happen either if the correct processes aren't in place to convert ideas into execution. And, as you would expect, the innovation programme won't have the strategic value anticipated if no one knows how to consider various innovative futures in a structured way.

In other words, the strategic leadership style is probably not that useful *until* an innovation programme has got to the venturing stage on its own. Institutions would be well advised *not* to appoint a CIO before this time. Lacking appropriate support, they will be unable to accomplish very much, and will quietly seek alternative opportunities elsewhere. In the meantime, the institution will likely suffer significant innovation trauma, rightly concluding that if it couldn't get innovative *even* with a senior-level executive in charge, it has no hope of doing so at all.

But once the innovators have become predictable in their operations – after managing has been reached – strategic leadership is probably the critical determinant of how successful they will be thereafter. There are several reasons for this.

The first is that the innovators have to insert themselves into the strategic planning processes of their institutions so that the results of its futurecasting can make a meaningful difference. As we've already seen in cases throughout this book so far, there are many examples where structured consideration of potential future states could have avoided significant institutional missteps. Sub-prime and declining housing prices. The emergence of alternative payments systems. The potential threat of mobile operators with their new NFC chips.

Without strategic leadership, however, the likelihood of any senior executive actually using the results of futurecasting is pretty low. Senior executives are much more likely to accept the unusual input of the futurecast if it comes from someone they regard as their peer.

The second reason strategic leadership becomes important after managing is that the kinds of innovations a programme will likely pursue will start to change in nature. Instead of concentrating on sustaining innovation, the programme will likely want to consider disruptions more closely. Certainly, it will need to consider how revolutionary and breakthrough innovations might add to the innovation portfolio, especially if the innovation strategy is Play to Win. To progress such innovation successfully, the innovators need senior-level support to enable them to make much larger, and more risky, investments.

The ideal leadership style

This discussion, no doubt, has served to illustrate an important point, which is that an innovation programme needs more than a single kind of leadership style during its development. At the start of a programme, a leader of the charismatic and interactive styles will likely provide the best results. Whereas a leader who focuses on strategic and instrumental leadership is better the more advanced a programme gets.

Most potential leaders have a preference for one style over another, and the remainder tend to be underdeveloped. The charismatic leader is probably not one to focus on the details required to make an innovation programme predictable, for example, even if they are fantastic advocates and great at sales. On the other hand, as I said earlier, there's little point in having a leader capable of only the strategic style if none of the supporting infrastructure that makes such a leader successful is in place.

In the end, this leads to an important conclusion: in general, it will be impossible to hire a single individual who will suit an innovation programme during all phases of its development through the five capabilities. Just as one doesn't take a start-up CEO and put them in charge of a major bank, one cannot expect an innovator who launches a programme to be successful when they are asked to run a Play to Win strategic programme with millions to invest. The management styles required are completely different. Actually, this leads to another point.

The more developed an innovation programme becomes, the *less* important it is that the leader has any knowledge of innovation science or practice. The reason, obviously, is that much of the infrastructure needed to do the day-to-day work is already built and should function on auto-pilot by the time the managing capability is reached. What *is* needed in an advanced innovation programme is a senior leader who knows how to play the political game at CEO or board level. The specific innovation processes – and indeed the innovations themselves – are less important than the ability to manage such senior stakeholders.

On the other hand, in the early stages of an innovation programme, deep knowledge of innovation process and science is a functional necessity. Someone has to build the innovation infrastructure into a state where it can be taken over by a senior leader, and to do this, one needs experience of doing actual innovation.

8.2   THINGS THE LEADERS SHOULD DO

This discussion of the leadership styles innovation leaders can adopt is useful when one looks at the overall timeline of the development of an innovation programme. But a key question remains, and that concerns the specific practices an innovation leader should adopt to get the most out of his or her innovation team.

There has been some decent research into this topic [66]. Most of it boils down to a few key signature actions that either help with the idea creation process, or the execution process, or both. We'll look at these signature actions next.

Role modelling

The first thing a great innovation leader does, particularly at the start of an innovation programme, is be a role model as an innovator him or herself. This goes beyond demonstrating high personal innovativeness, though functionally that is as important for an innovation leader as it would be for someone working at the innovation coal face. Role modelling, in this case, is about showing employees the kinds of behaviours they are expected to display to drive innovative outcomes.

The very best innovators combine two key skills: the ability to think creatively in such a way that they approach problems from alternate perspectives, with the result that they come up with new ideas that generate uniqueness. Then, with such ideas in hand, they create implementation approaches that avoid the natural tendency of institutions to slow down change. They have the ability both to create new ideas *and* to make them happen.

A leader who demonstrates creativity tends to encourage similar behaviour in their teams. In other words, if a leader is good at creating new ideas, staff will tend to be so as well. The leader acts as a catalyst.

This is also true for the execution part of the innovation problem. A leader with great execution capabilities – perhaps they have an instinctive ability to negotiate internal blockers, for example – will tend to encourage the same outcomes in their teams.

Conversely, there are great challenges for innovators ahead when their leader doesn't have the ability to think creatively *and* deliver execution. They come not so much from the fact that the innovation leader cannot themselves drive innovation outcomes (which becomes less important the more advanced the innovation programme is), but that the day-to-day decisions a member of the innovation team must make will likely be largely incomprehensible to his or her boss.

There is another aspect to role modelling which is important, and that is making sure the team can see positive evidence that the leader has belief in the role of innovation in an institution. Whether one likes it or not, most things the team will work on will fail. They will either be subject to internal-to-team puppy drowning, or will fail to win funding at the end of the innovation stage. In more extreme cases, they will fail because something has gone wrong during the execution phase.

Whatever the reason, the regularity with which failure occurs is sufficiently great that it could dishearten anyone. For this reason, the innovation leader must demonstrate faith in the value of the innovation journey to his or her team. There is nothing more unproductive than an innovation team that doesn't see the point in doing its work.

Stimulating knowledge diffusion

Collaboration and knowledge diffusion are key components to the innovation process. Who has not been in that common situation where a comment from someone triggers a whole avalanche of new thoughts from the rest of the group? Conversely, it is the rare individual who has not been subject to an information asymmetry, where someone 'in the know' failed to communicate important information because they were able to obtain a personal advantage from this lack of disclosure.

It is the role of the innovation leader to ensure that as much knowledge is shared as possible. The fewer barriers there are between innovators, other stakeholders, and the broader institutional community, the more rapid the pace of change becomes.

At my bank, we launched social media internally as a means of facilitating this kind of behaviour (see the case study in Chapter 2). The purpose was to ensure that if people wanted to share knowledge – on anything, not just their banking work – they would be able to do so. Initially, this was met with a degree of scepticism, even fear, from senior management. What inappropriate behaviour might occur when there were no formal controls on what people could publish? What if front-line staff spent more time chatting with each other than doing their jobs? The reality, of course, was that greater openness of communication enhanced, rather than detracted from, the overall operations of the bank. The chances that people could find the information they needed to make decisions were much greater when there was every possibility someone had already published the necessary material internally.

Online methods are not the only means an innovation leader has to foster information diffusion, though. Team meetings, road-shows, and other means to reach large groups of people are all excellent ways to make sure that as much knowledge as possible is shared.

Providing vision

A team without a vision is a team without much direction. Vision, in the context of the innovation leader, is the set of actions that make it clear to the rest of the team where, exactly, the innovation agenda is going. Without such clarity, things are much more difficult for the innovation team. What innovations are most likely to get acceptance? How could anyone know without a clear understanding of the path ahead?

Whether the innovation strategy selected is Play to Win or Play Not to Lose, providing vision is a key aspect of innovation leadership, because it sets the boundaries of what can (and cannot) be done to progress the innovation agenda. Let me give you an example. Most institutions have very complicated rules that govern how procedures may be modified in the retail branch environment. These rules are designed to prevent uncontrolled changes affecting the customer experience, which will likely be regimented, predictable, and highly systematised. They are rules which are in place for very good and proper reasons.

Let us next imagine that the innovation strategy is P2W, and that the overall vision for the customer experience segment of the innovation pentagram (Figure 3.1) is that the institution be the market leader. This leads the innovation team to several conclusions. The first is that ideas which are naturally aligned with this strategy and vision will be much more likely accepted than others. Their interest will be in more revolutionary and breakthrough kinds of innovations relating to branch, and they will actively seek to change the game in any way they can.

Naturally, those executives in charge of the branch network will not like this very much. Their entire operation is based on being as predictable as possible in order to meet specific customer service targets. They will do quite a bit to prevent the work products of the innovation team interfering with this.

Luckily, the innovation team is empowered by the vision of its leadership, so they know that breaking some of the rules in the interest of achieving market leadership will be tolerated. They are not put off by any resistance, and push forward with confidence.

But in the absence of any well-articulated vision for the innovation programme, what are the innovators to do? They don't have clarity of what will, and won't, be tolerated. They don't know, if they actually make the call to forge ahead with something that is clearly unpopular, what the consequences might be. And, because of this, they will certainly select innovations which have the least chance of ruffling any feathers.

Consulting and delegating

It cannot be overstated how strong the link is between involving innovation team members in everything that affects their work and the actual innovation outputs that result. Time and time again, research has shown that innovation works in a collaborative environment, and fails outside it.

There are two aspects of this. The first is that members of the innovation team have the opportunity to participate in the decisions which affect their day-to-day operations. And the second is that once decisions have been made, they are provided with sufficient autonomy to progress their ideas independently of any managerial oversight.

From a day-to-day operational perspective, there are many decisions made in an innovation function as a result of systematised innovation infrastructure. The scoring system inherent in ideation, for example, is one system that helps innovators make the decisions about what is sensible to progress. During the innovation phase as well there are many tools that govern the kinds of innovations that will be pursued, the portfolio planning process chiefly amongst them.

These systems and tools have their place, of course, but from time to time an innovator may choose to override them altogether. A good innovation leader will allow this, even when the evidence available suggests that the far better course is to drown the puppy.

Having made an effort to consult with team members on the things that affect them, the next thing an innovation leader will do is make sure sufficient delegated authority has been granted to actually make sure particular innovations can be progressed. Deciding how much, and on what to spend in answering the key questions, for example, is something that should be delegated to the innovation team members, especially when achieving volume is necessary.

Then, too, there is likely to be little time for the leader to be involved in these decisions in any case. There are many other accountabilities that leaders must take which can be done *only* by them. For example, ensuring that sufficient resources are available to support the innovation programme (we'll come back to this in a minute) is best done by the leader, whilst leaving their team to progress the day-to-day work of the programme.

Organising feedback

There are many times during the innovation process when feedback – from customers, business colleagues, and even other innovators – can be important. One of the key actions that must be facilitated by the innovation leader is the provision of the channels which enable such feedback to occur.

Consider the need to get customer insight during the ideation phase we've discussed earlier in this book. Now, in general, there will almost certainly be a business group somewhere in the bank which will feel it owns the customer relationship, and will likely take a fairly dim view of any interactions which it did not authorise. Providing access to customers for the purpose of screening ideas is pretty critical to being able to make decent decisions about which innovations to pursue, of course. Gaining access to customers without causing a massive political war is something the innovation leader is likely able to accomplish more successfully than his or her team members.

There are other feedback systems which are important for the innovation team as well. Chief amongst these is the need for individual team members to collaborate with each other in some structured fashion that enables a peer review of the activities which are being progressed. A very common configuration of innovation teams is where each member works in a semi-isolated fashion on a range of innovations. Collaborative culture aside, there are often few instances where specific innovations are discussed (and critiqued) by other innovation team members.

The perspective of a full-time innovator is, however, one that is very valuable. They are likely to know who are the key influencers, for example, when it comes time to sell the new idea prior to execution. Perhaps there will be positive inputs to the key question analysis which is underway. Or maybe a team member will provide a key insight that means the puppy can be drowned. There are so many ways that intra-team collaboration can be valuable.

The problem is that most innovators will not automatically seek such feedback on their specific innovations. They will generally not have any issue with feedback if it is given, but will usually need a structured mechanism provided for them if this is to happen on any kind of regular schedule. It is the role of the innovation leader to make sure this can happen.

Recognition of effort

Later on in this book we will discuss reward and recognition systems in quite a bit of detail. Those discussions are all about how to make sure that those *outside* the innovation team are compensated for going out of their way to do innovative things. Internally, though, recognition for effort undertaken is an important driver of team morale. Team morale, of course, has significant consequences for overall productivity.

The basic difficulty innovators face is the high failure rates they need to get used to in the course of their day-to-day work. Very few great ideas will ever manage to make it to execution, and of those that do, some will still go wrong.

The rewards and recognition an innovation leader can provide are a very significant part of balancing this out. When, for example, an innovation fails to live up to expectations and is killed off just before execution, it can be devastating for the innovator involved. They will likely have invested quite a lot of their time in answering the key questions. They will have gone out on a personal limb with many senior executives around the bank. The failure of the innovation to progress to execution even when it seemed everything was lined up for success can sometimes be inexplicable.

When this kind of thing occurs – as it most assuredly will in a great number of cases – the role of the innovation leader is clear. He or she must reinforce that no personal failure has occurred, and that, in the overall scheme of things, what actually has occurred is a success. Pushing forward with an innovation that would likely have failed later, at much greater cost, is never a strategy which has felicitous outcomes, and in some cases, can lead to severe innovation trauma. So, recognition of success, even in the face of failure, is very important.

Providing resources

It is usually destructive to the morale of an innovation function if innovators have to justify *why* an idea is a good one before they are given resources to progress exploration. It is better to allow the innovation team to pursue anything that fits within the context of the innovation system that has been created in the bank.

There are plenty of controls available to innovation leaders to ensure this does not get out of hand. In the first instance, there will be developed means of working out which ideas are relatively better than others during the ideation phase. And key questions, which are a large part of the innovation phase, make sure that only the most do-able of ideas actually get progressed. Even if all that fails to catch an innovation that probably shouldn't be pursued, the final hurdle of actually winning the money will normally ensure that bad ideas don't get too far through the process before they are killed.

So, the innovation leader will probably not be providing oversight concerning which specific innovations get developed. What they must do, however, is ensure that resources are available which may actually be used to develop the innovations. It is surprising how many times I've come across bank innovation programmes which have poor, or non-existent, capabilities in this regard. We will be discussing funding models for innovation later in this book, but suffice it to say right now, it is a key part of the leader's responsibilities to make sure that those resources needed to fund the ideation system and progress key questions investigations are available.

Innovation team members are accountable for getting innovations through to the execution phase. In the process they will spend money preparing sales materials for senior executives so they can make a buy decision. As a general rule, the resources an innovator will need to go through this process are likely to be microscopic compared with the resources they will be asking sponsors for in order to commence execution.

It therefore does not make sense that before they can commence the whole process of developing an idea, they must justify, and even win, the money they need to explore their ideas. When the innovation leader fails to make resources available for these activities, though, he or she forces the team to win control of resources *twice*. Once to start the investigations which are the key outcome of the innovation phase, and *again* to actually get the innovation into execution.

Most of the time, when you have to fight for resources, the time and influencing required is not related to the magnitude of the request. It takes just as long to get a small amount of money as it does to get a large one. Far better, then, for the innovation leader to provide the resources needed for the first iteration without much question. By doing so, the cycle time taken to get from idea to execution will likely be halved.

Monitoring

It is the innovation leader who is, in the end, accountable for whether the innovation programme is performing or not. And whilst I've been recommending throughout this chapter that he or she uses a very light touch with respect to managing the members of the innovation team, some controls are required to make sure that everything is on track.

At each phase of the futureproofing process, there are a number of specific activities that need at least some oversight. At the ideation phase, for example, it is important to know how many, and what kind of, ideas are being contributed. Even more importantly, it is essential to monitor the performance of the scoring system *and* how well it is helping the innovators do their jobs.

It is similarly the case with innovation and execution. One wants to make sure the portfolio of innovations being considered is correctly balanced with the dictates of the innovation strategy adopted by the institutions. And obviously, it is very important to examine how many ideas are being translated into the execution phase.

8.3   SIGNS OF A BAD INNOVATION LEADER

As I mentioned at the start of this chapter, the thing that makes the difference between a great innovation programme and the rest is the quality of the innovation leader appointed to drive the agenda. As in all things to do with people, it is easy to make a decision that turns out to be quite wrong in retrospect.

Now, of course it is impossible to be specific about *all* the things that can go wrong with innovation leaders, but there do seem to be a few specific types of problems that crop up. Here, then, are some of the top things to watch out for in your innovation leader if you want to ensure the team has the best possible chance of success.

The risk avoider

There are some kinds of managers whose day-to-day mantra is the elimination, as much as possible, of all risk associated with anything they do. This is the kind of behaviour you expect, of course, from security people or those entrusted with keeping mission-critical systems running. It is most assuredly *not* desirable, though, for anyone who has to do an innovation role. As we've seen throughout this book, innovation is a process of *managing* the inherent riskiness of what is an essentially speculative process to start with. Every new idea comes with significant unknowns, and it is only by exploring these uncertainties that it is possible to determine if driving whatever-it-is is possible or not.

It is absolutely important that an innovation leader exhibits a high degree of personal innovativeness. They need to be in the innovator or early adopter segments of Figure 2.2, since only individuals from those segments are capable of making the call to progress uniqueness in the presence of significant uncertainty.

Typically, risk avoiders are early majority or later when it comes to personal innovativeness. This means they require a great deal of peer-to-peer validation of their decisions before they feel they are in a position to commit with certainty. And once they've made a decision to proceed, they will seek significant feedback from others throughout the process to help convince themselves that the decision was, in fact, the correct one.

The likely outcome is that most innovations – especially breakthroughs and revolutions – will never be started at all. And you can forget any innovation that might be disruptive, because the level of risk involved is likely to be so substantive that no amount of peer reassurance will get the risk avoider over the hump of uncertainty involved. So, the risk avoider is unlikely to start many innovation projects which result in windfall gains. But what about the projects that *do* get started?

As we know, one of the key skills of innovators is the ability to drown the puppy. Or, in other words, to declare that a particular idea is a failure early enough that as few resources as possible are committed. Innovators want to have enough resources left that they can move onto something new with better chances. They know that *at least* three of four things they work on will be declared failures long before they get to execution. This does not sit well with the risk avoider. He or she is unable to accept that in an innovation context, failure is actually success. Instead, risk avoiders will not attempt anything that has no obvious path to success. They make sure their people don't either.

This kills an innovation programme, especially one that has a Play to Win strategy. There is no way to get a big enough pipeline to make a difference when the only things considered are those that are extremely obvious. It limits one to the most minor of incremental innovations.

In the meantime, any idea that is allowed to progress is most *certainly* not allowed to fail. The risk avoider, having taken a chance on something, will never allow it to fail, because he or she equates drowning the puppy with a team and personal failure as well. The consequence of all this is that when bad innovations get started, they are never stopped. And, conversely, good innovations never get started at all.

The autocrat

Another kind of innovation leader who is especially disagreeable is the autocrat, that manager who likes to control every single detail of their environment and their teams. They do so in an oppressive, perhaps even arrogant manner. Their view is that they know much more about the processes of innovation than anyone else, so they should make every single decision of importance. They even make decisions which are decidedly *not* of importance as well.

Autocratic leaders may have been, once, great individual innovators. Perhaps the reason they've been promoted into the leadership role is the track record of success they've demonstrated in the past. But, of course, the thing about management is that being a brilliant individual contributor has little or no relationship to the skills required to create great team performance. This is much more true for innovation leaders, who have to deal with a set of problems quite unlike those in normal institutional line management. The level of uncertainty is greater. The amount of creative input needed significant. And faith in people to deliver outcomes in the absence of any decent signposts with respect to the direction that ought to be followed unprecedented.

The autocrat may have been good at innovation when they were allowed to do these things themselves, but the fundamental issue is that they haven't made the leap of faith required to trust their subordinates to generate similar outcomes. This lack of faith tends to mean that very little is allowed to occur without the personal intervention of the leader. Such creative insights as the team might generate must happen only under the watchful eye of the leader. He or she may even take the view that only those innovations into which there has been a personal contribution can have any chance of success.

Naturally, this stifles team creativity monstrously, because, as we've seen earlier, creating the environment in which innovators are able to 'own' their innovations is a critical component of making the innovation process work. But the big issue with the autocrat is that they swiftly become a decision bottleneck. Those choices which would ordinarily be made in a systematic fashion – such as the scoring system implemented by ideation, for example – are interfered with. The autocrat likes to make the decisions about which ideas will be pursued personally. They will likely choose to interfere with the process of answering the key questions. And then, once execution is reached, if it ever is, they will attempt to control the implementation team as well.

Autocratic leadership can sometimes be deceptive to others outside the innovation team. It might *appear* as if innovations are being developed and successfully led to execution. There may even be a few big successes. But the issue, under the surface, is that these successes will inevitably be the result of the *personal* efforts of the leader rather than the team.

This makes innovation unsustainable in the long term, because sooner or later everyone leaves for new opportunities. But a much worse consequence is also waiting in the wings, and that is an innovation programme with the autocratic leader can never scale, since everything flows through one person. In other words, no matter how much resource is committed to an innovation programme, an autocratic leader will – perhaps unwittingly – be responsible for very slow development through the Five Capability Model. That's if the programme ever gets beyond the inventing stage at all, of course.

The traditionalist

Related to the autocrat in many ways is the traditionalist innovation leader. Traditionalists, when you examine the term from a workplace generations perspective, are usually those considered to have been born prior to 1965. They have specific behaviours and motivations which are quite different from those inherent in people who have been born in later generations. In our next chapter, I will discuss the traditionalist as well as the other generations present in most institutional workforces in detail. But suffice it to say here that traditionalists are individuals who have worked in your bank most of their lives, are very hierarchically driven, and for whom the impending maturity of their pensions is an important issue.

Now, before anyone accuses me of ageism, I must say that it is quite possible for a traditionalist to have high personal innovativeness, *and* very well-developed management skills. The problem with their leadership is not so much that they don't know *how* to do leadership well, but that the skills they have likely developed over the course of their decades of employment do not necessarily fit well with the kinds of cultures that an innovation team needs.

Innovation teams, as we've seen, are most successful when they exist in a collaborative culture that supports the innate creativity of the ideas generation process. They are teams that have to deal with substantial ambiguity. Quite often, no one has any idea ahead of time whether a particular concept is genius or stupidity.

All this requires that the innovation leader be able to empower his or her people in such a way that they can make mistakes with impunity. They need to experiment without fear. And they have to be able to create uniqueness, even if it means that other senior executives around them get irritated. Innovators *are* usually annoying in some ways to those who run more conventional parts of the business, who are just as likely to consider the innovators distracting as in any way adding value.

Anyway, this kind of an environment is an anathema to most traditionalists. They were trained in a command-and-control culture, and have great difficulty in accepting the kind of free-wheeling dealing that makes a successful innovation function. Traditionalists must either learn new ways of managing their new innovation team, or doom them to failure.

The politician

Let us now consider the next kind of bad leader, the politician, who focuses with laser-sharp accuracy on the amount of influence they control, both inside and outside the innovation programme. Now, this is a good thing in many contexts of course. Influence and money are the two main ingredients an innovator needs to get anything done. To a large degree, they are interchangeable. The problem with the politician, however, is that he or she is concerned with *personal* influence, rather than that of the team. Whenever there is an opportunity to enhance the team's value – perhaps in the context of a senior-level meeting or major presentation – the politician will find a way to make sure their own reputations are front and centre.

Practically speaking, all innovation leaders need to be politicians to a degree, since their personal credibility is likely to be one of the main reasons a programme can get past the managing stage to futurecasting and beyond. Gravitas is just so important when one is dealing with C-level executives. But the problem is that the team needs gravitas as well. When the innovation leader is the only one who is seen as sufficiently credible to take a meeting, or when he or she is the only person who can get a meeting in the first place, we come back to the problem that our previous two innovation leaders also have: they can't scale.

There is a further issue here, however. Because the politician is about creating personal influence, they will rarely, if ever, be interested in doing any innovations which are unpopular or have negative consequences that might reflect on them personally.

As we've seen throughout this book, though, doing failure well is a key skill for innovators. And it is the role of the innovation leader to create the environment in which failure is celebrated. A politician will likely not see the value in any of this: they know that their personal influence will be enhanced only with a track record of successes – preferably those that they can take all the credit for achieving.

When you have a politician in charge, there are several consequences. The first is that the innovation team will likely not accomplish very much. They won't feel comfortable with taking the necessary risks required to pursue really useful uniqueness. Neither will they have the mandate to do so, because the politician will only allow those endeavours which will make them look good.

The result is that the only innovations likely to go very far are those that are obvious. An obvious innovation has practically no risk associated with it. The key questions can be answered with the most cursory review possible. The chances that the innovation won't progress to execution are usually microscopic. And any risks associated with development and implementation are so tiny that they can be controlled completely. The politician likes such innovations – which will mainly be incremental in nature – because they are all upside, at least from a personal perspective.

The innovation team, on the other hand, has quite a different perspective. They will be happy to do incremental innovations, since they know the bills have to be paid somehow, so long as they get the chance to work on revolutionary and breakthrough stuff from time to time. It is unlikely this will happen, however, whilst ever the politician is in charge.

8.4   WHAT NEXT?

I hope I haven't given you the impression that only young, creative types have any chance at all of successfully creating an innovation programme and getting through all five stages of the Five Capability Model. Indeed, as we discussed at the beginning of this chapter, it may be a young-gun is just what *isn't* needed once the team begins its futurecasting and venturing phases. Nonetheless, though, it should be obvious that the successful innovation leader is quite different from the sort one normally finds heading up more traditional business lines in any bank. Finding just the right combination of skills and attributes that suit at a particular time of a programme's development is challenging.

This challenge is not insurmountable, and it is a pretty even bet that the right person to run your innovation team will be lurking around somewhere already in your workforce. Assuming that is the case, what might one reasonably look out for when recruiting an innovation leader?

Well, firstly, the best place to look is where a manager is already demonstrating success leading a team which is *not* process-bound. Strategy teams, for example, are good places to hunt for innovators, because they have to deal with similar kinds of uncertainty and ambiguity. A leader in this area will be well aware of some of the challenges involved in trying to predict future states, and will have a lot of experience managing people who are engaged in an inherently creative activity.

Look out for managers with high personal innovativeness. You can almost always tell these. They are the ones who are always trying to make their teams and operations better. They consistently seek unique ways to make the old things work more efficiently. And they're not at all afraid of taking a risk or two if they think the payoff will be worthwhile.

Examine the ranks of the average performers. Of course, most people who are average performers are rated that way because their performance *is* average. But managers who are just that little bit annoying, or just slightly out of the conservative box compared with their peers, will almost always be rated as average as well. It is this kind of individual that you want leading your innovation team, and you almost never find them with great performance ratings. Quite often, by the way, a great performance rating is a good way of finding the *most* conforming of your employees. You most definitely don't want that in an innovation leader.

And finally, find managers who *believe* in innovation. This is the most important aspect of all. Whilst it might not be hard to find people who have the other qualifications we've been discussing, finding people with the gut-held belief that an institution's future is in developing uniqueness is much more difficult. Locating people who *say* that innovation is important is hardly a challenge. What is needed – especially at the beginning of the innovation journey – is a rock solid faith in the power of innovation to make a real strategic difference.

The reason belief is so important is that the inevitable setbacks along the path to success – the pet project which is killed, or the fantastic new idea which no one will fund – all seem to tell innovators that what they are doing is not important. And because failure will happen so often, the innovation leader is the one who has to inspire his or her team with a vision of the end-point.

An unshakeable belief in the rightness of doing innovation is demonstrated in the values and behaviours of the leader. When the team see this, it reinforces for them the value of their work, *even* in the face of multiple rejections. There can be no more important task for the leader than making sure the team doesn't give up.

9

The Innovation Team

What you will find in this chapter

- How the workforce and especially the innovation workforce is changing.
- Four kinds of employees needed in an innovation function.
- Styles of team working in which innovators can engage.
- Signs you have a bad innovator.

Having a great innovation leader is a primary reason some innovation teams are successful and some aren't. If you don't presently have an innovation culture, a visible and charismatic leader can go a long way to helping establish one. Senior managers not interested? The right leader, coupled with some great success stories, can show them why spending some time would be a good idea.

But there is one thing a leader – no matter how good – won't be able to make up for, and that's an innovation team not well suited to, well, being innovative. This happens surprisingly often. It is rarely the case that any organisation has a ready-made group of individuals well skilled in the art and science of innovation, so what usually happens is anyone who is considered 'innovative' is slotted into the role.

In my experience, people are selected for such roles for two reasons: they have demonstrated their high personal innovativeness through early and frequent adoption of new things. Or, they are known for being 'visionary' and having 'great ideas'. Now, whilst these are great qualities to have if you are going to concentrate on innovation full time, they are not the only things that matter. As we'll see in a moment, there are a range of skills an innovation team needs, and it is a rare individual who has them all. Then, too, different demographic groups approach innovation in different ways.

These factors, when combined, mean that planning an innovation team, rather than taking any resource that is available, increases the likelihood of success in the long run.

We'll spend the rest of this chapter looking at an ideal composition for innovation teams, the kinds of things they need to do to be successful, and how the leader needs to manage innovators to get the predictable returns we've been speaking of throughout this book.

9.1 THE CHANGING SHAPE OF THE INNOVATION WORKFORCE

It is impossible to consider the best way to structure an innovation team without first understanding the changes that have occurred in the institutional workforce in recent decades. In a team of any size, there are likely to be at least three different groups of people: traditionalists, gen-Xers, and gen-Yers. Each has different needs, and because their formative environments were very different, have considerable diversity in their beliefs about the way that innovation should be approached.

Table 9.1 The generations of innovators

	Traditionalist	Gen-X	Gen-Y
Birth year	Earlier than 1965	1965–1984	1984–present day
Attitude to training	I did it the hard way	You will provide if you want to keep me	It's continuous, and everyone does it
Learning style preference	Classroom	I'll do it myself	I prefer to collaborate
Communication style	Message will be communicated through an hierarchy	Messages are communicated to me, and I have specific others I'll tell. I decide who I tell	I don't care where the message comes from. And I don't care who I tell
Problem-solving	I will take those bits of the problem I'm given to solve	I will decide what to solve	I'll work with my peers to work out what to solve
Decision-making	Seeks approval for everything	Team included in all substantive decisions	The team will decide what we do
Leadership style	Command and control	I will be a coach	I am a partner to my team
Feedback	I prefer to not know	I like structured feedback processes	I want it, and I'll have it without any particular schedule, on demand
Technology affinity	I don't like it, and prefer to avoid it if possible	I can't do my work without it	I can't even work out how to start doing my job without it
Job changing	Unwise	Necessary to career development	Something I do every day

Some of the key differences between each generation are shown in Table 9.1. This table is not original: it was adapted from an original in the seminal work *When Generations Collide* [67], a book that describes the challenges a multigenerational workforce presents in almost any context. This book, by the way, is highly recommended for anyone who has to deal with multiple generations in an innovation team. Increasingly, that is practically all of us.

Let us now examine the characteristics of each of these generations in an innovation team context.

The characterisation that follows will, no doubt, offend some by being overly stereotypical. But I don't make any apology for this, because the key point of this examination (which will be obvious later) is that you need all three generations of innovators in order to optimise the chances of a successful innovation programme.

Let us start with the traditionalists, those who have had careers in an institution for decades.

Firstly, it is a mistake to imagine that traditionalists, with their decades of learning and habit-forming, are incapable of being innovative. Personal innovativeness, that propensity to take risk and try new things, tends not to be age-specific. Innovators and early adopters can come from any age group. Naturally, it is necessary for anyone who is a part of an innovation team – no matter what their generation – to have a high level of personal innovativeness, and the traditionalist is just as likely to have these traits as anyone else.

Despite the fact that traditionalists are likely to be as innovative as the next person, they are potentially very challenging in an innovation team context. Firstly, they are likely to be less open to newness that is inconsistent with their established habits and norms. Their experience is likely to have come from the 'school of hard knocks', so they will have established views on the way things ought to be done right now. It is highly likely that these experiences will have left them in a situation where they feel they need approval – at every step of the way – before anything new can be done.

This is a function of being part of a command-and-control organisation since they started working. Theirs has been a hard slog through years of inability to make a difference until – finally – they have reached a time in their careers when their reputations and accumulated experience make them worth listening to. They have fought their way up through the ranks, and fail to see why others should not have to do so as well.

Traditionalists learned their initial skills in the classroom, but their own perception of personal value has little to do with formal training. Instead, they believe they are valuable *because* of their accumulated years of experience. It is highly likely, in fact, that this will be experience that has been gained entirely in a single institution. Traditionalists view the idea of changing employers as something risky, not as an opportunity to grow. This is starkly different from the views of subsequent generations, especially gen-Yers.

The traditionalist has a few other characteristics which distinguish him or her from later generations as well. They don't like to get feedback on their performance, for example, trusting they will be told if their outputs are less than acceptable. When this news arrives, their reaction is entirely defensive, and directed to mitigating any threat to their present position.

Technology affinity also distinguishes the traditionalists from their younger peers. Traditionalists grew up in a time when technology was either not used at all in banks, or was relegated to back rooms supported by white-coated technicians. They may even have posted ledgers manually, earlier in their careers! Their use of technology, therefore, is somewhat nervous. They do it, but can do without it just as easily.

But the most significant characteristic of traditionalists is that they have been trained to accept the idea that strategy, and its attendant uniqueness, is imposed by those above them. Their role is to implement that which is handed down, *not* to challenge the status quo themselves. This means they tend to solve those portions of problems which are defined for them, rather than taking on the whole problem themselves.

Let me enhance this discussion by introducing you to three innovators. Now, in reality, these are actual people I've worked with, but I've chosen not to embarrass them by naming them or their institutions directly. We'll be meeting David, Clarissa, and Tom, who are traditionalist, gen-X, and gen-Y, respectively.

David is a long-serving member of his institution, who has been with one bank for decades. He is personally innovative, and demonstrates this by always having the latest technological gadget in his arsenal of things he is able to talk about. He knows everyone, and is very much aware of the politics involved in any kind of change. However, he rarely uses either his ideas or his knowledge of the way things work to make substantive changes, because he will never take the risk of offending someone in authority. Concerned primarily with his retirement, which looms close, the risk of doing anything resulting in poor performance appraisals is so significant that he prefers to keep a low profile. Consequently, David limits his activities to those which are *additive* rather than *transformational*. He is happy to add his efforts to innovative projects which are already underway (knowing the primary risks have already been taken) or to start new incremental innovations (where there is little risk at all). In this role, David is exceptional. He knows his way around the institution, and is pretty expert at how to get things done. His track record is one of success, but he concentrates on the little things.

Unlike David who has never worked anywhere but his present bank, the gen-Xer has had a rather different career path. He or she will likely have worked in several institutions, and may even have worked in different industries. Their background is quite broad, and though they might not have the depth of experience that a traditionalist has in the specifics of their current institution, they make up for this with insights which you can only get from seeing how many places work.

The gen-Xer is confident and assured, and knows he or she has a value to the firm which will transcend failures when risks are taken. They like to reassure themselves of this value through structured feedback processes. When the feedback is negative, they will most often take active steps to correct performance, assuming they agree with the assessment. If they don't, they will often move employers, reasoning, perhaps correctly, that the mis-assessment is due to a failing of management.

Though the gen-Xer will also have learned the core skills of their trade in the lecture hall, their attitude to learning once they are in the workforce is quite different: they see training as something they are entitled to, since it provides them with the skills they need to remain independent of their employers. When this is denied them, they will probably seek other roles which they perceive as less likely to lock them in. They are constantly on their guard to avoid the biggest failing they see in traditionalists: a lack of substantive experience in the 'real world'.

Moving between roles is considered something that is essential, in any case, to development. So the gen-Xer will have little compunction about leaving an employer if their working environment doesn't suit. They will, however, keep one eye firmly on the CV when making such decisions, knowing that – at this stage of their career – they are likely to be dealing with hiring managers who are traditionalists, and who therefore don't like choppy employment histories.

In the meantime, a gen-Xer is much more self-directed than a traditionalist. They will look at big problems, and make their own decision about what parts they will solve. They feel their teams have a right to be included in all substantive decisions, even if, in the end, they have the ultimate call. And when they have to lead, they envision themselves as coaches, rather than didactic leaders.

Whilst the traditionalist may have spent most of their career without technology as a support, the gen-Xer will have had technological assistance for most of their time in the workplace. They are dependent on technology for their productivity, communication, and information management tools, and can't see how they could do their job without such supports. When these tools don't work, they will complain about lack of productivity and how 'terrible IT is here'. Such statements are a reaction to the constant need to demonstrate value through significant outputs. Whilst traditionalists demonstrate their value through *what* they know, gen-Xers do the same thing by seeking approval for what they have *done*. For such an individual, a computer problem is a very big deal.

Clarissa is a typical gen-Xer. She works in an innovation team in a bank, but hasn't spent all her time working there. She has also done project management, worked in other related industries, and now spends her time working on innovation projects. Her key skill is being able to drill down into a specific idea in order to get to something that might be workable for implementation. She's also pretty good at doing the implementation itself.

As an individual who is constantly seeking to prove her value, Clarissa prefers not to spend her time doing incremental innovation. As she said to her manager once 'that's not the kind of innovation I want to be doing'. Her preference is to work on bigger things, potentially breakthrough or revolutionary. Only that kind of innovation has the potential to reinforce her own need to demonstrate significant outputs for which she has *personally* been responsible.

However, Clarissa knows that she operates within the boundaries of an organisation that is largely traditionalist. She knows that she has to pander to a generation of managers who don't like rapid and transformational change, so she is cautious in what she chooses to support.

But Clarissa is different from David in one respect: she will take risks, and stand by any failures that come up. After all, her retirement is something she's managing independently of her employer, and she has a lot of time left to recover. But also, she knows that to be truly impactful, it is necessary to take some risks. She's happy to do so, as long as there is personal recognition and reward at the end.

Clarissa doesn't do additive, incremental innovation very well, but is very excited by the opportunity to make a difference. She loves things that are truly new, and will jump at the chance to work on a breakthrough or revolution. One thing she's less comfortable with, however, is doing disruptive innovation. She knows that the politics involved may be personally destructive to her reputation, so she steers clear of these kinds of innovations if possible.

That is not true of the gen-Yer, who is likely to be blissfully unaware of the political realities of a traditionalist's bank, and will therefore try anything. Clarissa makes a subjective assessment of the possibility of success before trying anything. The gen-Yer, on the other hand, imagines that anything can be successful given the right amount of tenacity and effort. This makes them, perhaps, the most challenging of all generations in a bank innovation team.

The gen-Y innovator probably doesn't have a lot of workplace experience, but this doesn't matter because they've been surrounded by work-like environments since an early age. They will have been using online collaboration and communication tools constantly, and certainly will win office records for how quickly they can send a text message on their mobile phones. Theirs is a world of teen jargon and abbreviations, which may be perfectly intelligible to them, but may as well be Martian to everyone else. And their mastery of the new technologically driven world makes them, perhaps unintentionally, intolerant of those in other generations who don't have their innate grasp of how the digital generation works.

The gen-Y innovator knows that training resources are available at the bank, but probably won't make much use of them. For the gen-Yer, training is a continuous and very personal process. They might go to one of the packaged courses on offer, but will almost certainly decide the skills and experiences they've learned would have been more easily acquired independently. Learning, in any case, is a collaborative activity best shared with friends and peers. The gen-Yer recognises that there are synergies to be had, and goes out of their way to make them happen.

Teaming is very natural to gen-Yers. Not only do they work together to solve problems, but they are likely to work together to define them as well. In fact, it is pretty unlikely they will be very much interested in any problem they haven't noticed – and decided to address – themselves. It doesn't occur to them that other people's problems could be as interesting as their own.

Gen-Y teaming is quite different from that of the previous generations. Whereas the traditionalist will certainly give orders and expect them to be obeyed, and the gen-Xer will take feedback and collaborate before making a decision, gen-Yers allow decisions to evolve as the problem defines itself. They don't make specific decisions independently, because they have a trust in the ability of the team to evolve, over time, to an optimum solution. Leaders of the gen-Y generation see themselves as partners to the team.

Even the conceptualisation of work is different for a gen-Yer. They don't define themselves in terms of their titles or positions as a traditionalist or gen-Xer would do, preferring instead to classify themselves by the kind of work they do. This results in their perception that job changes are something they do every day. The employer is pretty much irrelevant to the process.

They are completely reliant on technological aides to both their work and the rest of their lives. Having grown up in a digital age, they are unable to function without cell phones, Internet access, and the rich data of the Internet. They are simply unable to fathom how they could do anything useful without these technological props.

Gen-Yers, not having years of exposure to traditionalists or gen-Xers, rarely have much conception of what is, and is not, possible in an organisational context. But their understanding of the world, the one that is evolving as a result of the digital age, is unsurpassed. They naturally want to bridge between these two worlds, and spotting opportunities where this is possible is probably a daily occurrence.

The thing is, much of the time, such opportunities are very disruptive in nature. These are opportunities that are probably not obvious to traditionalists and the gen-Xers. And, in the long run, they are threatening to incumbent business lines. Gen-Yers, of course, don't care and may not even realise this to be so. In their joy at finding a better mousetrap, they run roughshod over the 'oldies', who do everything in their power to shut them down. It is a creative tension that rarely results in something worthwhile unless carefully managed.

Tom is a gen-Yer. He works in a bank innovation team, and is forever coming up against traditionalist barriers to his ideas. His peers, both inside and outside the team, intuitively 'get' what he is proposing, but no one else does. The failure to conform to existing organisational norms is a key limitation of his effectiveness. Though he is frustrated at work, he is working separately to build a start-up company of his own. Without the limitations of the traditionalists and gen-Xers, the company is quite a disruptive one, and he and his peers have very high hopes of being the next Google.

Tom never does incremental stuff, and wouldn't do it even if asked. He works on problems that he has defined for himself. When his managers ask him for more prosaic deliverables, the outputs will be less efficacious than might be expected. Tom doesn't care, though. He knows his value, and doesn't need it to be reinforced by his manager whom he probably doesn't respect anyway. Such feedback as Tom wants is provided on demand by lots of people and individual point opinions matter less than the consensus.

David, Clarissa, and Tom, though they come from different-generation workforces, are all critical to the successful innovation programme. If you refer to Figure 3.2, you will be able to deduce what sorts of people the programme needs to have on board at each different stage. During the inventing and managing stages, for example, the primary focus of the programme is going to be incremental innovations. The best kind of person to do that sort of work is the traditionalist, who prefers incrementalism anyway.

Getting predictability and process right is the first order of the day when the programme is young. As the innovation programme moves into the managing phase, however, things change. It becomes possible, even essential, to start working on breakthroughs and revolutions. The programme needs to do this in order to ensure that it not only meets its numbers, but exceeds them. Whilst incrementalism pays the bills, the more revolutionary work is what drives the windfall gains.

So, by this time in the programme's lifecycle, the team mix needs to be moving more towards gen-Xers rather than traditionalists. The gen-Xers will probably work on incrementalism if they have to, as long as they get to do the big things as well. But the traditionalists almost certainly won't want to be out of their comfort zone. Theirs is a role that decreases as the programme becomes more successful.

And once the programme gets to the futurecasting and venturing phases, what you really need is a nice group of gen-Yers. For starters, the really disruptive opportunities will likely be spotted by them first. And because they are young and lack the indoctrination of years in the workforce, they probably don't know that what they dream up is impossible (from a corporate perspective). When they propose a disruptive innovation that will, in time, eliminate the lending business, their view will likely be surprise when anyone suggests their better mousetrap isn't the obvious way forward. The gen-Xers, on the other hand, will worry about the politics that will have to be managed, making this somewhere they are uncomfortable to proceed unless they have already managed to obtain significant and powerful senior-level support.

The gen-Yers will take exceptional risks, because the downside for them is not especially significant. They are at early stages in their career, and practically any failure can be recovered from. This is why you see so many start-ups founded by gen-Yers. Why not go out on your own when you don't have a mortgage or a family to worry about?

9.2   CREATORS, EMBELLISHERS, PERFECTORS, AND IMPLEMENTERS

Not all innovators are alike. Though this may seem obvious, the fact of the matter is that most people align themselves to one, or at the most two, parts of the innovation problem. You can be the person who creates new ideas and then sells them to a willing public. Or you can be the one who looks at an idea and finds the flaws and then works around them to implement. But usually, a single person cannot do all these things equally well. Because this is so, the most successful innovation teams are designed around the preferences of their members. And when a vacancy occurs, such teams aren't just looking for an innovator, they are looking for an individual who has a particular innovation preference that supports the rest of the team.

It is usually agreed that there are four innovation preferences [68], and innovators can be classified by which part of the innovation problem their preferences make them most successful in solving. Let's spend a moment examining each of these innovators.

The first kind of innovator is the *idea creator*. We all know these kinds of people: they continually create a constant stream of newness. Theirs is the gift of being inspired by the things they see around them to invent new uniqueness that, conceivably, could be converted into competitive advantage. Idea creators see money growing on trees.

People are usually excited to be in the presence of idea creators. They are interesting people to be around, usually upbeat, and always ready to advance an out-of-the-box solution. They are distracting a lot of the time, but impossible not to like. But the idea creator suffers from a major flaw: he or she can't implement anything, no matter how many resources they are given to accomplish the task. Neither are they able to spot the flaws in their own ideas, and probably will lose interest in an idea the second something new pops into their head anyway.

I once worked with an individual who was the consummate idea creator of all time. Every single situation he was presented with resulted in a new idea for improving our bank. When we looked at the threat of near-field communications chips in mobile phones, his thought was a digital credit card. When we wondered how we could get more transactions through the grid computing systems used to calculate risk, he talked about quantum computing. Now, both these ideas are intuitively attractive. If the phone is going to replace the credit card, why *not* give the card itself the same capabilities as the phone? And if computing power isn't expanding as fast as might be demanded by an overnight batch window, why *not* implement a new kind of computer that might cut processing times by several orders of magnitude?

Here is the problem with both of these ideas: neither are physically possible. Whilst miniaturisation makes it *possible* to build a phone the size and shape of a credit card, the physical limitation is the amount of volume left inside the package for the battery. The device would have lasted about 10 seconds between charges. And whilst quantum computers are a field of active research, at the time of writing anyway, no one has managed to implement a general-purpose one that could be used for the general kinds of risk problems we were facing.

This is typical of idea creators. Their great gift is creating unique thoughts. Sometimes they lead somewhere, and sometimes they don't. Frankly, most of the time the thoughts of the idea creator *don't* lead anywhere, and that's usually because an idea creator, whilst inspirational to be around, is not well equipped to link their thoughts to the business problems at hand. Neither are they especially good at getting anyone to believe in their ideas. 'Another crackpot suggestion!' is something I've heard on more than one occasion.

That is why a rounded innovation team must have a few people in the next category: the idea embellisher. These are individuals who can take moments of great creative insight and fit them into the framework of existing needs. Not only are they able to spot how uniqueness might be used in a local context, they are experts at promoting and evangelising ideas as well.

The embellisher gets excited easily. They, too, see money growing on trees, but only after the idea creator has pointed out what looks like leaves are really bank notes. Having become a believer, the embellisher will then proceed to get everyone else excited as well. Usually consummate communicators, embellishers will immediately sell the 'vision' of an idea. That there is no reality at this point is inconsequential to the embellisher: he or she will believe that with enough support and excitement, any technical challenge can be solved. Why wait to work out if things are actually possible or not, when you can just rush in head first and get started?

The embellisher, being about creating excitement, is not one to bother much with the key questions which need to be answered by innovation teams before they do things. The answer to 'Should we?' will always be 'of course we should'. When asked 'When?', the answer is always 'now!'. And 'Can we?' will always be met with 'all it will take is a bit more effort'.

There have been a number of examples in financial services where idea embellishers have succeeded in getting an innovation out the door way before the time was right to do so. Mobile banking – in its first generation – was such an example.

Now, I've talked about mobile banking often thus far in this book. But current-generation solutions are nothing like what was offered the first time around when mobile phones first began to get access to mobile data. The initial technology was called WAP, or 'Wireless Application Protocol'. In 1999, when it was first released, there was much excitement, which led to vastly inflated consumer expectations. In Europe, for example, BT Cellnet ran advertisements showing users whirling through virtual realities on their handsets, something vastly in advance of what was possible at the time. Such over-inflation led some customers to ironically name the service 'Worthless Application Protocol' and 'Wait and Pay' in honour of its customer-unfriendly charging model [69].

Many banks were quite bullish as the service began to roll out in 2000. Halifax Bank of Scotland, for example, offered 150,000 customers free mobile phones if they would use the service – at a cost of some 15 million pounds. But adoption was patchy. In Asian markets, where mobile adoption was already accelerating ahead of the rest of the world, uptake was good. But elsewhere, it was appalling. The reason: the high cost of data at that time was a massive disincentive for customers. There were also user interface issues, and the performance of the service was poor.

Now, none of these factors were invisible to banks who decided to launch early in 2000, and in fact customer complaints were already a matter of public record even for non-bank WAP-based services. Idea embellishers, however, are good at selling new ideas, and this occasion was no different.

A large number of banks launched services, and practically none – excepting those in Asia where many of the issues with WAP were worked out early – were commercially successful.

Idea embellishers are all about creating the excitement needed to get things implemented. What they are *not* about, however, is thinking through the details of what that might take. With WAP, for example, the embellisher neither knew nor cared that the protocol would likely not support decent response times over existing wireless networks. Embellishers are all about creating the buzz that makes things happen.

That is why you need to have a third kind of innovator in an innovation team: the idea perfector. Unlike an embellisher, who is motivated by creating the social factors that will enable an idea to flourish, the perfector is interested in analysing an idea to find its flaws. By doing so, the perfector seeks to eliminate ideas which, though they might be aesthetically pleasing, financially attractive, or otherwise interesting, are unlikely to be practicable. Neither digital credit cards nor quantum computers were practicable, and only the strong words of an idea perfector prevented our institution from embarking on an expensive – and likely unfruitful – investigation of both innovations.

It is generally left to the perfector to find out why something cannot be done, and *then* to say something. It is remarkable, often, that this process occurs at all. When you have a great embellisher in the team, it is quite often the case that so much buzz has built up around an idea that 'drowning the puppy' can actually be an unpopular move for the perfector.

Perfectors like to know *how* an idea would translate into reality. They seek, always, to take uniqueness and determine the set of things that would have to be done to implement it. They are the 'Can we?' key question incarnated.

The thing about the perfector, though, is that they tip the balance so far to the side of do-ability that real breakthroughs are often not attempted at all. Resolving ambiguity is the key gift of the perfector, but also his or her chief weakness: left alone, an innovation programme comprised of perfectors alone would concentrate entirely on incrementalism. Now, that is probably a good thing in the early days of an innovation team, but it swiftly becomes a liability later when teams have to create ground-breaking newness in order to justify their existence. Embellishers and perfectors naturally balance each other out. You must have both for success.

Once an idea has been dreamed up, buzz created, and all the potential flaws ironed out, you need the fourth kind of innovator: the implementer. Implementers are those unique individuals who can take what is mostly conceptual and turn it into a plan of action. Now, of all the innovation preferences, the implementer is the least well understood. They don't usually come up with big ideas, nor are they quick to spot the opportunities that uniqueness generates. Neither are they all that good at creating excitement. But all these talents are useless if nothing happens. And the fact of the matter is that only implementers have what it takes to take uniqueness and make it into something real. They are the doers, the ones who are able to see the logical set of steps required to get from point A to point B.

It is a very special innovator who can see through the ambiguity involved in something that has never been done before, and turn that into a set of steps that result in real outputs. Implementers are the most rare of the innovation preferences. These are not process people or project managers. They are individuals with a unique combination of personal innovativeness, a focus on details when surrounded by a disabling amount of blue-sky thinking, and the stamina and discipline to get to the goal when everyone else has moved on to something else more interesting. Implementers are innovators with a decent attention span.

It is my experience that innovation teams fail to hire implementers at all. If they do have implementers, it is by accident. Innovation leaders often make the mistake of thinking that what they want is people who can create ideas, *not* those who can implement them. They fall prey to a mistake made by everyone else who doesn't do innovation for a living: thinking that a great idea will not only sell itself, but will also build itself. If the innovation leader also happens to be a creator or embellisher, then the probability of an implementer finding his or her way into a team is even lower.

In my own team, I am fortunate that I have Steve, who is an extremely good example of an implementer. When we decided to build Innovation Market, Steve was the manager who took control of all the details of getting it to a fit state to go live. Whilst I (being somewhere between a creator and an embellisher) was off with the pixies dreaming up the 'next big thing', Steve was patiently working through test plans, feature enhancements, and user feedback to make our Innovation Market a great success.

Steve, incidentally, is also the individual who first proofread this manuscript, and volunteered to do so just as the first chapter was completed. Implementers like to make sure anything they are even remotely associated with is *done right*.

In practice, no individual will have only one innovation style preference. Most people are a mix of at least two. As I mentioned a moment ago, my own preference is creator-embellisher. I like new ideas, and I am good at getting people excited about them. I don't much like the detail of getting things implemented, though, and prefer that task to be done by others. I quite enjoy the interplay involved in working with perfectors, as the challenge–response style of communication that is typically involved is especially intellectually stimulating. But by myself, I probably wouldn't go through the whole process of working out why something is a bad idea before starting the selling process. I am realistic enough to realise that this combination of preferences means that I can never be a successful innovator in isolation: I require the support of innovators with the other preferences to create anything of value.

This is true for all innovators, and leads to an important conclusion: the *minimum* number of people in an innovation team is, realistically, two. This is because the most likely combinations of innovation preferences are creator-embellishers and perfector-implementers. As long as all four styles are represented in a team, success will likely follow. Sizing up from this point is a matter of determining how many ideas need to be processed and what returns are desired from the innovation programme.

9.3   TEAM WORKING

Because no single person has a preference for all innovation styles, the next question is how individuals work together when they have to collaborate. Researchers have found that, generally, several different structures present themselves [70], evolving as a function of the specific mix of innovators, their generations, and particular preferences for working together. An examination of these structures is helpful, and it is to that we turn our attention next.

The first structure is the *genius team*. Now, most people imagine that truly breakthrough or revolutionary innovations come from single, great, minds. When Einstein composed the theory of relativity, it was his genius, and his alone, that led to this new understanding of physics. But the reality is quite different, because truly great minds rarely reach their full potential in a vacuum. They need other like-minded individuals in their circle to provide motivation and positive reinforcement.

The genius team structure often forms of its own accord when innovators get together. Its members are typified by strong positive outlooks, which are reinforced with very high levels of ambition. They are driven to make positive change, and feed off each other in order to accomplish this. As a self-forming structure, rather than one imposed from the outside, the genius team creates a set of rules and goals which form a very specific, very exclusive culture. They are out to achieve, they have the potential to do it, and they won't be stopped by anyone who is not in their 'inner circle'.

This, of course, is one of the primary problems of genius teams. Whenever you hear an institution has 'an ivory tower' innovation team, you can bet with practical certainty that what has happened is the innovation team has formed a genius culture. Now, whilst this might result in great outcomes when the overall programme is at the earliest stages of its development (innovators as inventors, see Figure 3.2), the same cannot be said later on. When innovators need to reach out to others to gain support for their work, as they will have to do in order to grow their influence, the genius structure tends not to work very well. Being exclusive, with strict barriers to entry of the group, other stakeholders tend to isolate the innovators. Inevitably, if left uncontrolled, this will result in programme cancellation.

Genius teams are also not likely to be very good at doing incremental innovation, which is certainly going to be the lifeblood of an innovation programme in most institutions. This means that by the time the programme has advanced to the managing stage, it will be poorly constituted to do the repetitive business-as-usual type work that is required for predictability. That is if it gets there at all, given a genius team is an exclusive one, and is unlikely to reach out to others to get through the championing stage in the first place.

Neither is the genius team structure very well suited to the kinds of work required later in the process. The more capable an innovation programme becomes, the more collaboration is required beyond the innovation team itself, and this is something very difficult for the genius team to succeed at. Such a team builds its self worth entirely on the positive reinforcement of peers in the group, who may compete with each other to be the best, but who certainly don't see anyone else as much competition at all. They don't naturally reach out to others, so they are practically useless at the futurecasting and venturing stages, which are so much about building rapport, gaining trust, and being inclusive of the views of the many. You can't run a decent scenario planning function, for example, when the only minds available to you are those in the innovation team itself.

Genius teams usually form around very strong gen-X thinkers, who are naturally exclusive in their dealings with others. As their sense of self worth is driven by reinforcement of the value of their outputs, they will tend to form into a genius configuration automatically, since only other 'genius' people will truly appreciate these outputs. Naturally, this excludes traditionalists completely, since they are hardly likely to have much affinity with those kinds of innovations that gen-Xers are interested in: the big, bold revolutions and breakthroughs. Neither is it likely to encourage much participation from gen-Yers, who may peripherally involve themselves in a genius team but will never truly engage. Gen-Yers are people for whom collaboration is their lifeblood. Exclusivity doesn't sit so well with them.

The thing is, most innovation teams of any size will have a fairly normal distribution of generations in them: about 20% traditionalists and gen-Yers, respectively, with the rest gen-X. The genius configuration will form by itself in this situation, unless active steps are taken to include everyone. If it does, 40% of the innovation workforce will perform at a sub-optimum level. It is for this reason that my advice is to eliminate genius teaming as soon as possible, and substitute one of the other configurations we will talk about next.

The *improv* team is an alternative structure in which things are much, much more collaborative. There isn't a specific genius around which the others gravitate. Rather, the performance is much like that of a jazz band: individuals take the lead as thoughts and actions occur to them, leading to synergies which can often be much greater than the whole.

Improv teams are founded on trust. Team mates have to believe that what they are being passed is something worthwhile. And they have to be sure that when it comes time to pass the baton to others, it will be picked up quickly.

Quite often, improv team members disagree with each other. But, because there is mutual trust and respect, individual team members subjugate their opinions to those of the group. That is quite a contrast to what happens in a genius team, of course, where a disagreement is seen as a healthy thing that leads on to personal competition. An improv team doesn't have disagreements at all: they are an interruption to the orderly flow of progress.

As you would expect, it is the gen-Yers who are best suited to working in improv teams. Their natural affinity for collaboration and personal interaction makes them ideal for the fast interflow of leadership and followership. If you have a preponderance of these people in a team, this is the sort of team structure that will practically always form.

I had the very interesting experience, once, of having a group of management trainees to watch as they formed a team to work on a project. A group of gen-Yers, they didn't do any of the things a gen-Xer like myself would have done. No team leader was elected, and there wasn't even the remotest hint of competitive positioning. An improv team formed of its own accord: there was a constant interplay of ideas and concepts, with one individual following on from the previous. The transitions were relatively seamless, and that extended even to the allocation of work units. People volunteered to resolve parts of the problem at hand, and the process worked almost as if they were part of a single group mind.

Such a performance, of course, is an anathema to gen-Xers, who have great difficulty in subordinating their personal sense of worth in favour of the success of a team. Since they measure their personal effectiveness in terms of how valuable other people find their outputs, their greatest difficulty in an improv team is finding a way of separating out their contribution for individual examination. Left to their own devices, they will practically always avoid participation in such a team.

That is true, also, for traditionalists, for whom the lack of command and control is very, very uncomfortable. A traditionalist needs a leader who is in charge. If they are not that leader themselves, they want to be told which part of the problem they are working on, and have their units of work minutely defined by such leaders as exist. And they have no time at all for the interplay of ideas relating to whatever someone else is working on. Theirs is a responsibility to work on what they are told, with no questions asked.

Practically speaking, though an improv team is a highly efficient way of organising for innovation, it is likely impossible when you have multiple generations of innovators involved. Later on, once the futurecasting capability has been attained, it becomes possible to have *only* gen-Yers in a team, but there are few teams which are in that situation to start with. It consequently becomes important to consider further alternatives.

One such alternative is the command and control team, a configuration not extensively described in the innovation literature. Such teams form where you have a preponderance of traditionalists. They are weighty on process, heavy on measures, and like to know that they can achieve a predictable outcome every time.

The problems that a command and control team work on will be largely dictated by outside interests. For example, if a decent ideation system has been deployed, and there is a reasonable idea flow through it, a command and control team will efficiently process those ideas.

Most people imagine that a command-and-control structure must be an anathema to innovation. How can a process which is inherently creative, often associated with that spark of genius that makes a real difference, have anything to do with a rigorous process? The answer is, not much, if what you want to do is focus on incremental innovation. It is breakthrough and revolutionary innovation which comes from creativity: incrementalism is about being able to repeatedly make small improvements on a regular basis.

This makes command and control teams perfect, of course, for innovation functions that focus extensively on incrementalism. Incremental innovation is mainly a numbers game, so you want a lot of command and control to ensure that quality control targets are met. In fact, for at least the first three stages of the development of an innovation programme – the 18 months that is typically available to get from invention to intrapreneuring, a command and control team is very much the most likely to succeed. Their focus on specific, measurable objectives and delivery of outcomes makes them perfect for this task.

Now, whilst command and control is a teaming arrangement that traditionalists will likely love, it is hardly going to suit gen-Yers. Younger innovators recognise that such a structure won't support the free flow of ideas supported by collaborative peers they are used to. When forced into the box of a traditionalist team, they will rebel at every opportunity.

Rebellion, of course, is the perspective on the situation you get if you are the manager of gen-Yers in a command-and-control box. But from their perspective, all gen-Yers are doing is trying to make a difference. Traditionalists (and even some gen-Xers) imagine that the behaviour is a direct challenge to their authority and try to impose even more control and process to stamp it out.

One of the management trainees I mentioned earlier came to me privately and told me he had been given a poor performance review for three quarters in a row. It was obvious to me (watching the performance of this individual working with his peers) that here was an individual who was anything *but* a poor performer. The problem was that the natural tendency to do things differently was seen by his management as an attempt to be distracting, even disruptive, to the smooth working of the team. This is a perennial problem for anyone who has to manage gen-Yers.

Gen-Xers, too, will probably have an issue with command and control. Even though they are very used to traditionalists, having grown up with managers of this generation, their personal sense of self worth will demand a certain profile that cannot be achieved whilst they remain confined by processes and measures. They want to do big, bold innovation, not the sort of incrementalism that is well suited to the command and control approach.

No matter what kind of team structure forms, one thing is almost certain: unless you have innovators who all come from a single workforce generation, the structure will certainly not be optimum for every member of the team. And since the process of building an innovation programme necessarily requires innovators from different generations as it grows and develops, there is inevitably going to be a degree of disagreement and friction. It is, as we saw in the previous chapter, one of the hallmarks of a great innovation leader that they can balance the generations of innovators in a sustaining, rather than a destructive, way.

Before we leave team structures, there is one more point that ought to be made. No matter how the innovation team configures itself, the relationships between team members themselves are, perhaps, the most critical determinant of overall success.

Working in a successful innovation team is quite unlike working for a traditional task-oriented one. The basic difference is that an innovation team concentrates on creating newness, on building processes that generate the unique. Ordinary teams tend to operate within existing frameworks and structures, so interpersonal dynamics (whether good or bad) usually have few significant effects, except in very extreme cases. That is not true of innovation teams. Research has shown a significant difference in innovation team performance depending entirely on the quality of the interpersonal relationships of team members [71].

The challenging conclusion of the research is this: superlative innovation team performance occurs if all team members are friends. That is, if team members are socially connected with each other both inside and outside their work environment. In many organisations, particularly very traditional institutions, the idea of a group of friends getting together to achieve good outcomes is somewhat challenging. It is imagined that there is something wrong with hiring all your friends to work with you. The fact of the matter is that the longer these external friendships have existed, the more likely it is that an innovation team will generate significant successes. It is not hard to see why.

The first reason is that innovation team members need to rely on each other extensively to get uniqueness into the hands of end-users or customers. Because no one innovator will equally prefer all four innovation styles, there is little choice but to cooperate with others. Friends are far more likely to have broken down any trust barriers which would prevent this.

But the second reason friends tend to form very successful innovation teams is that they are likely homogeneous in their beliefs and ambitions. Friendships form between people who have things in common. This common basis of mutual understanding means that an innovation team is far more likely to pull together than not. It makes them very effective.

Research also suggests something else. Innovation teams which are created of a diverse group of people who are *not* friends can also be successful if they are friendly in their interactions with each other. Now, these sorts of interactions develop naturally unless there are significant personality clashes, and that's a good thing. It makes it easy for people to communicate with each other, and friendly interactions are the foundation of a team that understands, at least at a high level, how to work with its members.

Friendly interactions are quite a different thing from *friendship*, though. The former is largely superficial, a patina that may be genuine but is not deep. Friendship is the result of shared joy and pain, deeply ingrained in the individuals involved, and able to survive significant interpersonal problems. Friendly relations have been shown to have an increasing effect on team performance as they develop. But this performance tails off and declines over time. The reason, many think, is that in order to avoid damage to a fragile relationship, team members actively avoid communications which have any potential to cause emotive or intellectual dislocation between participants.

One of the key measures of success in an innovation team is the ability to drown the puppy early. I can assure you there are few things more difficult for an innovator than for one of his or her pet ideas to be drowned by someone else in the team. Intra-team puppy drowning decreases as friendly relations increase. This means that an innovation portfolio will develop an increasing bias towards unprofitable investments.

A team founded on friendly relations can be successful, but will never be stellar. It will never generate significant windfall returns because it will almost always be dragged down by innovations which should never have been allowed to continue past the three key questions. Real friends, however, know they can cause an emotional or intellectual dislocation without the potential consequence of destroying the relationship. A deep relationship between two individuals is not likely to evaporate because one has drowned the puppy of the other. Individuals in such circumstances are therefore much more ruthless in their feedback, and more giving of their support. The greater extreme of response results in the high performance researchers have found.

This, then, is the reason the most high-profile innovators of our time invariably seem to be paired friends. Brin and Page at Google, who developed the world's most famous search engine whilst doing postgraduate research together. Jobs and Wozniak at Apple, who built their first personal computers together in a Silicon Valley garage. Even Gates and Allen, who together formed Microsoft with a vision of a personal computer on every desk.

But before innovators everywhere go and hire all their friends into their institutions, there is one final point I would like to make on this subject. Friends might make stellar innovation teams, but our objective here is to achieve predictable returns. In order to achieve that, one needs only friendly relations, *not* friendships. Good performance, carefully managed, is usually satisfactory.

Of course, if what is required is breakthroughs and revolutions, the situation might be quite different. But, as I've already outlined elsewhere in this chapter, these are innovations best left to much later in the development of an innovation programme, when the staffing mix should swing more towards gen-Y innovators. Conveniently, this is a demographic that has also optimised their ability to create deep friendships through digital media. The chances of a superlative innovation team are high.

9.4   WHEN INNOVATORS GO BAD

Having looked at the generations of innovators and innovation styles, one would imagine that it ought to be possible to determine with a relatively high degree of accuracy whether someone would make a good hire or not. Unfortunately, whilst these tools give us some insight into what is needed in an innovation team, they do not remove the risk – which is the same risk as in any hiring, of course – that things simply won't work out.

But for an innovation team, especially a new one, this risk is something that has to be managed directly. In a smaller team, one poor performer can have such a detrimental effect on the overall predictability of the innovation portfolio that it is pretty much essential to take steps as quickly as possible. The key reason for such significant effects is that a bad innovator burns influence more quickly than it can be recovered.

You will recall I said earlier that influence is the main currency an innovation team uses to progress newness in an institution. It is an almost perfect substitute for money, and like money, it can be wasted. You would never tolerate an employee who invested unwisely with the financial resources of the team, and neither is it advisable to waste influence. There is only so much available, and getting more is very, very hard work.

The problem of hiring innovators is much complicated by the fact that the optimum mix of generations and styles varies depending on the stage an innovation programme is at. As I mentioned earlier, you really want a lot of traditionalists at the start of the programme, preferably who have formed themselves into genius teams around some important incremental innovations. But by the time you're doing futurecasting and venturing you need gen-Yers, operating quite differently. Managing such transitions is something that would be difficult in any team, but is much more so for innovators. Innovators tend to love their jobs.

But assume, for a moment, you have determined the innovation style preference of a hire, and they supposedly fit in well with the existing team. What are the early signals that the innovator isn't going to work out? My advice is to watch out for the following archetypal bad innovation performers.

The gadgeteer

When you have an innovator who focuses most of their time on the latest and greatest technological thing, you are likely to have a gadgeteer. A gadget is a deceptively dangerous thing for an innovator. On the one hand, it seems the new thing (if only it could be sold correctly to stakeholders) would be a fantastic addition to the innovation portfolio. But on the other hand, there is practically no way to tie whatever-it-is back to any business problem. This is the hallmark of the gadgeteer – a pursuit of new things without any conceptualisation of what business problem is being solved.

Gadgeteers are dangerous for innovation teams because they burn influence at a fast rate. It only takes one poor meeting with a stakeholder (who will likely ask 'So what?') to close that door to innovators thereafter. A door slammed in one's face is one less avenue for the future to get predictability in the innovation portfolio.

But the worst thing about having a gadgeteer around is that they reinforce a stereotype that an innovation programme must try to undo as quickly as possible: that innovation is about way-out things with little relevance to the business. Whenever you spot an innovator continuously wasting influence pushing something that has no direct bearing on a business problem, it is time to call it a day.

The consultant

At the other end of the scale, you have consultant-innovators. They don't focus on the *answer* to the business situation (an answer that will, hopefully, be something innovative), and instead concentrate on defining the problem to be solved. Now, of course, it is necessary to have a pretty good definition of a problem before it can be addressed in any reasonable way, but the consultant-innovator will write reports and requirements documents till the cows come home.

A key sign you have a consultant-innovator on your hands is that they will try to run 'workshops' to get a group understanding of a problem. They will attempt to produce facts and figures that describe it. They will always seek more data to clarify things. And then, when it comes right down to it, they won't propose either a solution or a pathway to getting one.

The consultant-innovator's hallmark is such a narrow focus on the business problem that they don't ever get as far as using influence to push the next innovative thing. They would much rather study the issues and create PowerPoint. But the consultant-innovator is a deceptive creature, and that's because (at the start at least) their workshops and problem-definition work have actual value to stakeholders. Senior leaders call in consultants all the time in order to get independent views of their issues. Having an innovator do the same thing competently (probably for free) has an intuitive appeal.

Stakeholders, however, are unlikely to be thrilled with fact-finding that never terminates. That is the danger of the consultant-innovator, and influence-burning is the eventual result, as it was with the gadgeteer.

The talker

Now we come to the talker, one of the most destructive of all innovators. The talker is a superlative communicator, and when you put one on a stage in front of an audience, you get inspirational words that create excitement for the innovation experience. The talker is also great at networking, and is able to get to practically anyone in an organisation. Usually only once, mind you, because the great failing of the talker is that they never *do* anything.

If only innovation was about giving speeches and taking meetings, talkers would be the most successful innovators in the world. But unfortunately, it isn't. There's a lot of hard work involved, and a great idea may as well remain unthought-of if no one is going to work through the key questions to take things forwards.

Talkers, because they are great communicators and know how to open doors through their personal networks, will often have a greatly inflated view of their worth. They imagine that because people are enthusiastic about their ideas, they are successful. That, obviously, is not the case if an innovation team is being measured on *actual changes* they create.

Another thing to watch out for with the talker is the regular status meeting with the innovation leader to whom they report. Because they are such great communicators, it is likely the case that the innovation leader will be lulled into a sense of security just because doors are opening that were unavailable before. The talker will be excellent at doing smoke-and-mirror performances that make it *look* like progress is being made, even when it isn't.

The key signal of a talker is that you get the same status updates all the time, with promises they are 'close' to closing new innovations. Or that they have 'just one more meeting' to get agreement. A real innovator would drown the puppy, and forget the 'one more meeting'. Talkers, though, have nothing to back them up *but* the meetings they've been able to get.

As you would expect, the talker is also someone who burns influence. They do it at a great rate, because stakeholders, having met with them once or twice, realise that nothing is going to come of further interactions and *stop* letting innovators in. The talker, who needs to get meetings to justify him or herself, then moves on to the next stakeholder, where the same thing is repeated.

The defeatist

If you got to choose the kind of bad innovator to hire by mistake, you would want the defeatist. The only danger that comes from having a defeatist innovator is that you have to carry the headcount without getting any return. The reason? The defeatist will look at any new thing and be so overwhelmed by navigating the institution to get success that they are unable to do anything at all. These are the individuals whose first response to any innovation is 'that's too innovative for us'. The problem, of course, is that the defeatist doesn't have the correct amount of influence to get whatever-it-is accepted, and for some reason is unable to admit it.

Now, although the defeatist doesn't burn influence (as they probably won't get up enough courage to see anyone), they are insidious because they drag down all the *good* performers as well. Innovation is a tough game, and requires a great deal of self-confidence and poise: after all, the innovator is going to face rejection far more than he or she will have success. A positive outlook is essential. Having someone in the team who is negative just takes energy away from the main effort.

The lone ranger

Another kind of poor innovation performer, though one who is not internally destructive (as the defeatist) or externally problematic (as the talker), is the lone ranger. Lone rangers are innovators who prefer to work alone. They like to have everything under their personal control, cannot bear to delegate any work to anyone, and need to be personally involved in every single, little detail of their innovations. They imagine they, and they alone, are all it will take to get an innovation out the door.

The problem here is one of output. As we examined earlier in this chapter, people tend to have definite preferences for innovation styles, and any particular innovation needs a mix of all four if it is to have any chance of success. The lone ranger, of course, is no different from the rest of us, and is unlikely to have all four in equal measure. Consequently, lone rangers attempt to get their innovations out the door without all the necessary tools available. A creator-embellisher, no matter how good at creating uniqueness and the excitement that goes with it, is never going to be able to implement a new idea in such a way that it becomes real. A lone ranger in this situation will simply fail.

And the same is true for the perfector-implementer as well, if they also happen to be a lone ranger. They will almost never find the inspiration for innovation in the first place.

The cowboy

The final kind of innovator to watch out for is the cowboy. Such individuals are very, very committed to their innovations, so much so that no blockage can stand in their way. They go after what is needed to make the new thing happen, and they do so with gusto. Unfortunately, they also do it without much thought as to what will happen *after* they've rammed the innovation down everyone's throats.

If cowboys are lucky, they will at least get their current innovation out the door and into the hands of customers. But in doing so they will have locked themselves out of being able to do the next round of innovation. Cowboys are aware that they are burning influence to make things happen, but their focus is so much on the now that they don't permit themselves to consider how they will deliver the next innovation, or the one after that.

I've met innovators in this category, in fact, who feel that if they can just get *this* innovation out the door, all sins will be forgiven, no matter how heinous. That, of course, is never true, because as we discussed in Chapter 7 of this book, for every innovation there are both winners and losers. The losers will never be happy that the innovation makes it out the door at all, but the winners will also likely have a bad taste in their mouths: they might have a successful innovation on their hands, but to get it they were forced to do something they didn't want. There is very little upside here.

Another failing of the cowboy is that they will almost never drown the puppy. They get so invested in one particular innovation (which they have burned a huge amount of influence to promote) that failure is not an option. Even if the key questions turn out to be less than positive, they won't let things go. And they can't: their personal success is tied into achieving this one, great thing. They have no choice but to continue, since if they fail, they are left with nothing. That, of course, just highlights to everyone that their performance is sorely lacking.

What to do

Because influence is the currency of an innovator, as soon as it becomes obvious that a member of the innovation team isn't working out, drastic steps need to be taken as soon as possible. The problem is that a bad innovator will use up influence without creating any. And influence is generally in short supply.

Now, there is no good way to say this. Whilst good management practice might involve coaching a new hire into good performance, especially if the leader is the one responsible for making the hire in the first place, a new innovation team *does not have time* to deal with poor performance. As we've seen, the time between establishment of a new programme and its termination for non-performance is less than 18 months. 18 months is the amount of runway you have to get through at least the first three capabilities (inventing, championing, and managing – see Chapter 3), so a non-traditional way of dealing with poor performance is really the only available option.

Most countries have fairly strict employment laws, so it is impossible to eliminate the poor innovator immediately. But you can, at least, stop them from seeing key stakeholders who are the future of the innovation programme. That should be done as soon as possible. It is also possible to take other steps. One is that they are best isolated from the rest of the innovation team, physically if possible. Especially in the early days of an innovation team, there will be much negativity that surrounds the work of the team. Keeping a positive outlook is a daily battle, and the task of making sure the team is upbeat becomes more difficult when it is obvious that someone is being marginalised.

Ultimately, of course, care in hiring in the first place is the answer to the poor performance problem. My advice is to create diagnostic questions during the interviewing process to determine if you have one of the poor innovation performers I've described here sitting in front of you. For example, if you ask how a candidate has dealt with people who were trying to stop a project, and the answer leads you to believe that the candidate bulldozed his or her way through objections, you can be reasonably sure that you have a cowboy on your hands.

9.5   A LAST WORD ABOUT INNOVATION TEAMS

It is impossible to underestimate the importance of hiring the correct innovation team if you want to achieve predictable innovation outcomes. And it is usually a mistake to assume that you can hire someone 'close enough' and get good outcomes. It is essential to balance the mix of generations and styles correctly to optimise the chances of success.

The kinds of people most suited to being part of an innovation team will almost certainly already be employees of an institution. Because such people have a track record of performance, it is generally easy for the innovation leader to make a conclusive assessment of their innovation style and generation. This facilitates hiring appropriately to ensure the team is well rounded.

One final word on the innovation team: don't rush into hiring someone who looks *good enough*, even if there are significant pressures to get started. The dynamics of an innovation team are so very sensitive that poor choices will likely cripple outcomes until they are resolved. As I've mentioned here several times, most innovation teams have only 18 months to get from innovators as inventors to innovators as managers. There simply isn't *time* to correct a bad hiring decision and recover predictability.

10

Processes and Controls

What you will find in this chapter

- The why and how of innovation governance.
- Metrics and measures, and why they are important.
- Reward and recognition.
- Funding, press, and other miscellanea.

So far in this book, we've discussed the meat of the futureproofing process, and you will have developed a good idea of the set of things an innovation function should do in order to ensure its survival (and success). We've also looked at the way leaders and teams should function to drive an innovation programme's capability. With all that out of the way, there is one thing left to look at: the processes and controls needed to ensure innovators are doing their jobs correctly and that the institution is achieving maximal value.

Although, as an innovator, I hate formal governance systems as much as the next person, I can assure you they are fundamentally essential for any programme that expects to live more than one or two budgetary cycles. The reason is that innovators who are not seen to be part of a formal set of processes and controls in a large institution – as any other business unit would be – are almost always deemed to be *out* of control. It is a sure recipe for programme termination. Why should innovators be trusted more than a mainline business anyway?

In any event, the innovation programme is a business process pretty much like any other in all but one respect: it is about reaching into other business processes and changing them, hopefully in positive ways. Now, any function that successfully builds itself through the five capabilities of Chapter 3 will almost certainly be very influential. With a broad mandate to touch anything and everything, there is simply no possibility that appropriate controls on the innovation team can have failed to develop.

The question, of course, is determining what controls are appropriate. One wants to ensure the systems implemented are robust, surely, but without constraining the ability of the innovators to create uniqueness. This, it turns out, can be a bit of a tug-of-war.

Since every innovation results in both winners and losers internally, there will always be difficult struggles ahead for innovators. The powerful executive whose business is challenged by some disruptive innovation will certainly be able to eliminate anything which is not backed by a higher authority. What such an executive is unlikely to be able to do, however, is change the rules of the game to suit themselves on specific occasions. They, too, have to work within established process and control regimes.

An innovation which has been through the mandated corporate process for innovation, achieved funding, and entered execution – all without breaking any rules at all – is in a powerful position to challenge powerful internal dissenters. And the more robust the controls surrounding the innovation process, the more difficult it is to challenge the outputs generated. In other words, having a tight system of controls actually *helps* rather than hinders the innovation agenda.

Governance, as I will call such a system from now on, has always been an anathema to creative people. They hate it when process and control is placed on their work, arguing that it 'stifles' them and makes it impossible to work on creative big ideas. In the meantime, though, an innovation programme that has developed all five capabilities of Chapter 3 is such a powerful tool for change that no senior executive in a bank will likely have enough appetite for risk to allow it to go unchecked for long. It is better, in fact, to have an excess of controls – even to propose *new* restrictive controls oneself – than to allow senior leadership to feel out of control of their innovation investments.

Here is a truism learnt through bitter experience: innovators who are not transparent about how they do their work and don't have a robust set of control systems surrounding their methods are almost always shut down. On the other hand, the more highly regulated the innovation programme, the more likely it is to have big access to resources and large budgets.

Governance is an onerous overhead to be sure. It doesn't add very much to the specific output that an innovation programme was set up to deliver: predictable returns on innovation investments. But it isn't all bad: a decent governance system creates advantages for innovators that just aren't available in any other way.

Although the range of controls needed for an innovation programme will vary by institution considerably, there will certainly be several dimensions to the governance system eventually adopted. The system will probably evolve over time, as the innovation programme develops. However it happens, the advice I offer is this: propose much more governance than you actually need. It will make senior executives feel comfortable, and this will be incredibly valuable the more disruptive the programme becomes. And make no mistake about it: inevitably, innovators will need to get disruptive to ensure the returns their programmes generate are in line with expectations in the long term.

10.1   OVERSIGHT

Since we've been talking about the need to provide executives with as much transparency and control as possible over their innovation programme, it makes sense that we first discuss oversight, which is one of the most important control aspects of any innovation programme.

No matter how talented the innovation leader, or how competent the innovation team, theirs is usually not the final say in what objectives are to be achieved overall. More often than not, these are handed down by senior executives, usually the ones who provided the impetus to start the programme in the first place. Ultimately, the success or failure of an innovation programme is judged by these same individuals. It therefore makes sense that there be some kind of formal mechanism in place to enable them to correctly evaluate and guide progress, in the process ensuring it achieves the strategic goals that were initially intended.

When I spoke with various banks around the world on the subject of oversight of their innovation programmes, several models emerged. The most popular, by far, is the structure where oversight is accomplished by a committee of senior stakeholders who can be presumed to have an interest in innovation. At Royal Bank of Canada, for example, this body is known as the Innovation Council, and is comprised of senior people from both the technology and business sides of the bank. Collectively they control an investment budget and set innovation strategy for the group.

The Innovation Council (or similar) is an oversight mechanism replicated at banks around the world. It has the advantage of making sure innovation is on the agenda of a significant number of senior people. It allows the innovation team direct access to the strategic decision-makers of the institution, assuming the constitution of the committee is right. And, of course, it has the additional benefit of ensuring those who *should* know what is going on in the innovation space *do* know.

One of the biggest challenges with this model, however, is that it demands that busy executives take time out to deal with issues which are probably far removed from their day-to-day operational responsibilities. Though this may be helpful from a strategic perspective, it is not always welcomed by the individuals concerned. There is a very real danger of truancy from the committee, as many institutions have found to their cost when trying to establish their innovation programmes. Not being concerned with the day-to-day operational issues of a particular business line, the executive concerned finds it easy to delegate the innovation meeting to someone else. Sooner or later, the committee no longer has the mandate to decide anything, and the innovation team has lost any oversight it once had. This is why some organisations, such as Bank of America (as we saw in Chapter 3), have abandoned the committee method in favour of alternative models.

Advanta Corp, whom we met briefly in Chapter 5, uses one such model. Oversight of innovation is the direct accountability of the CEO, Dennis Alter, who prefers to keep a close watch on the uniqueness being explored by his institution. Alter spends a significant percentage of his time directing the innovation effort personally, and his close contact with the programme ensures that not only is it able to punch above its weight most of the time, it very rarely strays from the strategic path set down for it inside the corporation.

This model is very successful for Advanta, of course, but it is relatively rare in financial services groups as a rule. Most CEOs spend most of their time thinking about running their present businesses: they simply don't have the time to deal with the speculative nature of innovation on a day-to-day basis. In most cases, where the CEO is involved in innovation, it is peripheral at best, perhaps in the form of approving a few pet projects, or reviewing a status report from time to time.

A third model of oversight, one which is becoming increasingly prevalent in large institutions, is where a senior executive, probably only one step removed from the CEO in many cases, is given the task of innovation oversight as one of their full-time responsibilities. These chief innovation officers are not necessarily career innovators, but bring gravitas, resources, and access to senior management.

The popularity of this model (exemplified by institutions such as ANZ Bank of Australia, who moved its CIO into such a role in 2008) seems to be increasing. There is a good reason for this: when innovation features on the scorecard of a senior individual, greater attention – and therefore, better outcomes – is usually the result. Forward-thinking institutions are beginning to recognise this.

No matter how the oversight function is eventually structured, it is important to note one key thing: oversight is about governance and accountability, *not* about doing innovation itself. The overseers need to hold themselves apart from the actual processes involved in converting ideas to reality, because this necessary distance is what provides them with the objectivity needed to see if innovation is really working.

So what, then, *is* the role of the oversight function? The first and most important responsibility is to define the overall objectives of the innovation programme. This task is generally difficult, because so many people have different opinions – both as to the definition of innovation, and the best way it ought to be implemented. Nonetheless, without a consistent set of statements to guide it, any nascent innovation function will likely fail to accomplish very much.

You will recall from Chapter 3 that there are only two kinds of innovation strategies available to institutions. The first, Play to Win (P2W), is the scenario where an institution puts innovation front and centre of its competitive strategy. It puts most of its efforts into breakthrough and revolutionary innovations that enable it to outpace its competitors significantly.

On the other hand, a Play Not to Lose (PN2L) innovation strategy is all about using innovation to maintain market parity with competitors. Rather than trying to change the rules of the game, innovators spend most of their time trying to find uniqueness that improves existing processes, systems, or products. Usually dominated by incremental innovations, PN2L is a strategy that requires much less upfront commitment from an institution, as well as a smaller appetite for risk.

Whether the choice is P2W or PN2L, the end result is that strategy needs to be incarnated in a set of specific objectives and measures against which the innovation programme will be judged. The oversight function uses these as the means by which it is able to work out whether the overall strategy is delivering or not. We will come back to metrics and measures in the next section.

The second aspect of oversight is that it is the gatekeeper for the evolving innovation culture of an institution. The role of an innovation programme is to create new uniqueness for an institution, whether or not the strategy is P2W or PN2L. However, no matter how well funded a central team is, it will have bandwidth constraints, imposed by how many people are available to drive the innovation agenda. This is why a key part of any programme must be to instil innovative behaviours in the institution *regardless* of whether there is a central innovation function or not.

One bank I talked to on this subject said something surprising. I was told 'we don't want our front line staff being innovative! They are there to serve customers! We don't want queues building up in branches because staff are dreaming up new things to do.' And when I asked other bankers elsewhere about this conversation, they agreed it was behaviour they'd often seen in their own institutions as well. In other words, some bankers are of the view that establishing an innovation culture is a *bad* thing. Distracting at best, and deliberately destructive at worst.

Frankly, these opinions, traditionalist though they might be, are probably irrelevant. The reason is that as the capabilities of an innovation programme grow, tools and techniques supporting the innovation agenda will get released 'to the wild'. These encourage innovative behaviour in those outside the formal programme, regardless of what management might think. For example, when a tool for collecting ideas is available, especially if it has social features like the ability to comment and vote, there are consequences for the way that the overall institution responds to creating newness. When my team released Innovation Market internally, the initial offer was to people in the information technology and operations division. The concept caught on quickly, however, and soon this new way of managing ideas was spreading throughout the bank.

Collaboration tools such as these quickly create micro-communities of individuals who are passionate about changing things. But a command-and-control culture in an institution does not readily flex to accommodate such undirected changes, and without decent support from whatever innovation oversight function is present, it is easy for these initial efforts to cause disproportionate responses from management.

Line managers, of course, are focused on having their staff achieve their formal objectives first, *even* if there are better ways to achieve those objectives. They are naturally cautious about making changes, since their personal performance is based absolutely on managing the achievement of those objectives. It is far better to have the devil you know than the one you don't when your bonus is at risk. Then, too, what would staff know about the overall strategic scheme of things into which their little changes will be put?

But this mentality, whilst it creates stability and reliable execution, also locks an institution into a slow pace of change. Staff tend not to feel valued when their ideas for improvement are not considered. And an inability to make meaningful changes to the work environments of employees has been shown to be one of the key reasons that staff leave.

There is a more urgent reason for intervention in the development of an innovation culture by oversight. The increasingly common gen-Y workforce – and not just those working in innovation teams – cares little about silos and the boundaries imposed by traditionalists. They will change things *regardless* of the dictates of management.

In one institution I know, a feature of the work environment is a rigorously controlled personal computer environment. Now, this is true of most large organisations let alone banks, but at this particular institution the level of control imposed is very severe. The background desktop pattern cannot be changed. No software can be installed, and no settings can be accessed. Even connecting to the Internet when away from the office must happen through bank-approved providers so that everything can be monitored and controlled. Social networks are banned, and external email services other than the one provided for corporate use have technological restrictions in place to prevent their use.

Now, whilst traditionalists will just shrug and accept these restrictions, and gen-Xers will moan and complain without doing much about it, a gen-Yer will not tolerate restrictions like this without understanding the rationale behind them *and* agreeing with it. At this institution, circumvention of all these restrictions was commonplace, and the harried IT security folk spent a great deal of time dreaming up new restrictions to get around the hacks the gen-Yers created. That is when they knew about them, of course.

The gen-Yers were not really doing much harm, but they were very much interested in doing things differently than the corporate standard. They wanted to create new uniqueness in the way they were working, and their bank wouldn't let them. Perhaps a better approach would have been to accept that most restrictions placed on information technologies have a relatively short shelf life?

This brings us to the reason the oversight function of innovation governance must be involved in the development of innovation culture. Just as oversight sets the strategic agenda for the innovation programme, so must it define the allowable framework in which other individuals in an institution can be allowed to innovate. Such definitions include, for example, direction to line management that people be given freedom to try new things, as well as the assurance that when they do so, they will be protected from repercussions if things go wrong.

10.2 METRICS

The next thing we must cover is the question of metrics – the numbers or other measures against which innovation will be judged. Way back in Chapter 3, we first examined the importance of metrics. With them, innovation can be treated as a real business process, one that can be compared with other processes in an institution. Conversely, as I pointed out then, a lack of metrics means the innovation programme can never be considered predictable.

The most important metric of all is the one which determines how much difference the innovation programme has made, overall, to an institution. The obvious measure is return on investment in the innovation programme overall. However, there are at least two problems with this approach. The first, of course, is that not all innovations have hard numbers that can easily be attributed to the outcomes of the innovation. It is difficult, for example, to attach decent numbers to productivity improvements. That doesn't mean that innovators would not pursue projects which make employees better at their jobs, just that the business case associated with making such investments is more difficult to construct.

Of course, if the innovators are being measured on hard numbers only, they will tend to weight their work towards investments which produce either new revenue or take out cost. This may look good on paper, but it also means that lots of opportunities to make a bank better are being left on the table.

The second issue with return-on-investment metrics is much more significant, and is the lag between that time when execution starts, and actual returns are made. The more revolutionary or breakthrough an innovation, the longer decent returns take to come online. That is even more true if an innovation is disruptive rather than sustaining.

This presents a quandary for innovators who are measured only by returns. They are faced with certainty of development costs (which comprise winning the funding in the first place, then development, followed by launch and operating costs) in one reporting period. But they have no certainty of benefits, which will likely come much later, and certainly in a later reporting period than the one in which the big investments first occurred. This disconnect makes return on investment a fundamentally broken measure when used in isolation over the short term. That is why many innovation programmes in banks choose different metrics that take account of various efforts which go into bringing a new idea to end-users or customers.

It is impossible, of course, to provide any comprehensive list of the potential measures that might apply to an innovation function. These will be very specific to an institution. As we saw earlier, for example, Bank of America uses the number of products and patents it produces as the definitive measure of its innovation activities. On the other hand, my own programme considers any cost take-out or new revenue as a result of innovation an appropriate measure of success. The specifics of each institution are what matter.

In some industries the metric of choice is percentage of revenue from new products. Now this metric is a highly robust one. It represents, in the end, the total sum of all efforts from an innovation programme in a way that couples the effort to the bottom-line results. But even this has some challenges, because it can be hard to ascribe the specific work of innovators directly to the roll-out of new products. So whilst such a metric might be a good proxy for the amount of effort going into the development of uniqueness in an organisation, it tends *not* to be a good measure of how well an innovation programme is doing.

Boston Consulting Group [72], certainly one of the leading firms studying corporate innovation, surveyed senior executives in multiple industries and discovered that whilst practically everyone has innovation metrics, most companies measure five or fewer individual aspects of the process. And, by far and away the most used metric was the amount of money invested in the innovation process.

Now, on the face of it, this seems somewhat foolish. Of what value is a metric that measures only the input to a process without then determining if the result is actually positive for the firm? But of course, we have already seen why many firms take this approach: the disconnect between investment and returns.

Other research conducted by McKinsey [73] suggests that some innovation metrics are more popular than others. Among the top four in their results are revenue growth as a result of new products and services, customer satisfaction with new products and services, the number of new ideas in the innovation pipeline, and research and development spending as a percentage of sales.

One thing that all studies of this subject agree on, however, is that output metrics – measures that quantify what happens at the end of the innovation process – are inadequate as a means of instrumenting innovation. What is really needed is a way of looking at innovation metrics from end-to-end.

Looking at innovation end-to-end is useful because it gives us a way of examining all stages of the process for jam-ups that may affect the final result. What, for example, might the effect of insufficient ideas arriving at the ideation phase be? Have the selection criteria been set adequately to ensure that sufficient ideas pass through to the innovation stage? What is the correct distribution of projects across the range of incremental, revolutionary, and breakthrough in order to hit the expected value of returns needed to achieve the end goal?

Boston Consulting Group, in the study to which I previously referred, offer the suggestion that innovation metrics be divided into three categories, based on a process model which comprises inputs, processing, and outputs. This is an idea which seems to be gaining currency in institutions, since it offers a simple way of conceptualising the innovation process, whilst delivering some convenient, high-level measures that address many of the issues we've been discussing. Some example metrics broken down in this way are shown in Table 10.1.

Even when all that has been decided, there are a couple of final things to be wary of with innovation metrics.

Firstly, it is so very important to link the measures back to the innovation strategy of the institution. Clearly, if a PN2L strategy is adopted, then it is difficult to justify using metrics which focus on breakthroughs and disruptions, like cannibalisation. Obviously, the innovation team will not be focusing on developing uniqueness in these areas, so the metric will almost always report poor performance. Better choices might include, for example, the success rate of new ideas, or the cost savings generated over a period of time from innovative projects.

But the most important thing to consider with metrics is *how many* are actually needed. The temptation, given the broad range available, is to have more, rather than less. This is usually a mistake. I learned this to my cost when reporting to management in my first year doing innovation: we rigorously instrumented the whole innovation process, with traffic light status on every single aspect of the inner works of the programme. The result was that we spent quite a bit of time explaining how the numbers were generated, the underlying trends that made them up, and whether they were accurate or not. We spent so much time explaining this, in fact, that practically everyone forgot what we were really trying to tell them: that we were generating new uniqueness as outcomes. But, lost in the sea of data we were providing, no one ever got around to considering the results. As you can imagine, we greatly simplified the metrics we were reporting thereafter.

So, with metrics, what is really wanted is a few – five or less seems to be considered optimum – metrics that really tell the innovation story to senior leaders. What is the idea flow like? How balanced is the portfolio compared with the innovation strategy selected? And what has been the result of any execution that might be competing at present?

One last point ought to be made before we leave this topic, and that is that metrics have behavioural consequences. As you would expect, achievement of metrics will drive the actions of the innovation team completely. In one UK, bank, for example, a primary innovation measure was defined as the number of pilots the innovation team was able to drive in a year. It was assumed that having a lot of pilots would result in a much higher likelihood that innovative new products and services would arise.

Table 10.1 Sample process-based innovation metrics

Inputs	Employees engaged directly in innovation	A reflection of the scale of the innovation function. More people should result in more innovation
	Unique ideas generated	A measure of the success of the ideation phase. More ideas are generally better. It is sometimes useful to measure, also, the quality of ideas
	Operating expenses	The cost to run an innovation programme. It can sometimes be helpful to break this down in the futureproofing stage
	Capital expenditures	The amount of money actually invested in execution. Note this amount is quite different from those investments the innovation team will make in previous phases, which ought to be considered operating expenses
Processing	Time to launch	The amount of time it takes on average to go from a raw idea to something that customers or end-users can use. Obviously, an innovation function is doing well when the pace of change is increasing
	Puppy drowning	The number of ideas, by phase, which are terminated for the right reasons. For example, the number of ideas that are consigned to the deadpool during ideation, or are terminated because of a failure to answer key questions during innovation
	Innovation portfolio	The balance of incremental, revolutionary, and breakthrough innovations being examined
	Funding rate	The percentage of ideas in which the innovation team invests which achieve funding and move to the execution phase. This is a measure of how well the innovation process works
Outputs	New products and services	The amount of uniqueness the innovation team has managed to generate in the market
	Patents	A measure of how much new intellectual property is the result of the innovation team, whether or not the IP translates into revenue
	Actual versus projected financial performance	Illustrates how well the innovation team performs answering the key questions, and then how good it is at managing key questions compromises during execution
	Market share growth	Especially in a P2W scenario, a useful measure of the impact of innovation, even though it can be difficult to separate out the efforts of the programme from those of other areas (such as marketing)
	Churn	Again, especially in the P2W scenario, a reduction in this figure can be difficult to separate from other efforts, but can be a useful metric of the success of an innovation programme in delivering results that improve customer satisfaction with an institution
	Cannibalisation or existing revenues	A good measure of the effect of any disruptive innovations. In general, if customers are defecting to an internal innovation, this is a good proxy measure for churn avoidance in the event of a competitor's innovation
	Cost savings	A reflection of efficiency improvements an innovation team may have been able to drive across an institution

This turned out not to be true: the innovation team immediately focused its attention on doing innovative things with small groups of customers and internal end-users. There was no focus whatsoever on the full-scale roll-out of the innovation initiatives – only on producing demonstrations of what might be possible. Clearly, such a metric didn't result in very many new revenue or cost savings opportunities for this particular institution.

10.3   REWARDS AND RECOGNITION

Another aspect of the systems and processes which surround an innovation programme is the method by which incentives and rewards will be distributed to encourage staff to contribute to the overall innovation agenda. Now, in an ideal world, everyone would be sufficiently passionate about innovation that they would make their contributions without any encouragement at all. In reality, however, this never occurs. Some people like cash rewards for their efforts, especially if they've gone above and beyond the call of duty to make something exceptional happen. Some, especially those in the gen-X group (who, if you will recall from our discussion of this topic in Chapter 9, see their value in terms of their personal outputs and what others think of them), will prefer recognition over money. For this group, a reward system which doesn't elevate achievement for others to see will likely be ineffective. Preferred compensations for doing innovative things are highly personal.

What are the broad reasons one can expect innovative behaviour from people, then, especially those outside the innovation team? The first reason, obviously, is that some people expect to be paid. When there are economic incentives associated with innovation, such as cash rewards, revenue shares, or other monetary tokens which improve their personal situation, people will often do extraordinary things.

Secondly, they may be passionate about the activity, and the reward comes because they are able to work on something they are excited about. You often see this in technology people. Given the opportunity to work on something new or leading edge, there will often be an excess of individuals willing to take up the challenge, if only because their ordinary day-to-day work is mundane.

The third reason is that people feel they will be appropriately recognised for their efforts, perhaps through promotion, awards in the eyes of their peers, and so on. Recognition doesn't have to be about large, grand gestures though. Sometimes, even a word of thanks from a senior person is enough.

And the final reason people do innovation is that they are inspired by a vision providing a clear sense of purpose. This is more common than one might think. Everyone has had experiences of the inspiring senior executive, the one who is able to create a belief in some future state, and causes everyone to follow that belief. Quite often, such a vision is all it takes to get innovative behaviour from people.

A clever innovation programme will structure its reward systems to accommodate all four incentives. Here, as with practically everything we've been talking about in this chapter, the way this is done really depends on the innovation strategy selected. A Play to Win strategy, being about innovations which are designed to put uniqueness at the front and centre of the institution's competitive positioning, will demand longer-term rewards, such as stock compensation, rather than short-term cash bonuses. On the other hand, a Play Not to Lose approach, with its focus on incremental innovations, will likely need a quite different approach.

Table 10.2 illustrates the most important aspects of a reward system depending on whether the innovations being considered are revolutionary and breakthrough or incremental. Selecting the appropriate system depends on how the overall innovation portfolio is expected to be weighted.

The first aspect we will consider is the incentive system employed. For an incremental innovation, the most appropriate incentives are relatively short-term and will be weighted, most likely, towards economic compensations and recognition. Because incremental innovations are usually relatively small, and certainly deliver their benefits in a relatively binary fashion (i.e.

Table 10.2   Characteristics of reward systems

	Incremental	Revolutionary and breakthrough
Incentive system	Short-term incentives	Longer-term rewards
Compensation	Cash-based	Future value (i.e., stock)
Success criteria	Formulaic	Subjective evaluation
Metrics	Performance measures significant	Performance measures small component
Kinds of performance measures	Outcome-based	Input and process-based
Scope	Local and individual level	Company-wide

they either do, or do not work), it is often not difficult to link the benefits back to the innovation that generated them in the first place.

For revolutionary and breakthrough innovations, things are rarely so simple. In the first instance, such innovations are most often measured in terms of institution-level performance. One is interested, once such a large and risky investment has been authorised, in outcomes such as number of new product sales, or improved customer satisfaction. But how does one ascribe these outcomes specifically to the innovation, rather than any other initiative presently under way, such as a new marketing campaign, for example?

The sensible thing to do in this case is to switch the focus of rewards to much longer-term benefits. Now, whilst this can include some cash-based compensations, more often than not they will be in the form of benefits which accrue as firm-level success factors are achieved. One often-used way of doing this, for example, is to compensate with stock-based rewards, such as options. Another often-used method is the revenue or equity share: innovators are offered some percentage of the benefits they have generated for the firm, perhaps in some kind of time-bound way.

But for revolutionary and breakthrough innovations, financial compensations are not the only options, of course. Equally important are those that involve recognition of peers and superiors. For especially important innovations, for example, there is often an opportunity for innovators to progress more rapidly through an organisation. External recognition of achievement can also be important.

No matter how the reward system is designed, one thing is very important, and that is the objective criteria which are used to gate whether rewards are issued. It is impossible to underemphasise the importance of this.

As I mentioned, constructing appropriate gates is relatively simple for incremental innovations. A rather formulaic approach is possible, because the innovation is either implemented or it is not. If it is, whatever compensation scheme is appropriate can be applied. Some institutions use a tiered bonus system for this kind of thing, where the reward is matched to the scale of the benefit in some linear way. But other alternatives include small payments with a large prize draw option, and structured recognition processes, such as an annual event.

For other kinds of innovations, assessing whether compensations are due is much more difficult. Because it is often not clear what benefits are associated with the innovation, formulaic approaches are usually impossible. It is far better, in these cases, to use subjective methods to evaluate the success that has been achieved.

Consider the example of corporate venturing at Nokia we examined in Chapter 7. At Nokia, most of the innovations funded didn't actually result in new products, and a significant percentage were absorbed as new capabilities back into ordinary line of business units. Still others became patents, representing unique intellectual property without commercial consequence in the short term.

How best to evaluate the success of these innovations? Clearly, there were positive benefits, even though in most cases they would not have been financial. Some measures that might be considered, though, are expert opinion of the *future* benefits that might accrue. An assessment of the new capabilities now available through the development of the innovation. Or any cultural change effects that might have arisen.

Gating the success of innovation is pretty dependent on the use of metrics in order to achieve reliability. For an incremental innovation, these will largely be outcome-based. Did the innovation create new value? If so, hand over rewards. But for revolutionary and breakthrough innovations, it is better to base the reward metrics on the process model we've already looked at in the metrics section of this chapter. Doing so is a recognition that bigger innovation is a journey rather than a point outcome.

The final point to be made here is that just as metrics systems determine the behaviour of the innovation team, so reward systems affect the behaviour of those who *interact* with the innovators. One must therefore be careful to work out how to ensure you get the right behaviour, and often banks implement reward schemes which don't do this. Economic rewards particularly are a very powerful force and can result in quite destructive outcomes if misdirected.

One US institution ran a staff suggestion scheme for years based on a system of rewards that paid for original ideas collected through an elaborate online system. The cash reward for a single new idea was small. But each time the same person made another original contribution, the value of the payment increased. In the end, the motivation being driven was creation of new ideas. Unsurprisingly, this institution received lots of new ideas, but what happened to them? Very, very few got implemented. The rewards system encouraged creativity, but *failed* to reward execution.

10.4   INNOVATION AND THE ORGANISATION

In the course of my research for this book, I had the opportunity to speak with a large number of innovation teams in banks around the world. Of particular interest was the actual organisational configuration of these teams. I wanted to know where, in a typical organisational hierarchy, all these innovation functions were first started. But even more particularly, I was interested in knowing where they ended up.

Only a few themes emerged from these inquiries. Of great surprise to me was the fact that the most common case is innovation established as a sub-function of the IT organisation. CIOs – more so than any other senior executives, I would argue – are under incredible pressure to do things differently. They are always expected to cut costs whilst delivering more value. It is a natural tendency to think applied innovation is the answer to some of these challenges. We examined these dynamics in Chapter 3.

The second most common case is that multiple innovation teams are established in different parts of the business simultaneously. Now, these teams are not all known as innovation, of course. They often go by names such as business development, new product development, and so forth. The defining characteristic of such teams is that they have a laser-sharp focus on creating uniqueness for their specific business lines. They don't have the bandwidth or the mandate to consider innovation outside their local context, and neither have they any wish to do so.

Now, these distributed innovation teams, as I call them, usually operate in splendid isolation. It is not unusual for each team to be unaware of the existence of the others, in fact. In one institution I found three teams all working on the same mobile phone innovations, totally without knowledge that their work was being duplicated elsewhere.

Obviously, such duplication is fiendishly wasteful of resources, but in many institutions, there is no oversight that prevents it from occurring. Each particular business line feels an obligation to create uniqueness to remain competitive, and is loath to give up its own mechanisms for doing this. Coordinated responses are usually unacceptable because they reduce the pace of innovation in specific business units as a cost of *increasing* the average pace of change across an institution.

The third, but least common, way an innovation team gets off the ground is as an institution-wide shared service. This, as you would expect, implies a level of top-down support that is most unusual. It is also an indication, in many cases, that an institution has adopted a P2W innovation strategy.

In such circumstances, what usually occurs is that a very senior leader from elsewhere in the business is given innovation responsibilities, either as an adjunct to, or instead of, major line of business accountabilities. Such an appointment is expected to create, magically, an ability for the institution to do innovation as a core competence.

As we saw earlier in this book, though, such arrangements don't always work that well. The problem is that whilst such a senior leader will be highly competent at the strategic leadership style, able to influence innovation outcomes simply because they have the hierarchical power to do so, the lack of any mature innovation infrastructure limits their ability to scale up. Sooner, rather than later in most cases, the senior executive finds other things to do with their time. They recognise the potential career damage that is likely to occur when they don't show outcomes that are consummate in significance to their seniority.

So much for the ways that innovation programmes start out. Let us now turn our attention to the places they wind up.

I've already alluded to the fate of most shared innovation initiatives, especially in the presence of a senior leader who is expected to deliver significant outcomes without much in the way of support. Most of these top-down programmes are expected to work at the venturing capability level, but have not had any chance to develop through inventing, championing, managing, and so forth. As a result, they might have the organisational will behind them to create uniqueness, even of the breakthrough and disruptive kind, but they don't know *how* to do so.

Learning to do innovation is a multiple-year journey, and the skills cannot be magically conjured into existence, no matter the seniority of the executive appointed to lead the innovation team. That is especially true for the case where innovation is expected to be internally generated and led. The 18-month window institutions have to get from a standing start to managing applies just as much to such programmes as those that are led from the bottom up.

There are some institutions, of course, that have successfully run a top-down programme, but they buy themselves time to develop their internal innovation capabilities. They do this by focusing almost exclusively on open innovation and corporate venturing, or in other words, they've used their superior access to financial resources to buy innovation outcomes from outside. Another approach that has been successful in some cases is where the senior leader has built a small team around a portfolio of disruptive and breakthrough innovations and isolated it from the rest of the business.

The key success criteria for such endeavours seem to be how clever the accountable executive was in making his or her investments. Early demonstrable returns that hit the P&L in a meaningful way are the key predictor of the longevity.

The distributed innovation team in a particular business function has a much longer lifespan, so long as they deliver appropriate outcomes for their sponsors regularly. And they have the inherent advantage of being directly coupled to several slices at least of the innovation pentagram. About the only danger such a team has is that it gets reorganised out of existence. You would be surprised at how often this occurs. Function-specific innovation teams tend to be passed around line managers in their business units depending on the prevailing political climate of the day. Their accountabilities tend to get strengthened or diluted depending on the personal innovativeness of the currently in-power manager. But in the end, *someone* is always accountable for doing product development and innovation work, even if it goes only as far as tweaking the dials on interest rates and terms and conditions.

The great danger here, of course, is that such silo-based teams have little hope of executing anything other than a PN2L strategy. The kind of grand, front and centre disruptions and breakthroughs which a P2W strategy usually requires are simply impossible for a team that doesn't have an institution-wide mandate or budget.

Then, too, there is little incentive for such teams to move anywhere beyond the managing stage, if they get even that far. Being without a broad strategic mandate, and having no top-down incentive to get one, innovation teams in this situation usually settle for being predictable. That is why they are often known as new product development or similar. They have accepted their limited role in the overall scheme of things.

Finally, of course, there is the technology-based innovation team. Teams in this situation are in a particularly invidious position. As I explained in Chapter 3, most technology functions, and the CIO in particular, have very clear goals. They firstly want to make sure everything works. Then, they want to make sure any changes which compromise this objective are limited as much as possible. Finally, they want to accommodate any new developments which regulation requires and their business sponsors need. Then, and only then, do they consider the innovation agenda and how it might help them.

Because of this most innovations will be a low priority, and innovation teams in technology functions are especially prone to being perceived as not delivering value. The result is that such teams are usually disbanded the moment budgets become constrained – they are seen as expensive luxuries that can be ill-afforded when the rest of the IT agenda has its core funding reduced.

This examination may leave readers wondering whether any innovation function at all has much chance of being successful. Luckily, I was able to find examples of all three kinds of innovation programme that *had* developed successfully along the lines I describe in the Five Capability Model we first examined in Chapter 3. It appears there are a number of key predictors of success, common to all of these innovation teams, no matter where and how they started.

The first is a powerful oversight function, one that has either the ear of the CEO of the bank directly, or via one of his direct reports. Where top-table access is available, it tends to take less time to develop each of the five capabilities needed in a mature innovation programme. Probably, this is because less influence (the currency innovators need to make things happen) is needed to achieve each stage.

The second factor is that successful innovation teams focus with precision on the innovation pentagram, and use it to deliver a connection to the money as quickly as possible. Innovation teams will always struggle for relevance whenever they are not part of the money-making side of the business. The most successful innovation teams work this out quickly, and weight their portfolios appropriately.

The consequences of failing to get a connection to the money are predictable. One innovation team I interviewed (part of the technology function of a major global bank) learned this late. They were under threat of dissolution, and remarked to me that 'we realise now that business innovation was what we needed to be doing. We're irrelevant to the core business of this bank.' It seems this is a typical experience.

The final factor that predicts success in an innovation team is growing into a large budget, rather than being given huge amounts of money up front. Innovators have to earn the right to use the resources they are given. Programmes that grow into large budgets do so on the back of a track record of success. On the other hand, a large budget handed over without such a track record tends to be accompanied with extremely inflated expectations. When these are missed, as they will inevitably be, the innovation team gets into trouble.

Highly resourced programmes, especially when the budgets involved are material to the institution's overall results, need two things in order to deliver decent results. The bank must have committed to a Play to Win strategy, firstly, since nothing else will likely create large enough returns to justify the resources being committed. Secondly, it has to commit to a long-term journey, because as we've seen elsewhere in this book, innovation capabilities don't magically appear instantaneously, and neither do disruptive or breakthrough innovations make meaningful returns in the short term.

As you would expect, the combination of an executive inexperienced in the science and process of innovation *and* hugely inflated expectations of what can be achieved in the short term usually result in the big-programme failures we've been talking about. The fallout in terms of innovation trauma is usually severe.

There is one other thing that seems to have a great deal of influence on the success of innovation teams, and that is the way an institution approaches *paying* for innovation. We examine this topic next.

10.5   FUNDING INNOVATION

At the start of an innovation programme, one of the toughest questions is who is going to foot the bill. How this is managed is very significant, since it determines not only the shape of the innovation programme, but how the innovators will behave on a day-to-day basis. Because this is such a central question, I've spent quite a bit of time reviewing how various innovation programmes around the world manage this aspect of their operations. You will not be surprised to know that the range of possible funding models is not that great, and in fact, practically all of them boil down to some variation of what follows.

But before we examine those in a bit more detail, it is probably sensible to review a point that has come up several times already in this book: it is generally very difficult to link the money spent on innovation to specific financial outcomes, at least if you only examine the period in which the money is spent. This makes the funding problem for innovation quite difficult: whereas more traditional business operations can usually draw a direct relationship between investment and returns, most of the time innovations – especially those that are revolutionary, breakthrough, or disruptive – take quite a bit of time before they deliver anything substantive. In the meantime, the more unprecedented an idea is, the more money needs to be spent to deliver these returns. The upshot is that trying to fund an innovation group through ordinary business-as-usual means is usually not workable, and institutions have come up with many creative ways to get around this problem.

One approach – more common than you might imagine – is that an innovation team is set up with a level of investment that covers their operating costs (the people, computers, and so forth), but nothing more. The thought behind this is that dedicating people to a problem will result in progress being made towards a solution. If an innovation is so compelling, the thinking goes, the institution will find a way to fund it.

There are several problems with this model, of course. The first, which will be obvious to those who have been following this book from the beginning, is that it costs money to make an idea into something that is sufficiently well thought out that funding can be committed. Senior executives *never* invest in ideas: they only invest in well-constructed business opportunities. Constructing such opportunities requires putting the idea through the three key questions, a process which invariably costs money. Along the way, there is a need to get customer insight, build prototypes, and do futurecasts. So, an innovation team without any money to invest at all must spend most of its time dealing with these things itself. The results it will be able to obtain will likely not only take longer, but be less realistic in the absence of appropriate experts. Obviously this has a negative effect on the efficacy of the selling process that leads to a funding decision.

There is another, more problematic, issue with the operating cost-only funding model, and that is to do with the ongoing nature of the investments that the innovation venturing body must make to keep the innovation programme alive. When an innovation is 'sold' to a business executive, they will usually take ownership of any future returns that might devolve from the innovation once it is given to customers or end-users. In their view, this will be fair and reasonable: after all, they are the ones who have to put up the money for the execution phase. But this leaves the innovator in a predicament, of course. For the considerable effort involved in turning a raw idea into something that can be funded, what is the return they can expect? How do they recoup the investments they've made in a way that can be devoted to future innovation?

Quite often, in fact, there is little or no recognition of the efforts of the innovators, resulting in a budget problem: will the sponsors of the innovation team keep paying the bills when there is little demonstrable return to be had for *them*? So, obviously, the operating cost-only model is a relatively poor one.

Another model which is common is that where an 'innovation tax' is levied against all participating business units. Each sacrifices some portion of their budget to pay for the innovation function, and these funds are reinvested to support the development of innovative outcomes. Sometimes, these are cross business line, but often aren't. In this case, the innovation team is generally provided with sufficient budget to have the ability to operate a relatively large portfolio of innovations which are taken through the innovation phase and then handed off for execution. This, in fact, is the model advocated throughout most of this book. Innovators have sufficient budget to answer the key questions for themselves, but must win the money to take an innovation through execution.

The advantage of the innovation tax model is that it precludes the funding issues that normally come into play when a single business unit (such as technology, for example) is required to wear the whole cost, without seeing much return. The disadvantage, obviously, is that the innovation team can run into political problems if it is not seen to be delivering innovation in an equitable fashion amongst those business units that are participating. This is much more common than might be expected, actually. The innovation pentagram, and indeed, the ideation infrastructure which provides the raw material for the innovation programme, are unpredictable. It may be that many ideas arrive for, say, the branch, and none at all for the payments people. Balancing the natural question of value (for the tax payment) against the random arrival of new ideas with the potential to be turned into something new is a key challenge of the innovation tax approach.

There is one more approach to funding which is relatively common, and that is where a central investment fund – perhaps controlled directly by the CEO – is committed to paying for the innovation agenda. More often than not, this is accompanied by the appointment of the senior innovation leader we discussed earlier. We have already discussed the problems with this approach, especially when there are unrealistic expectations of the time it will take to create usable innovations. Nonetheless, there is an appeal to having significant funding of this kind available: as I've mentioned elsewhere, influence and money are largely interchangeable in an innovation context. Having more money means that less influence is needed in order to make significant innovation happen.

Now, all three of these common approaches to innovation assume one main thing: that there will be few, if any, financial returns that go directly to the innovation programme. Some institutions have tried to counter this by introducing constructs like an innovation dividend – essentially a means of double-counting benefits so they accrue equally to business units and the innovation team alike, but most of the time these measures don't work very well, if they are allowed at all. And they certainly don't address the fact that innovation, at least from an accounting perspective, is a cost rather than a profit centre.

Which brings me to the final model that one sees in institutions, one that is very uncommon, but addresses these funding issues head on: treating the innovation function as a cross-charged internal service. In this model, innovators internally charge for everything they do on a time and materials basis. In this respect, they are not substantially different from external consultants, excepting they have greater access to internal information and the people involved in making important decisions.

Innovation as a chargeable service works in some respects very well. As long as there is a sufficient pipeline of work to justify any overhead costs, there is no difficulty in justifying the innovation programme, since it appears to be paying for itself. Then, too, there is usually no argument from the business units paying for the service, since they are paying for only what they use.

But there are quite important issues with this approach as well, and chief amongst them is that it is utterly unsuitable for implementing any kind of P2W innovation strategy. The reason is simple: P2W requires concerted agreement from the entire institution that innovation will be front and centre of the bank's strategy. But a chargeable service is really an opt-in innovation approach, and those business units that don't feel like participating don't have to. This makes it practically impossible to get any kind of agreement on strategy at all, let alone one which will be appropriate for an entire bank.

So, given these points, which funding model makes sense for your institution? As usual, this is a key question that comes down to the innovation strategy adopted. If it is P2W, there is really no alternative to either centralised funding or an innovation tax, since the other options allow business units to opt in and out of innovation as they see fit. With P2W, opting out cannot be an option, since the whole institution is being bet on the innovation agenda.

On the other hand, there are many more options when the innovation strategy is PN2L. In this case, the objective is the repeated creation of innovations that enhance the ability of an institution to keep up with its competitors. Some business units will need to invest more to do this than others, and some will need do nothing at all. So, funding approaches which allow this individual flexibility tend to be more appropriate in this case.

But there is one final point I should make about funding, and that is that I was never able to find a case where the operating cost-only model resulted in sustainable innovation outcomes. That this is the most common model for innovation programmes is probably the reason that so few innovation teams retain their mandate for more than 18 months.

The lesson to new innovation leaders is clear: don't bother to start an innovation programme unless you have seed money available with which to progress an innovation agenda. Failure is the inevitable consequence.

10.6   THE VISIBLE FACE OF INNOVATION

Before we leave this chapter, there is one final aspect of an innovation function we need to look at, and that is the question of how visible an institution's innovation programme will be *outside* the bank.

I've already suggested multiple times that the process of innovation is slowed when knowledge diffusion is restricted. When you try to keep innovation a secret, the usual consequence is that less innovation gets done. The pace of innovation is also slowed when the innovation programme as a whole isn't allowed to collaborate with the external world. Innovators are more productive when they are able to talk with their peers in other banks. When they are allowed to go to conferences and see what other institutions are doing. And when they can invite comment on their activities through the use of mass media – like blogging.

Now, if there were difficulties trying to cause information diffusion *internally*, you can imagine executive response when it is suggested that *now* innovators should be allowed to blab their secrets all over the Internet, and to competitors as well. It is completely counterintuitive to most people, especially traditionalists who are used to protecting competitive advantage through trade secrets, that sharing more rather than less results in significantly better outcomes for an innovation programme. My own experience bears this out.

Early in my tenure in one institution, we decided that I would write a blog on the work we were presently engaged in at the bank [74]. This developed a significant following over the years I wrote it, and became a place that other innovation leads in banks would come. By the end of 2008, for example, I was receiving several invitations a week from bankers around the world for collaborative discussions. These often led to material collaborations which were of benefit to both sides.

The result of these contacts, of course, was that our innovation function had the benefit of getting insight into how some of the best innovators in the world were conducting their innovation programmes. I have no hesitation in admitting that we stole the best operational and procedural aspects of these programmes for incorporation in our ways of working. It is my understanding – and my hope – that many of the institutions we talked with *also* stole some of the things we were doing and made their own innovation functions better as a result.

'Ah-ha!' I can hear traditionalist readers exclaiming already. 'You copied what they were doing! We don't want anyone doing that for our unique innovation capabilities!' And you can imagine what people said to me when they discovered this kind of collaboration was going on from our side of things as well. The fact of the matter is that traditionalist views of what comprises competitive advantage are increasingly irrelevant in the new world in which innovation operates. In the old world, trade secrets and patents were the primary way of ensuring lasting competitive advantage over competitors. The intellectual property in anything valuable was represented by the uniqueness inherent in *ideas*. That is why so many people think it important to keep secrets as long as possible. Now, though, the modern world rewards *execution* way more than ideas. And this is more true than ever in an institutional innovation context. It is the idea, plus the unique way a bank implements it, that drives lasting competitive advantage now.

Every institution is unique in the way it operates, right down to the systems and processes it uses to implement the same product sets. The credit card and mortgage, which may seem undifferentiated to an outside observer, are very, very different when you examine the ways they are implemented and operated at an individual institution level. It is this uniqueness that provides the competitive opening for innovations. Some innovations make sense in the unique context of one institution that would never get past the key questions in another. This means each idea has value *only* in the specific context of the institution that created it in the first place.

With this realisation in hand, it is obvious that there is nothing to be lost by being very open with the progress of innovation at a particular bank. But there is a huge amount to be gained. Bank of America, with their Centre for Future Banking initiative (examined earlier in this book), is an exemplar of this approach. Not only are they collaborating with academia in a very open way, they've started a blog which explains exactly what is going on in their innovation laboratories [75]. They've worked out that sharing what they are doing has much greater upside than the more conventional approach of keeping secrets.

As a general principle, complete and open sharing with competitors will likely be unpalatable for most institutions. Despite this, however, an innovation team will be well served by challenging these boundaries. If it is at all possible, create a blog that explains what is going on inside the bank from an innovation perspective. Allow the innovators to speak at conferences. Permit them to take press interview requests and speak about their innovation processes. Let them write a book on the subject if they wish.

If you want further evidence that this approach works, one doesn't need to go much further than the fact that this book was made possible by the collaboration of a large number of banks around the world who were willing to share their experiences and processes with me. Most of them I was able to reach through social media, and the activity of my team and myself on the Internet.

10.7   AND FINALLY. . .

Building an innovation function from scratch is rather like climbing a mountain. At the beginning, it just seems as if no matter how much effort you put in, there's little chance of getting the whole distance in one piece. But mountain climbing is made much easier if you have the right apparatus to get yourself upwards with the minimum amount of energy. A climber who makes a few investments in ropes and supplies before starting has a much greater chance of getting to the top and planting their flag. The things we have discussed in this chapter are the ropes and supplies of an innovation team looking to get through the Five Capability Model. Futureproofing *is* a mountain, but it is one that seems far less daunting when you have a decent plan for oversight, metrics, and funding in place.

11

Making Futureproofing Work in Your Institution

What you will find in this chapter

- A set of recommendations you can follow if you are starting a new innovation programme.

The material presented in the previous chapters has hopefully been interesting and useful. But how does one turn it into an innovation programme that drives results for *your* institution? In answering this question, I present in this final chapter a set of things you might like to consider when creating an innovation programme of your own. The recommendations are organised by major subject of the book, and hopefully you will find these a useful summary, in addition to being a blueprint to the sorts of things you ought to consider for your own innovation programmes.

But before we get to the specifics of that, there is one final case study I want to share with you. It is the case of Caja Navarra, a savings bank in Spain, who used Play to Win innovation strategy successfully. Caja Navarra has created a new kind of banking, and the results of its efforts are an illustration of the way that a rigorous focus on innovation can have profound effects on the fortunes of an institution.

11.1 CASE STUDY: CIVIC BANKING AT CAJA NAVARRA

In Spain, there is a special sub-class of institution known as a savings bank, or Caja. As foundations, savings banks pay their dividends back to the communities that support them, so they are popular options for Spanish citizens. In 2001, Caja Navarra was number 41 of 46 savings banks in Spain, when compared on the basis of return on equity. But by 2007, it had leapfrogged its competitors and become number four. In a mere six years, the Caja left its competitors in the dust – literally. Employee efficiency (in terms of margin per employee) improved from 16th to 5th. And the number of branches it operated from increased by nearly 50%. Clearly, Caja Navarra did something which gave it a massive competitive advantage over its much larger rivals. The 'something' was to adopt a P2W strategy with a systematised innovation framework as the core of their business. How Caja Navarra got to this point is interesting.

In late 2000, post a significant merger with a competitor, the bank and its new board of directors were clear that the only way they were going to stay relevant to their customers was with a fundamental change in strategy. They knew that whilst the basic premise of a Caja was the return of value to the communities of which they were part, the financial services environment was swiftly evolving. Large Spanish banks such as Santander and BBVA were gobbling up rivals at a brisk pace. And customers were demanding much more from their financial institutions.

The question posed by the board was why – with their focus on community development – Cajas were not the preferred provider of financial services for a greater segment of the potential customer base. And the answer, found through an extensive research process, was that customers didn't have any personal connection to the investments being made on their behalf. Such social benefits as might be created from the Caja movement were so disconnected from customers there was little personal association with any positive outcomes. The millions invested made practically no difference to the financial services purchase decision.

With this realisation in hand, the board knew they could make an immediate change for the better simply by enabling customers greater participation in the investment process. It decided it would allow customers to specify how their investment money would be disbursed, offering a basket of projects – sourced worldwide – from which they could choose.

New organisations seeking funding now had to petition customers directly for enough votes to gain admission to the basket of investible projects. In some cases, non-profit organisations began to ask customers of other banks to join Caja Navarra just to make sure they had enough votes for inclusion on the investment rota. This contributed to a massive increase in customer acquisition – in 2007 it was estimated that non-profit recruitment helped drive 8% growth in new customers.

The decision to remove the board from investment decisions was the first of many innovations that would later be known as civic banking. The basic premise of this new strategy was that by empowering the customer with new 'rights' – such as the right to select the civic projects of which they would be a part – the overall business of Caja Navarra would improve as well. The initial success with this first right seemed to prove the point. So, the board adopted a new innovation model. They decided they would innovate by creating as many new 'rights' as they could, empowering customers and improving transparency.

The second right launched by Caja Navarra was that customers should know their individual profitability to the bank. This, it was felt, was an essential extension of the previous innovation. By telling customers their total value, they would then be in a position to know how much money they were personally contributing to social projects. Hopefully, this would increase their association with their community investment decisions, in the process driving additional stickiness to the Caja Navarra financial relationship.

Once again, this was a fairly unprecedented innovation, both from a business and a technical perspective. Very few institutions actually disclose profitability at an individual customer level, if doing so is technically possible at all. The ability to determine the actual cost to serve a customer (and therefore profitability) is influenced by individual channel and product mix. Most institutions are challenged with getting a single view of customers' holdings across various business lines, let alone factoring in channel costs as well. But these problems were eventually solved at Caja Navarra with diligent investment and effort.

The new right was met with incredulity from customers. They were simply unable to believe a commercial organisation would actually engage in such transparent behaviour. Caja Navarra had to launch an education programme to convince customers that it was serious about civic banking and had its customers' best interests in mind.

There were some unexpected benefits from this innovation. Most notable among these was a sharp upswing in corporate business Caja Navarra was able to win from competitors. Because these corporates were able to identify how profitable they were to the bank *and* were able to direct the way the profits were invested in social projects on their behalf, large companies began to use their Caja Navarra relationship as the centrepiece of their corporate responsibility programme. By switching their business to the bank, they were able to announce to their own customers that they were contributing to responsible programmes in communities. It turned out to be a massive incentive for business banking customers to switch.

With its new innovation model in place and the ability of rights to generate extra business for the bank proven, Caja Navarra continued to expand its innovation portfolio over the next few years. Its next innovation was to require the non-profit organisations that achieved investment to be transparent about what they were spending money on. This information was then reported back to customers along with their personal profitability figures they were now used to receiving.

So, not only were customers able to direct money towards those projects they were interested in, they could also see how well their projects were performing, at least from a financial perspective. In the process, Caja Navarra created additional stickiness for its own products: the amount of information available as a result of the new right was generally much greater than a private benefactor would get if they donated directly.

Then, working out that some customers might appreciate even further involvement in their projects of interest, Caja Navarra introduced its fourth right: a requirement that charitable organisations taking customer investment must also accept volunteers from its customer base if they are able to do so.

As you would anticipate, the effect of these rights was positive both on acquisition and churn – metrics which surged to record levels quickly. Caja Navarra's innovation framework was obviously working better than anyone could have dreamed. With these successes under its belt, the bank has continued to launch new rights to its customers.

The most recently launched right enables a customer to know how Caja Navarra is using its deposits. A customer, today, can see the kinds of organisations to which the bank is lending money. It is possible, for example, to determine what percentage of a given deposit is being used to fund social housing, construction, or other projects the bank lends to. Once again, such disclosure is wholly unprecedented.

The new right is important in one particular respect: one gets all the advantages of the peer-to-peer lending model *without* any of the personal risk or time commitments ordinarily required. By innovating with rights, Caja Navarra has come up with an effective counter to the potential future disruption of peer-to-peer *without* compromising its own business. At the time of writing, that is an achievement which has not been replicated by anyone else, anywhere.

Caja Navarra is an institution that put an innovative concept – civic banking – at the centre of its plan for success. By adopting a Play to Win innovation strategy, it is now in the top ten Cajas for all important metrics that measure institutions in its class. And it has begun a programme to expand into new markets in other regions in Europe. And so successful has Caja Navarra been with its customer rights innovation, it is now looking to take its model global. Not bad for an institution that was at the very bottom of its institutional league table just six years earlier.

11.2   STARTING YOUR INNOVATION PROGRAMME

Caja Navarra is an excellent example of what can happen when an innovation programme is allowed to materially affect the fortunes of an institution. Such dramatic results, however, are hardly normal in banking. The reason, more often than not, is that innovation teams simply don't have the buy-in of senior management at the beginning of the process. Senior executives may have an intellectual acceptance of the fact that innovation is important for the future, but this rarely translates into the kind of support which makes it possible for innovators to make a strategic difference, at least at the start.

Such support must usually be earned through the creation of a history of successful innovation. This is why, in the end, most innovation programmes develop through the Five Capability Model we looked at in Chapter 3. Each capability bootstraps on the success of the previous one, leading, in time, to a situation where innovators *are* supported in making strategic change. But every innovation programme has to start somewhere. So what follows is a set of recommendations that will give a new innovation team the very best chance of success.

1. Get agreement on what innovation means

Before anything at all starts, you need a definition of innovation. There are as many definitions of innovation as there are stars in the sky, and trying to settle on something everyone agrees with is usually contentious. Some people think the only innovation that counts is the breakthrough kind. Others are less ambitious and define innovation as anything even remotely new. Having a definition for innovation means it is possible to set down goals towards which innovators will be working. It makes it easy to define what success looks like. But without a workable definition, innovators will be condemned to a perpetual no-mans-land of no one being sure what is being achieved.

2. Decide on an innovation strategy

You need to be clear on your innovation strategy up front. There are only two high-level variations on innovation strategy. You can do Play to Win (P2W), which suggests your institution will put innovation front and centre of its competitive responses to the market. P2W is the strategy adopted when you can answer 'Yes!' when asked 'is innovation expected to be the primary source of competitive advantage for the future?'

When P2W is the selected strategy, the innovation programme will likely concentrate on revolutionary and breakthrough innovation, moving eventually to disruptive innovations as it gets its feet on the ground. Another characteristic of such a programme is that it needs to move through the five capabilities to venturing very quickly.

The other innovation strategy option is Play Not to Lose (PN2L), in which innovation is the tool used to maintain parity with competitors in the long term. One seeks to improve existing processes and systems in unique ways to maintain competitive position. A programme working this strategy will focus mainly on incremental innovation, and will need to ramp up quickly to volume in order to demonstrate value. Whilst there will be some revolutionary and breakthrough innovations, these will come as a bonus to incremental work, rather than being an end-goal in themselves.

It is critical that one of these two innovation strategies be identified up front, because the shape of the programme that results is absolutely determined by the decision. P2W programmes will have a very different constitution (they will have a portfolio of bigger, more risky investments) compared with PN2L (a sausage factory of small units of uniqueness). The fact of the matter is that most banks today will – even if they don't realise it immediately – adopt PN2L, regardless of what they say about innovation. Taking a P2W strategy forward implies a level of oversight, investment, and support which most institutions simply don't have, no matter how good their innovators.

3. Establish oversight and executive support mechanisms

You must have an effective oversight mechanism that is accountable for innovation outcomes. We looked at governance earlier in this book, and the most important aspect of that is the oversight function. It is critical that some body be established to review the outputs of the innovation function. Oversight is there to ensure that the programme is executing on the innovation strategy, and to make sure that innovation metrics are being reached.

But the oversight function has an even more important aspect, and that is showing there is senior-level support for the innovation function. Innovation in the absence of such support almost always fails. In fact, anecdotal evidence suggests an innovation function has only 18 months to live unless such a support structure exists to nurture and protect it.

Since that is the case, it is best to ensure that oversight is established early, *and* that it is made accountable for the right innovation outcomes. It is all the better if the CEO of the bank can be available as part of oversight, but if that is impossible, the next best thing is for several of his or her direct reports to be available.

4. Set five or less clear metrics to measure against

A set of metrics against which the innovation team will be measured is critical. Defining these metrics is likely to be an arduous process, and the temptation will be to have a large number of them. However, practically speaking, most institutions have found that five or less metrics is a good number. Having more means the data is too dense for effective decision-making against strategy. Whilst fewer are unlikely to provide sufficient instrumentation of the effective levers that drive the innovation process.

Whatever the metrics, the most important thing is that they provide an appropriate linkage to the innovation strategy. If the strategy is P2W, effective metrics are likely to include measures at the strategic level, such as customer acquisition, new product revenues, and so forth. A PN2L strategy, on the other hand, will likely use metrics which are more about process efficiency, cost savings, and other measures which relate to overall improvement of operations.

5. Get seed capital

Do not start an innovation programme without a budget. This may sound obvious, but so many institutions hire innovators and then expect the magic to occur. Almost always, such programmes are cancelled within 18 months, the average time an underperforming innovation team is allowed to continue.

The amount of money required to start a programme is that needed to answer the key questions multiplied by the number of innovations expected in the portfolio. This will be determined by the innovation strategy selected. Bear in mind, though, that breakthroughs and revolutions will be much more expensive in terms of key questions than incremental innovations. And expect that 25% or less of innovations investigated will go to the execution phase, so initial estimates should make allowances for this.

6. Hire an innovation team with the correct preference mix

Any innovation team that is hired must have competence in all four innovator styles we looked at in Chapter 9 if innovation is to happen reliably. Usually, innovators will have a preference for more than one style, which means you can get a completely functioning team with less than four people. It is a mistake, however, to have a team of less than two individuals: no one has all the innovation styles needed. At a minimum, there must be a creator and an implementer.

You *must* have all four styles available in an innovation team, or nothing will get done. At the very best, the team will operate inefficiently. The implication of this is that an innovation team must be designed rather than just thrown together. Unfortunately, it is often the case that innovation functions are built on the basis of who is available rather than who is best for the role. Then, too, innovation roles are often seen as glamorous and desirable. This combination of factors tends to mitigate against getting the perfect mix of people to run an innovation function successfully.

Taking the time to hire the correct mix of innovation styles is important. The temptation to 'just get on with it' will be strong, but should be resisted. All that will happen is that poor innovators will be fired, and the team will likely have to build its portfolio from scratch. And frankly, for a new programme, there is rarely enough time available to recover from a poor team before senior executives will conclude innovation as a discipline is insufficiently beneficial to justify the resources it consumes.

7. Set realistic expectations about the length of the journey

Building a reliable innovation programme will take time, probably years. All the capabilities of the Five Capability Model will have to be developed by an innovation programme at some time. There is no point trying to shy away from the fact that getting through all five is a process that is going to take years, and there isn't any shortcut.

It is unfortunately a reality that most business leaders don't have that long to wait for substantive results, however. Executives will tend to cancel innovation programmes in 18 months or less if they have no results to show for their efforts in that time. It is therefore essential that expectations be set early about what is realistic in terms of achievement.

Forming the team and getting initial inventions out the door is probably realistic for a start-up team in year one. It will likely take another year for the team to build out the infrastructures it needs to get to the predictable managing stage. And it may be much, much longer before the fruits of futurecasting and venturing stages take root.

8. Make sure the innovators understand the innovation pentagram

Innovation teams are often started in a siloed part of the organisation – very often in the technology department. If that is the case, it is important to understand that technology is *not* the point of the innovation programme. The point *is* creating new uniqueness in one or more of the five slices of the innovation pentagram we saw in Figure 3.1. It is critical the innovation team understands this at a very basic level.

One thing that will almost certainly terminate a nascent innovation programme is getting a reputation for being about gadgets. This will happen the moment that technology innovation – rather than business innovation – takes the upper hand.

11.3   MAKING IDEATION WORK

Ideation is the process of harnessing the creative capital of an institution. Every company has people with great ideas. In fact, great ideas are never the issue with the innovation process. In almost every case, the main issue is a lack of execution capability – the ability to convert a great idea into something that customers or internal end-users can use to do useful work.

When we examined the Five Capability Model in Chapter 4, I suggested that building out an ideation function was the first thing that needed to happen for any innovation programme as it gets beyond the invention stage. To help do that, here are the things that must be done to get this part of futureproofing started.

9. Acquire and deploy an ideas management system

Whether the innovation strategy selected is P2W or PN2L, collecting and managing ideas will be facilitated best if there is some kind of system available to manage the process. Ideally, it should be self-service, so potential contributors can be involved in the process as early as possible. And it should include wisdom-of-crowds features like user-generated content and voting to enable pre-screening of ideas.

Ideas are the lifeblood of an innovation programme, and the idea management system is a key tool on which to build volume. And volume is essential – more than 75% of all ideas collected will not make the grade for one reason or another. As the number of ideas scales up, it becomes less easy to manage the necessary processes – scoring, aggregating, and analysing – without such a system in place. So, investing in an ideas management system early is a good idea.

There are a couple of touch-points for such a system. When a programme is new, ideas management will likely be accessed only by those staff who are in conventional head-office roles. This is an easy demographic to reach, since such individuals will likely have access to email and other communications technologies which make it simple to get the message out about the new way of collecting ideas.

An innovation team, however, should not rest on its laurels here. A much more interesting place to collect ideas is from customer-facing staff – those in branches and call centres. These individuals have direct access to customers, and will likely be able to provide insights that are unavailable anywhere else.

And finally, an emerging trend in ideas management is to have customers access the ideas system themselves directly. Customer co-creation, as this concept is known, has motivated and passionate customers participate in the innovation process directly. In so doing, it is possible to gain insights about what the market is demanding that would be difficult and expensive to gain otherwise.

One last point on ideas management. Don't build a system yourself. It will take too long, and be less functional than something you can buy. It will also cost more.

10. Create a scoring system and apply it rigorously

Volume is the key to ideation, and the basic principle that must be applied is that as many ideas as possible should be examined for as little money (per idea) as can reasonably be managed. Preserve as much of the seed money as possible for the innovation phase, rather than spending it sifting through ideas. This will tend to optimise the returns available to the innovation programme.

A decent scoring system is the best way to sift through ideas cheaply, and there are several characteristics such a system should have if it is to be effective.

The first is that it must be quick and easy to use. Since individuals outside the innovation programme will necessarily have to do the scoring (no one inside the programme will be sufficiently expert that they will be able to render an opinion on every single idea proposed), if one wants to get decent turnaround, it must be possible for people whose day jobs are *not* innovation to respond quickly. And getting decent turnaround in a volume game is critical.

The next thing is that the scoring system must have a way of accommodating the different priorities of different business units around the bank. An idea likely to be adopted by the payments business may have no value at all to the deposits people. Failing to build in weightings that accommodate these differences means some ideas which could have been valuable will be abandoned prematurely.

The final thing to consider is the way the system will give feedback to the individuals who raised the idea in the first place. A mistake many institutions make is failing to feed back the results of scoring (and anything that happens later in the process). The result of this is that individuals will probably raise only a few of their ideas before getting bored of the process and giving up. This is where a self-service system with online access is so helpful. Individuals are able to log in for themselves and see where their idea is up to.

11. Build a network of people who can evaluate ideas

As I mentioned a moment ago, innovators will not ordinarily be sufficiently expert themselves to consider every idea that arrives. The best approach is to create a network of people in the business who are able to evaluate each idea in terms of their own business units. This evaluation will use the scoring instrument you have previously defined, and will ideally be quick and painless for the evaluator.

The evaluation network should be comprised of individuals who are sufficiently senior that they have a view of the overall strategy of the business unit, yet not so senior that they will eventually be the ones approving funding. Funding decisions should not be allowed to occur until the three key questions have been answered later in the innovation stage. Prior to that point, insufficient development of the idea has occurred: telegraphing something to a senior executive without adequate preparation can only have a negative outcome.

12. Work out gating conditions for innovation, parking lots, and deadpools

It is critical that the ideation system be eminently predictable in its behaviour. People who raise ideas need to be able to see why a particular idea was selected, compared with others. If they don't feel an appropriate process was followed, they will likely just give up on innovation altogether.

We talked about ideas being like puppies: when you have one, it is so cute and emotionally engaging that having it taken away (drowned) is often a painful experience. This is true for those who suggest ideas to an innovation programme: there must be a good and repeatable reason for the idea not to be progressed if the person contributing is not to be alienated.

Repeatability means that subjectivity must be removed from the ideation process. Subjective evaluations have their place, of course, but that time is during the innovation phase which follows. During ideation, what is needed is a purely mechanical means of evaluating ideas and selecting them for further investigation.

It is helpful to have three classes of ideas. The first are the ones that are selected for progression to the innovation phase. These are the ideas which score so highly that not investigating them further is obviously not an option. Then there are ideas which are either just above or just below average, compared with all the other ideas available. Such ideas should be added to the parking lot – in other words, they are good enough that they ought not to be rejected outright, but must wait their turn for future evaluation. And there are those ideas which score relatively poorly compared with all other ideas. These should be consigned to the deadpool – ideas which are never going to progress.

In Chapter 5 I suggested using the standard deviation of all ideas in the ideas management system as the gating criterion for innovation, parking lots, and deadpools. There is an intuitive attraction to this approach, since it is rigorous and repeatable. It also removes subjectivity entirely.

13. Create the processes that let you analyse the aggregate ideas data

Individual ideas are important, of course, but there is a wealth of information in the patterns that appear when you aggregate the raw ideas data. You need to be able to examine idea clusters – similar ideas arriving at the same time. You also need to be able to find idea trends – ideas whose volume increases over time – as this indicates something important is happening that may need a futurecast or other analysis. Spotting innovation clusters – groups of individuals who are especially innovative compared with their peers – is something that aggregate data can give you as well. And finally, removing duplicate ideas before too much money is spent means there is more budget left over for progressing true uniqueness which has a chance of making a difference.

14. Establish the ability to do customer insight cheaply

Although an idea may have been scored highly by business evaluators, there is nothing like getting insight into what customers or end-users think of an idea before committing sizeable amounts of funding. It is therefore appropriate to develop screening techniques which enable one to put many ideas in front of customers quickly and cheaply. Be mindful here that traditional market research techniques – such as focus groups, for example – are usually too expensive to use at this early stage. Luckily, idea-screening companies are now popping up that can cheaply provide customer insight for large numbers of ideas using panels of Internet respondents. These methods – and others like them – are great ways to get that initial sanity check one needs in order to validate an idea has sufficient merit that a little more money can be spent on it.

15. Create an appropriate incentive system

People need rewards for doing innovation. There are four aspects to an individual's motivation to do innovative things. There is the expectation of economic compensation. The possibility of recognition from peers and superiors. Individual passion for whatever-it-is. And, in some cases, the desire to follow a vision to some outcome in which there is strong belief.

To ensure innovative behaviour, one really wants to design a compensation system for individual contributors that includes all four of these factors, and the mix will be different depending on the innovation strategy adopted by an institution. For PN2L strategies, compensation tends to be weighted towards shorter-term rewards like small cash bonuses and peer and superior recognition. For P2W, however, compensations need to be more long-term. This reflects the natural temporal distance between the activities that initiate an innovation and the benefits that arise later.

11.4   THE INNOVATION STAGE

Once there is a working ideation function, the next thing to do is consider the steps to be taken in order to sell the idea to executives with money. Since it is almost never the case that innovation teams have sufficient funding in their own right to execute and launch without the support of their business colleagues, the process of getting an idea ready for the final pitch is the main determinant of how successful an innovation function will be.

What follows are the 10 things innovation teams need to consider once an idea has reached the innovation stage to maximise the chances of getting reasonable volume out the door in a predictable way. If you recall, I've been saying throughout this book that the goal of innovation teams must be to make innovation the most attractive investment opportunity available to their institutions at any given time. These pointers will help to do that.

16. Take a portfolio view and focus on expected returns

Although a significant number of very good ideas may be arriving from the ideation phase, further selection is necessary in order to optimise the returns on innovation investments. Bear in mind that innovation will have limited resources, and it is therefore impossible that *everything* which looks like a good idea can be done all at once. Some prioritisation is necessary. And the best way of prioritising is to take a portfolio view of all the innovation projects which are selected.

Taking a portfolio view means working through the expected returns an innovation is likely to generate. An expected return is the net benefit that will accrue to the institution if the innovation goes live (for example, the new revenue expected less the costs of getting the revenue), *multiplied* by the riskiness inherent in the innovation.

Risk, in this context, can take many forms. It may be that the innovation is unprecedented in the market – which means there are technical, regulatory, and procedural risks which must be taken into account up front. Perhaps there is a risk that customers won't like the innovation. Or, indeed, that the costs of operation, once live, make it uneconomic to continue. Innovation is a relatively speculative activity anyway, so getting a complete picture of the set of risks involved in an innovation is impossible in advance. This means that it is necessary to construct a proxy measure of risk (see Chapter 6) which enables one to get to expected values rapidly.

17. Weight the portfolio appropriately

If the innovation strategy is P2W, then the portfolio should be weighted towards breakthrough and revolutionary innovation. On the other hand, if it is PN2L, the portfolio should consist mainly of incremental innovations at volume. It is generally a mistake not to follow this advice. An institution that has no interest in leading front and centre with very significant uniqueness will also be unlikely to *fund* such uniqueness. This will likely leave an innovation team in the situation where it has an excellent portfolio, but little or no chance of converting it into actual change that makes a difference to whatever metrics are agreed. Programmes in this situation will usually be terminated within 18 months.

Conversely, an institution that looks to the innovation team for P2W kinds of uniqueness will hardly be delighted if what comes from the innovators are myriads of variations on, say, form redesign. In this case, the innovators will look incompetent or worse.

18. Make sure the key questions are front and centre

There are three key questions an innovator must be able to resolve before an idea is ready to be pitched to senior executives for funding. 'Can we?' is mainly technical, and is concerned with the technological, people, or process newness that comprises the innovation. 'Should we?' is mainly a question of economics, and should focus on the net benefit an innovation will provide if it is taken forward to execution. And 'When?' is mainly about timing, both in terms of overall market readiness and the institution's capability to execute. Unless all three questions can be answered positively, innovation practitioners should drown the puppy immediately.

Another consideration is how much effort it will take to get the answers to the three key questions. Some innovations, for example, do not have technological components available off-the-shelf. In these cases, the innovator may need to schedule the development of expensive prototypes in order to answer the key 'Can we?' question.

In general, unless the innovation has a very high expected value, there is little point in progressing an innovation for which the costs of answering the three questions are high. It is usually better to concentrate on those innovations which have largely obvious answers.

19. Recognise the real reason for business cases

One of the key outputs of the innovation phase will be some kind of business case document. Innovators need to recognise the *real* reason they create such documents: they are sales tools used to represent the potential value of an innovation even in the absence of the innovation team. It will likely be the case, for example, that breakthrough and revolutionary innovations will be the subject of much discussion at board level. Most of the time, innovators would not expect to be present during such discussions, so having a robust business case document – which deals directly with the sales mission – is one way of de-risking the executive decision process.

A business case document that works as an appropriate sales tool must address the stages of innovation decision process we first examined in Chapter 3. It must explain the 'How, Why, and What' questions that executives will likely have, as well as providing positive reinforcement that the potential decisions taken are good ones. Then it must link to evidence decision-makers can use to justify their decisions after the fact.

Ideally speaking, to maximise sales effectiveness, a business case document should be tailored to a specific target audience. If, for example, the objective is to create an innovative new payments service that is shared institutionally, it is better to create multiple business case documents addressing the decision process for each senior leader that might be involved in the go/no-go decision. Clearly, the executive responsible for credit cards will have a quite different perspective on the innovation than the one responsible for international payments.

There is another reason business case documents are important, and that is they act as 'get out of jail free' cards for executives *after* the decision to move to execution has been made. With a decent business case document, there is ample justification that the investment decision made was a good one. Executives need to be able to demonstrate their decision was not the root cause of any subsequent failure of the innovation. Failure to recognise this important aspect of the business case invariably leads to a failure to get funding. Executives, who are naturally risk-averse to start with, will not make significant decisions that have any degree of risk without protecting themselves in advance.

20. Drown the puppy

Most innovations – even those which have got through the comprehensive scoring stages that are part of ideation – will fail. It is senseless to rail against this, and innovators need to recognise that fewer than one in four ideas which make it to the innovation phase are likely to get to execution. Given that is the case, instilling a discipline of 'drowning the puppy' is important. The objective is to terminate ideas as often and as soon as possible in order to preserve cash for those ideas which *may* go somewhere.

This, however, is not as simple as it may seem. Once an innovator – or anyone else for that matter – has begun work on an idea about which they are passionate, it becomes increasingly difficult to drop it. Individuals get more emotionally engaged with ideas the more time they spend with them, and this clouds their judgement. Left unchecked, ideas can be pushed forward to execution even though they don't make much sense. It is therefore necessary to be rigorous in the puppy-drowning process. Ensure that innovators drown new ideas as soon as one of the key questions looks as if it won't be successfully answered.

21. Create an architectural design as part of the answer to the key questions

An important part of answering the 'Can we?' question is knowing *how* an innovation will be built if it gets approved. This is not only a matter of resolving technical considerations, of course. It also includes all the procedural, operational, and people questions as well.

An architectural design document is a high-level statement of how these inputs to the innovation will work smoothly together. Even more importantly, it is the information that is a key input to the 'Should we?' question: without knowing how the new thing will operate, it is difficult to know how much it will cost.

The architectural design document has another important function as well: it helps lock in the specific decisions an innovator needs to make in order to shape the innovation. Because the execution phase is all about managing compromise, having a set of statements about the way things are going to work earlier rather than later means it is easier to ensure the spirit of the innovation doesn't get lost when inevitable technical and financial pressures are applied.

22. Prototypes must be thrown away

There will be times when answering the key questions, especially 'Can we?', requires the creation of one or more prototypes. A prototype should always be considered something that will eventually be thrown away. Building anything that can do real work requires a great deal of investment – far more than is justified for an innovation that does not have any certainty of going ahead.

23. Don't bother to wait for autonomic innovations

Autonomic innovations happen when a perfect storm of factors – money, organisational will, and an urgent need – come together to create the situation where an innovation walks out the door regardless of the efforts of the innovation team. Naturally, if an autonomic innovation appears, it makes sense to pursue it. But waiting around for innovation to sell itself will rarely result in the kinds of predictability that an innovation team needs if it wants to keep existing. Instead of waiting for an autonomic innovation to present itself, innovators are far better off working the three key questions and managing their portfolios.

24. Make sure the discipline of creating influence maps assists the sales process

The process of selling innovations will rarely go smoothly. An assessment of the personal innovativeness of the executive with the money is an important part of the innovation phase. If this individual is late majority or later (see Figure 2.2), it is highly unlikely they will buy an innovation no matter how good the business case or how compelling the answers to the key questions.

In these cases, it is important to construct influence maps of those who surround the key decision-maker. As a general rule, finding two individuals who are personally disposed to the innovation (i.e., they are early majority or better) will be extremely helpful in convincing the executive involved that the innovation is a good investment.

If there are no appropriate influencers available, it is sometimes reasonable to examine the next layer for appropriate individuals: the influencers of the influencers. There will potentially be a positive payoff for such investigations where the innovation has a very high expected value, but not otherwise.

There is almost never a situation where investigation beyond the influencer of the influencer is justified. The reason is the geometric expansion of the number of people who must be coordinated for success.

Once again, the practice of puppy drowning should be called into play. If at two levels of influence insufficient people are found who are predisposed to the innovation, there is no point in progressing, no matter how positive the key questions were. The fact of the matter is that organisationally, your institution is simply not ready for whatever-it-is.

25. Get to managing as soon as possible

Anecdotal evidence from many failed innovation programmes at banks leads to one conclusion: a new innovation programme has about 18 months on average to start showing predictable returns. In other words, it has to create its initial first wins, build its networks, and get to managing quickly. At any time prior to this, a programme can be cancelled the moment its senior sponsors move jobs, or if economic conditions mean that innovation is seen as an 'expensive luxury'.

Managing is the third capability an innovation team must develop in the Five Capability Model (see Figure 3.2). For executives, this is the first time their innovation investments will start to make predictable returns they can rely on. People rarely eliminate something that is obviously working.

11.5 EXECUTION

Winning the money is the final step of the innovation phase, and the commencement of execution. Execution is all about the things that have to be done to convert the idea (which, at this point, is still pretty much just words on paper) into something customers and end-users can actually do useful work with.

In many institutions, there are developed processes which can be relied upon to turn ideas into reality. After all, most banks have to do project work as part of business-as-usual every day. Some innovations, however, do not lend themselves to standard bank processes. And others are so new that trying to shoehorn them into such processes will likely kill the innovation altogether.

No matter what the innovation, though, here are the key points you need in order to get successful execution.

26. Make sure you control the requirements document

Project managers (and other individuals working on the innovation) will base their actions around a requirements document. This document will describe in significant detail all the operating and technical parameters of the innovation. It should be a complete statement of what will be created and the functionality it will provide to customers or end-users.

Practically speaking, the innovation team does not need to control every aspect of this document. In fact, doing so will likely impose a rather significant, and unnecessary, burden on the innovators, who need to spend their time ensuring that the rest of their portfolios are getting sufficient attention.

What *is* needed, however, is that the document codify all the assumptions and decisions that were inherent in the key questions explored during the innovation phase. For example, if a positive answer to the 'Should we?' question assumed that a particular capability be available in the end product, that fact needs to be recorded in the requirements document.

27. Manage key questions compromise

The innovation team, having guided an idea to the stage when it will finally get built, needs to retain some influence over the execution process, and the reason is that converting an idea into something real is a journey during which significant compromises will be made.

Now, project teams will believe they control the three main inputs to this process: the schedule, the budget, and the deliverable. Practically speaking, they *do* in fact have to exercise considerable control over these parameters in order to do their jobs. Various compromises and trade-offs are necessary and reasonable during this process in order to get something out the door. Most of the time, innovators should not need to concern themselves with this process, which will happen whether they like it or not. Of great concern, however, is the situation where a project team feels they need to compromise one of the assumptions or requirements that support the answers to the key questions. A change in such an area is likely to materially affect the innovation in many dimensions. It may be, for example, that the project team recommends a slip in the launch date, which could materially affect the 'When?' question. This would be particularly the case where the launch strategy for the innovation predicates being *first* to market and later entry reduces the net benefits available.

Where a key questions compromise comes up, it is necessary to evaluate whether the innovation ought to be stopped outright. It is far better to kill off a project – even at this late stage – than run the risk of major innovation trauma (see Chapter 7, where we discussed the experience of Sun Microsystems). Severe innovation trauma is likely to kill an innovation programme altogether.

Project teams should be aware that whilst they have control over the significant parameters of an innovation during execution, if the projected net benefits of the innovation cannot be reached for whatever reason, the project will be cancelled.

28. Do schedule a pilot

For breakthrough and revolutionary innovations, it is a very good idea to schedule a pilot. The point of such an exercise is *not* to find defects in whatever-it-is: this is the role of testers. The main reason for running a pilot is to get operational experience with the new thing *before* a significant number of customers get a chance to form initial impressions.

Such initial impressions, by the way, are very, very important. Recall from our examination of innovation theory in Chapter 2, especially the adoption decision process, that most people seek reassurance from trusted third parties before they do something new. Then, once they've actually made the decision to try whatever-it-is, they seek *further* reassurance their decision was the correct one.

Whilst everyone exhibits this behaviour to a greater or lesser degree, it is the innovators and early adopters who are least dependent on the impressions of peers. It is therefore these two groups that will likely adopt the innovation first. But just because they will adopt early doesn't mean they will *stay* users if their initial impressions are poor. They are just as quick to dis-adopt as to adopt in the first place.

Of course, this group also comprises the influentials needed to get an innovation to the critical mass point. So forming bad impressions will almost certainly kill an innovation dead, leading to significant innovation trauma in the worst case.

Running a pilot makes sure that anything that would compromise the initial experience of these leading users is managed in advance.

29. Determine what involvement the innovation team needs to have post-build

As we discussed in Chapter 7, the execution phase also includes the launch and operations activities for the innovation. Frankly, building the new thing is likely to be the smallest part of the overall challenge involved in an innovation, especially for breakthroughs and revolutions. Usually an incremental innovation, operating within well-known and mature frameworks that already exist, needs no assistance from the innovation team. However, the more new something is, the less likely there will be an existing operating regime that can flex to accommodate the innovation. In these cases, the innovation team may need to be involved in helping to create the right environment for the innovation to flourish. The alternative, unfortunately, is that most institutions will try to shoehorn new things into existing processes and systems. More often than not, this results in a situation where the innovation is sufficiently compromised that net benefits are not reached.

30. Don't start disruptive innovations unless you have appropriate support

Disruptive innovation is very, very difficult for any large organisation to do, let alone do well. The reason is that disruptive innovations invariably threaten existing businesses. This leads to a dual issue for innovators: in the first instance, the disruptive innovation will generate microscopic revenues compared with those of the incumbent businesses, leading to questions of whether the new thing is a distraction that ought to be shut down. Then, once the disruptive innovation gets established, it begins to cannibalise the revenues of the main business. Invariably, powerful executives who have P&L responsibility take steps at this point. Why, they argue, would an innovation that will invariably shift an institution downmarket and be less rewarding in the short term be allowed to continue? Far better, they say, to close it down immediately.

The forces arrayed against a disruptive innovation are formidable in the extreme, so it is usually best to drown the puppy unless one has sufficient support to counter the invariable nay-sayers. Most of the time, attempting to do disruption before the programme has reached the venturing stage (see Figure 3.2) will be futile.

That is not to say disruption should not be attempted under any circumstance at all. The fact of the matter is that all industries – even banking – will be (or are already) subject to disruptive new entrants who are doing their best to change the way business operates. Peer-to-peer lending and alternative payment systems are both examples of disruption at work in financial services, and the sensible bank creates plans early to make sure any disruptions that might affect future revenues are its own.

11.6   DOING FUTURECASTING

Futurecasting is one of the most important parts of the futureproofing process, since it provides the early warning system that institutions need in order to address future competitive threats to existing business. The fact of the matter is that such threats are appearing with increasing regularity in our modern, global financial world, so having structured mechanisms for dealing with the potentialities is becoming increasingly important. I would argue, in fact, that doing good futurecasting is likely to be one of the most important competitive advantages that institutions can develop in coming years.

It ought to have been possible to predict the impact of sub-prime in a crashing housing market, and the boom in property pricing in the last decade was inevitably going to result in some kind of correction in the end. These facts were well known, yet *still* institutions went forwards with strategies which failed to consider potential outcomes. What was missing in this case was a structured process for considering the future in terms of what is known today. Futurecasting is the process used to do that.

There are other reasons to do futurecasts as well, of course. Perhaps the most important of these is that they enable senior executives to rehearse important decisions *in advance* of needing to make them. If, for example, a major strategic choice is to go after the nascent peer-to-peer lending market – even at the expense of existing lending operations – innovators will rarely be successful in getting a go decision without substantial preparation in advance. The preparation, in this case, is a set of stories that can be used to inform the thinking processes of executives.

As we explored in Chapter 4, though, there is yet another reason to do futurecasts, and it has to do with the failings of the traditional stage-gate method of innovation. Stage gates are all very well if what one wants to do is select prospective ideas from a large pipeline. But stage gates, by themselves, don't concern themselves much with *which* ideas should be in the pipeline. Neither do they provide a way to examine the competitive environment to influence the ideas that get processed. Futurecasting fulfils these roles.

Let us now examine the key things about futurecasting that should be considered by innovators.

31. Don't start futurecasting too early

The first thing to say about futurecasting is that it is usually a mistake to start this activity too early. Futurecasting is the innovator's key to participating in the strategic planning of an institution. Futurecasts will usually concern things which have long-term, significant impacts. They need to be handed to the most senior executives if they are to do any good at all. A futurecast that doesn't impact the strategic outlook of an institution is one that probably should not have been attempted in the first place.

The thing is, though, that a new innovation programme will rarely have access to leaders senior enough to make such strategic decisions. Such access is earned, rather than given. That is why, in the Five Capability Model I explained in Chapter 3, futurecasting comes after managing – that time when the innovation team can deliver predictable returns on demand. By the time things get predictable, the innovation team will have earned its stripes – they will be contributing material advantages to their institution.

32. Don't forget to start futurecasting

Whilst it is possible to start the futurecasting process too early, which is usually a waste of time, it is also possible to start it too late. As soon as the innovation team gets to the managing stage, it is time to consider implementing the futurecasting process. This is important because senior leaders will rarely be satisfied with predictable returns for long if they see their competitors doing breakthrough and revolutionary innovation. What, they will wonder, is the point of an innovation team that is so risk-averse that it takes no steps to counter strategic threats?

Strategic threats, of course, require strategic decisions. And strategic decisions are almost never taken without lots of consideration and preparation in advance. A futurecast, besides providing hints about the likely state of the future given the information known now, also allows senior leaders to consider what decisions they have to make ahead of time. This prepares them for the time they have to make the *actual* decision to proceed.

Sometimes, the point of a futurecast is not to create the environment in which a new innovation can be accepted. An equally valid reason to perform a futurecast is to inform senior leaders – as well as the rest of the employees of an institution – of the likely consequences of market or competitor innovations. Our examination of the prospects of peer-to-peer lending in Chapter 4, for example, is useful because it enables the consideration of any number of future states that might be the result of this kind of innovation. Whether or not an institution implements peer-to-peer lending is incidental to the process of considering the consequences of the innovation in a market context.

33. Tell stories

Senior executives don't have time to deal with lots of facts and figures about speculative future states. They will usually have their hands full just running the day-to-day businesses for which they are responsible. It is necessary, therefore, to find a way to provide a framework in which future considerations can be easily digested. One good way to do this is by telling stories. The stories can be framed in any format that makes sense – short histories of the future or fake newspaper articles are good means to do this – which enables them to digest information quickly and easily. The stories selected should be relevant to the bank, deal with a specific problem or strategic consideration that is known in the present day, and have a demonstrable and methodological linkage between the facts available and the projections for the future.

34. Don't have too many predictions that will be proved wrong

The art of the futurecast is to tell stories which are broad-brush approximations of what might come to pass, rather than making specific point predictions that will be proved wrong. And predictions will almost always be proved wrong eventually. It is far better, therefore, to make only those predictions which are necessary to colour the stories being told. And when a prediction *is* necessary, it is best to use multiple methods (for example, both a Delphi approach and statistical methods). This will at least prove to senior executives that numbers are not just being pulled out of thin air.

35. Make sure you collect signals from the rest of the futureproofing process

The most important futurecasts are the ones that have immediate strategic importance to your institution. The key question then becomes working out which futurecasts to do at any given time. The best way to determine this is to collect signals from the other stages of the futureproofing process.

For the ideation phase, for example, aggregated ideas data is very useful. If a particular idea is arriving with increasing frequency, there may be a trend at work in the market which would be a useful futurecast.

For the innovation stage, there are important signals to be obtained from the reaction of the business to various innovations that are proposed. Is there a particular segment of the innovation pentagram which the business is trying to avoid? Or perhaps a disruptive innovation which is prematurely killed? These may be signs that the forces of disruption are at work, and a futurecast may be necessary to inform senior leaders of possible consequences of failing to act.

And from the execution phase there are also interesting signals. What is the response of competitors and customers to a particular innovation? The lack of any response – as well as any energetic and rapid ones – are indicators of things that might be usefully explored using futurecasting methods.

11.7   INNOVATION LEADERS AND TEAMS

Of course, the futureproofing process is nothing without good people to operate it. And the fact of the matter is that whilst almost everyone is innovative to a greater or lesser degree, doing innovation as a discipline requires a specific combination of skills that make designing the innovation team a practical necessity. One mistake made by many institutions is failing to acknowledge this. It is often the case that people 'fall into' innovation roles, perhaps as an adjunct to responsibilities they already have, and are then expected to just do their best. This is almost never an optimum approach. Luckily, however, following a few simple pointers is all that is necessary to ensure the innovation function is well supported by people suited to the role.

36. High personal innovativeness is a necessity for all team members

We first examined personal innovativeness in Chapter 2 (see Figure 2.2). The defining characteristic of innovative individuals is that they don't require as much positive reinforcement of their adoption decision process from peers before they do something innovative. By contrast, the late majority and laggards require continual and constant reinforcement of adoption decisions before they will do anything new at all.

To be a professional innovator, one must accept that uniqueness will have to be considered and delivered without any positive messages from peers at all. In fact, the innovator must necessarily create these messages themselves to propagate to others. To do so requires a tolerance of risk, and an acceptance that innovation decisions may be viewed as ill-advised (even stupid) in the eyes of peers. Not everyone is able to do this, of course. It is therefore important that anyone working on the innovation problem be from the first two segments of the innovation distribution – either innovators or early adopters. No one else is likely to tolerate the unique circumstances the innovation practitioner finds him or herself in every day.

37. The role of the innovation leader is different at different times

The difference between a great innovation team and a poor one is leadership. And the innovation leader has a very great task in front of him or her: theirs is the task of protecting a team which will only create value in the long term, whilst simultaneously building out a corporate capability that many will find distracting. They will face a constant and uphill battle for relevance in the face of the demands of much larger business groups. And during all of this, will have to spend a great percentage of their time educating the rest of their institutions about innovation practice and value.

The fact of the matter, though, is that the combination of things needed from the leader depends on where the programme is on the Five Capability Model. The leader-inventor is very appropriate when the programme is established, but becomes a hindrance past the managing stage. On the other hand, a strategic visionary may be just what is needed at the futurecasting and venturing stages, but will not be much use when what is needed are those first significant wins on which the rest of the journey will be based.

The most important thing to recognise is that most innovation leaders are *not* equally capable of leading an innovation programme through each stage of the process. It is best to be candid with prospective innovation leaders up front: an institution will likely need several innovation leaders as it goes through its innovation journey, and the strategic importance of innovation as a competitive differentiator expands.

38. Fire bad innovators quickly

There is *nothing* to be gained by waiting for a poor innovator to come good. At the start of an innovation programme, such an individual will likely burn influence at a much greater rate than it is created. Influence is like money, and in similarly limited supply. There is only so much available, and an innovation team can do nothing without it.

But there is another reason to eliminate poor performers quickly. Any successful team will be made up of a combination of all four innovation styles we examined in Chapter 9. Losing any one of these styles will reduce the efficiency of a team dramatically. As I've said throughout this book, on average innovation teams in banks have about 18 months to get to the managing stage before they are terminated. Any reduction in efficiency just makes reaching this milestone much more difficult.

39. Recognise the importance of execution

In innovation, execution is everything. Ideas are like grains of sand on a beach: there are many of them, and finding the specks of gold is a question of having a deliberate process. But *doing* something with these great ideas is very difficult. It requires exceptional salesmanship, great analytical skills, and an overall passion for making a difference. These are commodities often in short supply in institutions. So making the team focus on execution is a very important part of ensuring success.

Having strong metrics and decent oversight is a key component of this, of course. But by far and away the most significant thing to do is ensure the innovation team is oversupplied with implementers, who are probably the least well understood of all the innovation styles. These are individuals who will ensure that the nuts and bolts that must be done to support innovation – dealing with the key questions, gunpowdering execution, and all the other things that precede a successful launch – will actually get done. Unfortunately, most innovation leaders tend to focus on creators and embellishers rather than the more practical perfectors and implementers. In doing so they make a very common mistake: assuming that great ideas result in a great innovation function.

Some Final Words

The points I've just outlined provide a basis for most institutions to get from a standing start to at least the managing stage of the Five Capability Model. And once there, generally, a programme is safe from cancellation whilst ever it continues to deliver predictable returns. Of course, the bigger picture is one that is somewhat more expansive than just being able to trot out incremental improvements on demand.

Whether the innovation strategy is Play to Win or Play Not to Lose, having a robust discipline for creating – and responding to – uniqueness is a key skill that institutions will have to develop if they want to stay in business in the long term. Because the fact of the matter is that the pace of change in our industry has accelerated, and will likely continue to do so. I often hear bankers complain about the amount of change they must accommodate every year. They wonder how they will ever be able to keep up, how they will pay for all the things that must be done reactively, and whether there is a tipping point beyond which it will no longer be possible to do what has worked quite well for several hundred years.

I am of the view that such a tipping point is just around the corner. The new reality of financial services is that the democratisation of the tools of our industry has just started. It is impossible to ignore the explosion of providers and the myriad of products and channels which are appearing. And every year, it becomes simpler to offer the kinds of services that banks do. Can there be any doubt that the answer to all this innovation in the market is to out-innovate everyone else?

Having said that, the temptation as a new innovator – one that I've fallen for myself in fact – is to be overly ambitious at the start. In order to make a difference as quickly as possible, it seems sensible to take big, game-changing ideas and work them to the ground in the hope that something – anything – will happen to justify the existence of the innovators. If nothing else, this book has hopefully explained the very great danger of taking this approach. Big innovations require big innovation capabilities. And these cannot be created overnight. They must be nurtured and developed over a period of years.

The innovation journey is a long one, but the prize at the end is significant. There can be little doubt that *the* competitive advantage of the future will be how good a particular institution is at identifying new uniqueness and commercialising it. Those banks that make this a core competence will be very successful. And those that don't will be forced to play an expensive game of catch-up, one which is probably unsustainable in the long term. Which leads me to my final point, one I often repeat to new graduates when they ask about careers in innovation.

In the past, the most senior jobs in banks – chief executives and their direct reports – have usually been appointed from the ranks of the business people in charge of the revenue. It is a rare circumstance when the computer guy takes the top job, for example, but there are lots of chief executives who have worked their way up from the teller window. Being connected to the money in a substantial way is what it takes to get to the top of the industry, apparently.

I am of the view that innovation will drive the greatest part of future revenues for our industry. It seems no great stretch, then, to imagine that some of the future leaders of our organisations will come from the ranks of the career innovator. Theirs will be leadership that is firmly grounded not in the traditions of the past, but systematised consideration of what it takes to be successful in the future. In the meantime, though, there is no time like the present to start putting the tools and processes in place that will make innovation a core competency in your institution. It is my hope this book has provided some of the necessary insights required to accomplish this task.

References

1. Jaruzelski, B. and Dehoff, K. (2007) The customer connection: the global innovation 1000. In *Strategy + Business*. Booz Allan Hamilton.
2. McGreggor, J. (2008) The world's most innovative companies. *Business Week*, April.
3. SRI International. ERMA and MICR: the origins of electronic banking. Available at http://www.sri.com/about/timeline/erma-micr.html.
4. Bátiz-Lazo, B. and Wood, D. (2002) Information technology innovations and commercial banking: a review and appraisal from an historical perspective. EconWPA.
5. Christensen, C.M. (1997) *The Innovator's Dilemma: When new technologies cause great firms to fail*. Management of Innovation and Change Series, eds M.L. Tushman and A.H.V.d. Ven. Harvard Business School Press: Boston, MA.
6. Bruene, J. (2007) Netbank falls but don't blame online delivery [cited 21 June 2008]. Available at http://www.netbanker.com/2007/10/netbank_falls_but_dont_blame_online_delivery.html.
7. Gartner (2008). Gartner says social banking platforms threaten traditional banks for control of financial relationships [cited 17 January 2009]. Available at http://www.gartner.com/it/page.jsp?id=597907.
8. Gardner, J. (2008) Social lending takes 10% share [cited 21 June 2008]. Available at http://bankervision.typepad.com/bankervision/2008/02/social-lending.html.
9. Yadav, S., Prabhu, J.C. and Chandy, R.K. (2007) Managing the future: CEO attention and innovation outcomes. *Journal of Marketing* **71**(Oct): 84–101.
10. Zhang, H. and Li, H. (2006) Factors affecting payment choices in online auctions: a study of eBay traders. *Decision Support Systems* **42**: 1076–1088.
11. Punch, L. (2001) The shakeout in online cash. *Credit Card Management* **Dec**(14).
12. e-Payments to become mega market (2006) [cited 12 April 2008]. Available at http://www.boozallen.com/capabilities/Industries/industries_article/7969275.
13. Garbade, K.D. and Silber, W.L. (1978) Technology, communication and the performance of financial markets: 1840–1975. *Journal of Finance* **33**(3): 819–832.
14. Bofondi, M. and Lotti, F. (2006) Innovation in the retail banking industry: the diffusion of credit scoring. *Review of Industrial Organisation* **28**(4): 343–358.
15. BACS (2008) History of BACS. Available at http://www.bacs.co.uk/NR/rdonlyres/48F498AE-1D4D-4F88-B5E7-1777CBACC047/0/HistoryofBacs.pdf.
16. Milligan, B. (2007) The man who invented the cash machine. BBC News, Monday 25 June 2007 [cited 5 May 2008].
17. Allison, D.K. (1995) Interview with Mr Don Wetzel, co-patentee of the automatic teller machine [cited 5 May 2008]. Available at http://americanhistory.si.edu/collections/comphist/wetzel.htm#I.
18. Gillan, S.L., Kensinger, J.W. and Martin, J.D. (2000) Value creation and corporate diversification: the case of Sears, Roebuck & Co. *Journal of Financial Economics* **55**(1): 103–137.
19. McVicker, E.D. (2007) From Wal-Mart to Prosper: where do banks fit in? *ABA Banking Journal* **99**(7): 18.
20. Orr, B. (1981) Home banking prospects: a status report on explosive growth. *ABA Banking Journal* **73**(10): 204.

21. Lunt, P. (1995) Welcome to sfnb.com: the paradigm just shifted. *ABA Banking Journal* **87**(1): 40.
22. ING Netherlands (2007) Our Virtual Holland – frequently asked questions [cited 15 June 2008]. Available at http://www.ourvirtualholland.nl/en/faq.
23. Hogan, J.E., Lemon, K.N. and Libai, B. (2003) What is the true value of a lost customer? *Journal of Service Research* **5**(3): 196–208.
24. Rogers, E.M. (2003) *Diffusion of Innovations*, 5th edn. Free Press: New York.
25. Bass, F. (1969) A new product growth model for consumer durables. *Management Science* **15**(5): 215–227.
26. Bruene, J. (2007) Mobile banking and payments. Online Banking.com.
27. Mahler, A. and Rogers, E.M. (1999) The diffusion of interactive communication innovations and the critical mass: the adoption of telecommunications services by German banks. *Telecommunications Policy* **23**(10/11): 719–740.
28. McKenzie, H. (2007) Collaborate & co-operate – new adventures in symbiosis – its ambitions in the mobile remittances space have led Vodafone to partner with Citi to extend the service beyond Kenya to provide international person-to-person mobile payments. *The Banker*, October.
29. Strothkamp, B., Johnson, C. and Tesch, B. (2007) Case study: metrics drive Wells Fargo's home page. A best practice home page driven by data, not opinions. Forrester Research.
30. Deutsche Bank (2006) Deutsche Bank of the future [cited 15 June 2008]. Available at http://www.deutsche-bank.de/presse/en/content/q110.htm.
31. Bruno-Britz, M. (2007) Decoupled debit presents threats and opportunities to banks. In *Bank Systems and Technology*. United Business Media LLC, New York.
32. Wesabe (2008) Wesabe: Get to know your money [cited 15 June 2008]. Available at http://www.wesabe.com/.
33. Sants, H. (2008) The FSA's Supervisory Enhancement Programme, in response to the Internal Audit Report on supervision of Northern Rock. Available at http://www.fsa.gov.uk/pubs/other/enhancement.pdf.
34. Davila, T., Epstein, M.J. and Shelton, R. (2006) *Making Innovation Work*. Wharton School Publishing: Upper Saddle River, NJ.
35. The Ponemon Institute (2007) *2007 Annual Study: U.S. Cost of a Data Breach*.
36. Gardner, J. (2008) Using the perfect storm. Available at http://bankervision.typepad.com/bankervision/2008/07/using-the-perfect-storm.html.
37. Vancity Credit Union (2008) We all profit [cited 7 September 2008]. Available at https://www.vancity.com/MyCommunity/OurVision/WeAllProfit/.
38. Schnaars, S., Thomas, G. and Irmak, C. (2008) Predicting the emergence of innovations from technological convergence: lessons from the twentieth century. *Journal of Macromarketing* **28**(2): 157–168.
39. Gardner, J. (2008) Bankervision: Blogroll [cited 3 September 2008]. Available at http://bankervision.typepad.com.
40. Trendwatching.com (2008) TrendWatching: 2008 [cited 10 September 2008]. Available at http://trendwatching.com.
41. Schwartz, P. (1998) *The Art of the Long View*. John Wiley & Sons: Chichester.
42. Heijden, K.V.D. (2005) *Scenarios: The art of the strategic conversation*, 2nd edn. John Wiley & Sons: Chichester.
43. Pang, C.-W. (2004) Consensus forecasts in business planning: their benefits and limitations. *The Journal of Business Forecasting Methods and Systems* **23**(1): 23.
44. Conroy, R.M., Fukuda, Y. and Harris, R.S. (1997) Securities houses and earnings forecasts in Japan: what makes for an accurate prediction. *Financial Analysts Journal* **53**(4): 29.
45. Linstone, H.A. and Turnoff, M. (eds) (1975) *The Delphi Method: Techniques and applications*, 1st edn. Addison-Wesley Educational Publishers.
46. Prendergast, G.P. and Marr, N.E. (1994) The future of self-service technologies in retail banking. *The Services Industries Journal* **14**(1): 94.
47. Bradley, L. and Stewart, K. (2003) A Delphi study of Internet banking. *Marketing Intelligence and Planning* **21**(4/5): 272.
48. Bruene, J. (2008) Online banking forecast: 2008 through 2017. In *Online Banking Report*. Online Financial Innovations.
49. Oracle Corporation (2008) *Crystal Ball*. Oracle: California.

50. Gartner (2008) Gartner says social banking platforms threaten traditional banks for control of financial relationships [cited 14 December 2008]. Available at http://www.gartner.com/it/page.jsp?id=597907.
51. Meyer, T. (2007) *Online P2P lending nibbles at banks' loan business.* Deutsche Bank Research: Frankfurt.
52. IBM (2006) IBM invests $100 million in collaborative innovation ideas [cited 7 September 2008]. Available at http://www-03.ibm.com/press/us/en/pressrelease/20605.wss.
53. Finextra (2008) London NFC trial shows customers want contactless m-payments [cited 17 January 2009]. Available at http://www.finextra.com/fullstory.asp?id=18919.
54. Thomke, S. (2003) R&D comes to services. *Harvard Business Review* **81**(4): 70–79.
55. Ogawa, S. and Piller, F.T. (2006) Reducing the risks of new product development. *MIT Sloan Management Review* **47**(2).
56. Royal Bank of Canada (2008) RBC P2P [cited 17 January 2009]. Available at http://www.rbcp2p.com/about.html.
57. Day, G.S. (2007) Is it real? Can we win? Is it worth doing? *Harvard Business Review* **85**(12): 110–120.
58. Andrew, J.P. and Sirkin, H.L. (2006) *Payback: Reaping the rewards of innovation.* Harvard Business School Press: Boston, MA.
59. Centre for Future Banking (2008) Frequently asked questions [cited 31 August 2008]. Available at http://cfb.media.mit.edu/faq.php.
60. Molden-Salazar, J. and Välikangas, L. (2008) Sun Ray's struggle to overcome innovation trauma. *Strategy & Leadership* **36**(3): 15.
61. General Electric (1961) Frontiers of progress sales meeting [cited 21 December 2008]. Available at http://www.smecc.org/frontiers_of_progress_-_1961_sales_meeting.htm.
62. McGrath, R.G., Keil, T. and Tukiainen, T. (2006) Extracting value from corporate venturing. *MIT Sloan Management Review* **48**(1).
63. Barsh, J., Capozzi, M.M. and Davidson, J. (2008) Leadership and innovation. *The McKinsey Quarterly* **2008**(1).
64. Bart, A.G.B. (2004) Effectiveness of innovation leadership styles: a manager's influence on ecological innovation in construction projects. *Construction Innovation* **4**(4): 211.
65. Bart, A.G.B. (2007) Leadership for sustainable innovation. *The International Journal of Technology Management & Sustainable Development* **6**(2): 135.
66. Jeroen, P.J.d.J. and Deanne, N.D.H. (2007) How leaders influence employees' innovative behaviour. *European Journal of Innovation Management* **10**(1): 41.
67. Lancaster, L.C. and Stillmann, D. (2003) *When Generations Collide: Who they are. Why they clash. How to solve the generational puzzles at work.* Harper Business: Wheaton, IL.
68. Roach, I. and Carol, S. (2000) Enabling innovation: leadership, tasks, and tools. *Annual Quality Congress Proceedings*, p. 289.
69. Wikipedia (2008) Wireless Application Protocol [cited 30 November 2008]. Available at http://en.wikipedia.org/wiki/Wireless_Application_Protocol.
70. DeCusatis, C. (2008) Creating, growing and sustaining efficient innovation teams. *Creativity and Innovation Management* **17**(2): 155.
71. Kratzer, J., Leenders, R.T.A.J. and Englelen, J.M.L.V. (2005) Information contact and performance in innovation teams. *International Journal of Manpower* **26**(6): 513.
72. Andrew, J.P. *et al.* (2007) *Measuring Innovation 2007 – A BCG Senior Management Survey.* Boston Consulting Group: Boston.
73. Chan, V., Musso, C. and Shankar, V. (2008) Assessing innovation metrics. *McKinsey Quarterly* **2008**(Nov).
74. Gardner, J. (2009) Bankervision [cited 1 January 2009]. Available at http://bankervision.typepad.com.
75. Bank of America (2008) Future Banking Blog [cited 7 January 2009]. Available at futurebanking.bankofamerica.com.

Index